"*The Complete Guide to Drea*... comprehensive, well-thought-out and thorough books on the principles of interpretation. Anyone who teaches this material should own and study this book as a vital part of their own personal development and as a brilliant tool in the curriculum. Any who dream regularly will receive much significant input from this powerful book, which will open avenues of revelation and application. This book blends both a scholarly treatise and persuasive, experiential and practical insights in how to move forward in this key area of spiritual growth. I highly recommend it!"

Graham Cooke, Brilliantperspectives.com

"*The Complete Guide to Dream Interpretation* is a treasure chest, a tool box and a compendium of practical principles for understanding the meaning of your dreams. Marsha Dunstan has packed these pages with biblical wisdom and experiential knowledge to provide a true road map for people to navigate their way into interpreting their dreams. This book will awaken your understanding, challenge your preconceptions and train you to hear the voice of the Lord through your dreams. I wholeheartedly recommend Marsha Dunstan, and I enthusiastically encourage you to add this volume to your library."

John E. Brown, senior pastor, Harmony Vineyard Church;
regional director, Midwest Ministers' Fellowship;
author, *Rhythm of a Captured Heart*

"I have had the privilege of working alongside Marsha as she has uncovered and discovered the mysteries of God. She operates from a place of intimacy with the Father, which releases deep revelation. What I appreciate is her heart to not simply be the dream interpreter but to equip others in the art of dream interpretation. In this coming age of Christianity it is vital to equip and release the Body of Christ into all they have been called to. Marsha is a kingdom builder, and *The Complete Guide to Dream Interpretation* brings this opportunity with kingdom intuition and pragmatic insight."

Byron Easterling, BHH, BHHInternational.com

THE COMPLETE
GUIDE TO
DREAM
INTERPRETATION

THE
COMPLETE
GUIDE TO
DREAM
INTERPRETATION

A SIMPLE, STEP-BY-STEP PROCESS TO BIBLICAL INTERPRETATION

MARSHA TRIMBLE DUNSTAN

Chosen
a division of Baker Publishing Group
Minneapolis, Minnesota

Published by Chosen Books
11400 Hampshire Avenue South
Bloomington, Minnesota 55438
www.chosenbooks.com

Chosen Books is a division of
Baker Publishing Group, Grand Rapids, Michigan

Printed in the United States of America

ISBN 978-0-8007-9857-4

Library of Congress Control Number: 2017963562

Unless otherwise indicated, Scripture quotations are from the New American Standard Bible®, copyright © 1960, 1962, 1963, 1968, 1971, 1972, 1973, 1975, 1977, 1995 by The Lockman Foundation. Used by permission. (www.Lockman.org)

Scripture quotations identified NIV are from the Holy Bible, New International Version®. NIV®. Copyright © 1973, 1978, 1984, 2011 by Biblica, Inc.™ Used by permission of Zondervan. All rights reserved worldwide. www.zondervan.com

Scripture quotations identified NKJV are from the New King James Version®. Copyright © 1982 by Thomas Nelson, Inc. Used by permission. All rights reserved.

Scripture quotations identified KJV are from the King James Version of the Bible.

Cover design by LOOK Design Studio

Author represented by Leslie H. Stobbe and by The Steve Laube Agency

18   19   20   21   22   23   24   7   6   5   4   3   2   1

With overpowering humility, I dedicate this labor of love
to my best friend, my Savior, my comforter and my guide, Jesus.
Freely You gave, and freely I am trying to give back to You
and to others. I embrace Your Word and thank You
for counting me among Your servants.

There is a God in heaven who reveals secrets. . . . Your dream, and the visions of your head upon your bed, were these: . . . He who reveals secrets has made known to you what will be . . . [that] you may know the thoughts of your heart.

Daniel 2:28–30 NKJV

CONTENTS

FOREWORD

As leaders in the Church of the Lord Jesus, we are to unite in our efforts to equip His people by putting tools in their hands to help them discern God's direction and love in a greater way. His sweet and precious voice is too often masked by the noise of the world. This has never been truer than today with the many pressures in our society. People are looking for answers. The privilege and mandate of leaders in the Kingdom is to equip the Lord's people to interact with Him—to abide in Jesus.

"Come to Me, all you who labor and are heavy laden, and I will give you rest. Take My yoke upon you and learn from Me, for I am gentle and lowly in heart, and you will find rest for your souls" (Matthew 11:28–29 NKJV). The Lord woos His people with these words of hopeful rest amidst struggles. We receive His promise of rest by believing and *abiding* in Him. Andrew Murray stated, "Abiding in Him is not a work that we have to do as the condition for enjoying His salvation, but a consenting to let Him do all for us, in us, and through us."[1] A consenting to let Christ do all for us. Dreams are one of several ways the Lord chooses to "do for us"—to help us by communicating with us. They are a gift from Him. *The Complete Guide to Dream Interpretation* is a helpful tool that may be useful in unwrapping this gift.

It is easy to read as it overflows with everyday stories and real dreams in colorful language. It will not be a onetime read but kept as a reference source or teaching tool to use many times.

This book goes beyond declaring that a dream may be from God, covered in symbolic meaning—it provides steps to uncover the dream's importance. It also seeks to assist the interpreter in discerning whether the dream is from God, from the enemy or from the dreamer's own body and soul. It seeks to help the interpreter avoid going down a wrong path. *The Complete Guide to Dream Interpretation* seeks to help the reader determine which symbols are helpful to the interpretation of various dreams.

Marsha Trimble Dunstan, trained by the Institute for Spiritual Development, has lovingly labored to put this powerful tool in the hands of God's people—to empower believers to grab hold of His touch. This book is well written and comprehensive. It is a tool for leaders and laymen alike.

Mike Bickle, director, International House of Prayer, Kansas City;
president, International House of Prayer University;
author, *Growing in the Prophetic*, *Passion for Jesus*,
The Pleasures of Loving God and *After God's Own Heart*

ACKNOWLEDGMENTS

This book has been a journey. Along the way, there have been many places of rest to which I have clung during times of need. These places have been the arms of people the Lord placed in my life at just the right moment.

As a student of John Paul Jackson and his Streams Institute for Spiritual Development, I credit much of my learning of dream interpretation to this gifted man of God who spent years serving the Lord with faithfulness by teaching "those who had ears." Even though John Paul's voice can still be heard in his many recorded teachings, the earth darkened a bit the day the Lord called him home. John Paul, your students miss you but are eternally grateful for the legacy you have left behind.

Graham Cooke, thank you for your dedication to helping the wounded and the weary. I was one of those. I consider you a mentor, as you have touched my life deeply. From your teachings I have learned it is okay to laugh and still love God, for God created laughter. Imprisoned by my own intensity at times, this was a divine lesson. I have tried to include God's laughter in this book. Thank you. You are brilliant.

I thank Carol Henningsen, a friend in arms, who walked this path with me and encouraged me when I needed it. Without you, this book would not have happened.

I am grateful to my sister Brenda, who shared her dreams and walked through John Paul Jackson's teachings with me. You are now with John Paul and Jesus in heaven. I will see you again someday.

To Pastor John E. Brown, thank you for being my friend, my pastor and my mentor and for helping me obtain a platform from which to serve others.

To Carol B., Theresa, Sally, Irma and all the other members of the Homer's Orphans writing group, I thank each of you for your critiques and encouragement during the construction of this book.

Because of your love and unwavering support in the research and writing of this book, thank you, daughters—Rebecca and Abbey.

Most especially, I thank my beloved husband, Steve, who encouraged me to use my voice and walk in the gifts God gave me. Your display of Jesus' unconditional love toward me has fueled me throughout this journey.

1

Where We Begin

In my dream, I floated above my body and watched myself sitting quietly on the swing. I looked strange—foreign, even. I did not know I looked like that. I thought I was homelier than the seven-year-old girl I saw. She sat motionless. Her small hands grasped chains that hung from the high, rusty gallows of the school swing. Frozen in time, she sat on the still seat. I hovered above.

Out of habit, I suppose, I inhaled. Like strong peppermint chewed during a cold January frost, the icy cold of subzero air whooshed into my mouth with a force greater than my inhale deserved—and the air did not stop. It went right through me and came out the back of my head.

Puzzled, I did it again. The same strange result.

I laughed. My disembodied spirit did not need breath, it seemed. I quit trying to breathe. It was not necessary, and it distracted me from a new focus: I could fly. I looked down at the lone girl with soft brown pigtails below me. She sat still.

I turned toward the playground. Kids were scattered. Some ran and yelled with glee. To the right, three boys scuffled on a painted blacktop foursquare box. One of them threw a large red ball hard, hitting another's head. The ball was immediately *abandoned, and instead, angry words bounced between the boys. Through the air, I soared and circled the boys.*

Nearby, four girls took turns on a crude hopscotch scrawled across the blacktop. A fifth girl hung back. She appeared shy as she watched them.

I moved on, passing a few feet above the girls' heads. No one could see me.

I flew faster. Experimenting with several twists and turns, I learned perfect control. This was fun! From one end of the playground to the other, I zipped. The wind had no authority over me.

Neither did the cold. But I knew it must be cold because the kids were wearing coats. A teacher on playground duty was bundled in her coat, too, and wore gloves and a knitted hat. To me, the air felt warm and cool at the same time.

I sensed a pull to go back into my body. I did not want to go back. But I understood it was time.

Reluctantly, I flew back and hovered above the skinny little girl, who was still seated, inactive, on the swing seat.

Okay. Here goes.

I dropped down to where she was. As I entered her body—my body—I felt smothered by its insufferable weight. My shoulders sagged under the burden. My chest seemed to be made of lead as I began to breathe in and out.

I woke into my 1960 world, rubbed my eyes against a pillow and struggled to make sense of the dream. Did this mean I could fly? How was I able to see my body sitting there? Could I do it again? I rolled off the bed in the upstairs bedroom I shared with my nine-year-old sister, then stumbled down the old, narrow, wooden stairs. With my seven-year-old vocabulary, I told Mama what happened.

A busy mother of six, she was already at work in the kitchen. She attempted patience and tried to listen but soon pigeonholed the dream as humorous nonsense and a waste of valuable time.

"But it was so real!" I protested. "And I saw the top of the teacher's head from above."

Mama frowned. "It is just a dream and does not mean anything."

Convinced against my will, for Mama knew everything, I decided the dream had no meaning. People do not fly.

How I Got Here

Thirtysome years later, I was firmly embedded in that mindset. My rationalism was further enhanced by an engineering degree in control systems, a branch of electrical engineering. A respected professional, I had proven to be, to my peers and superiors, a dependable, effective and sought-after engineer. In addition to technical duties, I provided project management, which required the selection and supervision of other engineers.

From Rationalism to Belief

Then one day, I stumbled upon two books by Frank Peretti: *This Present Darkness* and *Piercing the Darkness*. These books opened my eyes to the spiritual world. They helped me separate rationalism from the things of the spirit.

Until that time, I had felt there were evil and good forces in the world but that their strife was remote from me and my life. What did their battles have to do with me? In Peretti's books, I read that good and evil spirits are here with us on planet earth. My heart opened—my mind, my will, my emotions. But I could only ponder the ideas, as none of them fit into my world of thermocouples, human-machine interfaces, schematic drawings or engineering reports. I maintained the status quo, save for my private ponderings.

In my busy, rational world, I considered dreams "tomfoolery" and thought they were nothing more than electrical brain pulses that allowed our bodies to release tension—that is, until I experienced a dream that opened my blind eyes. In the dream, I saw the following:

A good friend I will call Anne was in a van I knew to be her vehicle. The van was underwater and sinking deeper. Anne sat

*in it, and I sat next to her. I knew, as you can only know in a
dream, that I could get out of the van at will. Instead, I chose to
sit beside Anne to support her. I knew she was trapped.*

When I awoke, I could remember the feel of the changing pressure
as the van dropped deeper under the water.

The dream stuck with me. A few days later, I called Anne and, in
a feeble attempt to be funny, said, "Are you sinking? I had a dream
you were underwater."

Anne's response stunned me. She muttered, sounding near tears,
"My business is sinking fast."

I told her my dream.

Then she said something to challenge my rationalism. She said, "I
have had that same dream three times in the past couple of months."

How could that be? Was it coincidence, the dream of her sinking
and the way she was sinking, metaphorically, in real life? Could a
dream show Anne's experience? What was this about? The odds
of her having the same dream I did three times were too great. My
analytical mind could not accept this as a coincidence. Yet if it was
not a coincidence, then dreams—at least some of them—must mean
something.

I began a search for the meaning of dreams.

From Ignorance to Understanding

In the mainstream churches I attended my whole life, there was
an assumed mindset that those who dabbled in the interpretation of
dreams were either nuts or "of the devil." There was zero tolerance
for dreams. I had to tread softly. So, doing what any engineering
professional and respected church lady who sat on a church board
would do, I went into the closet. I kept my hunt for the significance
of dreams hidden.

The first step in my search took me to the quickest information route I knew: the internet. There, I found a plethora of material pointing me toward interpretations having to do with Eastern

mysticism, horoscopes, New Age thinking and theories that said dreams were only about the dreamer. But nothing spoke to what I had experienced—dreams that offered words of knowledge about others or gave helpful direction or warning.

I revisited my university psychology courses on the teachings of Sigmund Freud and Carl Jung to deepen my understanding of those teachings.

As I searched, more dreams came to me—strange dreams of striving and seeking, and dreams in which I was given the interpretation. The Jungian and Freudian methods of interpretation did not hold up against the meanings given to me.

Finally, I discovered a largely ignored method of dream interpretation—ignored by those who chose to disregard the Bible, anyway. This method used symbols from biblical metaphors and allegories. These symbols were combined with the interpreter's openness to receiving what the Holy Spirit had to say about the dream.

In a leap of faith, I jumped into the world of biblical dream interpretation. Hungry for answers, I desired to hear clearly from the Holy Spirit. Starved, I was fed. I studied biblical principles, allegories and symbols. I prayed to God for proper meaning and direction. I began to apply the biblical metaphors to dreams.

The world of dream interpretation unfolded before me.

My ability to interpret dreams eventually helped in my engineering work. One day, I was nearing the end stages of a tedious project's final report. My preliminary final report had been sent to the required points of contact, supervisors and colleagues. I requested each one's comments, which I planned to incorporate into the revised document.

After I received their feedback, it took me two weeks to modify the detailed one-hundred-page report. Finally, on a Friday afternoon at four o'clock, I finished. It was time to incorporate the changes into the original document.

Stupid in my fatigue, I hit the wrong command. And in a second blunder, I clicked confirmation of the fatal error. The file closed without saving any of my changes. I lost those two weeks' worth of work and did not have time to make it up properly.

Panic ensued. I checked my computer's deleted files. But as I had been working on the company's server, the documents were not stored on my laptop. I ran to my company's computer department to plead for help and pull the documents off the server. The server gurus said the server was down and that files had not been backed up, due to its malfunction.

Stunned, I realized the information was lost forever. It was late afternoon on Friday, and my final report was due at an office in the Pentagon on Monday. All I had was my original, preliminary report, which included none of the required changes.

After a few minutes, I pulled myself out of a pit of despair. I took the feedback, my own notes and my laptop, and I went home. Working around the clock, I slept less than six hours that weekend and ate little. I had to reconstruct the entire final report. I must have saved the work in progress every twenty minutes—an overreaction to my former folly. I finished on Sunday night, around ten o'clock. I saved the file once again, then fell, exhausted, into bed.

The next morning, when I awoke, I remembered a vivid dream:

> The leader of my church spoke to me. He looked deep into my eyes and said, "There's something wrong with your appendix." I put my right hand on my abdomen and thought, I don't feel sick. But again he said, "There's something wrong with your appendix."

I woke up holding my stomach and said out loud, "There's something wrong with my appendix." My first lucid thought was, *I wonder if I'm getting sick.* But I did not feel sick. Again, I thought, *There's something wrong with my appendix.*

Then I remembered the grueling report. My appendix—of course! There was something wrong with the report's appendices.

I pulled it out and looked at it. Sure enough, I had forgotten a one-inch-thick attachment that had been a required addition to the report. That dream saved my hide. God spoke to me through it. He told me I had missed a crucial part of the report.

From Private to Public

For two or three years, I was content to study dream interpretation and use it for my own benefit. I took intense classes offered by John Paul Jackson through his ministry, Streams Ministries International.[1] The classes helped me to understand and hear what God had to say to me. My hunger was satisfied. I was content.

But the Lord would not let me keep my gift to myself.

On Mondays, prior to work, I met with a group of women for a Bible study at the home of one of the church ladies. I enjoyed the powerful, Spirit-filled women in the group. We prayed together and studied.

One particular morning, a woman I will call Ruth laid out a situation in need of prayer. She spoke of a person who had previously brought dysfunction into her life. This person now wanted to reenter her life. Ruth was torn between forgiveness and concern, due to her past experience.

As I listened to her, I heard the Holy Spirit say to me in a clear voice, *Ask her about her dream.* Without hesitation, I proclaimed a loud internal *no.* I was not about to go there. Sure, I was interested in dreams and knew they were real. Sure, they had helped me. But I was not about to put myself out there in a way that would cause others to raise their eyebrows and talk about me behind my back.

Ruth continued to release her anxieties at the kitchen table. I heard the calm voice repeat, *Ask her about her dream.*

This time, I disobeyed with a softer approach, as if to wheedle the almighty God, Creator of the universe, into changing His mind. *No, please, God,* I pleaded silently. *I cannot do it. I would be a laughingstock.*

I heard nothing. The conversation at the table changed to another prayer request brought up by one of the other ladies. *Thank You, God!* But just when I thought I was off the hook, Ruth brought up her concern again.

She said, "I have prayed and prayed for an answer, but I am just not getting anything."

A third time, I heard the voice say, *Ask her about her dream. Okay, okay!*

I turned to Ruth and said, "Have you had any dreams lately?" Embarrassed, I refused to look away from her eyes at the other women's reactions.

Ruth hesitated and then responded, "No. Well, actually, I did have one that was kind of weird."

"What was it?" I asked, still embarrassed. I just knew everyone believed I was having a breakdown.

Ruth shared:

> I dreamed I saw a little bear that was roly-poly and cute. He was so sweet. I wanted to play with him. But there, in the corner of the room, watching me, was a big she-bear that I knew to be the mother. I knew if I picked the baby bear up, the she-bear would come after me.

As I listened, I prayed in silence, *Lord, help me tell her what You would have her to know.*

Then I responded, "In a dream, a bear often represents something destructive. In this dream, you are considering, or 'toying,' with something that might seem innocent and harmless. But, in fact, if you go forward, it will cause something destructive to come at you."

Ruth told me she felt the Holy Spirit had spoken to her through the dream's interpretation. She felt the dream was about the problem she was facing with the individual who had come back into her life. She stopped toying with it. She felt the dream had been a direct answer to her prayer.

This lesson taught me that the Lord wanted me to use my learning and abilities for His service. After that day, I became braver and spoke of dreams to more people.

I am sorry to say I still sometimes hide when I am around those who do not believe God talks to people in this manner. I still hide from those who choose to judge me. Some people have known me too long to believe God would want to use me, someone they grew up with, in this way. I cannot say I blame them. Why me? Why the girl they played with, argued with, spent time with?

Many others simply do not believe dreams are real. They cannot get past the "foolishness" of this. And yet:

> God has chosen the foolish things of the world to shame the wise.
>
> 1 Corinthians 1:27

I am becoming bolder, but I am still working on it.

What I Want for You

I want this book to help people "hear," or understand, what God is already saying to them through their dreams. I am proof we do not have to be special to do this. We do not have to be into high, spiritual things. We do not have to be the pastor of a congregation. Even a boring engineer can get it!

Dreams are real, but an incorrect interpretation can mislead us. I am learning not to lean too much on my own understanding when it comes to interpreting dreams. The Bible warns us:

> Trust in the LORD with all your heart and do not lean on your own understanding.
>
> Proverbs 3:5

We need to ask the Holy Spirit for the interpretation—and then listen. We need to apply biblical metaphors, which are unchanging, instead of man-made interpretations, which change with culture, political agendas, personalities and paradigms.

To understand dreams, we need to study them. I hope this book helps others do that.

Biblical Foundations

Biblically, this book stands on the following foundations:

- God and the Holy Spirit are real and do exist.
- Jesus is God's only begotten Son and the Redeemer of all people (see John 3:16).
- The Bible is God's Word to us and is truth (see Psalm 119:30, 160; John 8:31–32).
- Jesus is Himself the Truth (see John 14:6).
- The Holy Spirit is the Spirit of Truth (see John 15:26; 16:12–14).
- Knowing God's Word as truth and relating to His Son, who is Truth, empowers us to comply with the exhortation that we "must worship in spirit and truth" (John 4:24).
- Satan, the enemy and adversary, exists and hates us (see 1 Peter 5:8).
- Where the Bible says "men," it includes women.
- God loves you and wants good for you, and this is true for everyone (see Psalm 23; John 3:16).
- Humans are tripartite—made of three parts (see 1 Thessalonians 5:23; note that this reference and those included below rely upon the New American Standard Version)—and these three parts consist of:
  1. Body, which includes bone, flesh and blood (see 1 Thessalonians 5:23; Hebrews 4:12);
  2. Soul, which includes the mind, will and emotions (see Genesis 27:4; 34:3–8; 35:18; 42:21; 49:6; Deuteronomy 12:20–21;

13:3; 14:26; 1 Kings 2:4; 8:48; Psalm 6:3; 41:4; 42:1–2; Proverbs 18:7; 21:10; Hebrews 4:12); and

3. Spirit, which includes wisdom, communion and conscience (see Ezra 1:5; Job 6:4; Psalm 77:3–6; Proverbs 18:14; Isaiah 57:15; Daniel 2:1–3; Mark 14:38; Luke 8:55; Philippians 2:2; Colossians 2:5; Hebrews 4:12).

I have spent almost two decades studying and teaching others about dreams and visions. This book is written based on those years of study and these biblical foundations. Even if you do not agree with all of these foundations, I hope you will get something out of this book. Who knows? You might experience a slight paradigm shift and begin to wonder whether some of these premises are true.

You will find many questions answered throughout this book. These questions are ones I have received in my years of teaching. You will also find many examples of actual dreams in these pages. In order to preserve the anonymity of the dreamers, I have changed their names, except where they have asked me to keep their real first names.

Relational Foundations

This book is a tool. Correct use of this tool relies on our discernment, which separates God's truth and voice from the noise of the world. Discernment, faith and relationship with the Holy Spirit are essential.

The Holy Spirit gives us understanding and the correct interpretation of dreams. To receive this understanding and interpretation, our spirit, on some level, must commune with the Holy Spirit, for the Bible says it is only by the spirit in us that we recognize the Holy Spirit:

Just as it is written, "Things which eye has not seen and ear has not heard, and which have not entered the heart of man, all that

God has prepared for those who love Him." For to us God revealed them through the Spirit; for the Spirit searches all things, even the depths of God. For who among men knows the thoughts of a man except the spirit of the man which is in him? Even so the thoughts of God no one knows except the Spirit of God. Now we have received, not the spirit of the world, but the Spirit who is from God, so that we may know the things freely given to us by God, which things we also speak, not in words taught by human wisdom, but in those taught by the Spirit, combining spiritual thoughts with spiritual words.

But a natural man does not accept the things of the Spirit of God, for they are foolishness to him; and he cannot understand them, because they are spiritually appraised.

1 Corinthians 2:9–14

These verses indicate that spiritual things cannot be taught; they can only be received as a gift. I love the way my senior pastor, John E. Brown, author of *Rhythm of a Captured Heart*, puts it. He says, "Some things are taught, and some things are caught." In Romans, Paul speaks of things caught:

For I long to see you so that I may impart some spiritual gift to you, that you may be established.

Romans 1:11

And in Matthew, Jesus speaks of things taught:

Go therefore and make disciples of all the nations, baptizing them in the name of the Father and the Son and the Holy Spirit, teaching them to observe all that I commanded you.

Matthew 28:19–20

For us to catch, or receive, spiritual things, we should seek after them, all the while being open to the Holy Spirit's leading.

People This Book Is For

This book is for people who believe God speaks to us through the Bible, His written Word, and who believe He speaks to us individually and, at times, may use dreams and visions to do so. The book of Job says:

> In a dream, a vision of the night, when sound sleep falls on men, while they slumber in their beds, then He opens the ears of men, and seals their instruction.
>
> Job 33:15–16

This book is also for those who believe that the words Moses spoke in the book of Numbers still apply to today's world:

> He said, "Hear now My words: If there is a prophet among you, I, the LORD, shall make Myself known to him in a vision. I shall speak with him in a dream."
>
> Numbers 12:6

Many believe there is substance to their dreams and would like to understand them better. They believe that the words in Joel 2, later quoted by Peter in Acts 2:17–18, speak of today's era:

> It will come about after this that I will pour out My Spirit on all mankind; and your sons and daughters will prophesy, your old men will dream dreams, your young men will see visions. Even on the male and female servants I will pour out My Spirit in those days.
>
> Joel 2:28–29

Imagine! Consistency between the Old Testament and the New Testament—from Joel to Acts. It is almost as if God knew that some of His children would throw out one or the other. Maybe He wants us to *get it*. I believe these verses tell us it is not quirky to believe God speaks through dreams and visions. Instead, it is what we *should* believe.

Is God the same today as He was when He made those statements? Some believe so. I believe so. The books of Malachi and Hebrews assure it:

> For I, the LORD, do not change.
>
> Malachi 3:6

> Jesus Christ is the same yesterday and today and forever.
>
> Hebrews 13:8

Again, these verses show consistency between the Old Testament and the New.

Dreams have puzzled people since the beginning of time. Many are driven to seek out spiritual mysteries. Others may not actively seek them, but they know in their spirit there is something more, something greater than themselves, out there. Unexplained experiences, or rumors of unexplained experiences, such as extrasensory perception, clairvoyance or apparitions, lead to even more questions. There is an abyss of unanswered questions.

Dreams fall into this mystical chasm. Whether they be vivid or frightening, whether they relay commonplace activities or strange occurrences, dreams often leave people with a yearning to understand their significance.

In biblical times, it was commonly accepted that dreams had meanings. The Bible is full of such accounts. But the rationalism movement that began with René Descartes (1596–1650) brought with it an era of reason based on the five senses. Consequently, many people in today's rationalistic society subscribe to the theory that dreams are irrelevant, nonsensical or an immaterial clearing of the mind during cycles of sleep. Indeed, many people scoff at dreams and visions.

However, there are those of us who do not. Many of us believe that dreams are lucid, living and accurate. We are convinced that a lot of our dreams have meaning and are given for a purpose. We do not enjoy going against the flow of societal thinking, but that does not keep us from receiving revelatory dreams or visions or knowing others who do.

Freely we have received from the Lord, and this volume is an attempt to freely give in return. This book, with its dictionary of symbols, offers you an alternative method for dream interpretation. May it be a helpmate to you, a useful tool to understand and discern the meaning of dreams and their symbols.

2

Common Dream Questions

A missionary gave me my favorite old-time Bible verse when I was a child. I bonded with it in the old King James Version: "Study to shew thyself approved unto God, a workman that needeth not to be ashamed, rightly dividing the word of truth" (2 Timothy 2:15). Early on, I embraced this verse and took it to mean that I must study the Bible and learn what is in it so I will not be shamed by my ignorance and can "rightly divide" God's Word. To me, this meant that I should think and pray upon Scripture to get its full meaning and understand what He is saying to me—and then apply it to my life. And I should prepare, so that when I hear someone say, "It is in the Bible," I can "rightly divide," or sort out, whether that is true. If so, I can determine if it is being quoted the way the Bible intended it to be quoted—or if it has been taken out of context. I have followed this verse my whole life and have questioned my way through the Bible, many times.

Because I believe the Lord wants all of us to question—according to His plumb line, not our own—whether what we are hearing is right or not, I encouraged questions during my years of teaching and working with dreamers. Many questions were asked over and over.

In this chapter, I have pulled out a few common questions that new learners, as well as skeptics, of dreams have asked, and presented them here for a short study.

What Source Is behind My Dream?

Do all dreams originate from one source? If not, what sources can affect our dreams?

Many believe God is a powerful spiritual entity, quick to dole out punishment. They may say He does not have the time or the inclination to nurture us, and these people might find it hard to trust that God wants to talk to us, much less talk to us in dreams. Others have their own paradigm system and beliefs. Still others do not have a clue what to believe about God.

For all of these people, it might be difficult to believe that God gives us dreams to communicate with us. But does He?

To answer this question, I will share a couple of stories with you. The technology company where I worked was involved in engineering projects. For one project, a wastewater treatment plant's sewage system was being contaminated with jet fuel on a regular basis. Someone in the giant spider-webbed system was dumping fuel down the drain—a big no-no. We had to figure out a system to expose the culprit.

On another project that needed underground water control to avoid leaching into a nearby river, we injected microbial "bugs" into the ground and fed them a form of molasses until they got big and fat—well, at least big and fat for a microbe. The fat microbe's excrement formed a barrier that was then used as an in-ground dam for underground water control. When the project was over, we quit feeding the microbes, and they died, leaving the barrier in place.

In engineering, to find a project solution it is vital to fully understand the project and determine the source of the problem before using insightful prowess to resolve the issue. Each engineering project arises because of its own unique set of circumstances that create a hindrance or occurrence needing resolution. In like manner, dreams are easier to understand if we consider their cause—their source. It is useful to know why it was created, and who, or what, created the dream. In other words, what is the source behind each dream? Is it brought on by the body, the soul, God or the enemy? The reality is that any of these could be the source.

Body

Some dreams are brought on by physical reactions. These are sometimes caused by chemicals in the body that affect the nervous system and manifest dreams as their by-product.

As a teenager during the drug years of the 1960s, I heard of devastating drug-induced dreams. Hallucinatory foods, drugs, prescription medicines, over-the-counter medicines and chemicals can all cause strange dreams.

To consider whether the body has caused a dream, look at the dream's timing. Did it occur during recent drug usage or while on new medication? Has the dreamer taken the same prescription for a long time with no dream side effects, or was a strange or unusually spicy food eaten by the dreamer recently? The answers to these questions can determine whether the body caused the dream.

One person who used drugs told me about a dream in which his arm hairs turned into worms that ate away his skin. I am grateful to say it scared him enough that he decided to give up his drug of choice before he became addicted.

When I was eight years old, I dreamed a lion was biting my leg. I awoke to find my sound-asleep sister, with whom I shared a bed, scratching that leg with her toenail. This was a body dream in which my mind identified, in a bizarre way, the pain being inflicted upon me.

Embarrassed, several individuals have reported dreaming that they were peeing—only to awake and find the bed wet underneath them where they had apparently peed in their sleep. Ouch! Not a fun dream, but another type of body dream.

Body dreams are of no consequence, other than to reflect a physical intrusion into the dreamer's body. Ignore them. Shake them off.

Soul

Remember that we said in the last chapter that humans are tripartite, or made up of soul, spirit and body. Additionally, our souls include the mind, will and emotions, each of which can affect our dreams. For example:

- A dreamer's *mind* says, "I think . . ." The mind is the paradigm through which a person views the world. It is the dreamer's analyses.
- A dreamer's *will* says, "I want . . ." The will connects with a person's desires and ambitions.
- A dreamer's *emotions* say, "I feel . . ." Feelings are built from anxieties, hurts, joys, life experiences, sentiments and teachings that a person has stored and draws upon to determine their perception of and reaction to a situation. Emotions are the dreamer's impressions.

Soul dreams are dreams that originate in the dreamer's mind, will or emotions. They may originate from an overflow of desire, fear or other feelings that manifest as the dream. The dream allows for the release of the strong emotions or pent-up anxieties.

Let me give you an example of this. Jeri called me on the telephone one day. Immediately I knew something was wrong. Her voice shook, and I heard sobs between her words.

"I need to tell you about a dream I had," she said. Her words were thickly enunciated, possibly in an attempt to keep her emotions from shutting down her ability to speak.

"Sure. Go ahead," I replied.

"I dreamed my son fell off a cliff and died," she said, her words ending with a loud wail.

God, help me tell her what You want her to hear, I prayed.

"Tell me the full dream, Jeri," I said, stalling to give me time to hear from the Lord.

"In the dream, my son drove a truck off a cliff," she began. "He crashed."

As I listened to Jeri unfold the details of the horrific scene, a peace from the Holy Spirit swept over me, that peace the Bible talks about that "surpasses all understanding" (Philippians 4:7 NKJV). The peace was so powerful I had to stop myself from laughing out loud.

Because the peace I felt was not compatible with the graphic scene she was detailing, I believed the Holy Spirit had let me know everything was all right. I surmised the dream was not a true dream from the Lord, not a vision of things to come.

Then I remembered many past conversations I had shared with Jeri. She struggled against an overprotective fear for her son and grandchildren. She lived a life of anxiety, worried about them because of the seriousness of their living situation. They dealt on a day-to-day basis with severe dysfunction in their family.

"Jeri, I believe this dream is not of the Lord," I said. "I believe it is a soul dream brought on by your own fears." Then I explained some of the different types of dreams.

"Also," I continued, "since dreams are usually metaphorical, if this *was* a dream from the Lord, dying in a dream is often a metaphor for dying to an old lifestyle and birthing something new."

I spoke more on the subject until I could feel she had calmed down.

"Okay," she said. "I'm going to hold onto that and claim that this isn't about him getting killed."

"Time will prove it right or wrong," I said, wincing a little at my lack of tact.

Time did prove it was just a fear dream. Several years have passed, and her son is still fine. I believe the dream's purpose was to act as a pressure relief valve for the anxiety of her soul.

God

Some dreams are given to us by God through His Holy Spirit. He might use a dream to give us help or to educate us. He might give us a dream to guide us, to give us insight or to warn us. Sometimes He gives us a dream to tell us about something that will happen or something He is going to do. The Bible says He does nothing without first telling us:

> Surely the Lord GOD does nothing unless He reveals His secret counsel to His servants the prophets.
>
> Amos 3:7

Most often, dreams given to us by God are given so we can understand ourselves better. They help us know why we react the way we do. He is working to help us understand our attitudes, perceptions, motives and habits:

> But there is a God in heaven who reveals secrets. . . . Your dream, and the visions of your head upon your bed, were these: . . . He who reveals secrets has made known to you what will be . . . that you may know the thoughts of your heart.
>
> Daniel 2:28–30 NKJV

Here is an example of a God dream. Rebecca was a thirty-one-year-old woman freshly back from a tour of duty in Iraq. Relieved from military service, she tried to get a job in her field of expertise in the civilian world. After several unsuccessful months, she moved across the country to be close to her parents and continued to seek employment.

In June, she received a dream and shared it with me. I interpreted her dream in this way:

Around Christmastime, you will receive a job in your field.

Strapped for cash, Rebecca continued to apply for positions, with no success. Just before Christmas, during the holiday hoopla, she received a good job offer. The dream was true. It was a dream God gave her to fill her with hope and assurance and to let her know that God was with her.

Enemy

Spiritual dreams may also come from a wrong spirit, meaning one of Satan's minions, such as a devil or a demon. This type of dream is usually given to inflict fear, to confuse or to instill condemnation.

Here again, it is wise to ask, What source is behind the dream? Jeri's dream about her son driving off a cliff could have been viewed as an enemy dream that aimed to inflict fear. So, was it a soul dream rooted in her own fear or an enemy dream meant to inflict fear? We can usually find clues that point to one or the other.

As I already shared, my previous experience with Jeri had proved she was prone to extreme fear on behalf of her grown children and young grandchildren. I believe that is the clue that her dream was likely brought on by her soul. A clue that a dream might be given by the enemy is when the dream includes hints of darkness or dark coverings on the people in the dream—as in the following example.

Tom, a strong, Spirit-filled Christian man, was a good dad. He had his hands full because he juggled two families—his sons by his first marriage, which ended in divorce, and two sons from his current marriage. Tom tried hard to meet the needs of both sets of offspring.

One morning, he awoke confused and hurting from a dream. He relayed the dream to me:

I dreamed I was running and trying to get to my boys. They were in two different places. I knew they all needed me. I had to choose which group to run to. I chose the most urgent need, the two who were waiting for medication. [In real life, the children did not need or take prescriptions but were healthy.]

When I got there, I was too late. My sons were critically sick because I had not arrived in time with the medicine.

As I was grieving over my sick sons, a man came into the room. He was dressed in black and had dark hair. He pointed his finger at me accusingly and said, "Your other sons were injured because you did not get there in time to prevent a car from hitting them." I knew he was right and that I had failed all my children. I felt worthless and devastated. I woke up.

Did God give Tom this dream, or did the enemy? Or had it originated from his soul? To determine whether Tom's dream originated from God, we ask, Does it follow the character and nature of God as the Bible has revealed it to us?

The twenty-third chapter of Psalms displays God's character as He relates to humans:

> The LORD is my shepherd, I shall not want. He makes me lie down in green pastures; He leads me beside quiet waters. He restores my soul; He guides me in the paths of righteousness for His name's sake.
>
> Even though I walk through the valley of the shadow of death, I fear no evil, for You are with me; Your rod and Your staff, they comfort me. You prepare a table before me in the presence of my enemies; You have anointed my head with oil; my cup overflows. Surely goodness and lovingkindness will follow me all the days of my life, and I will dwell in the house of the LORD forever.

Or how about Romans?

> Therefore there is now no condemnation for those who are in Christ Jesus.
>
> Romans 8:1

As these verses indicate, God's character is to guide, provide, restore, comfort and do away with fear by using loving-kindness. Tom condemned himself in his dream for not being able to meet the needs of others in spite of his best efforts. This does not sound like God. It sounds more like self-degradation (a soul issue) or condemnation from a devil.

So, which was it? Self-degradation? Or was a devil in the middle of this?

I believe this was a spiritual dream from the enemy because of the dark symbols in the dream. The man who appeared in the dream could be symbolic of an outside source or spirit that was bringing accusation against Tom. His dark hair and clothes could be metaphors for a dark covering on him. (See the "Dictionary of Theme Symbols" section of this book for more on this.) This dream was probably an accusation made against Tom by a force of darkness we will politely call the enemy.

Poor Tom! As a child, he had suffered under a hard, controlling, abusive father. Because of his past experiences and in spite of his best efforts to let go of the baggage, he still struggled to see Father God as a kind and loving but revered God. When Tom first told me about this dream, he thought God had given him the dream to criticize him. Always determined to "help" God out, Tom beat himself up pretty well. He told me he felt like a failure, so much so that it threw him into depression.

Why would the enemy give Tom this dream? What is a devil's purpose in giving any of us dreams? The enemy's purpose is always to attack or misdirect us. That is likely what he was trying to do to Tom. He likely sought to "freeze" Tom, in order to keep him from progressing in life, to confuse him or to instill a sense of worthlessness in him so he would not be productive.

> Be of sober spirit, be on the alert. Your adversary, the devil, prowls around like a roaring lion, seeking someone to devour.
>
> 1 Peter 5:8

This passage confirms that it is not God's will for us to live in fear or depression but that the enemy tries to distract or defeat us any way he can, including through the use of our dreams.

To learn the source of a dream, ask where the dream came from: the dreamer's body, the dreamer's soul, God or a devil. If the dreamer believes the dream is from God, encourage the dreamer to look for confirmation. People who rely on dreams alone for guidance and decisions open themselves up to deception and error. Words from God are followed by confirmation from Him:

> Every fact is to be confirmed by the testimony of two or three witnesses.
>
> 2 Corinthians 13:1

God Himself asks us to obtain confirmation. And He gives it in various ways. The dreamer may receive confirmation from the Scriptures of the Bible, from unsolicited comments or advice, from books or through circumstances. God designed creativity! He will be creative in His confirmation.

Correct interpretation of a dream should be obtained biblically. Additionally, because it is difficult to interpret our own dreams, we should seek to obtain the counsel of an interpreter who applies the biblical interpretive process. Our strong souls influence us often in our interpretations. Godly interpretation will be easier to receive if the interpreter is abiding in Jesus, because then he or she has a better chance of hearing the Holy Spirit. The Holy Spirit may speak to the interpreter and to the dreamer's spirit. Understanding will come if the interpretation is correct.

What Do You Mean, "God's Voice"?

It is difficult for some to believe that God wants to reach out to them. They might believe He reaches out to others but not to them. It is hard for these people to benefit from God dreams.

One example of this is my friend Jeff. My husband and I sat across from Jeff and his wife at a restaurant and listened to him proclaim, "Anyone who says they have visions from God is either a liar or of the devil!" He did not appear to notice the venom that spewed out with his words.

My heart sank, for he had been a part of my life for many years. A member of a mainstream denomination where visions were traditionally unpopular, he could not receive my testimony. His ears were shut, and his heels dug in. He would have none of it. He was a strong, God-fearing man, but he was standing on the legalistic doctrines of his lifelong belief system.

My enthusiasm often gets me in trouble, and never more so than when I speak of hearing God to one who does not believe God exists— or, worse, to another believer who is convinced those who hear God are evil or liars or even schizophrenic.

I have a circle of comfortable friends. We talk at warp speed and jump from talking about the alligator snapping turtle removed from the front yard to the latest word we heard from God without a blink. Who thinks we are strange? We certainly do not, and I have been told I am perceptive.

But an acquaintance, Lydia, who overheard our conversation one day, stopped us short by saying, "What do you mean, 'God's voice'?"

I paused. (I must *not* be very perceptive, or I would have considered my audience better!)

An innate people-pleaser, I had been working with God on my character. I do not mean the character I had been in the past. Rather, He was building a *new* character in me, one of integrity in Christ, and part of that process was to consider those around me.

When Lydia asked, "What do you mean, 'God's voice'?," I realized I had been insensitive to those within hearing distance. I knew I needed to meet Lydia where she was.

So I slowed down. We had a long talk about God—who He is to us and how we can hear His voice. Today, Lydia is a Spirit-filled woman of God who relays dreams and words from God to me and others on a regular basis.

I have found that God speaks to me in many ways. I have had words of knowledge given to me, which means information has appeared in my understanding in a way that could only be divine. I have also received words that were timely and fitly spoken by others, as well as dreams and visions.

The Bible says God speaks to us in many ways:

> God, after He spoke long ago to the fathers in the prophets in many portions and many ways, in these last days has spoken to us in His Son, whom He appointed heir of all things, through whom He also made the world.

> Hebrews 1:1–2

Sadly, some God-fearing people interpret this passage in a way that closes their ears to the many windows and doors the Lord may use to speak. A man named Jerod remarked, "That verse says God *no longer* speaks to people in many ways and that in these last days, God *only* speaks to us through His Son, Jesus—and He only uses the Bible to do that!"

In fact, a more appropriate interpretation of this verse might be:

> In the past, God spoke in different measures and in many diverse ways, but in these later years He also speaks through His Son.

This expands the way the Lord speaks to us. He used to speak one way. Now He speaks that way as well as in this additional way, through His Son. I believe this interpretation is confirmed by these verses:

> In a dream, a vision of the night, when sound sleep falls on men, while they slumber in their beds, then He [God] opens the ears of men, and seals their instruction.

> Job 33:15–16

> It will come about after this that I will pour out My Spirit on all mankind; and your sons and daughters will prophesy, your old men will dream dreams, your young men will see visions.

> Joel 2:28

It is written, "Man shall not live on bread alone, but on every word that proceeds out of the mouth of God."

Matthew 4:4

However, as it is written: "What no eye has seen, what no ear has heard, and what no human mind has conceived"—the things God has prepared for those who love him—these are the things God has revealed to us by his Spirit.

The Spirit searches all things, even the deep things of God. For who knows a person's thoughts except their own spirit within them? In the same way no one knows the thoughts of God except the Spirit of God. What we have received is not the spirit of the world, but the Spirit who is from God, so that we may understand what God has freely given us. This is what we speak, not in words taught us by human wisdom but in words taught by the Spirit, explaining spiritual realities with Spirit-taught words. The person without the Spirit does not accept the things that come from the Spirit of God but considers them foolishness, and cannot understand them because they are discerned only through the Spirit.

1 Corinthians 2:9–14 NIV

If anyone thinks they are a prophet or otherwise gifted by the Spirit, let them acknowledge that what I am writing to you is the Lord's command. But if anyone ignores this, they will themselves be ignored.

Therefore, my brothers and sisters, be eager to prophesy, and do not forbid speaking in tongues.

1 Corinthians 14:37–39 NIV

He said, "Listen to My words: When there is a prophet among you, I, the LORD, reveal myself to them in visions, I speak to them in dreams."

Numbers 12:6 NIV

Then there are those who do not believe that God takes the time and effort to talk to individuals. Stuart was one of these people.

"God Himself talking to individuals is more of that *egocentric* teaching," he told me. "You know, where the world revolves around the individual instead of God."

His comments indicated that those who do believe God still talks to people are putting themselves as a center point of focus, and thus taking the focus off of God. This is part of his paradigm.

But the following verse states that, indeed, the Lord does seek out individuals:

What man among you, if he has a hundred sheep and has lost one of them, does not leave the ninety-nine in the open pasture and go after the one which is lost until he finds it?

Luke 15:4

In this verse, the number ninety-nine represents the majority, or the corporate Church. The number one represents the individual in need. And the shepherd represents Jesus.

Or how about the tenth chapter of John?

The sheep hear his voice, and he calls his own sheep by name and leads them out. When he puts forth all his own, he goes ahead of them, and the sheep follow him because they know his voice.

John 10:3–4

Jesus gave these two parables to tell us He will seek us out individually. He calls us by name because He wants communication with each of us. We learn to recognize His voice.

He speaks in dreams, in visions and through other prophetic methods. Both the Old Testament book of Joel and the New Testament book of Acts say He pours out His Spirit on *all* people:

It will come about after this that I will pour out My Spirit on all mankind.

Joel 2:28

"And it shall be in the last days," God says, "that I will pour forth of My Spirit on all mankind; and your sons and your daughters shall prophesy, and your young men shall see visions, and your old men shall dream dreams; even on My bondslaves, both men and women, I will in those days pour forth of My Spirit and they shall prophesy."

Acts 2:17–18

Okay. The "pouring forth of the Spirit" part appears to be a little more comfortable to most Christians. Many might believe this refers to the Spirit being poured out through Bible readings. Others may see this happening through God-inspired human kindness and helpful intervention into needy lives. People can make that verse fit most of their paradigms in one way or another.

But when they hear people sitting at the table next to them at their favorite burger joint talk about a personal revelation received in dreams or visions, they pretend to have no interest. Their intellect—or their denomination—does not want to go there. So they eavesdrop. After all, it might be good material for their next judgmental or humorous conversation. This is the kind of stuff only kooks believe. (*Merriam-Webster* defines a *kook* as "one whose ideas or actions are eccentric, fantastic, or insane; a screwball.")[1]

My friend Sam believes that way.

"What do you mean, 'God's voice'?" Sam asked. "Dreams are just our thoughts coming out. They're nothing. They mean nothing. Anybody who believes they do is a kook!"

Sam was intellectual. In fact, he was *an intellectual*. And he was proud of it. He was not going to fall for one of those old wives' tales.

Going back to what we learned in the last chapter, if the mind, will and emotions make up the soul, then intellectualism falls under the category of the soul. Sam's mind, made up of his intellect, his knowledge and other worldly teachings, could not recognize spiritual things. And his will, made up of his habits, desires, preferences and actions, did not identify with spiritual things. His emotions were comprised of feelings and thoughts he was comfortable with. His

45

paradigms and belief systems controlled his reactions and processed his emotions so he would feel upset or happy. All of these operated in his soul.

According to the Bible, because Sam was using his intellect, he was never going to understand the spiritual aspect of God speaking to us through dreams. As 1 Corinthians 2:12–14 teaches, we know spiritual things by the spirit. If we believe what the Bible says is true, then when Sam operates out of his intellect, he is not able to recognize spiritual things.

But Sam *can* know spiritual things. How? By his spirit. Since his spirit is comprised of wisdom, communion and conscience, then he must receive spiritual things through these channels. If he allows his wisdom to receive the ultimate wisdom of God (for, as Ephesians 1:17 indicates, who other than God is truly wise?), he will obtain spiritual wisdom. If he communes with God and is open to receiving what God has to say to him, he will receive spiritual direction. And where Sam's conscience aligns itself, using God's Word as his plumb line, then his conscience will be in line with God. He will begin to receive a conscience based on absolute truth, not a conscience based on truth from his biased culture and paradigms. For the only real truth is from God (see John 14:6). Through these channels, Sam can tune in to spiritual things.

Maybe because Sam was too proud to lay down intellectualism, he found it easier to believe that God does not communicate to us through dreams. Maybe he found it easier to peg those who believe this way as kooks.

But if only kooks get dreams and visions, then how do we explain Acts 2:17—the part about seeing visions and dreaming dreams? Or how do we explain what the book of Joel says?

Who Are the "Old Men" and "Young Men"?

Again, in Joel 2:28 and Acts 2:17, God promised us He would pour out dreams using His Holy Spirit. So, what does it mean in these passages when it says "old men" shall dream dreams? I am not an old man, yet I have dreams. "Old men" and "young men" in these verses must be metaphors, then.

In fact, in Job, Ezekiel, 1 Kings, Psalms and Proverbs, we learn that the "old men" referred to those who were wise, able to understand, experienced, mature, continually fruitful and of strong faith. (See the "Dictionary of Theme Symbols/People and Beings" section of this book for the chapters and verses.) If the phrase "old men" is a metaphor for these traits, then the phrase "young men" would be a metaphor for the opposite.

And, indeed, in Exodus, Proverbs and 1 John, we find "young men" were those who had immature spiritual knowledge, lacked discretion and had less wisdom. In 1 Kings 12:8–14, "young men" represented unwise counsel. In Luke, it represented restlessness and impatience. (Again, see the "Dictionary of Theme Symbols/People and Beings" section of this book for the chapters and verses.) Therefore, the references to "old men" and "young men" in Joel 2:28 and Acts 2:17 may be metaphors for these traits.

Now, these verses say the young men shall see visions and the old men shall dream dreams. What is the difference between dreams and visions?

What Is the Difference between Dreams and Visions?

There are primarily two different thoughts/ideologies on the differences.

The first ideology compares "awake" versus "asleep." Visions are things seen while awake. Dreams are things seen in your sleep.

The second ideology compares "what actually is" versus "symbolic representation." Visions are a display of "what is—a real happening." Dreams are metaphors or symbols representing something else.

I believe the second concept is more accurate. I see dreams as symbolic and visions as snapshots of actual happenings—whether that happening is currently taking place, occurred in the past or will transpire in the future. Dreams are metaphors, analogies and similes. Therefore, we must look at their symbols to understand them.

The second concept also connects with what we have said about the biblical definitions of "old men" and "young men." Since there is little need to interpret a vision because a vision is "what actually is" and therefore needs no explanation, the immature, or "young men," are able to understand it, even with their limited experiences.

However, a dream is more difficult to discern. It is a metaphorical picture and requires analysis using biblical symbols and interpretation. Therefore, wiser, more experienced "old men" are often needed to discern them.

Putting this together, the verses that say "old men shall dream dreams" and "young men shall see visions" might be reworded in this way:

> The spiritually wise primarily, but not exclusively, will receive dreams or things that are more difficult to understand. And the spiritually immature primarily, but not exclusively, will receive visions or things that are easier to understand.

Ultimately, I believe these verses speak of different levels of spiritual maturity. They make an analogy between our ability to perceive and the Lord's ways of communicating with us, based on our ability.

Complicated? No. What is complicated is a project management system for engineers. Dream interpretation is simpler than you might think. Dreams consist of metaphors, as we have discussed, and simply put pictures inside the text of a story. Remember the childhood books where we read things like, "I saw a [picture of a train]"? Did we not feel smart in our ability to "read" such big words? This is no different. The problem is that our analytical and intelligent minds no longer recognize pictures as part of the story. We need to go back to basics.

Now, these verses refer to men, and there is no mention of women. What about women, then? Again, do not forget to look at the big picture. Remember that Acts 2:17–18 says, "Your sons and your daughters." Here, we go back to one of the biblical principles outlined in the first chapter, where we said that "men" includes women.

And what about the beneficiaries of these dreams and visions—who gets to receive them? These verses say *all* flesh, not just those who believe in God, which must mean that all people get dreams from God. Not all will understand them, or even remember them, but we all get them.

What if we do not realize that a dream was given to us by God? Well, then we will not give the dream the credence it deserves. And we will miss out on the very words we often seek—an answer to a prayer or an insight into a troublesome situation.

Use caution, though! Not all dreams come from God. God says to test it. In fact, He says to "test them all; hold on to what is good" (1 Thessalonians 5:21 NIV). It is through the Holy Spirit and biblical interpretation that we can be sure "the dream is true and its interpretation is trustworthy" (Daniel 2:45 NIV). In other words, there is need for discernment and counsel in interpretations. We will look more closely at this later.

What about Psychological Views on Dreams?

"I know all I need to know about dreams! And they don't mean nothin'!"

I could not help hearing the loud proclamation of the thin-haired man whose gelatin belly hung four inches below his waist. He waddled down the pavestone path and pointed his authoritative finger at his friend, his voice trumpeting several decibels too loud and appearing to embarrass his demure friend. My ears grew in their effort to catch the quieter man's reply, but all I could hear were murmurs.

They must know I'm eavesdropping, I figured as I caught their glance. But it made me think. What had the pontificator been taught about dreams? What had I been taught about dreams?

My college psychology classes used the theories of Sigmund Freud and his student Carl Jung to explain dreams. Like most of the other engineering students in the class, I accepted these theories as fact—that is, until several years later, when I realized the theories did not hold up against my own dreams.

Freud's[2] and Jung's[3] teachings were based on their mutual assumption that humans pull from within themselves to figure out problems and come up with solutions. In other words, people fix themselves.

But this makes about as much sense to me as a malfunctioning electrical system's ability to fix itself. In my experience, a fix does not happen without input from a programmer or other knowledgeable source. Additionally, the Bible clearly states we cannot fix ourselves and that, in fact, only God can fix us:

> There is a way which seems right to a man, but its end is the way of death.
>
> Proverbs 14:12

> Those who trust in themselves are fools.
>
> Proverbs 28:26 NIV

> Cursed is the man who trusts in mankind and makes flesh his strength.
>
> Jeremiah 17:5

> There is none righteous, not even one.
>
> Romans 3:10

These verses short-circuit suggestions that people progress to higher levels of goodness and perfection through their own hard work. They say we should not trust in our own efforts to improve ourselves.

Freud taught that dreams expose our inner thoughts and camouflage a dreamer's forbidden or secret desires. These emotions and desires are so unconscious, according to Freud's teaching on manifest content, that what the dreamer remembers possesses no meaning whatsoever. Freud's teaching takes God and the dreamer out of the picture and leaves the interpretation to an outside party: the interpreter.

Jung differed from Freud in some respects. He did not teach that dreams were as base or animalistic as Freud did. To Jung, dreams were not an attempt to conceal the dreamer's true desires but instead were a spyglass into the dreamer's unconscious. He said dreams originate with the dreamer and are all about the dreamer. Also, the dream helps the dreamer reach inside and fix himself.

Freud's and Jung's theories may be true in my work situation when I try to recall the correct equation to obtain the amperage output from a circuit's known resistance and voltage. I need to reach inside my engineering mind (intellect) and recall Ohm's Law, which says $V=IR$ (voltage across an element is directly proportional to the current flow through it and resistance). Their theories fall flat, however, when faced with the Bible's perspective on human nature and on spiritual versus intellectual things.

I am bold enough to say that human nature follows the same scientific rules that apply to most other systems on earth. The scientific principle of the Second Law of Thermodynamics states, "Everything left unchanged will move toward more entropy, or disorder." Or, as I have heard a couple of scientists paraphrase it, "For all increase in order, somewhere within the system disorder increases at a greater amplitude." This simply means that things do not fix themselves without some helpful input.

I believe this law also applies to the closed-circuit system called a human. As individuals endeavor toward order by their own effort, somewhere within themselves a greater measure of disorder, or chaos, develops.

Let's look at an example of this law. A young woman, heartbroken by her last two boyfriends, determines to avoid future bad experiences in her love life. She may attempt to create protection [order] by making an inner vow to never give another man a chance to hurt her. Subsequently, she becomes harsh to men and develops an instantaneous dislike of any man who comes into her presence. Her actions and the self-induced hardening of her heart create a greater disorder that becomes a dysfunction in her life. Freud and Jung claim that humans can reach inside and fix themselves, but in my observation, this is not natural for a human. We usually need outside input—perhaps in the form of wise counsel or God's Word.

Furthermore, we can dispute Freud's theory that "the parts remembered have no meaning." The dream about the sinking van I relayed in the first chapter disputes this, as we learned that my friend Anne truly was sinking under the weight of her business.

Another dream of mine further disputes Freud's claim. One morning I awoke shaken. I had been having a dream about logs falling off of a truck.

> I was driving my car [but it was not my car in real life]. I looked out the windshield and saw a semitruck pulling a flatbed of long logs in front of me. The logger was stacked high, and the rear corners of the bed were L-shaped metal brackets that held the logs on the bed. As I drove fast down the highway, I saw the right rear-corner bracket break off and the logs start to fall onto the road in front of my vehicle. I knew I could not stop in time. I knew I would hit with full force the fallen logs. Then I woke up.

The dream scared me. I prayed it would not happen. I was living in the northwest part of the United States and frequently found myself driving behind logger trucks. I prayed protection for myself against an accident of this nature.

As I thought about the dream, I remembered the car I had been driving had not been my real car. I thought maybe I had been looking through the eyes of someone else, so I began to pray for the person I might have represented in the dream—because who knew? I wanted to cover all my bases.

I relayed the dream to Anne, and we agreed to pray for safety for whomever the dream was about.

I tried to put the dream out of my mind over the next few months, but I would recall it every time I found myself driving behind a logging truck, and I would quickly cease following the truck.

Months later, I received a call from Anne.

"Do you remember your dream about the logs falling off a truck?" she asked.

"Yeah, hard to forget," I responded. "I'm still paranoid every time I see a logger truck."

"Well, the dream was about Sharon."

"Why do you say that?" Sharon was a mutual friend of ours.

Anne continued, "Sharon called and told me something interesting. She was driving home and had been driving for a couple of hours when she sensed an urgent demand to pull over."

Goose bumps crept up my arms.

"'Pull over! Pull over! Pull over,' she heard." Anne's intensity increased with each command as she told the story.

She continued, "Sharon kept hearing this screaming inside her head. It shook her up enough that she pulled her car over onto the side of the highway. She sat there and tried to make sense of it."

"What happened?" I asked, anxious.

"About twenty minutes later, she felt a release and pulled back onto the highway. She drove a short distance. Just around a bend, she saw logs all over the road."

Anne's voice softened. "The logger truck Sharon had been following before she felt she was supposed to pull over was stopped in the road. A side of the truck's bed had broken off, and logs were all over the place. They were spread like pickup sticks covering the highway. Sharon told me, 'If I had not pulled over when I did, I would have hit the logs.'"

My dream was about Sharon! Even though Sharon had renounced God and claimed to no longer be a believer, God's divine intervention told her to pull over. He did not renounce her. And He sent me the dream to pray for her. He saved her and answered our prayers.

So, is Freud's theory true, that "the parts remembered [in a dream] have no meaning"? To answer that question, let's consider the scientific method, which *Merriam-Webster* defines as a way of pursuing knowledge through "the recognition and formulation of a problem, the collection of data through observation and experiment, and the formulation and testing of hypotheses."[4]

The steps for research development speak of hypothesis, theory and law. A hypothesis is an educated guess. It may be disproven but not proven to be true. A theory is a hypothesis supported by repeated tests; it is valid only until there is evidence to dispute it. A law has no exceptions to it.

Again, the dreams about the sinking van and the falling logs dispute Freud's theory that "the parts remembered have no meaning," as we have seen that they *did* have meaning. Also, the dreams dispute the Jungian theory that everyone in the dream is the dreamer, for these dreams were not about me at all, though I was the one who dreamed them. The sinking-van dream was about Anne, and the falling-log dream was about Sharon.

Since hypotheses are only valid as long as there is no evidence to dispute them, I submit these two dreams as evidence—and these are only two of many dreams I could submit to provide a more substantial quantity of evidence. Based on the scientific method, these dreams and the stories connected to them nullify Freud's and Jung's theories of dream interpretation.

However, both men had brilliant minds and were on to something in the dream interpretation process. Freud, and later Jung, said dreams are made up of symbols. The symbols in Anne's sinking-van dream and the symbols in my dream where something was wrong with my appendix prove that part of their symbol theory is true. The van was a symbol of Anne's work. The act of the van sinking was a symbol of the business failing. The appendix in the other dream was a play-on-words symbol for the report's appendices.

However, Freud and Jung claim the meaning of a dream's symbols only originates from the dreamer's psyche. They ignore biblical symbols, and this often results in incorrect dream interpretation.

Later, Jung diverged from his earlier teachings and said that dreams are more "spiritual" than Freud had presented. My friend Ruth's dream about the she-bear watching over her cub, which I shared in the first chapter, was spiritual in that it was a direct answer to Ruth's prayer.

Jung missed it, though, when he taught that all dreams originate from the dreamer. The Bible teaches that spiritual dreams are not always creations from the dreamer's spirit. They may also originate from an outside spiritual source, like the Holy Spirit, or they may come from a spiritual representative of the devil. Yes, folks. In engineering you learn quickly that the devil is real and active. Or is that the law profession? Or the fast-food industry? No matter. The Bible says the devil is real, so I believe it.

Many spiritual dreams are given to the dreamer instead of being created by the dreamer. The interpretation of these dreams must come from God:

> Then they said to him, "We have had a dream and there is no one to interpret it." Then Joseph said to them, "Do not interpretations belong to God? Tell it to me, please."
>
> Genesis 40:8

We have a choice to apply biblical interpretations or psychological interpretations to dreams. I suggest we go back to basics and turn to God and His Word for interpretations.

Does the Bible Reference Dreams and Visions?

Throughout the Bible, we find references to dreams, visions and their meanings. Here are a few of the most familiar ones:

1. Gideon and his servant overheard their enemies fearfully relate a dream that Gideon's army would destroy them (see Judges 7:9–15).

2. King Abimelech, king of Gerar, was given a dream to warn him that Sarah was the wife of Abraham and that the king should leave her alone (see Genesis 20:1–14).

3. Jacob was given a dream that told him to return to the land of his birth (see Genesis 31:11–13).

4. Joseph, the son of Jacob, was told in a dream that his family would bow down before him (see Genesis 37:5–10). Of course, this came true later (see Genesis 42:6).

5. Joseph also interpreted the dreams of the Pharaoh's baker and butler (see Genesis 40:8–23).

6. Later, Joseph interpreted the dream of Pharaoh (see Genesis 41).

7. Daniel interpreted King Nebuchadnezzar's dream (see Daniel 2:1–47).

8. Joseph was told in a dream that he should take Mary as his wife (see Matthew 1:20–23).

9. Later, Joseph was warned in a dream to flee to Egypt to keep young Jesus safe (see Matthew 2:13).

10. And again, Joseph was told in a dream that the danger to Jesus was over and he could go home (see Matthew 2:19–23).

11. John was given the whole book of Revelation in a vision (see Revelation 1:1–2).

From the beginning of the Bible to the end, in both the Old Testament and New Testament, dreams and visions are tools the Lord uses to communicate with us. God put enough importance on dreams and visions that He referenced them throughout the Bible. (For more of these references, see Genesis 28:12–19; Numbers 12:6; Deuteronomy 13:1–5; 1 Samuel 28:6; 1 Kings 3:5–15; Job 7:13–14; 33:15–16;

Jeremiah 23:25–32; 27:9; 29:8–9; Daniel 1:17; 4:1–37; 5:12; 7:1–28; 8:1–27; 10:1–21; Joel 2:28; Matthew 27:19; Luke 1:11–38; Acts 2:17; Hebrews 1:1–2; Jude 8; and the book of Revelation.)

Why Should I Pay Attention to My Dreams?

God could use other methods than dreams to speak to us, and He often does. But dreams are one of His chosen methods. He uses them to give guidance, direction, creativity, prophecy, warning, healing and understanding. If we deny His dreams, we reject a means by which God receives glory. We also miss out on a wonderful blessing from God. When we do not believe God speaks to us through dreams, we ignore one of the great ways in which we can hear Him.

I believe this passage says that if we do not pay attention to our dreams and visions as a method of communication from God, then, little by little, we will receive fewer and fewer dreams and visions.

> To you it has been granted to know the mysteries of the kingdom of heaven, but to them it has not been granted. For whoever has, to him more shall be given, and he will have an abundance; but whoever does not have, even what he has shall be taken away from him.
>
> Matthew 13:11–12

These things will become less clear to us, as what we have been given will begin to slip away from us. The Bible seems to confirm this in Paul's first letter to the Corinthians:

> Or did the Word of God originate with you? . . . But if anyone ignores this, they will themselves be ignored.
>
> 1 Corinthians 14:36, 38 NIV

God wants us to be eager to explore and use the gifts He gave us. Jesus, in the book of Matthew, tells us that God wants us to search our dreams and speak them out:

What I tell you in the darkness, speak in the light; and what you hear whispered in your ear, proclaim upon the housetops.

Matthew 10:27

Additionally, the book of Proverbs teaches:

It is the glory of God to conceal a matter, but the glory of kings is to search out a matter.

Proverbs 25:2

Why Does God Speak in Metaphors Rather Than Directly?

By studying the dreams in the Bible and their interpretations, we see that God uses symbols and metaphors to represent various aspects of dreams. But why does God do this? In fact, the apostles asked Jesus this question:

And the disciples came and said to Him, "Why do You speak to them in parables?" Jesus answered them, "To you it has been granted to know the mysteries of the kingdom of heaven, but to them it has not been granted. For whoever has, to him more shall be given, and he will have in abundance; but whoever does not have, even what he has shall be taken away from him. Therefore I speak to them in parables; because while seeing they do not see, and while hearing they do not hear, nor do they understand. In their case the prophecy of Isaiah is being fulfilled, which says, 'You will keep on hearing, but will not understand; you will keep on seeing, but will not perceive; for the heart of this people has become dull, with their ears they scarcely hear, and they have closed their eyes, otherwise they would see with their eyes, hear with their ears, and understand with their heart and return, and I would heal them.' But blessed are your eyes, because they see; and your ears, because they hear. For truly I say to you that many prophets and righteous men desired to see what you see, and did not see it, and to hear what you hear, and did not hear it."

Matthew 13:10–17

Jesus' answer says that some people are granted the gift of understanding veiled things, or the mysteries of the Kingdom of heaven, but others are not able to understand them because they have become complacent, meaning dull to the Word, unconcerned and without interest. These ones do not try to understand. They close their ears and eyes.

So, why does God speak in metaphors and symbols? Additional verses in the Bible also speak to this (see Isaiah 6:9–10; Mark 4:10–12, 22–25; Luke 8:9–10). These verses imply that Jesus speaks to us in parables to get through our walls of complacency so we can understand.

During His walk on earth, Jesus taught people using everyday language full of word pictures, parables and metaphors. Some of these are shown in the following word pictures:

Christians are the salt of the earth (see Matthew 5:13).

Christians are the light of the world (see Matthew 5:14–16).

Do not let your left hand know what your right hand is doing (see Matthew 6:3–4).

Do not store up treasures on earth (see Matthew 6:19–21).

The eye is the lamp of the body (see Matthew 6:22–23).

Ask, seek and knock (see Matthew 7:7–12).

Beware false prophets (see Matthew 7:15–16).

Pay attention to the fruit (see Matthew 7:16–20).

Build houses on rock and sand (see Matthew 7:21–27).

Jesus is the Bridegroom (see Matthew 9:15).

Jesus has a true family (see Matthew 12:46–50).

Additionally, He gave many parables:

The parable of the four soils (see Matthew 13:3–9, 18–23)

The parable of the weeds (see Matthew 13:24–30, 36–43)

The parable of the mustard seed (see Matthew 13:31–32)

The parable of the yeast (see Matthew 13:33)

The parable of the hidden treasure (see Matthew 13:44)

The parable of the pearl merchant (see Matthew 13:45–46)

The parable of the fishing net (see Matthew 13:47–50)

The list goes on—these are taken from just part of the book of Matthew. Whew! Jesus used metaphors and parables a lot. He ministered that way then, and He does not change. In fact, since the beginning, God has used symbols, parables and metaphors to communicate with us. His Bible is full of metaphorical explanations and teachings.

So, then, in a dream, it is unwise to assume a tree is a tree, a dance is a dance and a dog is a dog. For example, in the Bible, trees are often representative of people (see Psalm 1:3). Dancing might mean taking the same view or moving together (see Matthew 11:17), or it may be a metaphor for joy (see Jeremiah 31:4), worship (see 2 Samuel 6:14) or idolatry (see Matthew 14:6–7). Dogs may be unclean people, like the negative meaning found in 1 Kings 14:11, or servants of the master, meaning Jesus, like the positive meaning found in Matthew 15:27. By researching the symbols in the Bible and praying for guidance from the Holy Spirit, the correct interpretation may be reached.

I hope these answers supply a few morsels of new, or old, information to chew on as we have addressed many common dream questions. I encourage deeper study into each question and answer—being diligent to "rightly divide" the word of truth (see 2 Timothy 2:15). The Bible says now we know in part, but later, when Jesus is fully known, we will know fully (see 1 Corinthians 13:12). In Proverbs 25:2, King Solomon said that it is the glory of God to conceal a matter, but the glory of kings is to search out a matter. These verses remind us that it is okay to have questions about God's ways—and God encourages us to seek and find their answers. It is exciting to learn about new things God has done and is doing. In the process, we learn His ways and begin to take back for His Kingdom things the enemy has stolen. So ask questions, but do not stop there. Seek out the answers by knocking on the door of God's Word and listening to the Holy Spirit.

In the next chapter, we will look at the steps of interpretation.

3

The Steps
of Dream Interpretation

How do we get dreams? When we get them, what are the steps for interpreting them? Is their meaning cut and dry? If not, what are some ways to discern the meaning of dreams that seem convoluted?

Receiving Dreams

Remembering and keeping track of our dreams is not as easy as we might think. I have often been asked, "Why does God tell us things we already know?" A good question. What purpose is there in that? Those anxious to get started in dream interpretation may ask, "How do we receive dreams, or is there a way to increase the number of dreams we receive?" We are going to look at these questions.

If God is talking to me in my dream, then it must be important, so why do I not remember it?

It can be a process to remember our dreams and interpret them. To remember a dream, first pray and ask the Holy Spirit for the full dream and its interpretation. Often He will bring back to us the important parts of the dream. He might choose to reward us immediately with its meaning. But sometimes it may be days, months or years before we understand a dream. Why?

> In a dream, a vision of the night, when sound sleep falls on men, while they slumber in their beds, then He [God] opens the ears of men, and seals their instruction.
>
> Job 33:15–16

Pastor John Paul Jackson, of Streams Ministries International, has said that we sometimes do not remember our dreams because God "seals" the instruction.[1] I believe the above verse in Job tells us God will sometimes give us a dream only to "seal" it; in these cases, either we will not remember it, or we will not receive an interpretation.

Can it be that God gives answers, comfort and guidance to our spirit? For reasons only He fully understands, He wants to speak solely to our spirit. Perhaps He knows we are not ready to receive the answers in our mind, will or emotions, so He "seals" it from us. Since our spirit never sleeps, possibly the spirit will retain the words of God, and it will be there to guide us at the appropriate time.

The following verse indicates that the Lord has a desire for us to aggressively search out the meanings of hidden things of God:

> It is the glory of God to conceal a matter, but the glory of kings is to search out a matter.
>
> Proverbs 25:2

Often God may not reveal a dream to us because we are too complacent and do not seek its meaning. God wants us to be proactive.

The Lord may also seal a dream to protect us from pride as He tells us of prophetic things to come. By protecting us, He will not have to judge us for that errant pride.

While I do not know the specific reasons God might choose to seal a dream or its meaning, the Bible *does* say that God opens our ears and then seals what He has given to us. Interesting.

If you are having trouble remembering a dream, ask the Holy Spirit to reveal it. It is up to Him to remind us of what we need to remember.

How do I keep track of my dreams?

Write them down. Put a notepad and a pen by the bed before sleeping. Do not forget the flashlight; you do not want to rouse a slumbering spouse!

Instead of writing down the whole dream upon awakening in the middle of the night, eyelids heavy from sleep, use notes or sketches to represent the dream. This will be quick and will keep you from losing good sleep. Usually notes or sketches are enough to later jog your memories.

First thing in the morning, write down the dream. Assuming you'll remember the dream usually does not work. A dream fades into oblivion, second by second, until it is forgotten. Capture it as soon as possible.

As we log our dreams, some handy tips may help us capture each dream successfully: title it, date it, write it in scenes and log it.

Title each dream with an easy title that will jog your memory in the future as to what the dream is about.

Post a date on the dream. Often, the date matters because the dreamer might look back and compare occurrences in the dreamer's life with the date of the dream. Months or even years after the dream, the situation might come true, and the date will validate the dream's authenticity.

Write down the dream in "scenes." Instead of trying to take the dream from the first scene to the second, as our rational minds would want to do, simply write down the dream as Scene 1, Scene 2, etc. Do not try to explain how the jump was made to the next scene. Explanations risk diverging from the actual dream and recording information that was never in the original dream. This could corrupt the interpretation.

Store the dreams in a computer log or print out each dream and insert it into a three-ring binder for keeping. For easy reference, these may be stored according to dream type. (See the "Types of Dreams" section of this book).

Why does God give us dreams about ourselves? Why is He telling me something I already know?

Daniel said that God gives dreams so that the dreamer "may understand what went through your mind" (Daniel 2:30 NIV). The implication of this verse is that we often do and say things out of reaction, habit or even from strongholds that carve out our responses without fully understanding why. Also, sometimes, while we may know something intellectually, we do not always grasp the fullness of it in our hearts. Dreams cut through the packaging and reveal the inner truth.

Okay! I'm beginning to believe some of this, so sign me up! How do I make God give me dreams?

What a great question! If anyone out there knows how to "make" God do anything, let me know . . . I think. As God is almighty, I believe I am safe in saying we cannot, and should not, try to *make* Him do anything. He's the one in control, not us. Dreams are revealed to us by His discretion.

However, like all gifts of the Spirit, we may seek and pray for them. We may ask. And if we do get dreams from God, let's pay attention.

Seven Steps to Interpretation

The dream interpretation process may be illustrated as a basic triangle. *Revelation* (the dream) defines the top angle. *Interpretation* defines the lower right angle. *Application* defines the lower left angle. This simple triangle takes the pressure off of immediately having to "know" what a dream means. It can also help us deal with time pressures, as this multi-step process allows for prayer and reflective input from others. This triangle is a simple way to get people to connect with God concerning what they've seen in the dream, what it might mean and how it should impact their life.

There is no single pathway to interpreting; often the Lord just gives the dreamer the interpretation. But if an interpretation search is necessary, there are some additional steps that might help us stay on the right road. Let's look at these steps, as well as questions that interpreters sometimes face.

How do we interpret dreams correctly?

It can be easy to get off track and come up with a wrong interpretation. No matter how hard we try to interpret correctly, we will not get it 100 percent all of the time. But our goal is to be accurate as often as possible and to grow in accuracy as we gain experience. So, how do we stay on the right path when interpreting dreams? To help, here are some basic steps.

Step 1: Pray for guidance from God;
Step 2: Write down or read through the dream to "process" it;
Step 3: Look at the beginning and end of the dream to set the scene;
Step 4: Find the focus, sub-focus and details;
Step 5: Look at the symbol meanings;
Step 6: Replace the symbols with their meanings;
Step 7: Seek counsel.

Step 1: Pray for guidance from God.

Pray. Always ask in Jesus' name: "Father, help me give them the interpretation You want them to have." Ask for the Lord's help. Remember, interpretations belong to the Lord. Do not try to figure it out without Him.

Step 2: Write down or read through the dream to "process" it.

I have found that "processing" the dream by making notes, writing it down or even by reading through an already-recorded dream helps me receive from the Holy Spirit what He would speak to me. It gives me time to download interpretive things about the dream. Identify the dreamer's feelings about people and situations in the dream. Where is the dreamer throughout the dream?

Reflect how parts of the dream affect the dreamer's emotions.

Ask the dreamer how the dream made him feel. Or listen and watch the dreamer give the dream to you. If he frowns when he mentions some unknown man in his dream, it is a safe indication that the man made him feel uneasy. If there is someone besides him in the dream, but he has no bad feelings toward the person, it is possible the person represents an angel or a friendly companion.

Does the dreamer feel happy as he is running naked down the street in his dream? Perhaps he does not seem to care or even notice. Or maybe he notices it and wonders why he is naked, but makes no effort to cover himself. How the dreamer feels about it is an indicator. Pay attention to emotions, as they might give a clue as to what that particular symbol in the dream represents. We will discuss this more in our examination of symbols.

I do not know where I was in the dream. It is like I was just watching from somewhere. What does that mean?

Where is the dreamer in the dream? Is he a player and participating? Or does the dreamer feel he is just watching? Does he feel like he's offscreen, just seeing things unfold? What the dreamer is doing in a dream tells the interpreter something.

If the dreamer is actively participating, helping others or going along with things, it is an indication that the happenings of the dream are about something that the dreamer is involved in—although the dreamer may not be running the show.

If the dreamer is very active, telling others what to do or making major decisions in the dream, it might be an indication that the dream is about something over which the dreamer has control.

However, if the dreamer is watching, then the dream might not be about the dreamer at all. It might be a dream about someone or a group of people that the dreamer is observing or is connected with. It might be a dream to give the dreamer an understanding of someone's problem or a situation. The dream might also be a revelatory dream about circumstances that will unfold in the future on a personal level, a family level, a regional level, a country level or even a worldwide level. It could be about anything that the Lord wants to reveal to that dreamer.

I woke feeling glum. What is that about?

How did the dream make the dreamer feel? Look at the atmosphere during the dream. Was it bright and sunny? Or dark and foreboding? Was it gray? Nondescript? This can affect the dreamer's mood and give the interpreter a clue as to the meaning of the dream.

Bright colors or a bright, sunny dream often indicates a dream from God (sunlight = radiance of God; see Habakkuk 3:4). Dark, foreboding dreams might represent the plans of the enemy (darkness = plans of enemy; see Revelation 22:5). Gray dreams might represent trials (gray rain = trials; see Matthew 7:25–27). Nondescript colors might represent worldly issues or things that are without relevance. A symbol that stands out in a bright color might mean, "Pay attention to this symbol!"

What *about* colors in dreams? Every dream is filtered through God; after all, He's the ultimate authority and has ultimate control. However, just as in all aspects of our life, the Lord often allows other dreams to come to us. So it is a good idea to determine the origin of the dream. Who actually sent it? The dream's colors will often help clarify that.

If the dream's colors are dark: (1) These dreams might be from the Lord to show the dreamer she is going through hard times, or a dark night of the soul, to help the dreamer understand what is going on; (2) These dark dreams might be plans of the enemy[2] or, rather, dreams given by the Lord to expose the enemy's plan of attack; or (3) These dreams might be from the enemy.

If the dream is in gray tones: (1) These might be soul dreams, or dreams that originate from the dreamer's mind, will or emotions; or (2) These, too, may be plans of the enemy that the Lord is exposing to the dreamer.

If the dream is without color: (1) These might be soul dreams; (2) This might be a plan of the enemy the Lord is exposing to the dreamer; or (3) This may be to accent something. Look to see if there are things in the dream in color—possibly only one thing. If so, this could be calling attention to what that symbol represents.

If the colors of the dream are bright, they are usually God dreams.

When interpreting a dream, ask, *Why that color? Why was the shirt worn in the dream green instead of brown—or any other color?* Green, for example, could represent (on the positive side) life or growth. On the ambivalent side, green could represent inexperience (a "greenhorn"). And on the negative side, green may represent envy, lust, decay or rot. To make matters even more complicated, green could be the name of a person (Marsha Greene) or a company (Green Electronics).

We can be sure there is a reason the Lord saw fit to make the shirt green in the dream. Study it; look in the "Dictionary of Theme Symbols/Colors" section for some of the biblical meanings of colors. And, most importantly, ask the Lord. Colors, bright and dark, might be important in a dream. Seek more in-depth study on colors in dreams.

Let's return to the original question about how the dream made the dreamer feel for a moment. Remember Jeri's dream? (See chapter 2, "Common Dream Questions/What Source Is behind My Dream?/ Soul.") She was in a panic. After awakening, confusion can rule until the dreamer decides that fear may not be a valid response—which it almost never is—for God says, "Do not fear, for I am with you" (Isaiah 41:10).

During the dreaming process, dreamers might find themselves in a semi-lucid state where they are dreaming in symbols, but at the same time their mind analyzes what is happening and they realize that what is happening is not conducive to society.

An example of this might be where a dreamer finds himself in a dream calmly peeing in a toilet bowl located in the front yard while many people look on. Although in the dream he appears to be okay doing the action, at the same time, he is thinking, *It is weird that I am using a toilet in the front yard instead of in my house.*

These semi-lucid dreams create a dilemma for the dreamer because the dreamer's spirit is fine with going along with the dream's happenings, but another part of the dreamer (the dreamer's mind/soul) is fighting against it. In these types of dreams, the dreamer is in two states at the same time. He is in a partial dream state, responding to the symbols in the dream, but he is also in a partial lucid state, where his mind is tracking with the real world.

Which wins out? The real world or the dream world? Actually, they both take a toll upon the dreamer. For example, Jeri was in a semi-lucid state in her dream. She saw the vehicle falling off of the cliff with her precious son behind the wheel, and in her semi-lucid state, she panicked. When she awoke, her fear grew even greater because she forgot that dreams are metaphors and, instead, looked at the dream as reality (or as a vision). She was sure her son was going to drive off a cliff. In Jeri's case, it was only after the interpreter discussed this distinction at length with her that she began to lay down her fear and see the dream as the fear soul dream, or even as the metaphor, it might be. Keep this in mind when interpreting: Often dreamers will create feelings in their confusion and forget the dream is only a metaphor.

It is weird! It is like I just showed up in this room and I do not know how I got there. Should I try to figure it out?

Tell the dream in scenes. Think movie! Scene One: I was _____. Scene Two: There were _____. Do not try to connect the dots between the scenes. Trying to connect the dots forces the dreamer to speak out things that were not actually in the dream, i.e., "Well, I must have been going for a walk because I found myself _____."

"Going for a walk" was not actually in the dream; it was a connection the dreamer added to create cohesiveness. It is not necessary, and it hinders the proper interpretation.

Do not help out the dream! Accurate interpretations depend upon not diverging from the dream in any way. Tell only what is actually in the dream.

Whoa! My dream used a word I never use, and I would be embarrassed to let others think I use that word. What do I do with that?

Tell the dream in the language it was given. Do not make the dream politically correct or up-to-date in terminology. There might be a reason that particular word was given. Remember the dream I related in chapter 1, "Where We Begin," in which I dreamed that something was wrong with my appendix? I woke up holding my stomach and wondering if I was coming down sick. Instead, the dream was about an error in the appendices of the report I was working on. What if I had relayed the dream to an interpreter—"I woke up thinking I was sick"? We would have missed the whole point of the dream. That particular word was crucial. Do not try to fix 'em or sanitize 'em.

Likewise, because of embarrassment, we sometimes want to "modify" our dreams. Jane, a Spirit-filled Christian woman who was faithful and loved her husband, woke from a disturbing dream.

> I dreamed I was in bed with George, the husband of my good friend. We were having sex. I was horrified because I would never do that, and, in fact, I have never even thought about such things with him.

Poor Jane. She trusted me very much to tell me that dream. I reminded her that dreams are metaphorical. Her stiff body language eased a little with that reassurance. I told her having sex in a dream might mean "in union with/united" (see Genesis 4:1; Matthew 1:15) or "sharing an intimate or closely personal thing with" (see Ezekiel 16:8).

Relieved, Jane said, "You know, my husband and I were having dinner with George and his wife the evening before I had the dream. At the dinner, George and I began to argue vehemently about our religious differences. We rarely do that, but for some reason, we both laid down grace and felt compelled to make the other understand. We got almost angry with each other until we finally agreed to disagree. Thinking back on it, I believe that was the 'sharing of personal, intimate things' in my dream. After all, what's more intimate than our personal spiritual views?"

The dream convicted Jane that she and George had stepped over an appropriate boundary of their friendship. They were both Christians, but of different denominations. She felt the Lord was telling her "not to go there."

Sex in a dream can be completely unrelated to a physical sexual act. One day Christy stopped me and blurted out the following confession: *"I'm so embarrassed. I dreamed I was having sex with my husband in the church sanctuary."*

Christy's dream confused her. I showed her where "husband" in the Bible often refers to Jesus (the Bridegroom; see Jeremiah 3:14–20; 31:32; 54:5; Hosea 2:14–20 [*ishi* = husband]; Ephesians 5:22–32; Revelation 19:7). And the "church" may be a metaphor for God's people (see 2 Corinthians 11:28–29; Ephesians 2:22). If sex can represent "intimacy with," then where better to have an intimate relationship with Jesus than among God's people? This tears Freud's theory all to pieces.

Do not let the dream be intimidating. And do not try to clean it up. It does not need our help.

Step 3: Look at the beginning and the end of the dream to set the scene.

It can be overwhelming to try to interpret some Christian brothers' and sisters' dreams. They are often convoluted. They sometimes go on and on, and three days later, our good Christian friend is still rambling on about the dream. Where to start?

Look at the first two sentences of the dream. Then look at the last two sentences of the dream. Often, they seem to "set the scene." Here is an example of a short dream given to me by a friend where the beginning and the end not only "set the scene" but almost sum up the dream. Here is the full dream.

> I am in a two-story apartment complex building in the upper-floor apartment. I am sitting in front of a big picture window, and my ex-wife is on the couch sleeping. An unknown man is also in the apartment. It is a small apartment; nevertheless, I yell out that there is a tornado, and we all head downstairs to the basement for shelter.
>
> We get downstairs, and the other man wants to go up to look out the door. I yell at him not to do it, but he does it anyway. Now he cannot get the door shut due to the suction of the tornado.
>
> After the tornado passes, we look around outside. My little car (which in real life I used to have) is still in the parking lot and is okay, but has turned 180 degrees. Then I wake up.

To "set the scene" let's look at the first two sentences and the last two sentences of this dream.

1. I am in a two-story apartment complex building, and we are in the upper-floor apartment.
2. I am sitting in front of a big picture window, and my ex-wife is on the couch sleeping.
3. After the tornado passes, we look around outside.
4. My little car (which in real life I used to have) is still in the parking lot and is okay, but has turned 180 degrees.

Look at the symbols and their meanings in these four sentences. You may want to refer to the symbols dictionary section in this book to see how the meanings were derived.

- In a two-story apartment = the dreamer is "residing" in a high-level place (is close to spiritual things).
- Big picture = looking at "the big picture."
- Window = able to see revelation.
- Ex-wife is sleeping = ex-wife is in a state of unawareness.
- Tornado = damaging trouble coming.
- My little car = dreamer's life.
- Turned 180 degrees = turned around in a completely opposite direction.

Put these meanings together and interpret the beginning and ending sentences:

> The dreamer is able to see the big picture by revelation. His ex-wife was unaware of the damaging trouble that came and passed. The trouble resulted in the dreamer's life being turned around in a completely opposite direction.

These few beginning and end sentences not only set the scene for the dream but also summarize it. In real life, the dreamer and his wife had gone through some destructive behavior that destroyed their marriage. The dreamer, now a strong, Spirit-filled man of God, had turned his life around. The dream detailed "where the dreamer is now and what the dreamer had been through." Looking at the first couple of sentences and the last couple of sentences may be very helpful.

Step 4: Find the focus, sub-focus and details.

How do we break down a dream full of metaphors and find out what it is about? Why does God give us some of these dreams? How do we know the right direction to go? Let's take a closer look at how to figure out our dreams.

My dream is so convoluted; how do I ever figure out who, or what, my dream is about?

I often get this question. The would-be interpreter is overwhelmed by the dream's detail and cannot sort it out. There are some steps the interpreter can take to cut through descriptions and determine what is going on. Pastor John Paul Jackson, in the Streams Ministries' teaching series *Understanding Dreams and Visions*, taught interpreters to separate the dream's focus and sub-focuses from the details.[3] We will look at how to do this.

The focus of a dream is the main thing the dream centers upon. Who or what is it about? Sub-focuses are primary issues in the dream. There is usually more than one sub-focus. The focus and sub-focus(es) alone are enough to provide a basic dream interpretation. Everything else in a dream is detail. These details describe, give reasons for actions and may define the degree of the problem or issue, etc. Details can easily get in the way if the interpreter is not careful.

A 77-year-old woman named Emma told me the following dream on April 28, 2009. This dream turned out to be prophetic and is useful to illustrate some interpretation techniques. We will dissect it to point out the focus, sub-focuses and details.

> I was visiting a friend's home. It was a big, beautiful home. I looked out and saw lots of circles in the fields everywhere. I could see a long ways. I wanted to figure out what the circles were, so I went outside to view them. I was wading in water ankle deep. There was a man walking alongside me.
>
> He said, "I have come to look over my property. Do you want to go along?"
>
> I agreed. I realized there was water everywhere, and the circles were farmhouses sticking up on their foundations with water all around them. We walked together.
>
> The man said to me, "No. Do not go that way. There is a ravine there. Come this way."

I looked out, saw the dangerous edge, but I was fine because I had listened to him. I said, "I need to go home. I have got to drive back."

He said, "You cannot see the road. Where do you live?"

I said, "Kansas City."

"You cannot get out from here. There is water over the roads," the man replied. "Do you have a big house?"

"Yes," I said.

"High ceilings?" he asked.

"Yes."

The man said, "You must be enjoying that."

In the next scene, I was back in the friend's house but concerned and felt like I needed to go home.

My friend said, "But you cannot see the road. Stay here. Now you can teach."

I said, "But I do not have my stuff."

My friend said, "You can use my Bible."

I knew I had to stay there, but it was okay. I woke up.

Focus

The focus of a dream is the main thing, or person, the plot is centered upon. Ask the question, "Who, or what, is the main subject of the dream?" In this dream, the subject of the dream was the dreamer herself. She is the focus.

The next question to ask is, "What does the focus represent?" In other words, "Is the focus a metaphor for something else?"

In Emma's dream, the focus is the dreamer. Since people may be symbolic, like everything else in a dream, the interpreter should ask, "Does the dreamer represent someone else?" To determine whether people in dreams are themselves or represent others, there are clues we can follow. We will look at these clues later. For now, in this dream we will assume the focus is the dreamer herself and not representing anyone else.

Okay. We have found the focus. Now let's find the sub-focuses of the dream.

Sub-focuses

Sub-focuses are problems or issues the dream is dealing with. Or they might be a person, place or thing upon which the dream pivots. Without the sub-focus, there would not even be a dream.

In this dream, I believe the sub-focuses are:

- The field
- The water
- The inability to get home
- Being at a friend's big house

The focus and the sub-focuses together show the basic interpretation of the dream. This dream's focus and sub-focuses are: focus = *I, or the dreamer;* sub-focuses = *field, water, inability to get home, at a friend's big house.*

Remember, the interpretation of the focus and sub-focuses will be enough to provide a very basic interpretation of the whole dream, so we will delay analyzing the details for a few moments. As we apply Step 5 and Step 6 to the focus and sub-focuses, we will get the interpretation.

Step 5: Look at symbol meanings.

Dreams are made up of metaphors. The symbols, colors and people in dreams might represent all kinds of things. What are some possible meanings of the sub-focuses in Emma's dream?

The "field" might be representative of life (see Genesis 27:27; Deuteronomy 21:1; Proverbs 23:9; Jeremiah 6:25; Matthew 13:24; 14:44).

The "water" might be representative of overwhelming trials (see Genesis 6:17; Job 20:28; Matthew 7:24–27).

The "inability to get home" might represent the dreamer's concern about going back to her old life on earth (Kansas City) or to her old pattern of life, either physically or mentally.

Her location "at a friend's big house" might represent a new place of existence where the dreamer finds herself. It is a place where her friend is also. Or, it is possible that "at a friend's big house" might represent our mansion in heaven as talked about in the book of John: "In My Father's house are many mansions. . . . I go to prepare a place for you" (John 14:2 NKJV).

Step 6: Replace the symbols with their meanings.

While interpreting a dream, often the interpreter does not know which of the different symbol meanings to apply. I have found that I can do an unusual thing if I do not know which meaning to apply: I can insert all of the meanings in place of the symbol within the context of the dream. Then, as the dream unfolds, the Holy Spirit will reveal the correct meaning.

In Emma's dream, inserting the suggested symbolic meanings of the focus and sub-focuses might yield this interpretation:

The dreamer's life has (or will have) an overwhelming trial. She wants to get back to her old way of life but is unable to. This will result in her being in a new place (either physically or mentally).

Or, if we want to assume that "at a friend's big house" is symbolic of heaven, then the meaning might be:

The dreamer's life has (or will have) an overwhelming trial. She wants to get back to her old way of life but is unable to. This will result in her being in heaven.

Wow! Pretty strong stuff.

The woman who relayed this dream to me was my mother, Emma! And she asked me to give her the interpretation. Talk about a tough job.

I asked myself, *How do I handle this? Do I tell her the truth—what I really think it means? Or do I play dumb? Will it scare her? What if I have it wrong? Will I lose her respect? And if she tells others in the family, will everyone think I am nuts? I mean, more than usual, that is.* The old fear of rejection and of what others would say rose up within me. Then I laid down my personal selfish fears and thought, *Will she lose her respect for the integrity of dream interpretation?*

After prayer, I sat down with her and spoke carefully about the dream. I said, "Mom, it looks like you are the focus of the dream, so the dream is about you."

She quickly agreed.

With care, I tiptoed forward. "I believe this dream is about your life and other people's lives [the field]. And the water over these lives could be some overwhelming trials. It is saying that you cannot get back to your old life [inability to get home], but you find yourself in a beautiful place that is okay. It is saying, 'It is all going to be okay,' Mom."

Emma was no dummy. I am sure the Holy Spirit spoke to her because she quickly responded, "I think this means I'm going to die and go to heaven."

I took a deep breath and said, "Well, it is possible that's what it means." Then, being the ever-hopeful chicken that I am, I added, "Or it could mean you are just going to be living in a better way in your future." Maybe I was not all that chicken after all. "Living in a better way" really could be another interpretation of the dream, even though some of the details pointed the other direction.

Over the next two years, Emma mentioned the dream to me several times. She would always smile and say, "If it happens, it happens. I guess I'm ready." I knew she was at peace with it. But I also noticed that she set about making some end-of-life preparations.

Two years later, on January 2, 2011, Emma stepped off a curb incorrectly. This resulted in a fall that caused a compound fracture to her left ankle and a bad sprain to her right ankle. A few days later, she underwent surgery to rebuild her left ankle. She worked hard, went through the appropriate rehabilitation process and expected a full recovery, sooner than later. On January 21, 2011, while at the rehab facility, I visited with her. Then she sent me on an errand to a nearby store. I was told later that, after I left, Emma read awhile. Then she took off her reading glasses and tried to lay them on her bedside table. They slid off, landing on the floor. Her roommate's visiting daughter picked them up and laid them on the table for her.

"Thank you, honey," Emma said. "I think I'll take a nap now. I'm a little tired." She closed her eyes and within five minutes left peacefully to be with the Lord. The emergency room doctor told me he believed a blood clot from her injured ankle traveled to her heart and took her. After her death, I found Emma's notes about this dream tucked away in her china cabinet. I miss my mother terribly.

But back to her dream. In retrospect, I see that the focus and the sub-focuses were right on! Within a short period of time after the dream, Emma found herself facing an overwhelming trial. It turned out that this trial kept her from her former life routine. And eventually the trial caused her to live in heaven (Jesus/her friend/God's house).

Details

Remember, details describe the problems, issues, objects and results of the dream in clearer terms. So, what is the rest of the dream about? What is the next step for interpreting? Do we even need to look at the details? After the interpreter has pulled out the focus and the sub-focuses, we can stop there if we want—since these are the essence of the dream. Everything else is detail. But details are interesting and can add flavor and confirmation. In Emma's dream, the details and their meanings might be as follows:

- Friend = Holy Spirit/Jesus (see John 14:16, 26; Matthew 26:50)
- Circles = covenantal promise to earth (see Genesis 41:42; Haggai 2:23; Isaiah 40:22)

- See a long ways = understand much (see Deuteronomy 11:7; 29:4; Psalm 115:5; 135:16; Jeremiah 5:21; Ezekiel 12:2; 40:4; Matthew 13:13; Ephesians 1:18); insight (see Judges 8:7; Revelation 1:14; 4:6)
- Water = overwhelming trials (see Genesis 6:17; Job 20:28; Matthew 7:24–27); God's Word (see Nehemiah 9:15; Psalm 73:10; Isaiah 55:1; John 4; Ephesians 5:26; Revelation 7:17)
- Wading in ankle deep = going through trials. (Could the trials have to do with the ankle?)
- Man walking beside me = someone or some spirit besides the dreamer. Because the man was felt to be good: Jesus, an angel or the Holy Spirit; Jesus beside me
- My property = earthly things that belong to me
- Farm = those who sow and harvest (seed or fruit) the Word of God in others (see Matthew 9:37–38; 13:3; Mark 4:14); those who toil and work hard (see 2 Timothy 2:6)
- Farmhouses = places to sow and harvest the Word of God in others (see Matthew 9:37–38; 13:3; Mark 4:14; Luke 8:5); places where there are those who toil and work hard (see 2 Timothy 2:6)
- Foundations = Jesus (see Isaiah 28:16; 1 Corinthians 3:11; Ephesians 2:20); God (see 2 Timothy 2:19)
- Ravine = low area (of life) that is hard to get out of (see Isaiah 57:5–6)
- Edge = dangerous divider; walking on the edge
- Kansas City = earthly home (Emma lived in Kansas City)
- Drive = in control of (see Exodus 6:1; 11:1; 23:31; Deuteronomy 4:38; Judges 2:23; Psalm 36:11; Isaiah 22:23; Jeremiah 46:9; Joel 2:20; Matthew 10:1)
- Water over the roads = trials hindering the pathway of life going forward (see Isaiah 57:14; Jeremiah 31:21)
- Big house = a fullness or largeness to personal life and relationships (see 2 Samuel 13:7–8; 14:24; 17:23; 18:17; 19:8; 23:5;

Isaiah 38:12; Proverbs 15:25; Jeremiah 35:2–9; 37:15; Matthew 7:24–27; 10:11–13; 24:42; Hebrews 3:6; 2 Timothy 2:20–21)

- High = toward God (see Psalm 78:39; 97:9; Isaiah 55:9; Matthew 5:14; Ephesians 2:6; Colossians 3:2)
- Ceiling = covering; a limit to going to higher levels
- Stuff = worldly acquisitions (see Exodus 25:9; 31:7; 1 Kings 7:48; 1 Chronicles 9:29; Proverbs 19:14)
- Bible = God's Word (see Colossians 2:17; 1 Timothy 1:7–10; 2 Peter 1:20–21)

Now, to get a feel for what the details add to the dream, I will rewrite the dream, substituting the meaning for each symbol. It will read choppily, and the grammar will be poor—but it will demonstrate the process.

*I was visiting **Jesus'** home. It was a beautiful **mansion in heaven**. I looked out and saw lots of **covenantal promise to earth** everywhere. I could **understand much**. I wanted to figure out what the **covenantal promises to earth** were, so I went **on the outside of the mansion in heaven** to **understand** them. I was going through **trials**. There was **Jesus** beside me.*

*He said, "I have come to look over **earthly things that belong to Me**. Do you want to go along?" I agreed.*

*There were **trials and God's Word** everywhere and the **covenantal promise** were **places where there are those who sow and harvest the Word of God in others** on **foundations of Jesus** with **overwhelming trials and God's Word** all around them.*

*We walked together. **Jesus** said to me, "No. Do not go that way. There is a **low area that is hard to get out of** there. Come this way!"*

*I looked out and saw a **dangerous divider**, but I was fine because I listened to Him. I said, "I need to go **earthly home**. I have got to **control of** back."*

*He said, "You cannot see the **pathway of life**. Where do you live?"*

I said, "Kansas City."

*"You cannot get out from here. There is **trials hindering pathway of life**," Jesus replied. "Do you have a **fullness or largeness to personal life and relationships**?"*

"Yes," I said.

*"**High limit to going toward God**?" He asked.*

"Yes."

***Jesus** said, "You must be enjoying that."*

*In the next scene, I was back in the **beautiful mansion in heaven** but concerned and felt like I needed to go **earthly home**.*

***Jesus** said, "But you cannot see the **pathway of life**. Stay here. Now you can teach."*

I said, "But I do not have my worldly acquisitions."

***Jesus** said, "You can use **God's Word**."*

I knew I had to stay there, but it was okay. I woke up.

That was hard to read, but hopefully you struggled through it. Did the details add much to the dream interpretation? They do witness to Jesus reflecting on Emma's earthly life and telling her she cannot go back the way she thought she could. Even though details might not provide the essential part of a dream, they are nevertheless wonderful. They give us information to help understand the fullness of the dream.

Some of the details of Emma's dream are interesting. Remember, in the dream, the trials were surrounding her ankle (she was "in water ankle deep"). In Emma's real life, it was her ankle that caused her death. Interesting!

In a dream, the details might also describe the effects of the situation on the focus or sub-focuses. For example, in this dream, Emma felt that where she wound up in the dream was beautiful; she was given a job to teach (in real life, teaching was Emma's passion); and it was all "okay" with her in the end. These details speak of Emma finding, in her transition to heaven, a place of great beauty, peace and personal worth.

Do not get caught up in the details of the dream; otherwise, the interpretation might miss what is most important. In fact, it could change the whole interpretation of the dream. If the interpreter grabs a detail and pays more attention to it than it deserves, the interpretation could get off track.

Does God try to scare us? Why would He give Emma a dream like this?

Why would God give Emma this dream? I believe the Bible, and it says that God wants good for us.

> Because Your lovingkindness is good, deliver me.
>
> Psalm 109:21

> For the LORD God is a sun and shield; the LORD gives grace and glory; no good thing does He withhold from those who walk uprightly.
>
> Psalm 84:11

The Bible also says that God meets all our needs.

> He himself gives to all people life and breath and all things.
>
> Acts 17:24–25

I believe this dream was given to Emma to meet her needs in a loving, kind way. The meaning "she was going to die" was so embedded in ambiguity that another interpretation was quite possible. This knowledge kept fear at bay.

However, on some level, the Holy Spirit spoke enough into Emma that her spirit came to terms with her impending death. She even stepped forward and made some final preparations. For example, she purchased a burial plot, she labeled personal articles in her home to let her children know where the items came from, she told me where she had hidden a stash of money "in case I die," and she spoke of the possibility of her death to me on several occasions. She told her roommate in the rehabilitation center just two days before her death that she "was ready and could go anytime."

I believe the ambiguity of the dream was purposeful—not only to keep fear away, but to allow Emma to continue to live her life as if she would live another thirty years. She rarely spoke of her dream to others—indicating that she did not dwell on it. She even planned for retirement. (Yes, it is hard to believe, but at 79, Emma was still not retired. She loved to work.) The Lord met all her needs, even her need for a gentle, subtle prophetic word so she could put things in order. He loved her that much.

What about the step of looking at the beginning and the end of the dream?

Remember, the first and last couple of sentences in a dream often set the stage and help summarize it. Emma's dream was fairly complicated. It could have been intimidating. But let us look at one more step in dream interpretation to see if we got it right. Let us check out the beginning and the end of the dream. Do they set the stage and give a synopsis?

> Beginning: I was visiting a friend's home. It was a big, beautiful home. (Interpretation: I was visiting Jesus' home. It was a beautiful mansion in heaven.)
>
> End: I knew I had to stay there, but it was okay. (Interpretation: It was okay that I was there.)
>
> The summation is: I was visiting Jesus' home. It was a beautiful mansion in heaven. I knew I had to stay there, but it was okay.

Looking at the beginning and the end of this dream gives us the same interpretation as looking at the focus and sub-focuses. Amazing, isn't it?

Step 7: Seek counsel.

Remember, in our basic definitions (see the "Biblical Foundations" in chapter 1 of this book), the spirit is not the same as the soul. And the Bible says we cannot understand dreams unless we look at them spiritually (through our wisdom, communion and conscience) instead of soulishly (through our mind, will and emotions).

> However, as it is written: "What no eye has seen, what no ear has heard, and what no human mind has conceived"—the things God has prepared for those who love him—these are the things God has revealed to us by his Spirit. The Spirit searches all things, even the deep things of God. For who knows a person's thoughts except their own spirit within them? In the same way no one knows the thoughts of God except the Spirit of God. What we have received is not the spirit of the world, but the Spirit who is from God, so that we may understand what God has freely given us. This is what we speak, not in words taught us by human wisdom but in words taught by the Spirit, expressing spiritual realities with Spirit-taught words. The person without the Spirit does not accept the things that come from the Spirit of God but considers them foolishness, and cannot understand them because they are discerned only through the Spirit.
>
> 1 Corinthians 2:9–14 NIV

I have found that the most important part of the dream interpretation process is to seek the dream's meaning using counsel.

> But examine everything carefully; hold fast to that which is good.
>
> 1 Thessalonians 5:21

The first and foremost source of counsel should be the Holy Spirit. It is through the Holy Spirit and biblical interpretation that we can be sure "the dream is true and its interpretation is trustworthy" (Daniel 2:45).

After seeking the Holy Spirit's guidance by prayer, it might be wise to seek the counsel of a trusted, Spirit-filled interpreter who will also look to biblical symbols and meanings for confirmation.

Sometimes we just cannot figure out a dream. And using ungodly counsel will not help.

> Now, in the morning his spirit was troubled, so he sent and called for all the magicians of Egypt and all its wise men. And Pharaoh told them his dreams, but there was no one who could interpret them to Pharaoh.
>
> Genesis 41:8

> Pharaoh said to Joseph, "I have had a dream, but no one can interpret it; and I have heard it said about you, that when you hear a dream you can interpret it."
>
> Genesis 41:15

Even though we might be using God's Word to interpret accurately, it can still be tough interpreting our own dreams. Things are not always as they seem. This is because our souls are so strong they often blur our insight and ability to hear the Holy Spirit.

Let's look at a dream that did not follow basic interpretation rules. Using counsel to interpret the dream was, in this case, imperative. One morning I awoke and remembered having this dream:

> *A rabbit was in my backyard. I had put my watch over its head and the watch had slipped down around its neck. I was chasing the rabbit trying to get my watch back. I threw a cap over the rabbit and caught it. The watch was not there. I knew it had slipped off the rabbit.*

To interpret the dream I looked at the symbols.

Rabbit = multiplication and fertility; harmless; destructive; timid; fast growth; sexual torment

Yard = area you have authority over; domain

Watch = time on earth, life span (to whom does it belong?); watch over

Neck = beauty; warrior; will; humility; strength/tenacious

Chasing = will not let you alone; oppression of the one being chased; harassing

Cap = covering

I prayed, applied the symbols—and nothing! Worse than nothing . . . I came up with such strange things as "I'm watching and chasing destruction, but lost watch over it," or "I'm chasing after a time of sexual torment, but the time is lost."

What? None of these interpretations seemed to apply to me and my life. And some were just downright creepy. Finally, I called my friend and said, "I have a simple dream, but I cannot get its meaning." I told her the dream.

She said, "That's easy. You're losing time chasing rabbits."

Of course. That was it. Forget the symbols. This dream was a wordplay. And the dream was an answer to my previous prayer: *God, give me the time to write my books if You want me to do it.*

The dream helped me realize what was occurring during my writing forays. I would research a specific thing for my writing text. The research invariably brought up an interesting tidbit of information that I found fascinating, so I would digress. I would read about and contemplate the new tidbit of data. Pretty soon, I found myself in a far-off field on a "rabbit trail." I was losing time chasing rabbits.

I found it especially interesting that God used the very expression I was fond of using as I talked to craftsmen and others working on my engineering projects. When I found we were going down a wrong path, they would hear me say, "We're losing time chasing rabbits."

In my dream, God had used my own phrase! But I still could not interpret it on my own. I had to have help. It happens often. It is hard to discern your own dreams. Seek counsel.

This lady at church told me my dream meant one thing, but I'm not convinced. I felt it meant something else. Who is right?

This question really deals with souls getting in the way of interpretations. This intrusion can come from two directions: the dreamer or the interpreter.

It is not easy for dreamers to keep their souls out of the way when they try to interpret their own dreams. We often try to make interpretations fit our preconceived outcomes. Our mind, intellect, will, desires, emotions or feelings get in the way and cause bias.

The interpreter's soul will occasionally impede a true interpretation as well. The interpreter may have a prejudice (good or bad) toward the dreamer and allow it to get in the way. The interpreter might also make a mistake because of inexperience or simply because he or she is "off" that day.

> For we know in part and we prophesy in part, but when the perfect comes, the partial will be done away.
>
> 1 Corinthians 13:9–10

> For now we see in a mirror dimly but then face to face; now I know in part, but then I will know fully, just as I also have been fully known.
>
> 1 Corinthians 13:12

Until our soul is out of the way and only the Holy Spirit's words come, we will make mistakes. Every human on earth (with the exception of Jesus incarnate) has made mistakes. Even men after God's own heart, like David, have made mistakes. Just as David handled his mistakes, we, too, must handle ours. We must not give up or quit seeking God but go forward in communion with Him. We should strive to live righteously and pick ourselves up each time we fall.

> For a righteous man falls seven times, and rises again.
>
> Proverbs 24:16

Note that this does not say a righteous man gets it right all the time. Instead, it says he falls; he makes mistakes. The spirit can only receive as much as the soul does not block. It is easy to make mistakes. Making mistakes does not make us bad; it just makes us mistaken—and human. Since none of us wants to make mistakes, it is wise to be discerning. Ask the Holy Spirit for the truth.

The sum of Your word is truth.

Psalm 119:160

We are from God; he who knows God listens to us; he who is not from God does not listen to us. By this we know the Spirit of truth and the spirit of error.

1 John 4:6

God tells us to be careful. We should not say, or even imply, that God has said something if He has not.

But the prophet who speaks a word presumptuously in My name which I have not commanded him to speak, or which he speaks in the name of other gods, that prophet shall die.

Deuteronomy 18:20

What does God say about someone who claims to speak something from God, but is wrong? God implies He knows who is falsifying His word for their own purposes and who is simply mistaken. We must not overreact in fear of making a mistake. If no one had been brave enough to speak out God's Word for fear of making a mistake, then we would not have any of the biblical translations, not even the King James. Nor would we have preachers in pulpits or witnesses on the streets. We have all misspoken on occasion due to our inexperience. But as we grow, our understanding grows, and hopefully our mistakes lessen. God knows this. He made us immature, and He helps us grow.

Deuteronomy 18:22 says we are not to be afraid of those who speak incorrectly:

> When a prophet speaks in the name of the LORD, if the thing does not come about or come true, that is the thing which the LORD has not spoken. The prophet has spoken it presumptuously; you shall not be afraid of him.
>
> Deuteronomy 18:22

No, we are not to be afraid of their words, but we are to test them. How do we know if their word is of God? Verse 22 says we know because it comes true.

What kind of timeline does the Bible say we should give these words to come to pass? It does not! So be careful. In Emma's dream, anything less than two years (the time from when she first received the dream that she would die until the actual date of her death) and the prophetic dream could have been misjudged by us to be false, i.e., not a word from God. If we judge too quickly we might find ourselves judging a prophetic word or a person who knows the Lord harshly.

> Therefore there is now no condemnation for those who are in Christ Jesus.
>
> Romans 8:1

Truth comes from God. And He is still speaking to us.

> He said, "Listen to my words: When there is a prophet among you, I, the LORD, reveal myself to them in visions, I speak to them in dreams."
>
> Numbers 12:6 NIV

> Let them acknowledge that what I am writing to you is the Lord's command. But if anyone ignores this, they will themselves be ignored.

Therefore, my brothers and sisters, be eager to prophesy, and do not forbid speaking in tongues.

1 Corinthians 14:37–39 NIV

It will come about after this that I will pour out My Spirit on all mankind. And your sons and daughters will prophesy, your old men will dream dreams, your young men will see visions.

Joel 2:28

The Bible says to judge not—yet it also says to be judging. A distinction is being drawn between being judgmental and judging rightly (using discernment to weigh the facts). Do not throw the dream interpretation process out simply because it can be misused and abused—and *is* misused and abused at times. Be discerning. Test it. The Lord says His Word is a lamp to our feet and light to our path (see Psalm 119:105). Shine the light of God's Word fully on the interpretation.

A Closer Look at Dream Symbols

The Bible is a wonderful source for symbols. In fact, I have found that opening ourselves to understand and receive symbols helps our Bible-reading comprehension. It makes those obscure, hard-to-understand verses jump out and clarifies their meanings.

The symbols dictionary section is designed to be a beginning source for symbol meanings. Most of the symbols in that section are based on Scripture.

However, I encourage everyone to create their own symbol book, since a symbol for one dreamer may be different for the next. For instance, consider the appearance of a cat in a dream. If the dreamer hates or is indifferent to cats, a cat in a dream might represent independent thinking or the occult. However, if the dreamer loves cats and her best friend is her cat, a cat in a dream might represent something close to her or a pet issue.

When looking at a dream's symbols, ask yourself, "Why? Why did the dream have a motorcycle in it instead of a car? Why were some of the people drinking milk and others eating steak? Why was there a horse in the dream instead of a goat?" The symbols chosen for the dream were selected for a particular reason. We cannot discern the reason without the help of the Holy Spirit, so include Him in the process. This chapter and the symbols dictionary section of this book have some suggestions to aid in your discernment of the symbol's meaning.

Let's look together now at an example of how this works. Karen was a good mom. Her seventeen-year-old daughter lived with her, along with her daughter's small cocker spaniel, Tolly, the love of her daughter's life. Early one morning Karen awoke and remembered the following dream.

> My daughter's dog, Tolly, came into our house with a frog in her mouth. I woke up.

When Karen came to me with the dream, I quickly prayed for help, then suggested we look at the symbols.

Dog, as a pet = might represent their child (as our pets often become extremely attached to us and we "baby" them)

Frog = might represent "lust" or "sex" (see Revelation 16:13–14)

In the mouth = might represent "tasting" or "experimenting with the thing"

If these symbols apply here, then the dream might say: Your daughter is experimenting with or tasting lust or sex. Ouch!

Karen took this to heart. She scheduled a formal lunch with her daughter so the two of them could sit and talk uninterrupted. Karen started the conversation by saying, "The Lord gave me a dream that says you are experimenting with sex." This is *not* the recommended approach, but Karen's enthusiasm to resolve the issue overpowered her normal humble and sensitive approach in dealing with her daughter.

Karen's daughter did a double take, then petulantly whined, "That's not fair! God's telling on me."

The daughter was, indeed, experimenting with sex with her boyfriend, and the dream gave her mother an opportunity to address the activity.

How important are symbols? What if in the dream the dog had come in carrying a fish! That could have meant that the daughter was experimenting with good, clean nourishment. A little different! In addition to counsel from the Holy Spirit, symbols are the key to understanding dreams.

As an interpreter, ask, "Why this symbol and not another?" That symbol was given for a reason—so let's look at symbols.

Who is in the dream?

Just because the dreamer's friend "Mary" is in the dream does not mean the dream is about Mary or that it is even really Mary in the dream. This is the biggest error I have seen with dream interpreters. Too many automatically default to the assumption that the person in the dream is actually the person in the dream. To make matters worse, they will run to that same person and say, "I had a dream about you." They will then proceed to explain their dream to the confused person, assuming it will mean something to their listener. The listener takes about two steps backward and says, "Okay," but is now bewildered and less likely to believe the dream interpretation process.

Like all other dream symbols, the people in the dream are likely to be symbolic. Determining what the people represent and why they are in the dream may become clear if you ask yourself, "What are the relationships of the people in the dream to each other and to me?"

For example, if the people in the dream are all from your church, this might be a clue that the dream is about a particular group within the church, about your church or about God's universal Church.

Are the people in the dream co-workers? Then this might be a dream about your job or issues relating to your job.

If there are numerous miscellaneous people you do not know in the dream, then this might be a clue that this is a prophetic dream about your city, your country or the world. What is happening to these people? What is your part in it?

Are the people in the dream your family members? This is usually a clue that the dream is about personal or family issues. If the people are your immediate family members, this might be a dream about what is going on in your personal life as it relates to your family or what is going on at home. Are the people in the dream your deceased parents? This might be a dream about your source, about the paradigms you were raised with or about issues dealt to you by your parents. Are the people in the dream your parents, your grandma and an uncle? This might be a dream about generational issues that have affected your family and yourself.

Look at the relationships of all the people in the dream—not only their relationships to each other but also to the dreamer.

What about the dreamer's role in the dream? How does the interpreter determine if the dream is about the dreamer or someone else? Is the dream centered on the dreamer? For example, is the dreamer an active leader, or an active victim, in the dream? If so, this might be a dream about the dreamer himself.

Is the dreamer an active participant with others, but not taking the lead? This might be a clue the dream is about something the dreamer is actively involved in.

Is the dreamer in the crowd and participating, but not in a pivotal role? Then this might be a clue the dream is about something that will affect the dreamer and others.

Lastly, if the dreamer is just watching the dream unfold, this might be a clue that the dream is not about the dreamer at all, and the events may not even affect the dreamer. These may be prophetic dreams giving the dreamer information about something or someone else.

Rarely, but on occasion, the dreamer may be "looking through the eyes of someone else." In these dreams, the dreamer is actually a stand-in, representing someone else. This type of dream was displayed in the first chapter when I was driving a car down the interstate, and logs fell off of a tractor-trailer truck in front of me. It was later determined that I was representing someone else in the dream. I was looking through her eyes. This is an unusual occurrence in dreams.

The people in a dream might represent any of the following: themselves; another person of "like or similar" relationship; another person with the same name; another authority figure; a "play on words," e.g., a brother or sister-in-law; the meaning of their name; or someone or something else. Because of this, an important question to ask in interpretation is, "Who does the person or the people in the dream really represent?" They may represent many things. Let's talk about each of these a little more now.

Represent themselves

People in dreams can confuse the interpretation. Of course the person in the dream may represent himself—however, equally often, he does not. It is important to be open to the idea that the person in the dream may actually represent someone else.

Represent another of like/similar relationship

People in a dream may represent another person who is in a like or similar relationship with the dreamer. The dreamer's close Christian friend Carol might really represent her good Christian friend Sharen, especially if they are both in the same prayer group with the dreamer. Or the dreamer's co-worker Jared showing up in the dream might represent another co-worker Doug, if both men are on the same project or in the same department as the dreamer.

What about family members in a dream? Penny dreamed her sister Cheryl had died. In the dream, Penny said to Cheryl's husband, Brian, "Are you okay?"

Brian responded, very annoyed, "Of course I'm not okay. My wife just died."

Disturbed, Penny dwelled on this dream for over a year. She was concerned it might be saying that Cheryl was going to die—but Cheryl appeared to be healthy and fine. In fact, all her sisters were fine. Unexpectedly one morning, Penny got a phone call that her sister Sandy had died. Penny rushed over to Sandy's house, and upon seeing Sandy's husband, Don, Penny blurted out, "Are you okay?"

Don responded with a frown, "Of course I'm not okay. My wife just died."

The minute she heard the words, Penny was flooded with the memory of the dream. The dream had not been about Cheryl and Brian; it was about Sandy and Don.

Think about the people in the dream and what they might represent. Look at their relationships with each other and with the dreamer. Do not forget to ask the Lord.

Represent another person of the same name

Mary Groves in a dream might really be speaking of Mary Swearingen. Or Joe Black in a dream might really be speaking of Joe Petrolli. People may represent another person of the same name. Ask the Lord who is represented by the person in the dream.

Represent another authority figure

Your father in your dream might represent your holy Father—God. The military, police or guards in a dream might represent angels. Your boss, a president or a pastor in a dream may represent Father God. Keep in mind that we are speaking of symbols, not reality.

Represent a "play on words"

I love it when God uses a play on words in a dream. A brother might represent a "brother in Christ." And your sister-in-law showing up in a dream might represent a Christian sister or brother who is too much into legalism. (The word *law* may indicate something legalistic.)

Represent the meaning of their name

Arlan told me a dream he was confused about:

All I remember of my dream is that Nan was coming through a door toward me.

I silently prayed for help, then asked Arlan what his relationship with Nan was. He answered, "She goes to my church. She's a nice person, but I have not had too many conversations with her. I really do not know her that well. I do not have a clue why she would be in my dream."

Since Nan did not have any special relationship with Arlan, I looked up the name Nan in a Christian name book. It meant "grace." Okay! I felt the Lord had revealed it to me, and it now made sense. "Arlan," I said, "are you facing a difficult choice or decision right now?"

"Yup. I sure am," he quickly responded. "I have been praying and praying to God to tell me what His will is in it, too."

"Well, if you look at the symbols, a door is often a choice or a decision," I replied. "It appears to me the dream is saying, 'With regard to your choice or decision, God is allowing grace to come to you.' I believe this means that God is giving you grace to go either way in the decision, and He'll be with you."

"Makes perfect sense to me." Arlan smiled.

God answered Arlan's prayer. In his dream, Nan did not represent Nan herself. Nor did Nan represent another of like relationship. It was Nan's name that was the key to understanding the dream. Do not forget to look at the name's meaning. Nan means grace.[4] In determining name meanings, use a Christian name book.

Represent someone or something else

People may represent someone or something else in a dream. In the book of Revelation, a woman is metaphorical for the large Church of

God (see Revelation 12:17). This same metaphor might show up in your own dream. Are the people in the dream unknown to you and wearing black? A black covering might be a clue that this is a dream about dark spiritual forces. Look at whom the forces are coming against. Are they watching you or someone else?

Are there unknown people in the dream helping you? This dream might be reminding you that God's forces are assisting you. These people may represent angelic or human help. A faceless man might represent the Holy Spirit. God is creative. Ask Him whom the person in the dream represents.

How in the world do I ever figure out what the symbol means?

There are many choices of what the symbol or person can mean. How do we figure it out? The greatest help comes from the Holy Spirit. If we pray for the proper meaning, I believe the Holy Spirit will speak to us and help us.

At times, I have noticed that if all the different meanings are inserted into the dream in lieu of their symbols, then the context of the dream—or the relationship that symbol has with the rest of the symbolic meanings—causes the proper symbolic meanings to fall out. Remember our dissection of Emma's dream? Let's look again at Karen's dream as an additional example:

My daughter's dog, Tolly, came into my house with a frog in her mouth. I woke up.

Let's substitute several possibilities for each symbol in the dream.

My (those I am mentoring; actual daughter; result; heir)'s (friend; dreamer's child; of no worth; strife; pet thing) came into my (actual house; life; family) with a (actual frog; lust; sex; materialism) (actually in her mouth; experimenting with; receiving; learning).

, Okay. What makes sense? My actual daughter came into the family situation with lust/sex learning/experimentation. See, it falls out.

Notice that in the dream there were two symbols of home/personal life: the daughter's dog and the dreamer's actual house. This double symbol of home/personal life is a clue that the dream is about the dreamer's personal life/home situation and not about someone she is mentoring elsewhere. Look at the symbols. What are they saying?

I do not hear clearly from the Holy Spirit about dreams.

Often I hear, "What about me? I do not think I hear clearly from the Holy Spirit when it comes to dreams. It is easy for you, but it does not work that easily for me."

Be open to receiving what the Holy Spirit might want to say to you and do with you. The Bible says that we are to ask for things from the Lord.

> Ask, and it will be given to you; seek, and you will find; knock, and it will be opened to you. For everyone who asks receives, and he who seeks finds, and to him who knocks it will be opened. Or what man is there among you who, when his son asks for a loaf, will give him a stone? Or if he asks for a fish, he will not give him a snake will he? If you, then, being evil, know how to give good gifts to your children, how much more will your Father who is in heaven give what is good to those who ask him!
>
> Matthew 7:7–11

If we ask God in the name of Jesus, He promises to answer us. The following verse says that we are not only to ask, but to ask with the right motives.

> You ask and do not receive, because you ask with wrong motives, so that you may spend it on your pleasures.
>
> James 4:3

He promises to help us if we ask with the right motive, but He will oppose us if we move into pride and worldly motives. Remember, the act of helping others understand their dreams is not a matter for pride. It is a ministry—in which we help others open up to spiritual communication with their heavenly Father.

Ask the Lord for help. Then "step out" into the process in faith. Look at the symbols and try to figure them out, trusting that the Lord will guide you and speak to you. The Lord wants us to work at it . . . to seek out the matter.

> It is the glory of God to conceal a matter; but the glory of kings is to search out a matter.
>
> Proverbs 25:2

Ask. Then go forward, and He will lead you and teach you. If you are abiding in Him, you are not really doing the interpretation—the Lord is. And He will use you if you let Him.

How do I know if the symbol's meaning is the correct one for my dream?

If the dream makes sense and speaks to the dreamer as "truth," it is probably the correct symbolic meaning for the dream. Let the Holy Spirit tell the dreamer whether it is correct or not.

So, if I just plug the meaning of these symbols in, I get the correct interpretation. Right?

Again, the Holy Spirit will help us know what symbolic meaning to use. Pray for His help. He will guide you as to whether the tree in a dream may be understood as a symbol or is, quite literally, a tree.

4

Types of Dreams

What are some of the different types of dreams? I have been asked, "Aren't all dreams either warning dreams or prophetic dreams?" The answer is definitely "No." In previous chapters, we discussed the four sources behind our dreams: body, soul, God or the enemy (see chapter 2, "Common Dream Questions/ What Source Is behind My Dream?"). These sources send dreams for different reasons, which results in different types of dreams. The book of Daniel confirms that we receive different kinds of visions and dreams.

> As for these four youths, God gave them knowledge and intelligence in every branch of literature and wisdom; Daniel even understood all kinds of visions and dreams.
>
> Daniel 1:17

But not all dreams have meaning. Some are brought on due to other reasons than communication from God. So, to understand dreams, we must dissect each dream on its individual basis, and, as it says in the book of Timothy, rightly divide the word of truth (see 2 Timothy 2:15 KJV). To interpret dreams, we need to understand the various types of dreams. Some, but not all, of the different types of dreams include the following:

1. Body dreams: chemical, food;
2. Soul dreams: fear, desire, deception/false, falling;
3. God dreams: self-condition (90 to 98 percent of all dreams), courage, calling, correction, direction, plans of the enemy, warning, intercession, invention/business development, spiritual warfare, deliverance, healing, prophecy and revelation;
4. Enemy dreams: fear, false.

Body Dreams

Body dreams are dreams that are brought on by physiological needs or reactions within our bodies. Body dreams might be chemical/drug or food induced.

Chemical/Drug Induced:

Drugs or chemicals might affect our dreams. Remember the drug user's dream in which his arm hairs turned into worms that ate away his skin? (See chapter 2, "Common Dream Questions/What Source Is behind My Dream?/Body.") Even prescription medicine might cause us to dream wildly. Discernment is needed while taking medication.

Food Induced:

Sometimes food can cause us to have strange dreams. Some refer to these types of dreams as "pizza dreams." This is our body fighting back against what we have stuffed into it. Some people are more susceptible to this than others.

Soul Dreams

The Bible speaks of soul dreams—dreams that we cause to happen through our minds (see Jeremiah 23:16), our wills or our emotions and feelings. These are false dreams in that they do not have any meaning other than to reflect the wishes or fears of our hearts.

> A dream comes when there are many cares.
>
> Ecclesiastes 5:3 NIV

Soul dreams are inadvertently brought on by our fears, desires, deceptions and anxieties.

Fear Dreams

If the dreamer is afraid of losing his job and dreams he was fired, this might be a fear dream created from his own soul. Should he take stock in it? No. If there is a strong fear, and then a dream occurs, it is wise to be discerning. Chances are the dream is a creation of the dreamer's mind or feelings.

Remember Jeri's dream? (See chapter 2, "Common Dream Questions/What Source Is behind My Dream?/Soul.") She was a fearful mother who worried a great deal about her son and her grandchildren. This fear resulted in a false dream—a fear dream in which her worst fears were realized and her son drove off a cliff. Throw these dreams out! Better yet, pray against them in the name of Jesus.

Desire Dreams

A teenage boy named Caisson heard me talk. Afterward, he came to me and said, "I have been in love with Melia for a long time. She does not like me, but I try everything I can to be where I know she's going to be. Or I keep trying to speak to her."

"Sounds like you're pretty hung up on her," I replied.

"Yeah, I have been obsessing over her for a long time and even stalking her on Facebook," he said. "But the good news is I dreamed we were together." He grinned knowingly at me. "We were kissing and dating. This must mean it is gonna happen, right? I just need to keep it up."

Wow! As you can imagine, I handled this one carefully. This is a type of dream I hear about often. It could be a woman who dreams she got a job she is silently, but passionately, wanting. Or a man who wants to move to Tennessee and gets a dream that he is living there. The dreamer creates desires such as these in his dream. And, as in Caisson's case, the dream could encourage the dreamer to stalk someone or do something he should not be doing.

> Yet in the same way these men, also by dreaming, defile the flesh, and reject authority, and revile angelic majesties.

> Jude 8

I explained to Caisson that often we create dreams from our strong human desires. If there is not confirmation of the dream, we should not trust it.

> [W]ill be like a dream, a vision of the night. It will be as when a hungry man dreams—and behold, he is eating; or as when a thirsty man dreams—and behold, he is drinking. But when he awakens, behold, he is faint and his thirst is not quenched.

> Isaiah 29:7–8

In these wishful cases, the only way to be sure is to wait and see. Chances are, however, that the dream is not a revelatory word but a vivid manifestation of the dreamer's desire.

Deceptions/False Dreams

The Bible refers several times to deception or false dreams (see Jeremiah 23:32; 27:9; 29:8–9; Zechariah 10:2; Jude 8).

Deception or false dreams are simply not true. I am not talking about a misinterpretation. Nor am I talking about a dream in which the dreamer mistakenly substituted wrong dream information that changed the dream's actual meaning. A deception or false dream is not about a false interpretation. Instead, the dream itself states a lie. The dream is interpreted correctly, and the dreamer has relayed the dream correctly, but the dream itself is false—a lie.

Since some dreams are lies, we do not know if a dream is correct unless we get confirmation from another source. Be discerning and judge the dream.

Remember, even though the Bible says not to judge others, it also counsels us to be judging. This means we must exercise discernment.

> Do not judge so that you will not be judged. For in the way you judge, you will be judged.
>
> Matthew 7:1–2

> Do not judge according to appearance, but judge with righteous judgment.
>
> John 7:24

Look at the complete picture the Bible paints on judging. It says we are to judge right from wrong, but we are not to judge an individual as a person. The implication is that there is more to an individual than we can know, so unless we are God, we cannot know another person rightly. In this same way, we must judge dreams and interpretations, but not judge the individual—even when we suspect the dream might be false.

Deception and false dreams may come from a dreamer's mind, *any* dreamer's mind. Even a strong Spirit-filled Christian man or woman at times gets false dreams.

> Then the LORD said to me, "The prophets are prophesying falsehood in My name. I have not sent them nor commanded them nor spoken to them; they are prophesying to you a false vision, divination, futility and the deception of their own minds."
>
> Jeremiah 14:14

Ouch! This verse in Jeremiah states that some dreamers/prophets can be deceived. So beware! We must never take a dream or vision and run with it, unless we have confirmation in other ways, for the dream or vision might be false. A fear dream (e.g., Jeri's dream in which her son drove off a cliff) is also an example of a false dream.

Deception and false dreams are also given because the one relaying the dream is flat-out lying. In this case, the dreamer is not deceived but is purposefully trying to deceive others.

> How long? Is there anything in the hearts of the prophets who prophesy falsehood, even these prophets of the deception of their own heart, *who intend* to make My people forget My name by their dreams which they relate to one another, just as their fathers forgot My name because of Baal?
>
> Jeremiah 23:26–27,
> emphasis added

I believe these verses in the book of Jeremiah speak of intentional lies—falsehoods given on purpose to control and manipulate others. Be wise and be wary.

Falling Dreams

What are falling dreams? You know, the ones where you fall off a cliff and never land? You fall and fall. There are debates about these types of dreams, but generally they are thought to be soul dreams functioning to dispel anxiety.

So, does it work? Do these falling dreams help us unload our anxieties? Rather than a cure, they might be a red flag to remind the dreamer to release his fears and anxieties to the Lord.

> "For I know the plans that I have for you," declares the LORD, "plans for welfare and not for calamity to give you a future and a hope."
>
> Jeremiah 29:11

Come to Me, all who are weary and heavy-laden, and I will give
you rest.

Matthew 11:28

God Dreams

The Bible speaks a great deal about God dreams. These are dreams
in which the Lord is communicating to us. Since we have many needs
and there are multiple things the Lord communicates to us, He sends
us all kinds of God dreams.

A rule of thumb for believing (or not believing) the dream is of
God might be to ask if the dream's interpretation goes against the
character and nature of God and God's Word as outlined in the Bible.

So do not listen to the words of the prophets who speak to you . . . for
they prophesy a lie to you; for I have not sent them.

Jeremiah 27:14–15

If the interpretation disagrees with the truth (the Word of God),
then it is not of God and is false.

Self-Condition Dreams

Self-condition dreams make up about 90 to 98 percent of our
dreams. We will learn about other types of God dreams, but most
dreams will not fall into any of these other categories. Instead, they
fall into this self-condition dream category. Self-condition dreams
are dreams the Lord gives us to tell us where we are and what we
are doing.

My friend Mike told me he received the following dream.

*A few other people and I were trying to help sparrows that
were in a building get outside. We were coordinating opening
the doors. There were two sets of doors, inner and outer. And*

we were shooing the sparrows along toward freedom. Some got out. Some took more effort to get out. One was weak and needed water and food before flying away.

I looked at the symbols:

Sparrow = God's care and provision to those who feel unworthy (see Matthew 10:29–31)

2 = discernment (see Exodus 2:12–14; Matthew 18:19); division (see Genesis 1:6–8; 1 Kings 12; Matthew 6:24; Hebrews 11:37)

Door = choices/opportunities (see Genesis 4:7; Matthew 7:13; Revelation 3:8, 20)

I told Mike, "It looks like this dream points to you, and others with you, who are helping to get God's care and provisions to those who feel unworthy [sparrows]. You are helping them find 'freedom' especially as it relates to things needing discernment [2] or which cause division [2] and with the choices/opportunities [doors] that they need to deal with."

Mike said he was involved in a ministry at his church in which he and his fellow workers reached out a helping hand to others in just this way.

So, why are most of our dreams self-condition dreams? Why is the Lord telling us something we already know? Daniel said that it is so the dreamer "may know the thoughts of his heart" (Daniel 2:30 NIV). We are all on a journey through life. Our mind, willfulness and emotions need help to process what is going on. I believe self-condition dreams are given by God to help us in this processing. Self-condition dreams might be given to us for the following reasons:

- They let us know that God knows what we are dealing with. This helps us battle the feeling of being forgotten by God.
- They let us see ourselves honestly, not through our own filters.

- They let us take time to realize we are acting out of reactive responses, and not necessarily with wisdom.
- They let us see our own habits and actions that may cause us grief.
- They let us see the strongholds we have built in our lives and how they affect us and others.
- They let us see the sins and issues we ignore, thinking, *They are minor.* This shows us God notices these things and their damage to our lives.
- They let us see that even though we know things intellectually, we often do not apply the correct principle.
- They remind us of things forgotten.

Basically, self-condition dreams reveal truths that we have forgotten or are unable to see easily. They set us up to receive healing and redirection in our lives. As in Mike's dream—or the dream that follows—they may also speak to us about our anointing and our good work.

Jane was in a huge, tall, four-wheel-drive pickup truck. She was driving. The truck was able to climb a very high embankment with no trouble. It was very powerful.

The interpretation of this dream might say:

Jane is in charge of (is driving) a ministry or work (truck) that is able to climb over high hindrances and is powerful.

Cool! Self-condition dreams cover a multitude of situations. Jane's dream spoke of a work she was active in. In the following dream, Rebecca is given insight into a bothersome situation at her local church. She had this self-condition dream:

I was with a group of people. This group of people was giving out bread to their members only. I was given bread. I knew that if I ate the bread I would not die. I also knew that very shortly (in the next day or two) there was going to be some sort of end to the world and that the only people who would live were the ones who had eaten the bread.

I was sad that only the group's members would live, so I took my piece of bread and broke it into little pieces. The piece I had was very little to begin with, and I was worried I would not have enough to pass around. But I did what I could. I found all my loved ones, including my sister and friend, and gave them each a piece. As the end time neared, I worried that there was not enough bread for me to be saved, but I figured that the risk of having a smaller piece was worth it, because if having a small piece was enough, then more people would be saved by eating part of my piece.

The end came, and I and my bread friends all lived. Everyone else disappeared.

Metaphorically, who is the "bread"? Yes, Jesus (see Matthew 26:26).

So, this dream might speak of Rebecca's frustration with a body of believers who were keeping Jesus to themselves, while Rebecca has a heart to spread Jesus to all she can. This self-condition dream might explain to Rebecca where the anxiety she feels regarding a particular group of believers or church originates.

In the following simple self-condition dream, Jim (the dreamer) is able to see a bit more clearly into his own habits. This is a common dream.

Jim dreams he is driving his car through traffic in a hurry because he is late for class.

Often we have self-condition dreams that indicate we are in some kind of school, college or class. These might speak of the dreamer going through a "learning" phase regarding some issue in his life. Dreams in which the dreamer is late often speak of getting caught up in some kind of distraction that has kept him from dealing with the issue.

> This dream may indicate that Jim is not learning what he is supposed to learn because he's caught up in the distraction of other people's lives or other works (traffic). And he feels it (he is hurrying).

Occasionally a dreamer might awaken from a self-condition dream with a strong sense of fear. This type of dream might be given to the dreamer by the Lord to highlight an issue wherein the Lord wants the dreamer to break free from fear. This dream is not to be mistaken for a "fear dream." A fear dream is given to the dreamer specifically to instill fear in the dreamer (if given by the enemy) or as an overflow of the anxiety and fear living in the dreamer's soul (if created by the soul).

All self-condition dreams are dreams from the Lord to expose behaviors, fears or situations in order to encourage dreamers to take action or to receive understanding on a deeper level.

Courage Dreams

A courage dream is given to the dreamer or ultimate recipient of the dream to provide courage. Gideon did not directly receive one of the most famous courage dreams in the Bible, but it was definitely meant for him:

> When Gideon came, behold, a man was relating a dream to his friends. And he said, "Behold, I had a dream; a loaf of barley bread was tumbling into the camp of Midian, and it came to the tent and struck it so that it fell, and turned it upside down so that the tent lay flat." His friend replied, "This is nothing less than the sword of Gideon the son of Joash, a man of Israel; God has given Midian and all the camp into his hand."

When Gideon heard the account of the dream and its interpretation, he bowed in worship. He returned to the camp of Israel and said, "Arise, for the LORD has given the camp of Midian into your hands."

Judges 7:13–15

The metaphors in this dream seem obscure and strange to us, but notice that the friend of the dreamer, the Midianite, was not confused and did not question the validity of the dream. Verse 14 indicates the Midianite knew immediately that barley represented Gideon. This is a stretch to us some 3,200 years later. We might guess that Gideon was a baker—thus a loaf of barley represented him. However, I choose to believe that the friend knew the barley loaf represented Gideon because the Lord spoke it to him. It does not truly matter. What matters is that the Lord sent Gideon there to hear the dream and to receive courage. This might not have been a courage dream to the dreamer, but it certainly was to Gideon.

Calling Dreams

A calling dream speaks to the dreamer of her calling, vocation or mission in life. Jane's dream spoke of her new work:

> Jane dreamed she reached out and took a new baby from its mother. The baby was scrawny but pretty, sweet and loving— and did not cry. Jane carried the baby around a bit in a house with strange turns and bends and steps. The baby peed on Jane, and she realized that the baby did not have a diaper on, but Jane did not mind. Jane cleaned out a bottle and put milk in it for the baby. She gave the baby the bottle.

Symbolically, a baby is most often a new work, new ministry or new beginning.

Therefore, this dream might be saying there is a new work that Jane is just starting that has not been fed much yet. It is a good work as it is pretty, sweet and loving. Jane will have to go through some unusual obstacles to tend to the work, and she will have to put up with some toxic stuff and messes (pee). But Jane will begin to nourish the work and handle it properly. Jane's dream speaks of her calling to nurture others or assume responsibility for a new work or ministry.

Calling dreams might also be a little more dramatic, as shown in the next dream the Lord gave me one awesome night.

I was lined up with several other men and women. I was showing them how to fly. I said to them, "It is easy. You just lean forward a little, and you jump upward." Then I would take off and fly around the room, controlling the turns and landing back in place.

The lady next to me tried. She leaned forward and jumped and flew a bit. Several other men and women tried. Some were able to do it but could not control their flying very well. Others could not get off the ground. Some did it well. We all laughed and had a good time in the efforts.

This dream may indicate my calling to come alongside others and show them things in the spiritual world (air).

Could this thing I am showing them be "dream interpretation"? I believe so.

Correction Dreams

A correction dream is a dream the Lord gives to "tweak" us. It is gently telling us that if we keep going the way we are going, we will run into some form of trouble or hindrance to keep us from getting where we want to go. One important rule of thumb in interpreting correction dreams is to be as kind to yourself (or the dreamer) as the Lord is.

Sean dreamed he went into his parents' house and stabbed them with a knife. There was blood all around.

When Sean gave me this dream, he was very upset. As a young man who lived in a college dorm, it scared him, and he was almost in tears as he cried in anguish, "Does this mean I'm going to kill my parents?"

I quickly assured Sean that most dreams are metaphors, so we needed to look at the symbols of the dream instead of the literal happenings. A knife in a dream is most likely not a knife but a symbol to represent sharp words (see Revelation 2:16). Stabbing with a knife is likely symbolic for inflicting sharp, hurtful words on someone else.

I said, "The dream is probably saying you are inflicting sharp words on your parents, and it is causing them a great deal of pain."

Sean said, "You got that right! It seems every time I go home I'm yelling at them, and we get into big fights."

I asked Sean, "Why did God give you this dream? It might indicate that Father God is aware of what is happening, and He loves you and your parents enough that He wants you to know this is causing them a lot of real pain and could permanently kill your relationship with them."

"I guess I better stop it," Sean said. "I never really thought of it this way before." Sean's response was right on. He took the "correction" to heart and realized it was a loving call to change his behavior.

The following gentle correction dream opened Jenny's eyes a little:

Jenny dreamed she went to visit Sue at her house. Jenny knocked and called through the screen door and then went inside. Sue was angry that Jenny had come inside. She turned away to take a bath and left Jenny standing there. Jenny then went back outside to her car under the pretense of getting something but was really waiting for Sue to finish her bath.

This dream might be saying that Jenny is trying to help someone whom Sue represents. Jenny does not have favor, however, and her help will not be received well. She should wait for Sue to receive some spiritual cleansing first.

This correction dream is a little tweak from the Lord. Note: The Lord is certainly not scolding Jenny for trying to help. Instead, He is trying to give her some wise discernment on the situation.

Correction dreams are not to scold us. If we believe in the Lord Jesus Christ and have accepted His salvation and cleansing of our sins, then God has already dealt with His penalty for our sins . . . through Jesus. No, these tweaking dreams, or correction dreams, are to help us help ourselves. They gently point us in the right direction.

Caution! If the dream interpreter, while interpreting and relaying the meaning of a correction dream, conveys condemnation, or anything other than the love of God and His desire to gently redirect us, then she has crossed the line into falsehood, for the Lord did not include condemnation in the dream. Be careful how an interpretation is delivered.

Therefore there is now no condemnation for those who are in Christ Jesus.

Romans 8:1

Here are a few more correction dreams:

Rachel dreamed she was in the front seat of a car waiting for her husband. Rachel's friends were in the back seat of the car waiting for a ride home. In the dream, Rachel fell asleep; she wakes up later and realizes that her friends are still waiting patiently for her to take them home. She feels bad because she should have driven the car and taken them home instead of sleeping. She wakes up.

The interpretation might be that Rachel has been lacking in awareness; she should become more responsive and take control of whatever work/ministry she is supposed to be doing. Others depend on her responsiveness.

The following dream is also a correction dream.

Dana dreamed she was in a locker room. She had to pee and headed for the stall, but she started peeing before she got there. She peed on other things and had to clean up her urine.

This might mean Dana is trying to get rid of toxins, or toxic issues, in her life. This is good. She's heading the right direction, but she's going about it in an incorrect way. The incorrect way will cause messy issues that she'll be forced to clean up.

Remember, try to be as kind to yourself (or the dreamer) as God is! By your tone or words, do not relay anger or condemnation in the interpretation. God is tweaking us, not reprimanding us, in our dreams.

Direction Dreams

Direction dreams help us choose the proper direction to go. Remember Ruth's dream about the she-bear? (See "Where We Begin.") Ruth was trying to decide whether to allow someone back into her life. The dream spoke of a destroyer that was waiting and watching, and would attack if the idea she was playing with came about. This is a type of direction dream. It could also be considered a plan of the enemy dream.

Amanda was given the following direction dream:

Amanda was with a guy she had just met, and they were doing some kind of work. He was okay, but she did not especially like him. The guy gets into Amanda's car, but he is too big, and his feet are hanging out the back.

This dream might be showing Amanda that a new person in her life (car) or work (car) is not a good fit for her life or work.

Just before I received the following dream, I joined a ministry I will call Prayer for Others. This ministry was led by a friend of mine. I did not pray about it before joining. Instead, I ran full-force into it because I thought it would be great fun to spend time with my friend. Then I received the following dream:

I was driving a red car that belonged to Ingrid. It was neatly loaded with a lot of stuff. I pulled up to a parking garage. I knew as I pulled into the garage that I was wrong and needed to go another direction. I get out and talk to the woman in charge of the garage. I tell her that even though I just brought the car there, I needed it back because I needed to go the other direction. She smiles and says, "Okay." She tells me that she has a car just like it, but it is another color. She sends someone to get the car. I recognize her as Ingrid's sister. I ask if she is, and she says, "Yes." She says she is thinking of joining the Prayer for Others group. I invite her to do it, knowing that I was not going to be a part of it. I wake up.

The dream contains the following symbols:

Red = not to go forward; stopped (red light)
Car = work or ministry
Car that belonged to Ingrid = ministry that is Ingrid's
Garage = place where individual ministries are kept
Woman in charge of the garage = woman in charge of the ministries
Car like it, but a different color = same ministry, but not stopped
(a different color than red)
Ingrid's sister = sister in Christ to Ingrid

These symbols might indicate that this dream means:

119

I am in a ministry that is not mine. I am going a wrong direction. I need to talk to the woman in charge of the ministries and tell her that I need to go a different direction.

I believe this dream confirmed to me that I should not be in the Prayer for Others ministry. Note: It does not say there is anything wrong with the ministry. It just says I am not to go forward. Possibly I am overcommitted, or the Lord knows something is going to come up that will make this commitment a bad choice for me.

This was a dream from God telling me that I need to change direction. A direction dream might be a type of correction dream if the dreamer is already in the middle of the issue.

Plans of the Enemy Dreams

In a war, covert operations succeed much better than plans broadcast loudly on international television. A great deal of time and governmental assets are spent either on determining plans of the enemy or in trying to keep a plan secret. Why? Because a plan is only good if it is successful. And there is less likelihood of success if a plan is known, because it allows preparation to come against it.

Plans of the enemy are only as good as they are covert or not acted against; therefore, they do not have to come true if we act against them. These dreams are not necessarily warning dreams, because they might not happen if the dreamer, or the focus of the dream, prays and steps out proactively.

Jim gave me the following dream he received.

In my dream, it was gray and overcast everywhere. I was driving a vehicle to a work-site location. I was followed by another engineer whom I often do work for. It was a cold, muddy, snowy day. I made a left-hand turn and started up a trail.

Now I was climbing the trail on foot. It was very steep, almost cliff-like, and I was using rocks, roots of trees, etc., to get my

*footing. I slipped a lot. I was mostly on my knees during the
climb. I noticed the sole and the inside of the heel had come
off of my left shoe. I woke up.*

I told Jim it appeared from his dream that he would be experiencing some difficulty at work. The gray and overcast sky might be a clue that this is a plan of the enemy. "Heel" could be a symbol for betrayal (remember, Jacob grabbed the heel of Esau at birth, only to betray him later). And "left" may be symbolic for worldly things. See the symbols dictionary section of this book. If these symbols apply, then this dream might say:

Jim would experience betrayal at work.

Immediately, Jim confirmed that there was a difficult challenge for him at work, and he was going along a lousy pathway. There were several people coming against him, and he was having a lot of trouble.

Sometime later, Jim found me and said, "Remember that dream about the betrayal? Well, it happened. I found out Paul had been bad-mouthing me to my boss. I always considered him one of my mates. Paul's one I have counted on for years. I could not believe he did that."

Could this have been averted if Jim had prayed against it? Maybe so. As a plan of the enemy dream, this might have been stopped or changed if someone had prayed and requested godly action to thwart the enemy's plan. I believe dreams that are plans of the enemy might be cancelled if we intercede, but often we fail to do so.

Warning Dreams

Warning dreams tell the dreamer, "Something is going to happen, so be prepared." I believe most warning dreams are somewhat set; we may be able to change some particulars of the happening or the effects of the happening, but we cannot completely prevent it.

Look, for instance, at the warning given to me in one dream:

In my dream, I am going to an army plant to work. I look down and notice I only have flip-flops on my feet instead of the steel-toed boots I am supposed to be wearing. A bus picks me up.

In Ephesians 6:15, shoes are symbolic for the gospel of peace. Therefore, having no shoes, or incorrect shoes, may be symbolic for a lack of peace. The implication of this dream might be that circumstances will be coming at me that will try my patience, temper, stress level and frustration. The interpretation of this dream might be:

I am not prepared to protect my peace in an upcoming business situation.

This dream was a warning to protect my peace. So what does "protect your peace" mean? According to Ephesians, we are to be proactive and "put on" peace as we go forward.

Usually, warning dreams will happen, and prayer does not change that fact. The dream is to prepare us on some level for what is coming.

Bart dreamed he was in Tom's home. Bart notices that Tom's clock on the wall is broken and stopped.

This dream may indicate that Tom's time has run out. It could be an indication that Tom is nearing the end of a season in his life. Or it might mean Tom is going to die.

As it turned out, Tom died a few weeks later. This was a subtle, gentle dream to prepare Bart for Tom's upcoming death.

Notice the goodness of God that He did not speak harshly of the death, thus invoking fear in Bart. On some level, Bart wondered if this dream meant Tom was going to die, and he was able to prepare emotionally. This dream is typical of the way our God warns us of death. He does it lovingly and a little ambiguously so as to be gentle.

Dreams in which someone is killed or dies are usually metaphorical for a change in their spiritual life. They are symbolic. Rarely are they "visions" that actually represent a death. Remember, dreams are metaphors.

While warning dreams will usually happen and prayer does not change that fact, often they are given to allow us to pray for safety or deliverance for the victim. Remember the "Logs Falling off a Truck" dream in chapter 2, "Common Dream Questions/What about Psychological Views on Dreams?" section of this book?

> I was driving my car [but it was not my car in real life]. I looked out the windshield and saw a semitruck pulling a flatbed of long logs in front of me. The logger was stacked high, and the rear corners of the bed were L-shaped metal brackets that held the logs on the bed. As I drove fast down the highway, I saw the right rear-corner bracket break off and the logs start to fall onto the road in front of my vehicle. I knew I could not stop in time. I knew I would hit with full force the fallen logs. Then I woke up.

This dream has already been dissected and discussed. But this is a good example of a warning dream. In this particular case, the warning was not for me, but for someone else. Nevertheless, it is a good example of a warning dream. The incident did happen, but because of prayer intercession, the full effects were not suffered by the individual. Let's take a closer look at intercession dreams.

Intercession Dreams

An intercession dream is given so that the dreamer, the interpreter or the person to whom God brings the dream may pray on behalf of the victim in the dream. The "Logs Falling off a Truck" dream is also an example of an intercession dream. And in that particular case, the intercession was effective. I prayed for safety for the driver, and it was granted, although the occurrence still happened. The dream allowed me an opportunity to see the need for prayer, to pray and to observe God work through the prayer.

Janet brought to me the following dream of intercession.

> *Janet dreamed there were two men. One of them was behind. He grabbed Lily [a doll that belonged to Emily when she was a little girl. Emily is Janet's now thirty-year-old daughter]. When the man grabbed the doll, he turned into a framed picture of a gun. Janet grabbed the frame and beat it until it broke. Then she grabbed the picture of the gun and tore it up. Janet woke up.*

I have got to say, I was confused on this one. But we sought godly counsel and found that the following symbols fell out of the dream.

Lily = purity
Doll = innocence of childhood
Gun = spiritual power and control
Picture = memories from the past
Frame = framed

Substituting the symbols into the dream, the interpretation relays the following story:

> The enemy desires Janet's daughter's innocence, but Janet will break the spiritual power and control of the demonic attack. There were dark things going on in Janet's daughter's life, but Janet was given the ability to break them through intercessory prayer and intervention.

Afterward, Janet told me Emily had been abused as a child; in her later life, she faced problems dealing with the memories and repercussions of the abuse. In a sense, Emily was "framed" by someone with power over her purity and childhood innocence. The dream was a welcome word to Janet, as it gave her something she could do for her daughter. It told Janet that she was given the ability to intercede and break this hold on her daughter.

I receive many different kinds of dreams. I understand the importance of them and know they are often a call to pray. So, when I was given the following dream, I got on my knees immediately.

I dreamed a tornado was coming. I was safe, but it hit my sister and brother-in-law's house.

When I received the dream, I began to pray that whatever was coming against my sister and brother-in-law would be tempered by the Holy Spirit. I prayed for safety, guidance and deliverance for them. After prayer, my concern caused me to call my sister, who lived in another state.

I said, "Hi. Are you all doing okay?"

"Why? Did you get a dream?" My sister Brenda was on to me. She knew of my dreams.

I confessed the dream to Brenda.

We discussed how a tornado in a dream can often represent a large upheaval in life.

I told her I was praying and asked her to also pray. About two days later, Brenda and her husband, Andy, were driving on narrow winding roads near a lake. It was pouring down rain, and the car hydroplaned and went off the road. They were okay, but the highway patrol told them it was a miracle they weren't killed because of the steepness of the ravine they landed in.

Intercession dreams are given so that we know how to pray and intercede for others.

Invention/Business Development Dreams

In the "Where We Begin" section, the dream "There's Something Wrong with My Appendix" was told. In this dream, a report was due, and I had forgotten about a large section of the appendices. This dream was a business development dream and given to help me do my job well. Yeah! God cares about how we do our jobs. Inventions and business development dreams are hard to grasp because we often find it difficult to believe that the master engineer, developer and builder of the universe has time to care about whether we left out a portion of our appendices. But He does.

Many great composers and songwriters have claimed that dreams inspired their work. Maynard Solomon's *Beethoven Essays* reports on some of the dreams of Ludwig van Beethoven. Beethoven remarked of one dream that "no music was performed, yet it was a musical dream." It is believed that the deaf Beethoven received inspiration through his dreams.[1] According to Wikipedia, the full melody of the song "Yesterday" by Paul McCartney was composed in a dream one night.[2]

Spiritual Warfare Dreams

One night, I was having a restless sleep. I kept awakening, tossing and turning. I was anxious but did not know why. I began to wonder if God was convicting me about something I did wrong. Finally, I prayed to the Lord to show me why I was having such a hard time sleeping. Immediately, I fell into a good, deep sleep and had this dream:

> I was in a car sitting in the front passenger's seat. Right next to my face on the outside of the passenger's-side window was a man/spider. He had on a horrible, wicked spider costume. He also had a leering grin and creepy eyes that were looking at me. In one of his claws, he had hold of a sheet that was wrapped around me as I sat in the car. He would pull the sheet tight, grinning, and it would choke me and tighten around me. We drove up to a bunch of men in military uniforms. I asked them, "Will you take care of this guy because he is harassing me?" They said, "Yes." The spider/man disappeared, and I woke up.

Spiders are often a symbol for demonic activity, and the military is often a symbol for angelic protection (God's army). I believe this dream was in answer to my prayer.

It said that I was not able to sleep due to demonic spiritual activity. It also said I had the ability to ask God to have His angels take care of the problem.

Penny relayed a dream to me.

I was running and fighting in my dream. I did not know what I was fighting against, but I was lashing out wildly and trying to keep my balance. Finally, I saw this huge head of a demon come at me. The head was growing larger and larger and was many times bigger than I was. It was ugly and black and had an awful mouth that opened up and seemed to try to swallow me. I woke up.

I told Penny that the dream showed she was involved in some spiritual warfare.

Why did the Lord give Penny this dream? Or did it even come from the Lord?

If the Lord gave Penny the dream, likely it was to disclose to her what she was facing in her life situation. Something was coming against her and causing her problems, and this dream showed Penny she could come against it with prayer or fasting. However, if the enemy, perchance, gave the dream to Penny, it would have been because the enemy's minions were trying to scare her and cause her further distress.

Either way, Penny took a proper stance and reaction to the dream. She gave the situation to the Lord, asked for His help in dealing with it and refused to kowtow to fear, knowing she was protected under God.

Deliverance Dreams

Sometimes the Lord allows us to fight spiritual warfare battles within our dream. We can receive a deliverance from demonic attack on our lives in this manner. I had the following dream.

I was in the bathroom with some force binding me to the bathroom wall. My arms were locked against the wall just as if there were invisible clamps around them. I fought against it and could pull away a little, but the force kept pulling me back to the wall.

I felt a tremendous heaviness press against my chest. It was hot, and I could feel rancid hot air in my face—like someone's breath. I turned my head sideways to avoid the pressing force as much as possible. I could hardly talk, but I called out to my daughter, who was located in the next room.

"Abbey, will you come and see what is binding me to the wall?"

Abbey came, looked on the other side of the wall and said, "I don't see anything." I pulled with all my might and pulled myself free. I realized it was a spiritual darkness that was trying to bind me.

Then Abbey and I walked through the bathroom and looked around. I walked out into the hallway with Abbey a few steps behind me, but the door immediately tried to close behind me, trapping Abbey inside. I pushed against the door, and a strong invisible force pushed back. It was trying to push the door completely closed. I pushed and pushed. Again, I finally realized I was fighting an evil spiritual force.

I called out loudly, "In the name of Jesus Christ, our Lord and Savior, the Son of the living God, I command you to leave." It released the push and immediately left. The door opened, and there was Abbey.

It took some time before I was able to go back to sleep, but the next morning when Abbey came into the kitchen for breakfast, I said, "I know what's been going on this week. We've been under spiritual attack. But God has taken care of it in my dream." Abbey understood because, during the entire week, one thing after another had gone wrong. Abbey and I had been pretty beaten up with car trouble, work trouble, people trouble and injuries, etc.

> I believe this was God's way of showing me that Abbey and I were in the midst of spiritual warfare. I felt strongly that God was saying to me, "Quit fighting under your own strength. Call on My name, and I will handle it. Be faithful and pray."

This was the third dream I had received that week regarding being bound or held down. But this dream actually delivered us from the warfare. No more dreams occurred, and things smoothed out on the life front.

Healing Dreams

Healing dreams are one of God's tools to reach inside dreamers and heal the soul wounds inflicted upon them by the world. As declared in Isaiah 61, one of the Holy Spirit's jobs is to rebuild us from former devastations. I believe the Holy Spirit uses healing dreams to help this process.

The following dream is fascinating because it is such a simple dream, but the symbolic meaning is profound and deals with Peg's need to heal her bitterness.

> *Peg dreamed she had a lot of garbage in a milk carton. Nan yells at Peg and says, "Put it down." Martin tells Nan she did not have to yell at Peg. Nan is defensive. Peg is doing the dishes, and her hands are in soapy water. She says, "Would you please just drop it?" Martin says, "Thank you. Yes, we'll drop it."*

Some healing dreams tweak us to let go of something that is causing bitterness in our lives. Or they might open our eyes to truth so we can accept and deal rightly with issues we face.

Peg had no idea why these two people showed up in her dream. They were not particularly close to Peg, and she had no real relationship with them. I looked up their names. Martin means "truth," and Nan means "grace." So this is a dream where "truth" is in conflict with "grace" over some of Peg's "garbage."

Peg's healing dream might mean:

> God's grace says that Peg needs to drop some garbage she is carrying around. If Peg listens just to the truth or facts, it will defend her right not to drop it. But as Peg is trying to clean the vessels of her works, she needs to ignore the truth and, with grace, just drop the issue.

Peg was holding on to stuff she should not, and it was causing her problems. Unfortunately for Peg, the stuff she was holding on to was true and real. She did not know what to do about it. This dream told her to ignore the fact that it was true, and just lay it down and go on in the interest of cleaning up her life. What a healing dream! It is one we all can apply to our lives at times.

How about a healing vision? On January 24, 2011, in the wee hours of the morning, I had a vision. I was sitting in my living room chair playing stupid computer games on my laptop. I had been unable to sleep because I had lost my mother to an unexpected death just three days before, and I was grieving and heartbroken. (See the story about Emma in chapter 3, "The Steps of Dream Interpretation/ Seven Steps to Interpretation/Step 4 Find the Focus, Sub-focus and Details.") As I sat there, out of the corner of my eye, I saw a vision.

> *Jesus was standing there, laughing very hard and in complete joy about Emma's excitement. He was facing me. Facing Jesus, with her head turned slightly to see me, stood my mom. Mom was scrunched in a gleeful, funny, nutsy way, totally immersed in excitement. She was laughing so hard it was funny to look at her.*

She was pointing to Jesus, and the impression I received was that she was saying with her laughter, excitement and body language, "Look! Look! Look who I am with. Look! Look! Look!"

She was so happy. She was on Jesus' right side and was so close He would bump into her if He moved an inch.

Jesus had His hands spread out and upward as if to say, "What can I do? She loves Me so much!" He was happy and rejoicing with her. They were both glancing over at me in their love, laughter and fun, excited to share their joy with me. It made me laugh to see them.

As I leaned inward to get a closer look, the vision disappeared, but the imprint remained in my mind. And it still does. It has been very healing. Even though my loss was great, her gain was so much greater. It helped put things in perspective. Wow! God is good.

Prophecy and Revelation Dreams

Prophetic or revelatory dreams are amazing. They speak of things in the future. They may be on a large scale pertaining to all mankind (like the book of Revelation in the Bible) or on a small, individual scale.

Remember our discussion about the difference between visions and dreams? (See chapter 2, "Common Dream Questions/Who Are the 'Old Men' and 'Young Men'?" and "What Is the Difference between Dreams and Visions?") For an example of a large-scale prophetic vision (other than the book of Revelation in the Bible), I recommend reading "Vision of the Lord's army" in chapter 5, "Examples of Dreams/Visions and Interpretations" of this book to any readers with patience. It is long, but amazingly prophetic about how the Lord is creating His army, and the world's response to the Lord.

Here is an example of a prophetic dream that Kay received years ago.

I was in a hollow on top of a barren, rocky mountain. I looked out and saw some houses built on the side of the mountain. I

saw a beautiful new home turn all the way around, rotating. I
saw the back wall collapse and fly against the mountain wall. I
saw all the clothes, still on hangers, fly out and hit against the
mountain wall. I saw the rest of the house collapse and also
fly against the mountain wall. I then knew I was witnessing a
cyclone, although I never actually saw the storm, just the ef-
fects of it.

I walked around and saw some other damage done on the
mountaintop. I then remembered that the houses damaged
belonged to Adam or Bernard . . . so I knew it was all right. I
woke up.

In this dream, I believe some of the symbols represent the following:

Mountain = things high in the Spirit (see Genesis 49:26; Exodus 3:12; 19:23);

House = Church/God's universal Church without denomination/ total Church (see 2 Samuel 7:5–10, 13, 25–29; 1 Kings 8:13; 1 Chronicles 22:7, 19; Psalm 23:6; 31:20; 65:4; 66:13; Isaiah 2:3; Jeremiah 26:2–7, 29:26; Haggai 1:3–7; 2:3; Matthew 15:24; 21:13; John 14:2; Ephesians 2:19–22; Philemon 2; Hebrews 3:6; 10:21; 1 Timothy 3:5–15; 1 Peter 2:5);

Clothes = what we are walking in or doing (see Psalm 35:26; Proverbs 31:25);

Cyclone = stormy chaos from God to tear down things that need it (see 2 Kings 2:1–12; Isaiah 40:24; 66:15; Jeremiah 4:13; 23:19; Ezekiel 1:4; Hebrews 12:18);

Adam is a person in Kay's family with whom she does not agree on important principles = represents our universal Church family that is not right on important principles;

Bernard is a secular friend of Kay's who is hostile to God = represents the secular world.

The interpretation of this revelatory dream might be:

Even though the church [house] is high in the Spirit [mountain], it is without real substance [hollow, barren and rocky] and will come against the tearing-down judgment of God [cyclone]. God will bring down fortification [wall] behind the scenes [back wall] first. Then the self-righteousness and secular coverings [clothes] of the church [house] will meet the impact [cyclone] of God/ things high in the Spirit [mountain]. After that, the rest of God's universal Church [house] that belongs to the secular world [Bernard] or that is not correct on important principles of the Lord [Adam] will come down.

A revelatory dream may also be about just one person. Joann is a Christian woman who is active in understanding dreams. Margaret is her daughter. Joann's dream was as follows.

I was on a large, crowded bus. There was standing room only. The bus went to the top of a hill and stopped. It was the first stop. I knew it was my stop, so I got off.

I went into the house, and Margaret greeted me with pleasure. She wanted to show me the wonderful gift she was given. She opened a small keepsake folder and showed me a large cut of red hair, tied with a small ribbon. The hair was bloody. The blood made the red hair even redder looking. Margaret said the blood came from the person's nose who gave it to her. She was very pleased.

The interpretation of some symbols within the dream may be as follows. (See the symbols dictionary section for more information on each particular symbol.)

Nose = discernment;
Blood = covenant;
Hair = covenant;
Ribbon = covenant;

Red = anointing, wisdom;

Bus = movement of evangelism or ministry to many people;

First = God;

Top of hill = God.

Note the many references to covenant and God. Wow! This dream might mean:

> Margaret has been given a gift of an anointing by God for discernment and wisdom. This is a covenant between her and God. She will save this anointing until she pulls it out to use.

The dream indicates Margaret is not currently walking in the anointing and gift yet (she is saving it), but it is there for her future. This was a revelatory dream about Margaret.

Enemy Dreams

Unfortunately, in the spirit world, the Holy Spirit is not the only one talking to us. Demonic or spiritual influences from the dark side may also enter into our heads. (See chapter 2, "Common Dream Questions/What Source Is behind My Dream?/Enemy.") The enemy's forces may also give us dreams. We need to be careful not to believe every dream we get. The enemy mainly gives us the following two types of dreams: fear dreams and false dreams.

Fear Dreams

Fear dreams are not of God. The Bible says God does not wish to instill fear in His followers.

> Do not fear, for I am with you; do not anxiously look about you, for I am your God. I will strengthen you, surely I will help you, surely I will uphold you with My righteous right hand.
>
> Isaiah 41:10

Even though fear dreams often come from the dreamer's own soul, they might also come from a minion of the enemy. Soul fear dreams arise out of the dreamer's personal fears. But enemy fear dreams are given to get the dreamer off balance and to instill fear into the dreamer, probably in hopes that the fear will affect the dreamer's decisions or actions in an ungodly way. You cannot always tell what is behind fear dreams (your own soul or the enemy). Either way, they are not of God and are probably false. Therefore, a dreamer should never take a fear dream to heart. Instead, test the dream against the Word of God to see if the interpretation holds up.

Be proactive in ending fear dreams by recognizing them, renouncing them and then dealing with the "fear" issue in you through godly counsel. Recall Jeri's fear dream in chapter 2 in which her son drove off a cliff. To renounce this dream, Jeri may then work with the Lord and godly counselors on the root of that fear in her life.

The Bible says, "Fear the Lord," but this speaks of a reverential respect and honor, not "being fearful." The Lord does not want us to be fearful. Isaiah 41:10 says, "Do not fear, for I am with you; do not anxiously look about you, for I am your God. I will strengthen you, surely I will help you, surely I will uphold you with My righteous right hand." When we get fear dreams, whether from the enemy or from our soul, the Lord wants us to work on the root of that fear and not allow it to have any part in our lives.

Remember, fear dreams are not of God, because fear is not of God.

False Dreams

Another favorite way to get a revelatory dreamer off-center is for a minion of the enemy to give him a false dream. We discussed how false dreams may originate from the dreamer's own soul, but they may also be implanted by a dark spirit to attack the dreamer. They might be given to confuse us about our mission or the direction we should go. False correction dreams might also be put into our minds to instill guilt or condemnation. Here, too, it is difficult to determine whether a false dream has originated from the dreamer's soul or from the enemy, but either way, they should be disregarded.

Sometimes false dreams are given to a dreamer to keep the dreamer in captivity, or, in other words, to keep the dreamer in oppression and bondage, without healing.

> Your prophets have seen for you false and foolish visions; and they have not exposed your iniquity so as to restore you from captivity, but they have seen for you false and misleading oracles.
>
> Lamentations 2:14

The following verses indicate that divination, or receiving information from spiritual forces that are not of God, will cause people to prophesy falsely.

> Then the LORD said to me, "The prophets are prophesying falsehood in My name. I have neither sent them nor commanded them nor spoken to them; they are prophesying to you a false vision, divination, futility and the deception of their own minds."
>
> Jeremiah 14:14

Note, the next verse indicates the divination might be "flattering" to us. This should caution us that not all uplifting things said in a dream are from God.

> For there will no longer be any false vision or flattering divination within the house of Israel.
>
> Ezekiel 12:24

The following verse shows that those receiving false and lying words do not know they are not of God—and sometimes speak them out as a "word from the Lord."

Did you not see a false vision and speak a lying divination when you said, "The LORD declares," but it is not I who have spoken?

Ezekiel 13:7

God says He is not only unhappy with those who speak falsely, but also that He will come against them.

So My hand will be against the prophets who see false visions and utter lying divinations. They will have no place in the council of My people, nor will they be written down in the register of the house of Israel, nor will they enter the land of Israel, that you may know that I am the Lord GOD.

Ezekiel 13:9

I hope these verses are enough to convince the reader that he should not trust dreams on their own merit. There should always be confirmation from another source.

There are many types of dreams, and a dream may fall under more than one category. For example, a fear dream may also be a false dream. A correction dream may also be a healing dream. A spiritual warfare dream may also be a deliverance dream and a healing dream. The intent is not to diagram the dream to determine what "type" it might be, but to inform the dreamer and interpreter that there are various types of dreams out there. Because of this, be cautious and open to the Holy Spirit for guidance in dream interpretation.

5

Examples of Dreams/Visions and Interpretations

The following eleven dream examples are actual dreams relayed to me. These are worth looking at for the simplicity of the dreams and their easy interpretation. Look these over and see if you can get the same interpretation.

The twelfth example shown is not a dream but a vision. Remember, a vision does not use many metaphors. A vision is foreseeing an actual happening. This vision is profound and, I believe, prophetic. It was given to a young woman with a real heart for the Lord as she was in deep prayer.

Dream 1: A brother-in-law is killed in an accident.

Mark dreams that his brother-in-law is in a bad accident while driving an unknown, fast, red car. The brother-in-law is killed in the accident.

Could this mean that whoever represents Mark's brother-in-law in the dream will face a serious life-altering change very quickly?

Yes, it might. Or could this mean that Mark's actual brother-in-law will die in a car accident? Only if it is a vision. And it is likely this is a dream and not a vision. Remember, dreams are metaphoric. To die in a dream most often is symbolic and represents a life-altering change. It is also possible that the brother-in-law is himself, but the rest of the dream is metaphorical. Why did the Lord give Mark this dream? Possibly it is to let Mark know, on a more conscious level, for whom or for what he should pray.

As it turned out, shortly after this dream occurred, Mark's actual brother-in-law was unexpectedly diagnosed with cancer. The next fifteen years of intense treatments, surgeries and medicines were a life-altering change for him.

Dream 2: Jake is without pants.

Jake has a dream that while walking with friends he does not have on any pants.

Is Jake secretly having sexual fantasies about his friends? No. We are not going Freud's route. Might one of Jake's friends be interested in him in a sexual way? No. This is another Freudian concept.

And let's not be embarrassed about this dream, either. Clothes may represent putting on or taking off a characteristic (see 1 Peter 5:5); genitals may represent secret or private matters (see Genesis 3:21) or even shame (see Genesis 2:25; Ezekiel 23:17). If so, then exposing the genital region may be metaphorical for turning "loose secrets or exposing hidden things." To paraphrase: The exposure of this area may indicate being vulnerable and open with others and holding nothing back. Alternatively, since genitals might represent "being productive" (see Genesis 4:1), then exposing them may be metaphorical for being productive.

Yes! We do want to look at this dream symbolically. We will let Freud's followers get caught up in the worldly view of this dream. But symbolically, this dream is probably saying:

Jake is productive, open and vulnerable when he is with his friends.

A very good thing.

Dream 3: Nate has dinner on the fifth floor.

Nate dreams that he goes to a high hotel room on the fifth floor. The hotel was blue with gables. It was lovely. He had dinner there.

Could this mean Nate will be traveling to lovely places that have lots of blue—like the ocean? Well, possibly. A hotel could be a symbol for travel.

Might this mean that Nate will go on five trips and enjoy fine dining? Here, too, this interpretation uses the hotel, which might signify travel, so I can follow that. The interpreter is also trying to do something with the number five in the dream—i.e., five trips. But remember, neither the hotel signifying traveling nor five representing the number five are too metaphorical. A more symbolic approach to this dream might be:

Nate is in a temporary place of receiving grace and teachings from God.

What? How did I get that? Let's look at the symbols.

Hotel may be symbolic for a temporary place, a place of transition (see Luke 2:7) or a high spiritual calling (see Jeremiah 35:2–9). Or consider it as a metaphor for "high-rise apartment" (high: symbolic for "toward God"; apartment: symbolic for "place of living").

Five may be a symbol for grace (see Romans 5:2).

Blue may be a symbol for spiritual communion/heavenly things (see Exodus 26:1–36; 27:15–17; 28:5–15; Numbers 4:11–12) or

141

revelation (see Exodus 39:22; Numbers 15:37–39; 2 Chronicles 2:7, 14; Revelation 9:17).

A *gable* is a triangular head that often represents the Trinity—or God. *Dinner/food* is often symbolic for "being fed" or receiving learning.

Putting these symbols together, we might interpret the dream in this way:

> Nate, being in God's grace, is in a temporary state of transition where he is experiencing heightened spiritual communion with God and is being fed the Word of God through revelation.

So, why did Nate get this dream? Probably the Lord is giving him a word of encouragement and revelation.

Dream 4: Luke is barefoot as he walks into a restaurant.

Luke dreams he walks into a bar/restaurant with three of his employees to meet a fourth person, a man, who wants to work for Luke's company. Luke is barefoot.

If shoes represent peace, then being barefoot may be a metaphor for being without peace (see Ephesians 6:15). Therefore, this dream might say:

> Luke is not at peace with hiring this person under consideration.

Note: This dream does not say Luke should not hire the person; it just says he is ill at ease about it.

Dream 5: Zach is fighting with his dad.

Zach dreams repeatedly that he is physically fighting with his dad.

In real life, Zach does not have problems with his father, so he is confused about the dream. In a dream, a dad, or father, is often symbolic for "Father God" (see Psalm 68:5; Jeremiah 3:19; Matthew 10:33; 11:25–27). Therefore, this dream might say:

Zach is fighting against what God wants him to do.

Dream 6: Rebecca takes an elevator to the eleventh floor.

Rebecca dreams she entered an elevator in a high-rise office building in order to go to a new job. She needed to go to the eleventh floor.

Eleven is often a symbol for revelation from God (see Ezekiel 26:1; 30:20; 31:1; Zechariah 1:7).

An *office building* might be symbolic for work.

Going to a higher level in a dream might symbolize a higher calling or level of work.

In this particular dream, Rebecca needed to go to the eleventh floor; thus, this dream could be a calling dream and might mean:

Rebecca is entering into a higher new work in the revelatory arena.

Dream 7: David calls in sick, eats potatoes and carrots.

Scene 1: David dreams he was staying home and in his bedroom. In the dream, the bedroom was upstairs, and the wall was open to outside air. He was calling in sick because he felt he needed time at home. His boss said it was fine but that he would miss riding on the fire truck.

David then remembers he was going to take a ride on a fire truck that day.

Scene 2: David is home eating potatoes and carrots.

The interpretation might be:

> David is seeking rest (bedroom) and higher intimacy (bed) with the Holy Spirit (open air). He needs time to go back to basics (at home). God (his boss) says it is okay, but to do it David will miss being ready to deal with current events (riding the fire truck / putting out fires) that need attention. David chooses to do it and receives some healthy input (eating potatoes and carrots).

Dream 8: Jane dances with a clown ghost.

Jane dreams she is in an old house full of antique furniture. It is dark and spooky. She hears a scary noise and "knows" it is a ghost noise. She sees a ghost form in the corner. The ghost comes to Jane. He is taller than she and looks like a clownish and scary figure. His head and hair are white. He has a clown-ish smile. He wants to dance with Jane. Jane is repulsed and scared and says, "No." The clown becomes enraged and opens the door to the outside of the old house and says, "Then go!" Jane apparently did not want to leave, so she agrees to dance with him. They dance, and he sings loudly and joyously a song of nonsense words such as "O-lah-lah," etc.

The interpretation might be:
Jane is messing around (dancing) with her family's past (old house full of antique furniture). It is not a good past (it is dark and spooky) with lots of hidden issues (ghosts). To mess with this stuff is foolishness.

This may be a warning dream and a directional dream to Jane from God about what she is choosing to do. It might be encouraging her to go a different direction to avoid trouble.

Dream 9: Lisa mentors girls.

Lisa dreams she was mentoring a lot of girls. They were senior-high and junior-high age, and they were traveling on a bus. They were on their way to a college. They stopped along the way and did pleasant things.

This dream might mean:

Lisa will be mentoring others who are learning about things on a higher level, possibly spiritual issues. Some are spiritually immature (junior-high age), and some are more spiritually mature (senior-high age).

Dream 10: Ben's hotel room is messy.

Ben dreams he was in a hotel. His room was very messy with piles of his clothes lying all over the floor.

The interpretation might be:

Ben is in a temporary place of transition (hotel). There are things in his life in disarray that need to be put in place.

Dream 11: Joe is driving a Blazer.

Joe dreams he is sitting in a Blazer in the passenger seat, but he has stretched his leg over and is putting his foot on the accelerator trying to get the Blazer to go up the hill. The vehicle stalls and loses power. It rolls downhill with Joe steering it. Joe turns it into a side dirt/gravel road on the right. Joe gets it to stop. He starts it again and tries to drive it up the hill, but it loses power and rolls back down the hill again. Joe steers it onto the side road by looking into the rearview mirror. It rolls down quickly, and Joe stops it.

The interpretation might be:

> Joe is blazing (Blazer) a new trail, trying to go where others have not gone. But because he is not in the driver's seat, he is without power. Finally, through hindsight (looking in rearview mirror), he tries again to do it the "right" way. But, he is still without power (authority, guidance and might from God—see Matthew 28:18; Luke 24:49). He needs to stay on the right pathway/direction (road) until he gets power.

Dream 12: Vision of the Lord's army

The following is an example of a vision given to Rebecca. She had been praying to God for insight about what is true about heaven. Even though there are metaphors in it, for the most part, it is actually happening in the dream. This is pretty long but so awesome I wanted to share it with you. The person who had the vision was a thirty-year-old single woman with a strong heart for the Lord. The following vision was given to her as she silently worshipped the Lord.

> *First I see darkness, like space with purplish lines running in zigzags in really beautiful patterns, zooming past me—as if I was traveling through them. (Now, thinking back, it was like Space Mountain—but not white stars. They were a more purplish color.) All of a sudden in my vision, I am standing on a sidewalk in front of an office building. There is a rock-type garden landscape with bushes and flowers. (I do not know what they are called, but they have red, triangular flowers.) The rows began to bow, first the flowers, then the bushes and trees. They were all bowing.*
>
> *Then, in an instant, I am flying over a lake. It is beautiful and lit from the colors of a sunset (but I do not remember seeing a sun). There are forests on either side of the lake passage, and*

I am soaring fast over the water. I'm weightless, just zipping around. And I am taken aback by the beauty and calmness of it all. It is very peaceful, and I really enjoy flying.

Then I was in a forest with trees, and the trees began to bow. Next, I am standing near power-line poles, and they bow. Then I see rows of crosses, and the crosses begin to bow. Everything is bowing! Even the grass and wheat are bowing in awe and reverence. (There was a sense of honor in the bowing, not like we have—not an emotion that I know how to explain. Everything wanted to bow, but it wasn't like they felt subjected or obligated. There was excitement. It is really hard to explain—just not as you might bow to someone on earth.)

Next I was in an old arena (like the gladiator type). There was a path that led to the top of the arena, circling three times. On the path were many people on horses. I asked who these people were. The Lord said they were His army getting ready for a fight. I heard His words clearly in my head as I journeyed.

Off to the side I saw a large group of people behind a rope (like when you wait in line at the movies). The people had muzzles covering their mouths. Most prominent was a queen who was richly robed. All of them were wearing more muted colors—not rich colors like everything else I was seeing. I asked who these people were. The Lord said these were the people who will no longer speak out against Him.

Then I am on a sidewalk, a central sidewalk surrounded by grass (similar to a main campus walk at a university). I see a man in an army PT uniform running. I asked why I was seeing this, and the Lord said, "Wait." I watched the runner run down another sidewalk and around the corner coming toward me. In the background, I heard loud drums and marching. A bit after he rounded the corner, I saw a massive army marching in perfect step, each step thunderous. They were coming down the walk. And the Lord said the man was clearing the way for the army behind him. It is His army—meaning the Lord's army, not the runner's.

Then all of a sudden, appearing before the army were people in wheelchairs. I said, "This must not be Your army, God, because Your army would not have handicapped people" (meaning they would be healed already). Suddenly the wheelchairs turned into fantastic chariots. The people who were in the chairs were now piloting the chariots. The chariots were fierce, large and powerful, and they rode ahead of the army. I knew that those who had been bound to their chairs and were previously considered handicapped were now the greatest.

Then I was flying again. I flew over what looked like a concert venue with a stage and a crowd so large you could not see the end to the right or the left. I flew over row after row of people who were singing and worshipping, except it was as if they were at a concert for their favorite band. It wasn't worship in the sense that we do it. They were having a blast singing, dancing and worshipping God. In the background were beautiful lightning-like flashes.

Rebecca was wide awake when she had this vision. She was stunned and awed by it and immediately called me to share it. She understood it completely and did not even feel confused about what she saw. She said she felt this vision was showing her what heaven was "really like." It is more about our experience with the Lord, as opposed to our experience with the departed or our own actions and acquisitions. She was quick to emphasize that our heavenly experience is not about obedience as we, on earth, would define obedience—what we *have* to do. Instead, in heaven there will be a passion and excitement to be worshipping the Lord. We will not bow out of duty, but out of awe for the majesty and wonder of who the Lord is—excited to be partaking in Him.

I believe Rebecca's vision shows what the Lord is doing to prepare His army for upcoming spiritual battles—as well as giving us a glimpse into God's heaven. It is amazing.

Remember, a vision is a "seeing of what actually is" as opposed to symbols. In this vision, flowers, bushes, trees, rows of crosses and power-line poles bowed in worship to the Lord. These were not symbols in the dream; they were the actual physical articles, and this shows us that everything will be voluntarily subject to His authority and power. In the vision, people who were handicapped in the past became fierce, large and powerful—a word about how they will receive power and strength in heaven. This is a revelatory vision (a picture that exhibits a word from God), and it also happens to give us a peek into heaven.

6

Dictionary of General Symbols

When interpreting a dream, pay attention and ask, "Why? Why that person and not someone else? Why is the dreamer in a strange car and not his own? Why is the car black instead of blue? Why does the dreamer wear a formal, or is half naked? Why is the dreamer without shoes? Why does the dreamer have a polar bear on a leash instead of a black bear?" Do not shrug it off. Ask why. The symbols are usually there for a reason.

The "Dictionary of General Symbols" and the "Dictionary of Theme Symbols" are only a starting place for what a symbol in a dream might represent. These are a good start, because most of these symbols are taken from the Bible and are already symbols the Lord has used in communicating with us. As you discover your own personal dream vocabulary, jot them down for future use.

To use the "Dictionary of General Symbols" section, determine from the dream's context which direction to go in choosing a symbol's meaning. In other words, is the dog mean and bad? If so, the interpretation might best fall into the negative choices. Or is the person pleasant and helpful? If so, the interpretation might best fall into positive choices. Either way, never forget to ask the Holy Spirit for His guidance—as all interpretations belong to the Lord.

This general category is a miscellaneous category. For specific categories, e.g., places, body parts, animals and creatures, transportation, colors, people and beings, numbers or actions, see the "Themes" category in the next chapter.

Warning: To determine the correct definition of symbols in a dream, first seek the Holy Spirit's guidance (see Genesis 41:16). One symbol may have many different meanings. The meanings listed in this dictionary may not necessarily be the accurate symbol meanings for your dream.

Most of these dream symbols and their meanings come from biblical application and principles. Other symbols are derived from the characteristic of the item or animal; from the relationship involved; or from the function or use of the item, building, area or being. Other symbol meanings come from modern-day culture.

These symbols are listed with some positive meanings first, followed by some negative meanings. To determine whether to apply a positive or negative meaning, look at the dream context.

In seeking the definition of symbols in dreams, you must pursue the Holy Spirit's guidance (see Genesis 41:16). One symbol may mean many different things. A symbol meaning for one person's dream may not be an accurate meaning for the next person's dream.

Terms for deriving dream symbolic meanings:

- Char—This denotes the characteristic of the item or animal (based on Proverbs 6:6–8; 2 Samuel 2:18).
- Rel—This denotes a relationship inference (based on Hebrews 2:11; Matthew 12:46–50).
- Func—This denotes the function, or use, of the item, building, area or being (based on Nehemiah 12:44; Isaiah 39:2).
- General—This references "Dictionary of General Symbols."
- Themes—This references "Dictionary of Theme Symbols" and its specific theme category.

A

Abide: see General/Live.

Accent: designates where they "live" (are emotionally) or whom they represent (see Judges 12:5–6); of a foreign nation (see Zechariah 8:23).

Account: be accountable for (see Job 31:14; 31:37; 1 Peter 4:5); because of (see Psalm 59:12; 1 Peter 3:15).

Accuracy: consistent, but not necessarily true (see Psalm 51:6; 2 Corinthians 10:4–6).

Accusation: enemy trying to make you weak so you cannot go forward (see Nehemiah 6:1–9).

Adoption: qualified to share in the family and inheritance (see Colossians 1:12).

Adultery:
in agreement with (see Revelation 2:22);
come into intimate relationship for pleasure (see Judges 2:17);
unfaithful (see Hosea 2:20).

Affliction: problem (see Psalm 34:19; 2 Timothy 4:5); area of oppression (see Acts 7:10; Revelation 2:9–10).

Air: spiritual things [good or bad] (see Ephesians 2:2); see General/Wind.

Air balloon: see Themes/Transportation/Air balloon.

Alarm:
on guard (see 2 Samuel 4:1);
afraid (see 2 Chronicles 13:12);
warning (see Numbers 10:5–9; Jeremiah 49:2–3).

Alcoholic drink:
Holy Spirit (see Isaiah 51:21; Acts 2:15–17; Ephesians 5:18);
good spirits or bad spirits (as in slang term for alcohol);
brawler (see Proverbs 20:1);
causes confusion or error (see Proverbs 20:1; 23:29–35; Isaiah 28:7; Hosea 4:11);
see General/Wine.

Alive: in spiritual communion with Christ (see Ephesians 2:5; Colossians 2:13; Revelation 1:18).

Alley: direction you are going in life that is not easily seen [perceived] (see Numbers 22:32; Psalm 23:3; Proverbs 14:12); see General/Path.

Almond:
beginnings/prophetic (see Jeremiah 1:11–12);
to hasten/to be the first to blossom, *shoqed* [produce flowers and fruit early] (see Exodus 25:33; Jeremiah 1:11–13);
points to high priest [God/Jesus] (see Jeremiah 1:11);
watching (play on the original Hebrew word *shoqed*).

Aloe: used for healing (see Numbers 24:6).

Alpha:
God the Father (see Revelation 1:8);
first (see Revelation 1:8);
beginning (see Colossians 1:18; Revelation 21:6; 22:13).

Altar: where God can fill you in order to pour out to others (see Genesis 8:20; Leviticus 6:14; Acts 17:23).

Altar, under: persecution (see Revelation 6:9–11).

Altitude: your spiritual level (see Matthew 11:23; Luke 10:15); creates your attitude [as in flight] (see General/Attitude).

Ambush: waiting to do evil to the unsuspecting (see Judges 9:25; Proverbs 1:11).

Anchor: hope (see Hebrews 6:19); stability (see Acts 27:29–30; 27:40; Hebrews 6:19).

Anchor, tattooed on arm: strong hope (see Hebrews 6:19); [arm: strong] (see Themes/Body Parts/Arm).

Ancient: God's Church (see Jeremiah 5:15; 6:16); from the beginning (Psalm 119:52).

Ancient of Days: God (see Daniel 7:9–13).

Angel:
messenger of God or the enemy (see Exodus 33:2–3);
fellow servant of God—not to be worshipped (see Colossians 2:18; Revelation 22:8–9);

leader (see Revelation 1:20);
see Themes/People/Beings.

Antibiotic: slows down bad growth.

Antiques: things inherited from our fore-fathers (see Isaiah 23:7); relating to the past (see Isaiah 23:7).

Antique tub: old method of receiving cleansing (char); see General/Bath.

Appetites: set boundary for self (see Proverbs 23:2; Matthew 5:28–29); greed (see Isaiah 56:11).

Apple:

refreshing and healthy (see Song of Solomon 2:5; 7:8);

favored (see Deuteronomy 32:10; Psalm 17:8; Zechariah 2:8);

temptation [by tradition represents the fruit of temptation] (see Genesis 3:6).

Apple, gold: word spoken in the right circumstance at the right time (see Proverbs 25:11).

Apple of the eye: favor (see Deuteronomy 32:10; Zechariah 2:8); favorite/chosen (see Deuteronomy 32:10; Zechariah 2:8).

Aquarium: easy to see, but contained (char).

Aquarius:

pouring out water to others/Jesus Christ (see Numbers 24:7; John 3:5; 4:14);

astrology, not of God (see Deuteronomy 4:19).

Aries: the lamb/Jesus (see 1 Samuel 7:9; John 1:29; Revelation 5:12); astrology, not of God (see Deuteronomy 4:19).

Ark:

God's timing in life (see Joshua 3:1–5); God's rules for life (see Hebrews 9:4); Salvation (see Genesis 6).

Armband: loyalty (see 2 Samuel 1:10); identity (see 2 Samuel 1:10).

Armed: ready for battle (see Nehemiah 4:16–23).

Armor:

ready for battle (see Jeremiah 46:4, Romans 13:12, Ephesians 6:10–18;

shielded from the enemy's weapons/protection (see 1 Samuel 17:5; 17:38; 2 Chronicles 26:14; Nehemiah 4:16; Ephesians 6:13).

Army: army of God [i.e.: people of God and/or angels of God] (see Joshua 5:13–15; 1 Chronicles 12:22; Isaiah 52:12).

Aroma: a good gift (see Matthew 2:11; Ephesians 5:2, Philippians 4:18); good offering and good sacrifice (see Ephesians 5:2; Philippians 4:18).

Arrogance: idolatry (see 1 Samuel 15:23).

Arrow:

tool/worker of God (see Isaiah 49:2; Jeremiah 50:9);

to reach a target (see Lamentations 3:12; Psalm 64:3; Ezekiel 5:18);

one's children/son (see Psalm 127:4);

pierced/piercing (see Numbers 24:8; Lamentations 3:13; Psalm 38:2; 45:5);

something hurtful coming (see Deuteronomy 32:23; Psalm 64:7; Ephesians 6:16);

bitter speech (see Proverbs 25:18; 38:2; 64:3–8; Jeremiah 9:3–8);

false testimony (see Proverbs 25:18).

Arrow, blunt: without power or hurt (see Psalm 58:7).

Arrow, sharp: false witness against someone (see Proverbs 25:18).

Ash: repent (see Luke 10:13); destroyed (see Lamentations 4:5).

Ashes:

repented (see Matthew 11:21);

scattered (see Psalm 147:16);

humbled by sin (see 2 Samuel 13:19);

mourn (see Jeremiah 6:26);

things of the world (see Job 30:19);

lies (see Isaiah 44:20);

without sustenance or life (see 1 Samuel 2:8; Lamentations 4:5);

not pretty (see Isaiah 61:3);

of no worth (see Genesis 18:27; Job 13:12);

wicked (see Malachi 4:3).

Assembly:

council of holy ones (see Psalm 89:5–7; Isaiah 14:12–15);

praising God (see Psalm 22:25);

God presides over the great assembly (see Psalm 82:1–8; 89:5–7);

throngs of people gathered to watch (see Psalm 35:18);

Jesus is advocate and intercessor (see Job 16:19–21; Mark 14:62; 1 John 2:1);

Jesus on the right hand of Father God (see Exodus 15:6);

Lucifer wants to take over leadership (see Psalm 109:6–31; Isaiah 14:12–15);

Satan is the accuser (see Zechariah 3:1–10; Revelation 12:10);

located in second heaven (see Revelation 12:7–12).

Astute: counter for every move (see Psalm 18:26).

Ate: conquered (see Jeremiah 2:3; 5:17); see Themes/Actions/Eat.

Attitude: the degree to which you can see what is ahead (as in an airplane's attitude).

Audition: test [probably about what you will be tempted to say] (see Exodus 16:4; Judges 2:22).

Authority:

Jesus (see Matthew 7:29; 28:18; 1 Thessalonians 4:2);

those we should submit to and respect (see Matthew 8:8–10; Romans 13:1–7; 1 Thessalonians 5:12–13; Titus 3:1; 1 Peter 2:13).

Authority, false: teachers not teaching Jesus' words (see Matthew 7:29).

Awaken:

be aware and change what you are doing (see Psalm 57:8; 78:65; Revelation 3:3);

pay attention/alert (see Revelation 3:2; 16:15).

Axe:

book of Acts (play on words);

cut down people (see Jeremiah 46:22; Matthew 3:10; Luke 3:9);

destroy (see Jeremiah 46:21–23);

battle axe: battles/war (see Jeremiah 46:22; Ezekiel 26:9).

Axe, dull—more strength and skill is needed (see Ecclesiastes 10:10).

B

Babble: confusion [Babel] (see Genesis 11:9).

Babylon: organized rebellion (see Daniel 1–7; Revelation 1–7; 14:8).

Back:

behind you (see Isaiah 38:17; John 20:14);

not easily seen (see Daniel 7:6; Jeremiah 32:33);

not offered (char).

Back is on fire: something backfired (play on words).

Backsliding: perversion of way (see Jeremiah 3:22; Hosea 14:4).

Backward: not going the right way/away from God (see Jeremiah 7:24).

Bag: provisions (see Ezekiel 12:3–4; 12:9–12; Matthew 10:10; Luke 10:4; 22:35–38); things of the past we carry around with us (see 1 Samuel 10:22; Matthew 10:10).

Baggage: see General/Bag.

Balance:

true weight/God's viewpoint (see Job 31:6; Psalm 62:9; Proverbs 11:1; Isaiah 40:12);

in need of more fullness and balance (see Daniel 5:27; Revelation 6:5);

redemption/a purchase to balance (see Isaiah 40:12; Revelation 6:5);

stable or without swaying [of sober spirit] (see 1 Peter 5:8);

all things without excessiveness/staying centered (see Proverbs 16:11; Ecclesiastes 7:16–17).

Bald tires: ministry needs stability [needs God] (char; see General/Tire).

Balm: healing (see Jeremiah 8:22).

Ban: not to be touched (see Genesis 3:11; Joshua 6:17–18); will bring curses upon you (see Genesis 3:17–19; Joshua 6:18).

Banana: things that are slippery/unstable (char).

Band: come together (see Numbers 16:11; Psalm 94:21); bound (see Jeremiah 2:20).

Bankrupt: depletion of sources/without provision (char).

Banner:

proclaim truth/what God says (see Psalm 20:5; 60:4–5; Isaiah 5:26; 13:2; Jeremiah 50:2; 51:27);

Lord (see Exodus 17:15);

love (see Song of Solomon 2:4);

victorious (see Song of Solomon 6·4);

welcome of God (see Isaiah 49:22).

Baptize: outward expression of confession of sin (see Matthew 3:6; Ephesians 4:4–5).

Barb:

trouble [especially in seeing or understanding] (see Numbers 33:55);

painful afflictions (see Job 41:7);

see General/Thorn.

Barefoot:

without preparation (see Ephesians 6:15);

servant/slave (see Isaiah 20:2–4);

lost peace (see 2 Samuel 15:30; Jeremiah 2:25; Micah 1:8; Ephesians 6:15).

Barley: Gideon, personality—weakest/. cheapest/without honor/foolish (see Judges 7:13); able to overcome weakness/an overcomer (see Judges 7:1–25).

Barren: unable to be productive/without life (see Deuteronomy 32:10; 1 Samuel 2:5; Job 15:34; Isaiah 54:1).

Barrier: something keeping us separated out (see Ephesians 2:14).

Bars:

fortified (see Deuteronomy 3:5);

protection (see 2 Chronicles 14:7);

strength to forbid entrance/security (see Psalm 147:13);

contention that causes separation (see Proverbs 18:19).

Bars, none: unsuspecting (see Jeremiah 49:31); peaceful (see Ezekiel 38:11).

Basket:

preserving of God's people (see Matthew 13:48);

container (see Zechariah 5:6; Matthew 15:37);

day (see Genesis 40:18);

can hide what should be seen (see Matthew 5:14–15).

Basket, measuring: container judging sins of people (see Zechariah 5:6).

Basketball: competition/relationships (see 2 Timothy 2:5); striving/actions of life (see Proverbs 10:22).

Bath: cleansing from God (see John 13:10); see General/Wash

Bathroom, going to the bathroom: cleaning your life by getting rid of toxic things (see Exodus 40:30–37); see Themes/Places/Bathroom.

Bathtub: place of cleansing (see Exodus 40:30–32).

Battle:

struggles (see 1 Timothy 6:11–12);

fight against sinfulness (see Revelation 3:5);

spiritual warfare (see 1 Timothy 6:12);

see Themes/Actions/Battle.

Battle, axe: book of Acts (play on words); to fight spiritual battles.

Beard, half-shaved: ridicule/humiliate (see 2 Samuel 10:4–5).

Beauty: of the Lord (see Isaiah 33:17); make a prostitute (see Ezekiel 16:15).

Bed:

rest (see 2 Samuel 4:5–7; Psalm 63:6; 132:3);

where you choose to stay (see Job 7:3; Isaiah 57:7; Revelation 2:22);

intimate/place of intimacy/in private (see Micah 2:1);

sex (see 2 Samuel 13:11; Hebrews 13:4).

Bed, others in it: those you are in relationship with (see Isaiah 57:7); those you are of like mind with (see Isaiah 57:7).

Bed, short: too short to rest (see Isaiah 28:20).

Bed, wide: breaking commitment to God (see Isaiah 57:8).

Beer:

good things (see Micah 2:11);

things of the spirit/water from the Lord (see Numbers 21:16);

brawler (see Proverbs 20:1);

cause to forget the law (see Proverbs 31:5).

Behind our/my back: behind the scenes (char); sneaky (char); not obvious (char).

Behold: look for God/look upon God (see Isaiah 35:4).

Bellows: blow (see Jeremiah 6:29).

Belt:

truth (see Ephesians 6:14);

clinging to or bound to God (see Jeremiah 13:1–11);

support (see Exodus 12:11);

financial support (see Matthew 10:9);

preparation to go fast (see Exodus 12:11);

tied to you (see Psalm 109:19; Jeremiah 13:11).

Belt, around waist: bound, binding (see Jeremiah 13:1–11).

Belt, loose: not fit/fitting (see Isaiah 5:27).

Bent: something twisted a wrong way (see Ecclesiastes 7:13).

Bewitch: causing you not to see clearly (see Galatians 3:1).

Beyond: happening outside your control (see 1 Samuel 20:22).

Bible: see General/Scripture.

Bier: death (see 2 Samuel 3:31).

Bill: what we have to pay for our choices (see Colossians 2:14).

Bind: heal (see Isaiah 61:1).

Birdcage: house full of deceit (see Jeremiah 5:27).

Birth:

new membership in God's family (see John 1:11–13);

beginning (see Psalm 71:6);

bring forth (see Isaiah 59:4; Matthew 24:8; James 1:15);

time of pain before joy (see John 16:22).

Birth pains:

contractions and release [something over and over] (char);

shaking up and releasing, etc., to bring something about (see Galatians 4:19–20).

Birth, will not come: distress/rebuke/ disgrace (see 2 Kings 19:3).

Bit: forced to obey (see 2 Kings 19:28; Psalm 32:9; James 3:3); will direct entire body (see James 3:3); leads people astray (see Isaiah 30:28).

Bite: quick word that hurts (see Jeremiah 8:17).

Bitter:

hard to take (see Numbers 5:11–28);

curse (see Exodus 1:14; Numbers 5:27; Ruth 1:13);

judgment (see Revelation 3; 10:7).

Bitterness: trying to receive recompense by unsuccessful means (see Acts 8:23).

Black powder rifle: old-style power being exerted from a long distance away (char).

Blameless: without penalty from sin (see Psalm 18:23; Colossians 1:22); he who keeps accounts current by asking for forgiveness when he has sinned (see 1 John 1:9).

Blanket: covered in the consequences of your action or decision [good or bad] (see 2 Peter 2:13).

Blanket, narrow: too narrow to protect or cover you (see Isaiah 28:20).

Bleeding: wounded, hurt (see Leviticus 20:27; Deuteronomy 19:13; 2 Samuel 21:1; Revelation 14:20; 17:6).

Blemish:

not perfect/flaws (see Exodus 11:5; 2 Samuel 14:25; Malachi 1:14; Jude 12);

sin in life (see Leviticus 21:17–23; Ephesians 5:27; Colossians 1:22; 1 Peter 1:19; 2 Peter 2:13);

scars of life (see Leviticus 13:23, 28).

Blight: work of our hands judged by God (see Haggai 2:17); oppression (see 2 Chronicles 6:28).

Blimp: full of or from the Holy Spirit [air] (see 1 Kings 19:11; Psalm 104:4; Jeremiah 5:13).

Blind:

weak and unable to "see"/unable to understand/without "vision" (see 2 Samuel 5:6; Psalm 40:12; Isaiah

42:18–20; 56:10; 59:10; Lamentations
4:14; Zephaniah 1:17; Matthew 15:14;
John 9:39–41; Revelation 3:17–18);

living without understanding (see Matthew 23:24; Romans 2:19);

without qualities of faith, morals,
knowledge, self-control, perseverance, godliness, brotherly love,
kindness (see Isaiah 42:16; Matthew
23:16–19, 2 Peter 1:9).

Blocks: pathway in life is blocked (see
Lamentations 3:9).

Blocks, stumbling: wicked things (see
Ezra 4:3–4).

Blood:

covenant/binding promise (see Leviticus 4:6; Matthew 26:28; Hebrews
9:7, 12);

redemption/cover sins (see Exodus
12:23; Leviticus 17:11; Isaiah 4:4;
Ephesians 1:7; Hebrews 9:13–22;
10:4, 19; 13:12; Revelation 1:5);

offering (see Leviticus 1:5);

consecrate (see Leviticus 8:30);

weapon against the enemy (see Revelation 12:11);

life juices (see Deuteronomy 32:14);

defiled (see Leviticus 15:19; Lamentations 4:14; Psalm 106:38; Revelation
17:6);

death or killing (see Leviticus 20:27;
Deuteronomy 19:13; 2 Samuel 21:1;
Revelation 14:20; 17:6);

injure/unjust (see Proverbs 1:11; Isaiah
5:7).

Blood, bathe feet or walk in: to triumph
over (see Psalm 58:10).

Blood, drink: kill (see Numbers 23:24).

Blood, Jesus: weapon to combat evil (see
Colossians 1:20; Hebrews 12:22–24;
1 John 1:7; Revelation 12:11).

Blood, on land: polluted land without
atonement/without the ability to be
cleansed (see Numbers 35:33).

Blossom: burst forth (see Isaiah 27:6).

Blot out: remove from (see Revelation
3:5).

Blush: shame (see Jeremiah 8:12).

Board:

giving counsel/council (func);

direction (func);

providing communion and fellowship
(see Exodus 26:35; Matthew 8:11;
9:10–12; 26:20–29).

Board, wooden: see General/Wood.

Boil: affliction from the Lord (see Deuteronomy 28:27; Jeremiah 1:13–16).

Boiling pot tilted: disaster pouring out
(see Jeremiah 1:13–14).

Bond:

peace (see Ephesians 4:3);

guarantee (see Acts 17:9);

tied to (see Jeremiah 2:20; Philippians
1:1);

bondage (see Jeremiah 5:5; 30:8).

Bondage: caught up in sin (see Galatians
2:4).

Bone: dry bones/dried up (see Jeremiah
8:1–2); without God in your life; dead
(see Ezekiel 37:1).

Book: divine or preparatory knowledge/
learning (see Revelation 3:5); permanent record (see Revelation 3:5).

Book, of life: all are in (see Exodus
32:32–33; Psalm 69:28); blotted out
when an individual rejects Jesus
(see Revelation 3:5).

Boot, soldier: battle/warrior (see Isaiah
9:5).

Booth: where followers of Christ reside
(see Nehemiah 8:14–17); boxed-in
area (char).

Borders: boundaries others try to cross
(see Psalm 147:14).

Borrow: become a slave (see Proverbs
22:7).

Bottom: on the bottom of things (see
Deuteronomy 28:13).

Bound:

unable to minister (see Ezekiel 3:25);

unable to move (see 1 Samuel 14:24;
2 Samuel 3:34; Ezekiel 3:25);

caught up in something that is keeping
you from going forward (see Psalm
25:15; Proverbs 5:22; 6:2; Isaiah
8:14–15; 2 Timothy 2:26).

Boundary: limits in life (see Acts 17:26).

Bow: show reverence to (see Exodus
23:24); ability to be aggressive (see
1 Samuel 2:4; Psalm 44:6).

Bow (as in bowing down): be subservient to (see Genesis 37:9–10).

Bow and arrow: tongue shooting sharp words/lies (see Job 34:6; Jeremiah 9:8).

Bow, battle: warrior in Christ (see Zechariah 10:4; Revelation 6:2).

Bow, broken: unable to fight (see Jeremiah 51:56).

Bow, new: ready and effective (see Job 29:20).

Bow, old: not effective (see Job 29:20).

Bow, unstrung: no longer an effective defense (see Job 30:11 NIV).

Bowl:

vessel of God (see Isaiah 22:24; Revelation 5:8; 15:7; 16:1–21);

to be used by God, must be kept holy/kept clean (see Exodus 30:27–29);

vessels to hold offerings (see Exodus 25:29; 37:16; Numbers 4:7);

people (see 2 Timothy 2:9–21);

full (see Jeremiah 35:5; Zechariah 9:15);

used in service (see Jeremiah 52:18);

supply (see Exodus 37:16; 2 Samuel 10:19; Zechariah 4:2);

a vessel of judgment or consequences (see Revelation 17:1).

Bowl with shamrocks on it: a vessel that is a sham or a falsehood.

Bowling: doctrines (char: on the fast, straight path); see General/Sports game.

Bowling gutters: false doctrines that one cannot get out of (char); doctrines that do not work (char); human difficulties of life (char).

Box: container (see Numbers 19:15); covering (see Numbers 19:15); an enclosed group (func).

Bra: hidden personal things that are open for viewing (char).

Brace: human effort to compensate (see Job 38:3; 40:7; Nahum 2:1).

Bracelet:

adorned (see Ezekiel 16:11–12);

betrothal/one to whom you are pledged (see Isaiah 3:19);

pledge (see Isaiah 3:19);

friendship (see Genesis 24:22, 30, 37; 38:18; Ezekiel 16:11).

Bracelet, ankle: haughty (see Isaiah 3:16, 20).

Brake: able to be controlled (func); may be stopped (func).

Brambles: see General/Thorns.

Branch:

Jesus (see Isaiah 4:2; 11:1; Jeremiah 23:5; 33:15; Zechariah 3:8; 6:11–12);

Christians (see Isaiah 4:2; John 15:1–5);

appointed to serve God (see Zechariah 4:12–14; 6:12);

dominion/nation/section (see Jeremiah 5:10–11; Daniel 4:11–12, 22);

descendants (see Job 18:16–19).

Branch, broken and grafted in: Gentiles/people receiving the word (see Romans 11:17–19).

Branch, cut off: something not bearing fruit (see John 15:2, 6); someone not of God (see Isaiah 9:14).

Branch, trim (prune): something bearing fruit (see John 15:2); cleansing us (see John 15:2–3).

Branded: mark indicating who something or someone belongs to (see Galatians 6:17; 1 Timothy 4:2).

Brass: strong (see Micah 4:13); mirror (see James 1:23–24); judgment (see Isaiah 11).

Bread:

Jesus (see Isaiah 55:2; Matthew 26:26; Luke 22:19; John 6:35);

Word of God (see Deuteronomy 8:3; Matthew 4:4; John 6:32);

sincerity and truth (see Matthew 15:26; John 6:32; 1 Corinthians 5:8);

teachings (see Proverbs 31:27; Ecclesiastes 9:11; Matthew 16:5–12);

words already spoken (see Matthew 4:4);

sustenance (see Leviticus 26:26; Jeremiah 37:21; Lamentations 1:11; 2 Thessalonians 3:8);

earthly food (see Deuteronomy 8:3; Proverbs 17:1; Matthew 4:4).

Bread, dry: meeting minimum standards without much taste (see Proverbs 17:1).

Bread, flat and unleavened: being fed affliction (see Deuteronomy 16:3).

Bread, sweet: consumables obtained by falsehood (see Proverbs 20:17).

Bread, without yeast: sincerity/truth (see 1 Corinthians 5:8).

Breaker, water: to sweep over (see Psalm 42:7).

Breastplate: righteousness (see Isaiah 59:17; Ephesians 6:14); faith/love (see 1 Thessalonians 5:8).

Breath:

Holy Spirit (see Isaiah 40:7; Ezekiel 37:9–10; John 20:22);

life (see Job 7:7; Lamentations 4:20);

power to do God's will on earth (see John 20:21–23);

individual's spirit/He breathed the breath of life into us (see Psalm 39:5).

Breath, bad/offensive: someone you do not want to be around (see Job 19:17); religiosity/not the fresh breath of God (see John 20:22).

Breath, take away: die (see Psalm 104:29).

Breathe: life (see Genesis 2:7).

Bred: beginning of growth (see Isaiah 55:10).

Breeze: passes and does not return/ gone quickly (see Job 6:26; 8:2; Psalm 78:39); see General/Wind.

Briar:

consistent problems (see Judges 2:3; Job 31:40; Isaiah 32:13; 55:13; Ezekiel 2:6);

recurring problems often brought on by disobedience to God (see Judges 8:7–17);

malicious people (see Ezekiel 28:24); see General/Thorn.

Bribe:

a manipulation tactic (see Proverbs 17:8);

blinds wisdom (see Deuteronomy 16:19);

creates wrath (see Proverbs 21:14);

corruption (see Proverbs 17:23; Ecclesiastes 7:7).

Brick: hardness that is man-made (see Genesis 11:3; Exodus 5).

Bridle: control (see Psalm 32:9; James 3:2; Revelation 14:20).

Broken: old way of life come apart (see Matthew 21:44).

Bronze:

ruling crown (see Daniel 2:39; Revelation 2:18);

atonement/judgment (see Exodus 39:39);

strong (see Genesis 4:22, Job 6:12; 37:18; Jeremiah 1:18; 15:12, 20);

vanity/pride (see Jeremiah 6:28);

hard/unyielding (see Leviticus 26:19; Job 37:18);

substitute for gold [things of God] (see Isaiah 60:17).

Bronze, belly and thighs:

What is normally vulnerable (belly) is covered with hard, unyielding strength (see Leviticus 26:19; Job 37:18; Daniel 2:39);

possibly Greek or Hellenistic influence.

Brown paper bag:

fleshly humanistic issues;

see General/Paper;

see General/Bag;

see Themes/Colors/Brown.

Bruise: hurt (see Matthew 12:20).

Bucket: vessel (char); doctrine/tradition (see Isaiah 40:15).

Budded: chosen of God (see Numbers 17:5); begin to produce results (see Isaiah 27:6).

Buffet: self-discipline (see 1 Corinthians 9:27); ability to "choose what you partake in."

Burden:

work to be done (see Matthew 11:30; Galatians 6:1–5);

bearing things caused by someone else's sin (see Galatians 6:1–5);

bearing your own load (see Galatians 6:1–5);

idiosyncrasies and baggage that is carried (see 1 Samuel 25:31; Proverbs 28:17; Hebrews 12:1).

Burden, heavy:

oppression/persecution (see Matthew 11:28; Galatians 6:2);

legalistic/excessive religious demands (see Matthew 11:28; 23:4; Acts 15:10); rebellion (see Psalm 107:12); sin (see Matthew 11:28).

Buried: lay dead things down (see Colossians 2:12); something hidden (char).

Burn: through wickedness people are hurt/burned like fuel for a fire (see Isaiah 9:18–19).

Burnt: offering (see Leviticus 1:14–17).

Bush, in desert/wastelands: not able to see prosperity (see Jeremiah 17:6); survive on nothing (char).

Butter:
blessing (see Genesis 27:28; 45:18; Leviticus 3:16);
prosperity as a result of [churning] struggles (see Proverbs 30:33);
smooth words (see Psalm 55:21);
see General/Oil.

Buy: paid price of/obtain through recompense (see Revelation 5:9); give to receive (see Revelation 3:18).

C

Cage:
enclosed (see Job 18:9–11; Ezekiel 19:9);
captured/house (see Job 18:9–11; Ezekiel 19:9);
see Themes/Animals and Creatures/ (the bird).

Cage, dove: house of God's presence; see Themes/Animals and Creatures/ Dove.

Cage, eagle: church that is keeping their prophetic people from soaring (func); see Themes/Animals and Creatures/Eagle.

Calamity: disaster created for our own betterment by the Lord (see Isaiah 45:7).

Calf, image: false god (see Nehemiah 9:18).

Callous: unfeeling (see Psalm 119:70); mind, will and emotions so strong the Holy Spirit is unable to penetrate (see Deuteronomy 15:7; 2 Chronicles 36:13; Ezekiel 36:26; Ephesians 4:17–20; Hebrews 3:15–19).

Camera: way to make memories (func); see what is in the pictures (rel).

Camouflage: hide and try to obscure self (func).

Cancer:
reaching both far away and near [char of the crab];
reconciling two to one body [the Church] (see Ephesians 2:14–19);
astrology, not of God (see Deuteronomy 4:19).

Candle:
Christ (see 2 Samuel 22:29; 1 John 1:5);
life (see Job 18:5; 21:17);
ability to "see," understand (see Psalm 18:28; 119:105; Proverbs 6:23; 20:27);
each dip into the hot wax causes it to get stronger and its light to get bigger and to be "built up" but each time it is heated, it is painful (char);
a light for others to see (see Numbers 4:9; 2 Samuel 21:17; 2 Kings 8:19);
see General/Fire.

Candle, golden: Christ (see 2 Samuel 22:29; Zechariah 4:2, 11); the Church (see Revelation 1:13, 20).

Candlestick: influence (see Exodus 26); illumination (see Exodus 26).

Candlewick, snuffed out: dead (see Isaiah 43:17).

Candy: sweet teachings/things that appeal to man (see Psalm 119:103; 141:4).

Cane, in hand: old age; inability to go forward easily (func).

Cannon: very powerful attack (func); see General/Gun.

Canopy:
government (see Jeremiah 43:10);
a place to reside (see Isaiah 40:22);
shelter from trials (see Isaiah 4:6).

Canopy, dark: Lord's anger (Psalm 18:11).

Cap, marker: covering over a time period (cap—covering; marker—marking time).

Capricorn: scapegoat/Christ (see Leviticus 16:5, 17); astrology, not of God (see Deuteronomy 4:19).

Capstone: Jesus (see Isaiah 28:16; Zechariah 10:4); stone on top of arch (see Acts 4:11).

Captured: judgment of God (see Ezekiel 16:27); unable to fight (see Jeremiah 51:56).

Car wreck: a drastic life change (see Haggai 2:22).

Card: reveal (func); proclaim (func).

Cardboard: man-made covering (char).

Carmel: fertile field (see Amos 1:2).

Carnival:
festivity (char);
party-spirit (char);
competition (char);
worldly (char);
divination (char).

Carpet: soft foundational covering (func); see General/Floor.

Carpet, gray: foundation of compromise (func); see Themes/Colors/Gray.

Cart, on wheels: carried by spiritual things; see General/Tire; see General/Air.

Cast: healing to become strong (see Ezekiel 30:21); something crippling you (char).

Cataclysmic events: consequences brought by God to get people's attention (see Revelation 6:12–17).

Cauldron: vessel of offering (see 1 Samuel 2:13–14).

Cedar:
leader who overshadows others (see Ezekiel 31:3–10);
is fragrant (char);
man's work to honor God (see 1 Kings 6:18);
wealthy and fine (see Jeremiah 22:14–15);
tall (see 2 Chronicles 25:18; Psalm 92:12; Isaiah 2:13; Ezekiel 31:3–9; Amos 2:9);
takes deep root (see Hosea 14:5);
man-made (see 2 Samuel 5:11; 7:7);
sways (see Job 40:17).

Cedar, broken: voice of Lord (see Psalm 29:5).

Celery: salary (play on the word).

Cell phone: calling out from a place of imprisonment [cell] (char).

Cellular: about the body [biological cells] (play on words).

Cement: man-made "rock" [gods or idols] (see Deuteronomy 32:37); hard and cold rock (see Jeremiah 5:3; 23:29; Ezekiel 11:19; 36:26).

Censer:
Holy (see Numbers 16:37; 17:3);
vehicle for prayer or worship (see Exodus 30:7–9; 2 Chronicles 26:19; Revelation 8:3);
censor/cover up (see Ezekiel 8:11).

Census: to count (see Exodus 30:12).

Centaur: two-fold nature.

Center: position of distinction (see Revelation 7:17).

Chaff: those who have rejected Jesus (see Matthew 3:12; Luke 3:17); of no worth (see Job 13:25; Isaiah 33:11).

Chain, gold: honor (see Daniel 5:29).

Chains:
bound (see Psalm 107:10; Isaiah 52:2; Jeremiah 40:1–4; Ephesians 6:20; Revelation 20:1–2);
cords of affliction/affliction/oppression (see Job 36:8; Colossians 4:18);
weighed down (see Lamentations 3:7).

Chainsaw: Word of God under the Spirit that cuts down trees bearing bad fruit (see Matthew 3:10; 15:13); a word that leaders [trees: see General/Tree(s)] are accountable to the Lord (see Matthew 3:10; 15:13).

Chair:
position of authority (see 1 Samuel 4:13; Job 29:7; Daniel 4:30; Matthew 23:2, 6; 27:19; Revelation 20:4);
rest (see 2 Kings 4:10);
position of honor (see Jeremiah 22:23).

Chair, cover: covering over authority (func).

Chair, straight-backed: support that is straight (correct), not corrupt or bent (func); unbending authority (see General/Chair).

163

General Symbols

Chair, wooden: fleshly authority (see General/Chair).

Chalk: easily crushed to pieces (see Isaiah 27:9).

Charcoal: burns away impurities (see Ezekiel 24:11); strife and quarrels (see Proverbs 26:21).

Charge: to direct (see 2 Timothy 4:1); to take responsibility for the cost (see Philemon 1:18).

Chariot: life (see Judges 5:28).

Chariot wreck: God will change life (see Haggai 2:22).

Charm: able to control others (see Psalm 58:5).

Cherubim: guards of Lord (see Genesis 3:24).

Chiffon: light, airy [Holy Spirit] covering (char).

Child sacrifice: to hurt one's offspring or those one should be protecting (see Isaiah 57:5).

Childless: one who will not prosper in his lifetime (see Jeremiah 22:30).

Choke: put pressure on (see Matthew 18:28).

Chosen: one who meets the criteria (see Matthew 22:1–14; 2 Timothy 2:10).

Christmas tree: structure of Christ's birth (rel); around Christmas time (rel).

Chubby: see General/Fat.

Cigarette: pride/arrogance; people who say, "Keep away; do not come near me, for I am too sacred for you" (see Isaiah 65:5).

Circle:
earth (see Isaiah 40:22);
continuous (see Ecclesiastes 1:6);
covenantal promise (see Genesis 41:42; Haggai 2:23);
round (see Isaiah 40:22);
going in circles (see Ecclesiastes 1:6).

Circuit: designated path (see 1 Samuel 7:16); path of power (see 1 Samuel 7:16).

Circumcise:
spiritual covenant/promise to you (see Jeremiah 4:4; 9:25–26; Philippians 3:2–3; Colossians 2:11);

display of faith (see Colossians 3:11);
grafted into Christ's blood [saved] (see Ephesians 2:11–13);
human manifestation or attachment to religious laws/religiosity/legalism (see Galatians 5:2–6; 6:12–15; Ephesians 2:11; Titus 1:10);
of a religious spirit (see Titus 1:10).

Cistern: place to hold the truth [water]; man-made life (see Jeremiah 2:13); filled with the dead (see Jeremiah 41:9).

Cistern, broken: cannot hold God's ways (see Jeremiah 2:13).

Clam: opportunities, promises and prophecies that are not released until fulfillment to protect them from coming out prematurely [growth of the pearl] (char); things strongly closed (char).

Clap: express praise for (see Psalm 98:8); supports or approves the happening (see Nahum 3:19).

Claws: clause (play on words); documentation, laws.

Clay: people of God (see Isaiah 29:16; 64:8; Jeremiah 18:6; 19:1).

Clay, vessel:
a ministry (see 2 Corinthians 4:7–9: "we have this treasure in earthen vessels" to show that the surpassing greatness of this power is from God);
hard-pressed on every side but not broken (see 2 Corinthians 4:7–9);
city; nation (see Jeremiah 19:10–11);
work of the potter's hand (see Lamentations 4:2);
earthly/worldly things (see 2 Timothy 2:20);
easily broken (see Job 13:12; Daniel 2:42; 2 Corinthians 4:7).

Clay, wet and moldable:
open to the instruction of the Lord (see Job 33:6; Isaiah 45:9);
easily molded (see Job 10:9);
a follower/easily influenced (see Job 10:9).

Clean:
purity and obedience (see 2 Samuel 22:25);

without spiritual contamination (see
2 Chronicles 29:16; Ezra 6:20);

remove sin (see Psalm 51:2–7; 2 Timothy 2:21);

by confession of sin/and following the
Word (see Psalm 119:9; John 15:3;
Ephesians 5:26);

see General/Wash.

Cleft: shelter (see Judges 6:2; Revelation 6:15).

Clock: time, watchman (func).

Clod, dirt breaking up: preparing for
planting (see Isaiah 28:23–26);
breaking up years of thought patterns (char).

Clothing:

mantles/calling/what you are going to
be doing/what you are doing (see
Job 38:9; Psalm 89:45; Revelation
4:2–6);

covering/protection (see Job 8:22;
29:14; Psalm 30:11; 45:3; 65:13; 73:6;
104:1–6; 109:18–19, 29; Isaiah 50:3;
51:9; 52:1; 63:1; 64:6; Jeremiah 52:33;
Ezekiel 26:16; Matthew 22:10–13;
2 Corinthians 5:2; Ephesians 6:11–17;
Colossians 3:12; Hebrews 1:12);

motives (see Matthew 5:28; 7:15);

defines who the wearer is/who the
wearer has characteristics of (see
Job 30:18; Psalm 35:26; 132:9; Proverbs 31:25; Jeremiah 2:34; Matthew
22:10–13; 27:28; Luke 24:49; Romans
13:14; James 2:2; 1 Timothy 2:9–10;
1 Peter 5:5; Revelation 1:13; 19:16);

Holy Spirit (see Luke 24:49);

ready for service or work (see Luke
12:35);

tend to/take care of (see Ezekiel 16:4;
Matthew 6:30);

will wear out and be changed (see
Psalm 102:26; Isaiah 50:9; 51:6; Hebrews 1:11);

religious system (see Matthew 9:16);

covering of sin (see Genesis 3:17–21;
Zechariah 3:3–4; Matthew 27:28);

vengeance (see Isaiah 59:17).

Clothing, apron: protective covering
(func).

Clothing, baby: immature coverings and
immature ways (char).

Clothing, ball gown: Lord preparing you
for elegance (char); putting on luxuries of the world (char).

Clothing, black: covering of the enemy
(see Psalm 18:11).

Clothing, bloody:

proof of virginity (see Deuteronomy
22:13–18);

acts that cause spiritual death (see
Genesis 37:31);

pain (see Revelation 19:13);

guilty (see Jeremiah 2:34).

Clothing, casual: made comfortable
(func).

Clothing, changed: coverings/jobs that
are changing (see Hebrews 1:12).

Clothing, chiffon:

fine airy [of the Holy Spirit] (see Isaiah
66:15; Ezekiel 37:9; John 3:8);

soft, beautiful, valuable covering (see
Psalm 109:18–19); worldly and of
little substance.

Clothing, clean: pure acts of God's
people (see Revelation 19:8).

Clothing, cloak: see General/Clothing,
Coat.

Clothing, coat:

anointing (see Matthew 14:35–36; 21:8);

covering (see Psalm 109:18–19);

zeal (see Isaiah 59:17);

Holy Spirit (see Luke 24:49);

See General/Clothing, Robe.

Clothing, colorful coat: favor with humility (see Genesis 37:3, 23).

Clothing, cultural: foreign (char); relating
to that culture or country (rel); see
General/Foreign.

Clothing, cut to expose buttocks: ridicule/
humiliate (see 2 Samuel 10:4–5).

Clothing, embroidered: riches (see
Ezekiel 26:16); banner (see Ezekiel
27:7).

Clothing, expensive:

caught up into the world's finer things
(see Matthew 11:8);

rich (char);

see General/Clothing.

Clothing, filthy: our actions under our
own power (see Isaiah 64:6); sin (see
Zechariah 3:3; Revelation 3:4).

Clothing, formal: things of the world (char); formal (char); stiff (char).

Clothing, gaudy: greedy and selfish acts (see Revelation 17:4; 18:16).

Clothing, heavy: heavy covering (char); heavy protection (char).

Clothing, leopard skin material:

ready for warfare (see Jeremiah 5:6);

Jezebel spirit (see Jeremiah 5:6; Revelation 13:1–4);

see Themes/Animals and Creatures/ Leopard.

Clothing, linen: righteous acts of God's people (see Revelation 19:8, 14); no perspiration (see Ezekiel 44:17–18).

Clothing, old-style: old coverings from the past (char).

Clothing, pants: covering over productiveness (func).

Clothing, put on robe: acquire wealth (see Job 29:14).

Clothing, rags: poor (char).

Clothing, remove robe: stripped of wealth (see Micah 2:8).

Clothing, rich:

righteousness and holiness of God (see Zechariah 3:4; 2 Corinthians 5:21; Ephesians 4:24; Revelation 19:8);

finery (see Ezekiel 16:10);

righteous acts of God's people (see Revelation 19:8, 14);

wealth/worldly adornment/caught up into the world's finer things (see Micah 2:8; Matthew 11:8).

Clothing, robe:

adorned/royalty (see Revelation 1:13);

grab hold of (see Zechariah 8:23);

royalty (see 2 Chronicles 18:9; Matthew 27:28–31);

ruling/authority (see Psalm 93:1; Ezekiel 26:16);

immersed in (see Psalm 93:1).

Clothing, sash: see Themes/Colors—denotes calling [e.g., golden: of the Lord] (see Revelation 1:13).

Clothing, soft: covered with soft things/ soft and easy world (see Matthew 11:8).

Clothing, T-shirt and shorts: little covering, but enough (char).

Clothing, taken away on a cold day: singing or speaking lightly to a heavy heart (rel); an inappropriate action (see Proverbs 25:20).

Clothing, torn:

outward display of penitence (see Joel 2:13);

mourn/grieve (see Numbers 14:6; 2 Samuel 13:31);

vexed (see 2 Kings 5:7–8; Joshua 7:8);

lost or threatened protection (see 2 Samuel 1:2; 1:11; 13:19; 15:32).

Clothing, tuxedo:

Lord preparing you for elegance/righteousness and holiness of God (see Zechariah 3:4; 2 Corinthians 5:21; Ephesians 4:24; Revelation 19:8);

righteous acts of God's people (see Revelation 29:8, 14);

finery (see Ezekiel 16:10);

wealth/worldly adornment/caught up into materialism (see Matthew 11:8).

Clothing, underwear: without pretense or guile (char); transparent and open (char); unprepared (char).

Clothing, wearing someone else's: pretending/disguised (see 2 Chronicles 18:29).

Clothing, wedding:

clothes of righteousness and salvation (see Isaiah 61:10; Matthew 22:11–13);

coming into intimate agreement with (see Matthew 25:1–12; Revelation 19:7).

Clothing, white:

coverings of Christ (see Ecclesiastes 9:8; Galatians 3:27; Revelation 3:18; 4:4; 6:11; 7:9);

walking with Christ (see Revelation 3:4; 7:13);

overcoming evil (see Revelation 3:5);

occult covering (see Matthew 23:27).

Cloud:

God's leading (see Exodus 13:21; Numbers 9:15–23; Deuteronomy 31:15; 1 Kings 8:12; Ezekiel 10:4; Mark 9:7);

Glory of the Lord (see Exodus 40:34; 1 Kings 8:10; 2 Chronicles 5:13–14);

mental attack/emotional manifestation (see Ezekiel 30:3, 18);

cloud an issue (play on words);

cover up (see Numbers 9:15; Psalm 97:2; 105:39; Ezekiel 8:11);

will vanish and be gone (see Job 7:9; 30:15; Isaiah 44:22);

covering the land (see Psalm 105:39; Ezekiel 38:9);

reduces the heat of the ruthless (see Isaiah 25:4–5);

advances (see Jeremiah 4:13);

as high as (see Jeremiah 51:9).

Cloud, bright: of the Lord (see Matthew 17:5).

Cloud, dark:

dwelling of God (see Deuteronomy 5:22–29; 2 Samuel 22:10–12; 2 Chronicles 6:1);

will receive favor; blessings coming (see Proverbs 16:15);

repercussion from the Lord (see Psalm 18:9);

enemy (see Isaiah 5:30);

going to rain/go through hard times (see Psalm 18:11; Luke 12:54).

Cloud, gray: hard, confusing times (see Job 3:5; Psalm 18:11; Isaiah 5:30; Luke 12:54).

Cloud, lift: set out (see Numbers 10:11–12); embark on (see Exodus 40:36–37).

Cloud, moving: sensitivity to presence of God (see Exodus 13:21; 14:19); time for change (see Exodus 13:21).

Cloud, rain: will receive favor; blessings coming (see Proverbs 16:15).

Cloud, under: not able to set out (see Numbers 9:17; 10:12).

Clouds, white: from God (see Matthew 17:5); God's judgment (see Lamentations 2:1; Zephaniah 1:15; Revelation 14:14).

Clouds, with no rain: boasting of gifts not given (see Proverbs 25:14); gift not given (see Jude 12).

Clown: make mockery of (func); dealing in foolish things (char).

Club: false testimony (see Proverbs 25:18).

Clutter: unhealthy issues/blockage in the way (see Galatians 5:7); things of the world/clutter in life (char).

Coals/charcoal:

warm (see 2 Samuel 14:7);

burn away impurities (see Isaiah 6:6–7; Ezekiel 24:11);

Lord's anger (see Psalm 18:12; 120:4).

Coal, burning: source of warmth (see 2 Samuel 14:7).

Coat: see General/Clothing, Coat; see General/Clothing, Robe.

Coat, colorful: favor with humility (see Genesis 37:3, 23).

Coconut: fruits often refer to the fruit of the Holy Spirit, especially if the fruit appears in a "spirit" (alcoholic drink) (char).

Coffee: eye-opening/bringing alertness (func); bitterness (char).

Coffee pot: vessel producing bitterness.

Coffin: something dead (func); storing a dead issue (func).

Coffin, found an old:

something dead from the past that is being opened up again (func);

a dead issue is being "dug up" again (func).

Coin: something or someone valuable being paid or received (func).

Cold: stagnant (see Revelation 3:15); without warmth or life (see Matthew 24:12).

Cold, at harvest time: a faithful messenger (see Proverbs 25:13).

Collar: binds us (see Job 30:18).

Colored: altered (func); put forward as having a certain characteristic, but not really having it (func).

Colonoscopy:

needs help in getting rid of old garbage in life (see Genesis 2:16–17; Matthew 15:17);

needs help in getting rid of unclean things (func);

by-product/result (see 2 Kings 18:27; Isaiah 36:12).

Comb: holds sweet things [honeycomb] (see Psalm 19:10); tool that will

General Symbols

167

straighten out your covering or protection (see Genesis 9:20–27).

Comforter: God's Comforter/the Holy Spirit (see John 14:16–18, 26; Acts 9:31).

Commandment: holder of God's teachings/understandings from God (see Proverbs 6:23).

Commission: an order or calling (see Deuteronomy 31:14).

Communion: listening and speaking to God (see Luke 12:12; John 14:26; 16:13; 1 Corinthians 2:13).

Compact: agreement (see 2 Samuel 5:3).

Confirm: second or third repetition of something God is saying to you (see Hebrews 2:3–4).

Conflict: trials (see Hebrews 10:32).

Confusion: preliminary to change/destruction (see Deuteronomy 7:23); unable to think clearly (see Psalm 55:9).

Conscience:
God's absolute truth (see Romans 14; Hebrews 8:10);

listening to God/Holy Spirit (people heeding the voice of Jesus; see John 8:3–9; Acts 24:16);

listening to your spirit (see Acts 24:16; Hebrews 9:14).

Constellations: names given to stars by God and for His purpose (see Psalm 147:4; Isaiah 40:26); astrology, things not of God (see Deuteronomy 4:19).

Consume: destroy (see 2 Kings 1:10; Revelation 28:8); see General/Eat; see Themes/Actions/Eat.

Coordinator: one who arranges things (func); Jesus (see 1 Peter 2:25).

Copies:
reproduce/imitate (see Isaiah 54:1);

shadow of things of heaven (see Hebrews 9:23–24);

not the true one (char).

Copper: part left over after being refined (see Ezekiel 22:18); wealth that will corrode (see Matthew 10:9).

Coral: of great value (see Job 28:18–19).

Cord:
the drawing and holding power of God/the love of Christ (see Hosea 11:4; 2 Corinthians 5:14);

not separate (see Ezekiel 16:4);

not quickly broken (see Ecclesiastes 4:12);

still attached/encompassed by/an entanglement (see Psalm 18:4–5; 116:3; Jeremiah 10:20; 2 Timothy 2:4);

sin (see Proverbs 5:22).

Cord, blue: remember and obey the Lord's commands (see Numbers 15:37–40).

Cord, red: not to be touched; follower of Christ (see Joshua 2:18–21).

Corn:
God's seed (see Isaiah 55:11; Hosea 2:8; Matthew 12:1–23);

harvest (see Genesis 27:28; Deuteronomy 18:4; 2 Kings 19:30; Proverbs 14:12; Jeremiah 2:19);

food (see Leviticus 23:14).

Corners, four: all of earth and nature (see Exodus 25:12; Job 1:19; Revelation 7:1).

Cornerstone: Jesus (see Psalm 118:22; Isaiah 28:16; Zechariah 10:4; Ephesians 2:20; 1 Peter 2:6); model we measure from (see Ephesians 2:20).

Couch: rest (see Job 7:13; Amos 6:4; Acts 5:15).

Council of holy ones: see General/Assembly.

Counter: place of preparation (func).

Course: life's journey (see 2 Timothy 4:7).

Court: confront others (see Job 9:32; Matthew 10:17); resolve disputes (see Deuteronomy 25:1; Psalm 37:33; 84:2; James 2:6).

Covenant:
promise (see Genesis 9:9–17; Hebrews 8:6);

comes into force upon the death of the one who makes it (see Hebrews 9:16–18);

sealed by blood (see Hebrews 10:15–22);

Jesus (see Isaiah 42:6).

Covered area: a covering/protection (see Genesis 9:20–27); trying to put God in a controlled area (see Numbers 4:5).

Covering: authority (rel); protection (func); align self with (rel).

Crawling: under submission/submitting to (see Matthew 20:20; Mark 1:40; 5:6; Luke 5:8).

Cream: best of God's Word (see Isaiah 55:2); best foundational truth/prosperity (see Job 29:6).

Credit card: receiving credit for something done (char).

Crib: cottage/hovel (func); manger (func); bed for new work (func).

Crocus: burst into bloom (see Isaiah 35:1–2); strength to come out in hard (winter) times (char).

Crooked: deviation from God's way (see Deuteronomy 32:5; Psalm 18:26; Proverbs 2:15; 21:8; Ecclesiastes 1:15; Philippians 2:15).

Crop:

period of time of growth until harvest/ length of time (see Ecclesiastes 3:1–2; Matthew 13:30);

harvest (see Haggai 1:10);

results (see Matthew 13:8);

blessing (see Zechariah 8:23);

results of spreading God's message (see Matthew 13:23);

people (see Isaiah 60:21).

Cross:

plan of salvation (see Matthew 27:35–46; Mark 10:21; Romans 6:6; Galatians 6:14);

redeeming worldly things to God (see Ephesians 2:11–16);

pass by (see Joshua 1:2);

instrument through which sin is done away with (see Romans 6:6);

problems of life (see Matthew 16:24);

trials, including bullying, threats, ridicule, oppression (see Matthew 10:38; 16:24; 27:32; Luke 9:23).

Cross country: across the country/regional (play on words).

Crowd: public opinion (char); peer pressure (char); rise above status quo (char).

Crown:

of God (see Revelation 4:2–6);

adorned (see Psalm 65:11; Ezekiel 16:11–12);

covenant (see Lamentations 5:16; Revelation 3:11);

righteousness (see 2 Timothy 4:8);

those who love (see 2 Timothy 4:8);

ruler (see 2 Samuel 1:10; Isaiah 28:5; Matthew 27:28);

glory and honor (see Hebrews 2:7–9);

success (see Job 19:9; James 1:12);

excellent wife (see Proverbs 12:4);

grandchildren (see Proverbs 17:6).

Crown, gold:

rewarded/reached point of success in God (see 2 Timothy 4:8; 1 Peter 5:4; Revelation 4:4);

things we have held in high esteem (see Philippians 4:1; Revelation 9:7).

Crown, many crowns: Jesus (see Revelation 19:12).

Crown, removed: stepped down (see Ezekiel 21:26).

Cruise: on a "ship"/the large church/ community of God (see Genesis 6:18; 7:1; Matthew 13:2; James 3:4); see Themes/Transportation/Ship.

Crumbs: small bits of truth (see Matthew 15:27).

Crushed: destroyed (see Ezekiel 30:8).

Cry: because a person has perverted his way (see Jeremiah 3:21).

Crystal:

of God (see Revelation 4:2–6);

clearness (see Revelation 4:6; 21:11);

beautiful (see Job 28:17);

future (able to see clearly).

Crystal, store: in store for the future (char).

Cubit: 18 inches.

Cubit, long: 21 inches.

Cup:

communion/promise of relationship with/salvation (see Psalm 116:13; Jeremiah 35:5);

covenant in Jesus' blood (see Luke 22:20);

partake in (see Isaiah 51:17; Jeremiah 49:12; Matthew 20:22; Mark 10:38–39);

destiny (see Matthew 20:22–23; 26:39; Luke 22:42; John 18:11);

same fate (see Isaiah 51:22; Jeremiah 49:12; Lamentations 4:21; Matthew 20:22; Mark 10:38–39; Revelation 18:6);

suffering/trials (see Matthew 26:39–42; Luke 22:42);

wrath (the "containment of the cup of His wrath"; see Isaiah 51:17);

make stagger (see Isaiah 51:22);

isolation and death (see Matthew 26:39–42).

Cup, dirty inside: greed/self-indulgence (see Matthew 23:26; Revelation 17:4).

Cup, gold: offering that affects nations (see Jeremiah 51:7).

Cup, large and deep: experience holding much (see Ezekiel 23:32).

Cup, miniature: small communion (char).

Cup, others: share their experience (see Isaiah 51:22; Jeremiah 49:12; Ezekiel 23:32; Matthew 20:22; Mark 10:38–39; Revelation 18:6).

Cup, overflows: more than plenty/in abundance (see Psalm 23:5).

Curse: without cause, a curse is not effective (see Proverbs 26:2).

Curtain:

protector (see Numbers 4:5; Luke 23:45);

hidden/separation (see Exodus 26:7; Numbers 3:26; Isaiah 40:22; Hebrews 6:19–20; 9:3);

the end (as in performance or theater production).

Curtain, lush red:

hidden power (curtain: hidden; red: coming from a place of power; see 2 Samuel 1:24).

that appear good, "lush" (char);

hidden dangers (see Proverbs 23:31; Revelation 12:3);

Curtain, red: danger hidden (see Proverbs 23:31; Revelation 12:3).

Curtain, temple: protector of the Church (see Numbers 4:5; Luke 23:45; Hebrews 9:3); Jesus (Luke 23:45).

Curly: bend around (char); leaning toward (char).

Custom: worthless (see Jeremiah 10:3).

Cut: separate (see Leviticus 20:6; Isaiah 53:8; Galatians 5:4).

Cut down: driven away (see Daniel 4:23–24).

Cut off: died (see Job 27:8; Lamentations 3:54); destroyed (see Jeremiah 8:21; 51:13; 52:8).

Cut short: end quickly (see Matthew 24:22).

Cymbal: worship (see 2 Chronicles 29:25–28); praise God (see Psalm 150:5).

Cypress: things of earth that resist God's Word [water] (see Genesis 6:14).

D

Dance:

taking the same view/moving together (see Matthew 11:17);

joy (see Jeremiah 31:4);

worship (see 2 Samuel 6:14; Psalm 149:3; 150:4);

idolatry (see Matthew 14:6–7).

Dancing: see General/Dance.

Dark:

hidden (see Deuteronomy 5:23; Job 3:6; Psalm 97:2);

to be "in the dark" or not know where you are going (see Job 12:25; John 12:35; Ephesians 4:18);

time of privacy and learning (see Matthew 10:27);

ignorance (see 2 Corinthians 4:6);

hard times (see Exodus 10:21; Isaiah 5:30; Ezekiel 30:18; Joel 2:2; Zephaniah 1:15);

time of mourning (see Ezekiel 32:7–8);

without Jesus/not of the Lord (see Exodus 10:21; Job 3:4; 1 Samuel 2:9; Isaiah 5:20; Lamentations 3:6; Matthew 4:16; 6:23; 22:13; Luke 1:79; John 1:5; 12:35; Acts 26:18; Ephesians 5:8; 6:12, 1 John 1:5–6);

death (see Ezekiel 32:7–8);

of the enemy/evil one/wicked (see Proverbs 4:19; Isaiah 5:30; 50:10;

Matthew 8:11–12; John 8:12; Ephesians 4:18; 5:11; 6:12; Colossians 1:13; 1 Thessalonians 5:4–5).

Darkness: see General/Dark.

Darkness, thick: unapproachable (see Job 19:8); mysterious (see Psalm 97:2); time of predators (see Psalm 104:20–22).

Dart: painful, piercing experiences (see Job 41:26); to move quickly (see Proverbs 7:23; Nahum 2:4).

Darts: attacks (see Job 41:26); curses (see Ephesians 6:16).

Dawn:
Jesus (see Song of Solomon 3:1–5; Isaiah 8:20; 9:2);

break forth (see Hosea 6:3);

early (see Psalm 119:147);

is certainly coming (see Hosea 6:1–3);

removing the wicked (see Job 38:12–13);

righteousness (see Proverbs 4:18; Isaiah 62:1).

Daylight: exposed for all to see (see 2 Samuel 12:12); of the Lord (see John 11:9; 1 Thessalonians 5:5–8).

Dead:
pertaining to the end of an era in your life (see Mark 9:20–27; Luke 15:4–32; Ephesians 2:1, 16; Colossians 3:3; 1 Peter 2:24; Revelation 21:8);

life-changing experience (see Matthew 14:2; Mark 9:21; Luke 15:24–32; Romans 6:2–11; Ephesians 2:1, 16; Colossians 3:3; 1 Peter 2:24; Revelation 21:8);

salvation/dead on earth, but alive in heaven/baptized into Christ's death (see Matthew 22:32; Luke 20:33–38; Romans 6:2–11; Ephesians 2:1, 16; Colossians 3:3; 2 Timothy 2:11);

cannot help you (see Psalm 146:3–4);

those who are not of the Lord (see Proverbs 21:16; Matthew 8:22; Ephesians 5:14; Colossians 2:13; Revelation 3:1);

dead in the spirit/living with unforgiven sin/Christ is not in them (see Psalm 88:5; Romans 8:11; 1 Corinthians 15:12–20; Ephesians 2:1–5;

Colossians 2:12–13; 1 Timothy 5:6; 1 Peter 4:6; 1 John 3:14; Revelation 3:1);

name not written in the Book of Life (see Revelation 20:11–15);

to die (see Psalm 115:17; 2 Timothy 2:8; Revelation 1:18; 9:6; 20:12–114; 21:4);

without growth potential (see Psalm 31:12; Ezekiel 37; Romans 7:8);

cannot be restored (2 Samuel 12:23);

put aside (Romans 6:2, 11; Ephesians 2:1, 16; Colossians 3:3–11);

separated from God (see Luke 15:24; Ephesians 2:5; Colossians 2:13).

Dead, body: man without the Spirit of God (Luke 9:60; James 2:26).

Deaf: unable to understand (see Isaiah 42:18–20); cannot hear/will not listen (see Psalm 38:13).

Death:
spiritual change (see 1 Samuel 2:6; Psalm 88:5; Jeremiah 8:3; 2 Timothy 2:11; Revelation 21:8);

physical death (see Matthew 10:21; Philippians 2:27–30; 2 Timothy 1:10; 2:8; Hebrews 11:5);

change of clothes [your covering] (char);

spiritually not of the Lord (see Proverbs 16:25);

see General/Dead.

Death, of someone else:
dealing with character issues they may be "dying" to (func);

relationship with them is dying (func);

end to their old way of living (see Mark 9:21; 1 Peter 2:24; Revelation 21:8);

they are becoming "dead" to evil (see Mark 9:21);

change in their spiritual life (see Mark 9:21; 2 Timothy 1:10; 1 Peter 2:24; Revelation 21:8);

spiritually not of the Lord (see Proverbs 16:25).

Death, second: spiritual separation forever (see Isaiah 28:18; 1 John 5:16–17; Revelation 2:11; 20:14; 21:8).

Debt: unforgiveness/someone owes you recompense in your mind/penalty for sin (see Colossians 2:14).

Decree:

careful to follow (see Deuteronomy12:1);

God's laws (see Psalm 2:7);

legalism (see Daniel 6:4–16; Colossians 2:13–15).

Defect: sin (see Leviticus 3:1; 21:17–23; 1 Peter 1:19).

Defiled: without the Lord (see Isaiah 52:1).

Deploy: sent out against (see 1 Chronicles 19:11).

Deposit: Spirit in us guaranteeing what is to come (see 2 Corinthians 5:5).

Depth: God and His love (see Psalm 36:5–6; 42:7); the enemy's area (see Matthew 11:23; Luke 10:15).

Depression: struggle with anguish and sorrow in one's thoughts (see Psalm 13:2; book of Titus).

Desert:

place of spiritual refuge and protection from Satan (see Revelation 12:6);

land not sown (char);

trials/hard, trying times (see Jeremiah 2:2; Revelation 12:6);

time/place of trial/testing (see Deuteronomy 8:15; Psalm 106:14; Isaiah 25:4–5; Jeremiah 17:6);

parched places (see Jeremiah 17:6);

forsaken (see Isaiah 27:10);

see Themes/Places/Desert.

Desk: a place of communion equipped with compartments (func); a place of judgment (func).

Desk, sitting at with no pants on: God making spiritually reproductive (char).

Desolate: unproductive (see Isaiah 33:9).

Dessert: taste of God/power of the Holy Spirit/sweet things (see Numbers 13:27, 14:8); sweet things that appeal to man (see Psalm 119:103; 141:4).

Deviled eggs: seeds of Satan (play on words).

Dew, on grass:

blessing (see 2 Samuel 1:21; Proverbs 19:12; Hosea 14:5; Zechariah 8:23);

fleeting favor (see Proverbs 19:12);

words (see Deuteronomy 32:2);

everywhere/covering all (see Judges 6:39–40; 2 Samuel 17:12).

Die:

spiritual change/spiritual death (see Leviticus 22:9; 1 Samuel 2:6; Psalm 49:10; 88:5; Jeremiah 8:3; Colossians 3:3; 2 Timothy 2:11; James 2:26; Revelation 21:8);

will be with Christ in heaven (see Philippians 1:23–24);

physical death (see Matthew 10:21; Philippians 2:27–30; 2 Timothy 1:10; Hebrews 9:27; 11:5);

see General/Death.

Dimensions: know fullness of (see Ephesians 3:18–19).

Dinner:

see General/Eat;

communing with/communicate with (see Genesis 43:16; Job 1:4; Isaiah 25:6; Ezekiel 2:8; Matthew 26:20–29; John 4:26; 6:35; 13:26; Revelation 3:20);

learn or "feed on" (see Genesis 2:16–17; Leviticus 10:14–19; Proverbs 23:6; Jeremiah 3:15; Ezekiel 2:8–3:3; John 4:26; Hebrews 6:4–5);

partake in the Word/learn truth (see Ezekiel 2:8; Matthew 15:27; John 4:34);

partake in (see Genesis 2:16–17; Exodus 32:6; Proverbs 31:27; John 4:34; Revelation 2:7).

Dirt:

Lord providing a place of growth (see Isaiah 61:11);

large quantity (see Zechariah 9:3);

mankind (see Genesis 2:7; 3:19);

soiled/unclean (see 2 Samuel 16:13; 1 Peter 3:21);

sinful (see Revelation 3:4);

see General/Dust.

Disaster: intense trouble (see Genesis 19:19; Exodus 32:12; Judges 20:34; Psalm 57:1; Zechariah 8:1).

Discipline:

loving, nurturing action that will train, correct and instruct without provoking anger in order to teach

obedience, endurance and righteousness (see Hebrews 12:5–11; Proverbs 19:18; 23:13–14; Acts 17:24–31; Revelation 3:19);
brings wisdom (see Proverbs 29:15);
removes foolishness (see Proverbs 22:15).

Discouragement: enemy prophesying to intimidate and cause sin (see Nehemiah 6:10–13).

Disease: repercussion of sin (see Genesis 12:17).

Dish:
vessel of God (see Luke 38:40–41);
vessel to hold offerings (see Exodus 25:29; 37:16; Numbers 4:7);
people (see Matthew 23:25; Luke 11:39);
container of doctrine/tradition (see Numbers 4:7; 1 Kings 7:50);
giving to others (see Exodus 25:29; 37:16);
used in service (see Jeremiah 52:18).

Dish, broken: not wanted/disliked (see Psalm 31:12); an object no one wants (see Jeremiah 22:28).

Dish, dirty inside: greed/self-indulgence (see Matthew 23:26).

Divided: will fall (see Matthew 12:25–26); fighting within (see Matthew 12:25).

Divination: those who gain power from objects and not from the Lord (see 2 Chronicles 33:61; Ezekiel 13:22–23); power not of God (see Deuteronomy 18:10; Ezekiel 13:22–23).

Divine assembly: see General/Assembly.

Division:
different factions (see Numbers 10:14);
groups organized according to duties (see 2 Chronicles 26:11; 31:2);
to sort out (see 2 Timothy 2:15).

Divorce:
to put away (see Jeremiah 3:8);
can be cleansed by moving back to God (see Leviticus 22:13);
adultery (see Matthew 5:32; 19:9).

Divorce certificate: sent away (see Isaiah 50:1).

DNA: Holy Spirit (see Colossians 3:9–11).

Doll:
childhood issues (see 1 Corinthians 13:11);
childhood innocence (see 1 Corinthians 13:11);
childish ways (see 1 Corinthians 13:11);
one who is false/not authentic (a doll is a replica of the person).

Door:
choice (see Genesis 4:7; Matthew 7:13; Revelation 3:8; 3:20; 4:1);
decision (see Proverbs 8:3; Acts 14:27; Revelation 3:20);
opening/entry (see Genesis 4:7; 2 Kings 4:5; Job 31:9; 31:32; Luke 11:7; 13:24);
opportunity (see Genesis 4:7; 2 Kings 6:32; Matthew 7:7; 25:10–11; 1 Corinthians 16:9; 2 Corinthians 2:12; Colossians 4:3; Revelation 3:8);
revelation to be disclosed (see Revelation 4:1);
question/invitation (see 1 Kings 14:6; Matthew 7:7; Luke 11:10; 13:25; Revelation 3:20);
correct way to enter (see John 10:1);
Jesus (see John 10:1, 7–9);
lips (see Psalm 141:3);
near (see Matthew 24:33; Mark 13:29).

Door, back: what is happening in the background or behind the scenes (char).

Door, new: new area in life that God is opening up (see Genesis 4:7; 2 Kings 4:5, Luke 11:7; Revelation 3:8).

Door, open: opportunity to go forward (see Revelation 3:8; 4:1); opportunity to do wrong (see Job 31:9).

Door, screen: dealing with a screening issue in order to go forth (func); filtering out bad things [bugs] (func).

Doorpost: pertaining to what is hidden inside (see Isaiah 57:8).

Dot: [circle filled in], a covenant being filled (char).

Double: pay back double for injuries received (see 1 Samuel 1:5; Isaiah 40:2; 61:7; Jeremiah 16:18; 17:18; Revelation 18:6).

Dough: members of the Church (see 1 Corinthians 5:6; Galatians 5:9).

Down: bringing or coming down from lofty actions and views (see Jeremiah 49:16).

Dragnet: cast out to gather (see Matthew 13:47).

Dragon:

the beast (see Daniel; Revelation 13);

antichrist (see Revelation 13);

Satan (see Revelation 12:3–17; 13:1–11; 16:13; 20:2).

Drain: going "down the drain"; losing something/being without (see 2 Kings 19:26).

Dream:

metaphor of life (see Genesis 37:5–10; 40:5–16; 41:1–11; Judges 7:13–15; Daniel 2:1–36; 2:45; 4:1–28; Joel 2:28; Matthew 1:20–24; Acts 2:17);

seems unreal/too good to be true (see Psalm 126:1; Isaiah 29:6–8);

answers from God (see 1 Samuel 28:15; Matthew 1:20–23; 2:12);

visit from God (see Psalm 17:3);

revelation/word from God (see Genesis 20:3–6; 28:10–12; 31:10–11; 31:24; 41:1–26; Judges 7:13–15; 1 Kings 3:5–15; Job 33:15–18; Daniel 2:1–36; 2:45; 4:1–28; 7:1–16; Matthew 1:20);

warning (see Job 33:15–18; Matthew 2:12–13; 2:22–23; 27:19);

cares of the soul (see Ecclesiastes 5:2–4);

delusions of the heart (see Jeremiah 23:24–26);

direction/divine instruction (see Matthew 2:12–13, 19).

Dream, repeated: matter firmly decided by God, and He will do it soon (see Genesis 41:32).

Dressed: prepared, equipped and ready for good (see Esther 5:1); honed and chiseled down appropriately (see 1 Kings 6:7); ready for evil (see Proverbs 7:10).

Dried: easily broken off and destroyed (see Isaiah 27:11).

Drink:

real/eternal life (see Revelation 21:6);

become filled with (see Hebrews 6:7);

offering (see Genesis 35:14; Exodus 29:40–41; Leviticus 23:13; 2 Timothy 4:6);

commune with/communicate (see Exodus 32:6; Judges 19:6; 1 Kings 13:8, 16; John 4:10–13; 6:53; 7:37);

join in/partake in (see 2 Samuel 23:17; 2 Kings 18:27; Job 21:20; Proverbs 7:18; Song of Solomon 5:1; Ezekiel 23:32; Matthew 20:22–23; 26:42; Mark 10:38–39; John 7:37; 1 Corinthians 10:31).

Drink, alcohol:

becoming filled with the Holy Spirit [alcohol] (see 1 Samuel 1:15; Isaiah 28:7; 29:9–14);

filled with spirits [alcohol] (see 1 Samuel 1:15; Isaiah 28:7; 29:9–14);

see General/Drunk.

Drink, all: partake totally (see Psalm 75:8).

Drink, offering: given over and used up for things of the Lord (see Genesis 35:14; Exodus 29:40–41; Leviticus 23:13; 2 Timothy 4:6).

Drink, wine: communion with God (see 1 Samuel 1:15; Isaiah 28:7; 29:9–14); will cloud judgment (see Genesis 19:32–35).

Drip: abundance of (see Psalm 65:11–12); quarrelsome (see Proverbs 27:15).

Drive:

in control of (char; as in driving a vehicle [in control of the home, life, work or ministry]; see Jeremiah 46:9);

firmly established by God ("I will drive him like a peg in a firm place," see Isaiah 22:23);

removing and pushing away (see Exodus 11:1; 23:31; Deuteronomy 4:38; Judges 2:23; Psalm 36:11; Jeremiah 46:9; Joel 2:20).

Drop, in a bucket: of little importance (see Isaiah 40:15).

Dross: that which is discarded (see Psalm 119:119).

Drunk:

full of the Holy Spirit (see Acts 2:14–21; Ephesians 5:18);

high (see General/High);

intoxicated by/under the influence of (see Genesis 9:21; 2 Samuel 13:28; Esther 1:10; Acts 2:13–21; Ephesians 5:18);

caught up in our feelings/not having our wits about us (see 2 Samuel 13:28; 1 Thessalonians 5:7; Revelation 17:2, 6);

overwhelmed by (see Deuteronomy 32:42);

wicked (see 1 Samuel 1:15–16).

Dry:

easy passage (see 2 Kings 2:8; Nehemiah 9:11);

without the Lord (see Job 13:25; Psalm 63:1; Ezekiel 20:47);

empty (see 1 Kings 17:14–16; Job 14:11; Ezekiel 23:34; Hosea 9:14);

without life (see Isaiah 5:24; 19:5; Jeremiah 50:12; Ezekiel 17:24; 37:2–4);

unproductive/sterile (see Isaiah 56:3);

hard times (see Luke 23:31).

Dull: without clarity (see Matthew 13:15).

Dung: will disappear (see 1 Kings 14:10; Job 20:7).

Dust:

numerous (see Genesis 13:16; 28:14; Numbers 23:10; 2 Chronicles 1:9);

man (see Genesis 2:7; 3:19; Psalm 90:3; 103:14; Ecclesiastes 3:20);

inactivity/neglect (see Psalm 90:3–6);

fleeting and blows away (see Isaiah 5:24);

beaten down until pulverized (see 2 Samuel 22:43; 1 Kings 16:2; 2 Kings 13:7; Matthew 21:44);

atrophy/defile (see Psalm 44:25; 89:39);

those who turn away from the water [the Lord] (see Jeremiah 17:13; Micah 7:17);

place without sustenance (see Deuteronomy 28:24; 1 Samuel 2:8; Job 10:9);

of no worth (see Genesis 18:27; 2 Kings 13:7; Isaiah 29:4);

dirty, messy things/trials of the world (see Job 30:19; Psalm 78:27; 113:7; Isaiah 47:1; 52:2; Matthew 10:14);

death (see Job 2:12, 10:9, Psalm 22:15).

Dust, on head: humbled (see 2 Samuel 1:2; Nehemiah 9:1).

Dust, on scale: of no importance (see Isaiah 40:15).

E

Earrings: hearing (rel); adorned (see Exodus 32:2; Ezekiel 16:11–12).

Earth:

foundation (see 1 Samuel 2:8; Zechariah 12:1);

world's nature (see Colossians 3:2);

long (see Job 11:9).

Earth, cracks in:

foundational issues cracked (char);

wrong foundations (char);

life based on incorrect things (char).

Earthquake:

power of God (see Judges 5:4–5; Psalm 60:2; Matthew 27:51);

something to be shaken up (see Psalm 68:8);

storm (see 1 Kings 19:11);

voice of the Lord (see Psalm 29:5–9; Hebrews 12:26);

cataclysmic event not from God (see 1 Kings 19:11);

judgment of God (see 2 Samuel 22:8; 1 Kings 19:11; Psalm 18:7; 60:2; Ezekiel 38:19; Habakkuk 3:10; Revelation 6:12–16).

East wind:

hot, dry wind blowing off of the desert (func);

can wither crop (see Genesis 41:6, 27; Ezekiel 19:12; Hosea 13:15; Jonah 4:8);

sweeps away (see Job 27:21; Jeremiah 18:17).

Eat:

communing with/communicate with (see Genesis 43:16; Job 1:4; Isaiah 25:6; Ezekiel 2:8; Matthew 9:10–11; 26:20–29; John 6:35; 13:26; Revelation 3:20);

learn or "feed on" (see Genesis 2:16–17; Jeremiah 3:15; Ezekiel 2:8–3:3; Proverbs 23:6; Hebrews 6:4–5);

being fed by one another/learning something from someone (see Leviticus 10:14–19);

partake in the Word/learn truth (see Jeremiah 15:16; Ezekiel 2:8; Matthew 15:27; John 4:34);

destroy, consume (see 2 Samuel 20:19–20; 2 Kings 1:10; Isaiah 51:8; Revelation 17:16);

partake in (see Genesis 2:16–17; Exodus 32:6; Proverbs 31:27; John 4:34; Revelation 2:7);

overcome (see Psalm 124:3; Isaiah 25:8).

Education: learning to do good/learning Word of God (see Isaiah 1:17).

Egg:

new beginning (func);

reproduction (func);

wealth/bounty/nest egg (see Deuteronomy 22:6; Isaiah 10:14; Jeremiah 17:11);

non-productive (idiom: "to lay an egg").

Egg, did not lay: wealth by unjust means (see Jeremiah 17:11).

Egg, goose: of no importance (char); zero (Deuteronomy 22:6; Isaiah 10:14; Jeremiah 17:11).

Elegant: place of influence, favor and inheritance (char); see General/Clothing, ball gown.

Elegant, but dark and cold feeling: looks good, but not good.

Electricity:

power/energy (see Revelation 4:5, lightning);

Holy Spirit (see Revelation 4:5, lightning);

sorcery (rel).

Elevator:

going up faster (func);

choices made (func);

way of being lifted out of a situation (func).

Elevator, to ground floor: get grounded (func); back to foundation (func).

Embers: painful/burn (see Psalm 26:21; 102:3); last of the destruction (see Psalm 102:3).

Empty: without substance (see 1 Samuel 6:3; Job 35:13; Isaiah 16:6; 1 Timothy 6:20; 2 Timothy 2:16).

Encrusted: covered by sin (see Ezekiel 24:6).

Engaged: in agreement with/in intimate relationship with (see Hosea 2:14–20; Colossians 1:21; 1 Corinthians 7:36); doing (as in engaged in an activity) (see Colossians 1:21).

Enlarge: will spread out and grow (see Exodus 34:24; 1 Chronicles 4:10; Isaiah 54:2–3; 2 Corinthians 9:10).

Enroll: sign up (see 2 Samuel 24:4); make accountable (see 2 Samuel 24:2).

Entangled: caught up in (see Psalm 35:8; 2 Timothy 2:4; Hebrews 12:1); in bondage to (see Hebrews 12:1–3).

Ephod: priest (see Exodus 28:4; 1 Samuel 22:18).

Equipment: good things to use in working for the Lord (see Numbers 3:36; Hebrews 13:21); useful help (see Deuteronomy 23:13; 1 Samuel 8:12).

Erase: remove from (see Revelation 3:5); death (see 1 Samuel 24:21).

Eve: beginning/source (see Genesis 3:20).

Evening: rest from labor (see Psalm 104:23); beginning of "dark" trial times (see Psalm 59:14; Zephaniah 3:3); see General/Dark.

Evil: plans of Satan (char); an evil spirit can be sent with the permission of God (see Judges 9:23; 1 Samuel 16:14–16).

Exam: see General/Test.

Excrement:

old garbage in life one needs to deal with (see Genesis 2:16–17; Matthew 15:17);

unclean things (see Deuteronomy 23:12–14; 2 Kings 18:27);

by-product/result (see 2 Kings 18:27; Isaiah 36:12).

Exit: signs that show the way out of darkness (func).

Explosion: made a big impact (char).

Extortion: foolish (see Psalm 62:10; Ecclesiastes 7:7); unjust gain (see Leviticus 6:4; Isaiah 33:15; Ezekiel 22:12).

Extreme: avoid; seeking balance—not grasping one thing only to drop the other (see Ecclesiastes 7:18).

Eye shadow: vanity (see Jeremiah 4:30).

F

Faint:

unconscious—not of good conscience toward God (see 1 Peter 3:21);

not forceful (see Job 26:14; Lamentations 5:16);

ailing/weak (see Job 26:14; Psalm 6:2; 77:3; Isaiah 51:20; 57:10; Jeremiah 4:31; 45:3; Song of Solomon 2:5; Lamentations 2:11–12);

afraid (see Deuteronomy 20:8; Job 23:16; Luke 21:26);

depression/needs encouragement (see Psalm 61:2; 1 Thessalonians 5:14).

Faith:

a measure or measures of understanding and belief that is powerful (see Matthew 8:10; 9:2, 22, 28–30; 15:28; 17:20; 21:21–22; Mark 5:1–19; 9:23; Luke 5:20; 7:12–14; 8:48; 13:11–13; John 5:8–9);

sure of what we hope for, even though we do not see it (see Hebrews 11:1);

necessary to please God (see Hebrews 11:6);

understand the system/rely on proper authority (see Matthew 8:8–10);

one belief system that is true (see Ephesians 4:6);

will reflect good work if authentic (see Matthew 7:21–23);

will heal (see Matthew 9:22, 27–30);

hidden from intelligent and revealed to those without learning [infants] (see Matthew 11:25; Galatians 3:25).

Faith, without: must rid or reduce lack of faith before miracles can occur (see Matthew 9:18–25 [Jesus requested the "laughing" (without faith) crowd be put out before He performed His miracle]); will sap true measures of faith; lack of faith will subtract from the power that comes from true measures of faith, resulting in a reduction of power (see Matthew 9:18–25; 13:58 [Jesus did not do many miracles because of the lack of faith found in His hometown]).

Fall: brought down (see Proverbs 16:18; Jeremiah 8:12).

Fall, season: time of falling away (play on words).

Fall foliage: end signs, end result (char).

Falling: something out of control (char); often a "worry dream" from your soul (char).

Falling and waking up: releasing anxieties.

Falling down: heading in the wrong direction (see 2 Chronicles 28:23; Jeremiah 8:4).

Fallow ground: promises given up on or walked away from (see Hosea 10:12).

False: not for real (char); not of God (see Exodus 23:1; Psalm 4:2; Proverbs 11:1; Philippians 3:2–3).

Famine: warning/judgment of God (see Jeremiah 14:12; 15:2; 29:17; 34:17; Ezekiel 14:13, 21); death (see Lamentations 4:9; Job 5:20; Psalm 33:19; Revelation 18:8).

Fangs: ability to kill others (see Deuteronomy 32:24; Job 20:16; Psalm 58:6; Joel 1:6).

Fangs, broken: unable to be effective in wickedness (see Job 29:17; Psalm 58:6).

Fast:

humble oneself in preparation to ask the Lord for something (see 2 Samuel 12:23; Ezra 8:21–23; Esther 4:16; Matthew 9:15);

to make God hear your voice (see Isaiah 58:4);

humbled (see 2 Chronicles 20:3; Psalm 35:13; 69:10);

to loose bonds of control and wickedness (see Isaiah 58:6).

Fat: satisfied/plenty (see Psalm 63:5; 65:11; 73:4); caught up in fleshly things and not following God (see Leviticus 8:16; Judges 3:17; 1 Samuel 2:5; Job 15:22–27; Isaiah 10:27).

Fat, burned: sacrificing to the Lord (see Exodus 29:13; 1 Samuel 2:15–16).

Favorite: it is not of the Lord to show partiality (see Colossians 3:25).

Fax: a facsimile representation [not the original] (func); verification of documentation (char).

Fear: see Themes/Actions/Fear.

Feast:
celebration (see Genesis 21:8; 40:20; Nehemiah 8:10; Luke 14:8; 15:23);

communion with (see Genesis 26:30; Isaiah 25:6);

abundance (see Psalm 36:8; Isaiah 25:6);

partake in the Word/learn truth (see Matthew 15:27; Luke 14:15; 2 Peter 2:13);

laughter (see Ecclesiastes 10:19).

Feather: protection/cover (see Job 39:13; Psalm 91:4); a "whoo-hoo, look what I did!" feeling (as in the expression "a feather in your hat").

Feed: see General/Feast.

Feigned: heart not in it (see Psalm 66:3).

Felony: treason (char); treachery (char).

Fence:
barrier/boundary (see Psalm 62:3; Acts 17:26); at the beginning of/starting to unfold (see Acts 17:26);

noncommittal (to be "on the fence");

doctrines/inhibitions [to enclose or contain something].

Fence, tottering: ready to fall from high position (see Psalm 62:3).

Fertile: good for growth or for being productive (see Numbers 13:20; 2 Chronicles 26:10; Jeremiah 2:7; Micah 7:14).

Fettered: unable to move (see 2 Samuel 3:34; Psalm 149:8).

Feverish: hunger for (see Lamentations 5:10); sick (see Deuteronomy 28:22; Lamentations 5:10; Job 30:30; Matthew 8:14).

Field:
living area/your world (see Deuteronomy 20:19; 2 Kings 19:26; Psalm 23:2; Matthew 13:24; Luke 10:2);

people/others (see Matthew 9:38; 1 Corinthians 3:9);

opposite of wilderness (see Genesis 2:5; 3:18);

marked with a boundary (see Leviticus 23:22);

wealth (see Leviticus 27:17–18; Numbers 16:14);

life (see Genesis 27:27; Deuteronomy 21:1; Proverbs 23:10; Jeremiah 6:25; Matthew 13:24, 44);

livelihood (see Genesis 4:8; 30:16; 31:4; 34:5; 37:7).

Fig:
prosperity (see Zechariah 3:10);

God's people (see Jeremiah 24:1–10);

to receive blessings (see Jeremiah 24:3);

results (see Judges 9:11).

Fig, bad: people who have rejected God; cursed/to be banished (see Jeremiah 24:2–8; 29:17).

Fight: dealing with issues of life (see 1 Timothy 1:18; 6:12; 2 Timothy 4:7).

Filter: paradigms that we see through (func).

Fine linen: righteous acts (see Proverbs 31:22; Ezekiel 16: 8–10; Revelation 19–21).

Fire:
the Word of God in our mouth (see 2 Samuel 22:9; Jeremiah 23:29);

God/of God (see Deuteronomy 4:24; Isaiah 66:15; Hebrews 12:29; Revelation 4:2–6; 20:9);

Holy Spirit (see Matthew 3:11; Acts 2:3–4);

test from God (see 1 Kings 18:38; 19:12; Psalm 104:4; Malachi 3:2; 1 Peter 1:7; 4:12);

angels (see Hebrews 1:7);

testing quality of work (see 1 Corinthians 3:13);

refining/cleansing/purging (see Isaiah 4:4–5; Ezekiel 24:11; Zechariah 13:9; 1 Peter 1:7; Revelation 3:18);

warmth (see Jeremiah 36:22; Mark 14:54; John 18:18);

offering to the Lord (see Exodus 29:18, 25; Leviticus 8:21);

movement of God (see 2 Kings 1:10; 2 Chronicles 7:1; Psalm 66:12; 104:4; Isaiah 64:2; 66:15; 1 Thessalonians 5:19);

God's judgment/Holy Spirit in judgment/wrath (see Leviticus 9:23–24; Numbers 11:1; Psalm 97:3; Isaiah 4:4–5; 29:6; 30:30; 66:15–16; Jeremiah 4:4; Ezekiel 30:8; 30:16; Amos 1:7; Micah 1:7; Matthew 13:40–42; 22:1–7; Luke 9:54; 17:29; Hebrews 10:27; 12:18; Revelation 15:2; 18:8);

a division/separation due to Jesus (see Zechariah 2:5; Luke 12:49);

to light the way in darkness (see Psalm 78:14; 105:39);

tongue/words (see Proverbs 16:27; Jeremiah 5:14; James 3:6);

inflaming the minds of the people (see Proverbs 29:8);

never satisfied with enough (see Proverbs 30:16);

trials (see Isaiah 43:2; Zechariah 3:2; Mark 9:49–50; Ephesians 6:16);

will burn if you get too close (see Proverbs 16:27);

wickedness/destruction that is not of God (see 2 Samuel 14:30; 1 Kings 19:12; Job 1:16; Psalm 83:14; Isaiah 9:18; 66:24; Jeremiah 4:4; 32:35; 34:2; Ephesians 6:16; Revelation 9:17).

Firepot: consumes (see Genesis 15:17; Zechariah 12:6).

Firewood:

those people [ready to be set ablaze by the Lord]/people whom God's Word consumes (see Isaiah 7:4; 9:19; 30:33; John 15:6);

judgment to people who bear no good fruit (see Jeremiah 5:14; Ezekiel 21:32; Matthew 3:10; 7:16–19);

gossip (see Proverbs 26:20–21).

First:

belongs to the Lord (see Leviticus 27:26; Numbers 18:15);

Lord/Jesus (see Isaiah 44:6; 48:12; Colossians 1:17–18; Revelation 1:17);

will be last (see Matthew 20:16; 20:27–28);

self-appointed as the most important [narcissistic] (char).

Firstborn:

Jesus (see Colossians 1:15–20);

will follow in succession/will succeed (see 2 Kings 3:27);

most exalted (see Psalm 89:27);

first fruits (see Psalm 105:36; Colossians 1:15);

those who belong to God (see Hebrews 12:22–23).

Fishing:

evangelizing others (see Mark 1:17);

pull others out of sea of humanity (see Luke 5:5–10);

probing for information (play on words).

Fish tank: place where God's people are.

Fit/Fitting:

applies to you (see Judges 5:25 NIV; Acts 22:22 NIV; Ephesians 5:4);

is proper (see Ezra 4:14; Proverbs 19:10; 26:1);

is worthy of (see Matthew 3:11; Mark 1:7; Luke 3:16; 1 Corinthians 15:9);

the right way of the Lord (see Colossians 3:18).

Flank: shove (see Ezekiel 34:21).

Flashing: in use (see Psalm 76:3).

Flattery:

test (see Proverbs 27:21);

manipulation tactic/to gain advantage (see Proverbs 2:16; Jude 16, 19);

a net that will trap (see Proverbs 29:5).

Fleece: warmth (see Job 31:20); proof (see Judges 6:36–40).

Flesh:

tenderhearted and open (see Ezekiel 11:19; 36:26);

worldly; man (see Deuteronomy 32:42; Philippians 1:22–24; 3:3–4);

lusts (see Romans 13:14).

Flesh, tear: life's troubles that bring tremendous pain (see Judges 8:7; Micah 3:2).

Flint: hard (see Zechariah 7:12).

Flint, point: to inscribe (see Jeremiah 17:1).

Floating: see General/Flying.

Flock:

people (see Ezekiel 34:17; Micah 2:12); part of the "fold" (see Habakkuk 3:17); possessions (see Proverbs 27:23).

Flood:

Holy Spirit pouring through (see 2 Kings 3:16–20);

judgment of God (see 2 Samuel 5:20; Ezekiel 13:11; Psalm 104:6–9; Hosea 5:10; Nahum 1:8; Habakkuk 3:10);

overwhelmed (see Genesis 6:17; Job 20:28);

trials (see Matthew 7:24–27).

Floodgate: quarrel (see Proverbs 17:14).

Floor: foundation (see 1 Kings 6:15).

Floorboards of someone's house, beneath: below the surface of who the person is (char).

Flour:

offering (see Leviticus 2:1);

gift from God [play on word *flower* (see General/Flower); white: holy, Jesus, with Christ (see Themes/ Colors/White)];

messy, but made to look good [white: holy, purity, with Christ (see Themes/Colors/White)] (rel);

see General/Flower;

see General/Grain.

Flow: abundance (see Deuteronomy 31:20); Spirit of God moving (see John 7:37–39).

Flower:

fragrance (func);

blessings/gifts (see Psalm 103:15);

glory (see 1 Kings 6:32; Isaiah 40:6; Matthew 6:29; 1 Peter 1:24);

fades away (see Isaiah 28:1–4, 40:8);

observe the color (see Themes/Colors).

Flower, wild:

fleeting/will pass away (see Matthew 6:28–30; James 1:10);

offer themselves willingly and humbly, even though it seems no one appreciates them (char);

a new beginning with a "wild side" (see Song of Solomon 2:12);

untamed beauty (char);

uncultivated/doing our "own" thing (char).

Flute: worship of God (see Matthew 11:17); prophesying (see 1 Samuel 10:5).

Flying: high spiritual activity/advancing in things of the Spirit (see Isaiah 40:31; 60:8; Zechariah 5:1–2).

Flying, crash: a "crash" of some sort is coming (char).

Foam: volume without real substance (see Job 24:18); shame (see Jude 13).

Foam, sea: casting up own shame (see Jude 13).

Foil: to interfere with (see Psalm 33:10).

Folly: guilt, mistakes (see Psalm 69:5).

Food:

teachings/things learned [being ingested] (see Nehemiah 9:15; Proverbs 18:20);

work of God (see John 4:32–34);

consecrated (see 1 Samuel 21:4–6);

gossip (see Proverbs 18:8; 26:22).

Food, barley: second choice [compared to wheat] (char); inferior [compared to wheat] (see Judges 7:13–15).

Food, bitter: punishment (see Jeremiah 9:15).

Food, bread:

Jesus/teachings of Jesus (see Proverbs 18:20; Luke 14:15; John 6:32–35);

a present or gift from God (see Exodus 16:15; Nehemiah 9:15; Mark 6:30–44);

gift of first fruits to God (see 2 Kings 4:42–44);

consecrated (see Exodus 25:30; 29:2; Leviticus 2:4–16; 1 Samuel 21:4–6);

food (see Genesis 3:19; Numbers 21:5; Isaiah 3:1; 51:14; 55:10; Luke 15:17).

Food, candy: sweet words of God [as in: sweet food] (see Numbers 13:27; 14:8); gossip (see Proverbs 18:8).

Food, canned:

repetitious teachings that are not applicable to the individual; teachings and things being learned that are "canned" [produced by society and not by God's Word].

Food, ceremonial: of little value (see Hebrews 13:9); strange teachings (food: teachings).

Food, cheese: curdled (see Job 10:10).

Food, chocolate: see General/Candy.

Food, choice: indulgence (see Daniel 1:16).

Food, corn: God's seed (play on words); harvest (char).

Food, egg white: without flavor/no fun (see Job 6:6).

Food, feast: communion with God's people (see Matthew 8:11; Jude 12).

Food, first fruits or grain: offering to Lord (see Leviticus 23:40; Nehemiah 10:35).

Food, fruit: harvest/results (see Matthew 7:17–20; 12:33; Ephesians 5:9); actions (see Matthew 3:8; 7:20; Luke 3:8); see General/Fruit.

Food, grain: people (see Mark 4:7, 28–29); year of production (see Genesis 37:7; 41:5–7, 22–27).

Food, manna: spiritual nourishment (see Revelation 2:17).

Food, meat: solid Word of God, including discernment (see Hebrews 5:12–14).

Food, raisin: strengthen (see Song of Solomon 2:5).

Food, religious feast: despised by God (see Amos 5:21).

Food, rich: of the Lord (see Isaiah 55:2).

Food, seafood: teachings of man (see General/Seafood).

Food, solid: mature [wise] teachings good [Christ] versus evil [plans of the enemy] (see Hebrews 5:14).

Food, soup: receiving thin teachings (char).

Food, summer fruit: good results (see General/Fruit); almost at the point of being rotten (char); time for pruning (char).

Food, with gravelly rocks in it: things hard to understand/things hard to tolerate (see Proverbs 20:17).

Food, without salt: without flavor/no fun (see Job 6:6).

Fool: guilt, mistakes (see Psalm 69:5).

Football: dealing with competitive actions of life (see General/Sports game); messing with peace (see General/Shoes—feet carry the gospel of peace; see Ephesians 6:15).

Foothold: something to support you (see Psalm 69:2); way of entering (see Ephesians 4:27 NIV); door for the devil (see Ephesians 4:27 NIV).

Footstep/footprints: your actions and the direction, or way, you are going (see Psalm 77:19; 119:133).

Footstool: God's earth (see Isaiah 66:1); subservient to (see Psalm 110:1; Hebrews 1:13; 10:13; James 2:3).

Foreclosure: seizure of property [reminder that you have better and lasting possessions] (see Hebrews 10:34).

Foreign: not of the "world"/of God (see Hebrews 11:14–16); not of God (see Joshua 24:23; Psalm 114:1; Zephaniah 1:8; Ephesians 2:12–13).

Forest: God's people (see 1 Chronicles 16:33; Psalm 29:9; 96:12; Song of Solomon 2:3; Isaiah 7:2).

Fork: junction (see Ezekiel 21:21); to winnow/clean out/separate (see Matthew 3:12).

Fork, winnowing: tool God uses to separate His people (see Luke 3:17).

Former things: in the past (see Isaiah 46:4).

Fornication: idols (see Revelation 2:14, 20–21).

Forward: for God (see Jeremiah 7:24).

Foundation:
Jesus (see Isaiah 28:16; 1 Corinthians 3:11; Ephesians 2:20);
God (see 2 Timothy 2:19);
base/basis of belief (see Matthew 7:24–25; Hebrews 6:1–2);
support system/support (see 1 Samuel 2:8; Psalm 24:2; 104:5);
solid footing (see Psalm 24:2);
basement/undercover (char).

Foundation cracked: the foundation things are based on is cracked/the base is not right (see 1 Samuel 2:8; Psalm 24:2).

Fountain:

from which to draw life's needs (see Psalm 36:9; Proverbs 16:22);

Christ (see Zechariah 13:1);

cleanse from sin (see Zechariah 13:1);

fear of the Lord (see Proverbs 14:27);

wisdom (see Proverbs 18:4);

wise teachings (see Proverbs 13:14);

understanding (see Proverbs 16:22);

casts out life/casts out wickedness (see Jeremiah 6:7);

life in the Spirit (see Psalm 36:9).

Fourth grade: level of God's creative works (func); see Themes/Numbers/4.

Fragrance:

Christians (we are the fragrance of Christ; see 2 Corinthians 2:15);

fragrance of the Lord/Holy Spirit (see Ezekiel 8:11; John 12:3);

see General/Smell.

Frame:

how we/things are formed (see Psalm 103:14);

support system (see Exodus 26:15–29);

construct by fitting together (see Hebrews 11:3);

general strength (see Isaiah 58:11);

being framed or set up/appearance of (rel).

Frankincense: burned in the temple [implying a priest] (see Matthew 2:11).

Freckles: see General/Blemishes.

Free: not subject to yoke of slavery/no longer oppressed (see Galatians 5:1); uncomplicated (see Matthew 11:28–30).

Fresh: strong (see Judges 15:13–15).

Fringe: outskirts of [as in "on the fringes of"] (see Matthew 14:36—healed, but by touching on the fringe).

Frost: scattered around (see Psalm 147:16).

Fruit:

results/proof (see Psalm 92:14; 104:13; Proverbs 1:31; Isaiah 5:2; 11:1; 14:29; 27:6–9; Jeremiah 6:19; 31:5; Matthew 3:8; 7:16–20; John 15:4; Galatians 5:22–23; Philippians 1:22; Colossians 1:6–10; Hebrews 13:15);

bringing others closer to Jesus (see Matthew 21:43; John 15:2);

eternal salvation (see Proverbs 11:30);

results in people's lives (see Matthew 3:8; 7:16–20; Luke 3:8–9; 6:43–45; Philippians 1:11);

blessing (see Zechariah 8:23);

able to be productive (see Exodus 1:7; Matthew 21:43; Ephesians 5:11; Colossians 1:6–10);

love, joy, peace, patience, kindness, goodness, faithfulness, gentleness, self-control (see Galatians 5:22–23).

Fruit, early ripened: will be consumed quickly (see Isaiah 28:4); the best result/best fruit (see Micah 7:1).

Fruit, first:

Jesus (see 1 Corinthians 15:20–23);

Christians (see James 1:18);

first result of your labor (see Deuteronomy 18:4; Proverbs 3:9–10; Ezekiel 44:30);

set aside for God (see Jeremiah 2:3);

firstborn (see Psalm 105:36);

disciplined to seek God first (see 1 Corinthians 16:15).

Fruit, none: not productive (see 2 Kings 2:19; Matthew 21:18–21; Titus 3:14); pointless (see 1 Timothy 1:6).

Fruit, ripe: time is ripe (see Job 15:33; Amos 8:2–3).

Fruit, twelve types of fruit: government (see Genesis 17:20; Revelation 22:2).

Fruit, unripe: has not flourished/not yet time (see Job 15:33).

Fruit, wither/bad:

The harvest is taken away/is not coming (see Isaiah 16:8);

not blessed (see Isaiah 16:8; Matthew 21:18–20);

cannot be used (see Jeremiah 29:17).

Fundraiser: asking for God's favor (func).

Furnace: cleansing; purging/refiner's fire/place of intense trial (see 1 Kings 8:51; Jeremiah 11:4); day of the Lord (see Genesis 15:17; Malachi 4:1).

Furnace, iron: strong, fiery ordeal (see Jeremiah 11:4).

Furniture: worldly acquisitions/stuff (see Exodus 25:9; 31:7; 1 Kings 7:48; 1 Chronicles 9:29; Proverbs 19:14).

G

Gables: gable points are triangular [3: Trinity—may represent place of the Trinity or area of God] (see Revelation 1:4–6); if the dream is dark or gloomy, this may be speaking of an "imitation" of the Trinity or a dark spiritual presence (see Themes/People and Beings/Spirit, bad).

Gall: bitter (see Psalm 69:21; Proverbs 5:4).

Gambling: may be punished (see Proverbs 28:20–22).

Gangrene: bad teaching (see 2 Timothy 2:17); gossip/slander/words that spread death (see 2 Timothy 2:17).

Gap: separation (see Judges 21:15).

Garland: victorious (see Proverbs 1:9).

Garment:
wrapped up in (see Psalm 109:18–19, 29; Zechariah 3:1–7);
religious system (see Matthew 9:16);
see General/Clothing.

Gash: sin that is superficial [not vitally serious] (char); injury that is painful, but not serious (char).

Gate:
Jesus (see John 10:1–9; 14:6);
protection (see 2 Chronicles 14:7);
choice/direction (see Matthew 7:13);
place of decision (see Proverbs 8:3);
fortified (see Deuteronomy 3:5);
way to get inside (see Matthew 7:13).

Gate, does not use: thief/robber (see John 10:1).

Gate, high:
Deep, wide protection (see Jeremiah 51:58);
easy to get in (see Proverbs 17:19);
invites attack (see Proverbs 17:19).

Gate, none: peaceful; unsuspecting (see Ezekiel 38:11).

Gemini: two natures of Jesus [as in God and man] (see Themes/People and Beings/Jesus); astrology, not of God (see Deuteronomy 4:19).

Gestation: time when expectation is transformed to presence (char).

Ghost: see Themes/People and Beings/Ghost.

Gift:
life everlasting (see Revelation 22:17);
things from God (see 1 Corinthians 12:4–13; Romans 11:29; Hebrews 2:4; James 1:17);
unearned blessing (see Ephesians 2:8);
talent (see 1 Corinthians 12:4–13; 1 Peter 4:10);
honor bestowed (see Psalm 68:29);
subdues anger (see Proverbs 21:14).

Gird: to wrap around yourself [by covering or equipping]; to carry around (see 1 Kings 20:11; Psalm 65:12).

Glass:
ability to see/understand/see through (see Revelation 4:6);
revelation/revealed (see Revelation 21:21);
the place "beyond" (char);
man-made (char).

Glass, broken: access to a place "beyond"; not able to see/understand (char).

Glass, smoky: your ability to see is not good (see Matthew 7:5); smoke-screen (char); revelation not good or clear (see Matthew 6:23; Luke 11:34).

Glasses: ability to see or understand (see Deuteronomy 11:7; Matthew 13:13; Ephesians 1:18); prophecy (func); dreams (func).

Glasses, black, horned-rim: an accent on the ability to "see"; to see things through a dark perspective.

Glasses, colored: being overly optimistic (as in "rose-colored glasses"); looking through eyes of bitterness (see Matthew 6:23; Luke 11:34).

Glaze, over earthenware: has attractive, exciting words, but an evil heart (see Proverbs 26:23).

Glory: of the Lord (see Psalm 96:7; Ephesians 1:17).

Glow: of the Lord (see Genesis 1:4; Isaiah 5:20); attractive (char).

Goal: follow Christ (see Philippians 3:14).

Goblets:

containers of water/wine [people] (see Isaiah 22:24);

where one receives refreshment (see Proverbs 5:15);

communion/relationship (see Jeremiah 35:5; Luke 22:20);

partake in (see Mark 10:38–39);

see General/Cup.

God:

only one (see 2 Kings 5:15);

highest authority (see Exodus 1:16–17);

excessively held in esteem (see Psalm 96:5; Isaiah 45:21).

Gods, other: idols (see Psalm 96:5; Isaiah 45:21).

Goggles: seeing in the deep things of the Spirit (func); dreams (char).

Goggles, night vision: ability to "see" through dreams; knowing who you are in Christ (see 2 Corinthians 5:17–20); able to see through evil, "the darkness" (char).

Gold:

royalty, kingship (see Judges 8:26; 1 Kings 9:14; Daniel 2:36–38);

wisdom (see Matthew 6:19–20);

offering (see Exodus 25:3; 35:5; Numbers 7:14);

deity, of God (see Psalm 68:13; Matthew 2:11; Hebrews 9:4; Revelation 1:13);

beautiful (see Job 28:17; Ezekiel 16:13);

scarce/rare (see Isaiah 13:12);

wealth (see Exodus 12:35; Job 28:19; Psalm 19:10; Isaiah 60:9; Matthew 10:9);

greed/contamination/licentiousness (see 1 Samuel 6:4; Psalm 119:127; Jeremiah 4:30);

idols (see Psalm 115:4; 135:15);

false security (see Job 31:24).

Gold, building with:

good works on Jesus' foundation (see 1 Corinthians 3:12);

sacred/holy (see Matthew 23:17; Revelation 21:15);

ruling crown (see Zechariah 6:10–11).

Gold, corroded: wealth used wrongly (see James 5:2–4).

Gold, head: Babylonian kingdom (see Daniel 2:36–38).

Gold, refined with fire: life with God (see Revelation 3:18); tested by God (see Zechariah 13:9).

Good: things of the Lord (see Isaiah 55:2; Matthew 19:17; Luke 18:19); God/Jesus (see Matthew 19:17).

Goose egg: financial zero (see Deuteronomy 22:6; Isaiah 10:14; Jeremiah 17:11); producing nothing (char).

Gore: displaying power (see Deuteronomy 33:17).

Gossip:

dainty morsels that go to the innermost part of body (see Proverbs 18:8);

repeats a private matter/will not drop an issue (see Proverbs 17:9);

causes separation between people (see Proverbs 16:28);

gangrene which spreads and destroys (see 2 Timothy 2:17).

Gourd: vessel of provision (see 1 Kings 6:18).

Government: should have integrity and reverence for God (see Nehemiah 5:15); authority/structure (see Romans 13; Ephesians 1:10; 3:9–10).

Grace: a measure of mercy given according to God's gift (see Ephesians 4:7).

Grain:

thrive (see Haggai 1:11; Zechariah 9:17);

harvest (see Joel 2:24);

will be pounded to be useable (see Proverbs 27:22);

see General/Food, Grain.

Grain, cut and left behind by reaper: waiting to be gathered (see Jeremiah 9:22).

Grapes:

harvest/fruitfulness of people (see Matthew 7:16; Luke 6:44);

good results (see Matthew 7:16; Revelation 14:18–20);

reward (see Judges 9:27);

new wine (see Genesis 40:11; Amos 9:13);

things feeding upon/food/sustenance (see Deuteronomy 32:32 [people "feeding on, or partaking in, ugly, unhealthy things]; Psalm 65:9).

Grapes, dry: without the Word of the Lord [water/juice] (see General/ Water).

Grapes, juicy: good (see Isaiah 65:8).

Grapes, sour: bad results (see Jeremiah 31:29–30; Ezekiel 18:2).

Grapes, unripe: do not flourish/not yet time (see Job 15:33).

Grass:

mortal men/flesh/people (see 2 Kings 19:26; Psalm 37:2; 90:5; 92:7; Isaiah 40:3–8; 51:12; 1 Peter 1:24);

flourish (see Psalm 92:7; 72:16; Isaiah 66:12–14);

will wither (see Psalm 37:2; 90:5; 102:4–11; Isaiah 40:6–7; Matthew 6:30; 1 Peter 1:24);

here today, gone tomorrow (see Job 8:12; Psalm 90:6; Matthew 6:30; 7:30; Luke 12:28).

Grass, dried: men not living in the Word of God (see Isaiah 5:24).

Grass, on roof/on hard surface: withers before it can grow (see Psalm 129:6).

Grave: death (see 1 Samuel 2:6; Job 17:1; Isaiah 57:9; Matthew 27:59–60); dressing room for eternity (func).

Grave, unmarked: walking and living on top of dead issues and not being aware of it (see Luke 11:44); unclean corruption of those it contacts (see Luke 11:44).

Gravel: to cause one not to understand/ to break teeth (see Lamentations 3:16); something that is falsehood (see Proverbs 20:17).

Gravel in mouth: something acquired or learned by falsehood (see Proverbs 20:17).

Grease: frees things/people that are "bound" (char); fat (see Psalm 119:70).

Greatest: shall be a servant (see Matthew 23:11).

Greenery and trees: growth, prosperity and God's people (see 2 Kings 19:26; Psalm 1:3; 90:5; Matthew 3:10); soon die away (see Psalm 37:2).

Ground: humbled (see 2 Samuel 12:16); foundation in (see Ephesians 3:17); laid low (see Isaiah 28:1–2).

Ground, unplowed: needs to be broken to be productive (see Jeremiah 4:3).

Growth: chosen of God (see Numbers 17:5).

Guidepost: directions; direction to God (see Jeremiah 31:21).

Guilty, family: families held guilty for crimes of forefathers (see 2 Samuel 21:1–9).

Guitar: praises to Lord (see Psalm 144:9).

Gun:

exert power over (func);

power to reach beyond (func);

spiritual power or authority/good or bad (func);

Word of the Lord (see Jeremiah 23:28);

food for sustenance (see Nehemiah 5:2–3);

slanderous power (func).

Gun, battery-operated gun: weaker power (func).

Gun, bazooka: major spiritual attack (func).

Gun, cap gun: no power (func).

Gun, empty: no power (func).

Gun, holding gun: I have power (func).

Gun, machine: high-power weapon (func).

Gun, rifle: power from a distance (func).

Gun, water gun: shooting the Holy Spirit at someone (func).

Gutter: human difficulties of life (char); off-center of the desired pathway (char).

H

Hail:

Lord sweeping away lies (see Isaiah 28:17);

the work of our hands judged by God (see Psalm 18:12; Isaiah 28:2; 29:6; 30:30; Ezekiel 13:11; Haggai 2:17; Revelation 16:21);

hurls down/destroys sustenance (see Psalm 18:12; 78:47; 147:17).

Hair: promise or covenant that is covering (see Jeremiah 7:29); protection/control over (see Jeremiah 7:29).

Hair, bald: prophetic/intercessor (see Micah 1:16); no covenant [good or bad] (char; see Jeremiah 7:29).

Hair, bleached: covering is not natural (char; see Jeremiah 7:29).

Hair, braid: tied or bound up in something that is supposed to be your covering (char); your covering is in knots (char; see Jeremiah 7:29).

Hair, cut: break covenant (see Jeremiah 7:29).

Hair, dreadlocks: acting in rebellion (char; see Jeremiah 7:29; cutting off the consecration); this is a dream symbol for someone who does not wear dreadlocks on a routine basis. If hair is symbolic of a covering, then dreadlocks [a technique called "twist and rip"] is a covering that has been twisted, ripped and free-formed by the wearer—in rebellion of the usual lay of hair [covering].

Hair, fake: not a real covering from God (char).

Hair, goat: atonement (see Genesis 15:9; Leviticus 1:10–13; 16:15–17).

Hair, gray: aged (see 1 Kings 2:6, 9).

Hair, highly stacked and dark: under a large, dark covering.

Hair, kinky: something covering you [e.g., your thinking, a false doctrine, improper teachings] (see 2 Timothy 2:4; Hebrews 12:1–3); worldly covering (char; see Jeremiah 7:29).

Hair, long: acting in rebellion or defiance (char; see Jeremiah 7:29).

Hair, messy: entangled in messy things (see Leviticus 10:6; 2 Timothy 2:4; Hebrews 12:1–3); unwilling to submit to disentanglement (see Leviticus 10:6; 2 Timothy 2:4; Hebrews 12:1–3).

Hair, wavy: belonging to God (Song of Solomon 5:11).

Hammer:
Word of God (see Jeremiah 23:29);

to create through one's own effort (see Exodus 25:31);

makes smooth/breaks hard things (see Isaiah 41:7; 45:2; Jeremiah 23:29);

those who smash and splinter (char; see Jeremiah 50:23—as in the "hammer of the whole earth"—the evil empire that has pummeled the earth).

Hammock: resting in the Holy Spirit [air] (func).

Hamstrung: unable to go forward easily (see 2 Samuel 8:4); made lame (see 2 Samuel 8:4).

Handcuffs: bound/unable to work freely (see Psalm 149:8).

Hard to find: narrow is the way (see Matthew 7:13).

Harmonica: music/worship (see Psalm 92:1–3).

Harp:
prophesying (see 1 Samuel 10:5; 2 Kings 3:15);

music/worship and victory (see 2 Chronicles 29:25–28; Psalm 92:1–3; 98:4–5; Revelation 15:2);

praise of God (see Psalm 43:4; 71:22; 81:2; 150:3; Isaiah 16:11; book of Lamentations).

Harvest:
bringing others to Christ (see Matthew 9:37–38; Luke 10:2);

what God has given (see Jeremiah 8:13);

results (see 1 Samuel 12:17; Psalm 67:6);

end of age (see Matthew 13:29–39);

eternal salvation (see Matthew 9:37–38; 13:30; Revelation 14:15).

Harvest, none: not productive/unfruitful (see 2 Kings 2:19).

Harvest, varied by person: each person has different results/not uniform (see Matthew 13:8; 13:23).

Harvest, withered: harvest taken away or not coming (see Isaiah 16:8).

Harvest, workers: those evangelizing (see Matthew 9:37–38).

Hat: covering/may indicate under what authority you are operating (see Job 29:14; Zechariah 3:1–7; 1 Corinthians 11:6–7); protection for the mind (see Psalm 60:7; Ephesians 6:13–17).

Hat box: holds covering.

Hay, building with: inferior works erected on Jesus' foundation (see 1 Corinthians 3:12).

Hear: to understand (see Isaiah 6:9; 55:3; Matthew 13:14); to understand and act on it (see Revelation 3:20).

Heaven:

God's holy dwelling place/dwelling place for God's angels (see 2 Chronicles 30:27; 2 Corinthians 12:2–4; see Themes/Places/Heaven, third).

dwelling place for those who die in the faith of Jesus Christ (see 2 Corinthians 5:6–8—to be absent from the body and at home with the Lord);

sky around the earth (see Psalm 71:19; see Themes/Places/Heaven, first);

dwelling place for Satan and his minions (see Ephesians 6; see Themes/Places/Heaven, second);

high up/height (see 2 Chronicles 28:9; Proverbs 25:3);

things of God (see Colossians 3:2);

see Themes/Places/Heaven, first; Heaven, second; Heaven, third.

Heaven, open: ability to see into the third heaven (see Matthew 3:16); see Themes/Places/Portal.

Heavenly hosts: those other than angels in heaven (see Psalm 148:2).

Hedge: barrier/hedging/hide and protect oneself (see Job 1:10; Isaiah 5:5).

Hedge of thorns:

protection from the beasts (func);

protection by the crown of thorns of Christ (char);

lazy (see Proverbs 15:19).

Heel: betrayed (see Job 18:9; Psalm 41:9).

Helmet:

salvation (see Ephesians 6:17; 1 Thessalonians 5:8);

protection (see Psalm 60:7);

ready for battle (see Jeremiah 46:4).

Hem:

covering torn off/position removed (see 1 Samuel 15:27–28);

on the fringes/outskirts of (see Matthew 9:20);

enclosed behind and before (see Psalm 139:5).

Herd: possessions (see Proverbs 27:23).

Heritage: what God has in mind for you (see Isaiah 54:17).

Hidden:

secret things of the Lord (see Genesis 18:17; Deuteronomy 29:29; Joshua 7:19);

will be revealed (see Matthew 10:26);

turn away from (see Deuteronomy 31:18; 32:20);

in fear (see Exodus 2:3);

ashamed (see Genesis 3:8).

Hiding place: in the Lord (see Psalm 32:8); falsehoods (see Isaiah 28:15).

High:

rise high (see Deuteronomy 28:43; Isaiah 52:13);

toward God (see Psalm 78:39; 97:9; Isaiah 55:9; Matthew 5:14; Ephesians 2:6; Colossians 3:2);

life is not about yourself (see Revelation 12:11);

cannot be hidden (see Matthew 5:14).

High place: of God (see 1 Kings 3:3; Psalm 97:9; Isaiah 55:9; Matthew 5:14; Ephesians 2:6; Colossians 3:2).

High stuff:

things up high in the Spirit (see Deuteronomy 33:2; Psalm 43:3; 48:1; 68:16; Isaiah 2:2–3; 25:10; 52:7; 55:12; 65:11; 66:20; Ezekiel 20:40; 28:14; 38:21; Micah 1:3; Zechariah 9:3; Hebrews 8:5; 12:18; 12:22);

evil things or altars lifted up/high places (see Leviticus 26:30; 1 Kings 14:23; 2 Kings 23:13–16; 2 Chronicles 20:33; Isaiah 2:14; 26:5; 40:4; Jeremiah 7:31–32; 32:35; Ezekiel 6:3–4; 43:7);

what your focus is on/what is important to you (see Psalm 49:2; Matthew 4:8).

Highway:

Christian path (see Proverbs 15:19; 16:17; Isaiah 62:10; Jeremiah 31:21; Matthew 3:3; 22:1–14);

living and walking uprightly/path to holiness (see Proverbs 15:19; 16:17; Isaiah 2:3; 35:8; 40:3; 62:10);

to depart from evil (see Proverbs 16:17);

see Themes/Places/Highway.

Hill, high: see Themes/Places/Hill, high.

Hinder: sufferings that cause spiritual growth (see Philippians 1:29); obstacles that keep you from trusting and going forward (see Romans 14:21; Galatians 5:7; Hebrews 12:1).

Hinge: rusty and needs oil:

your pathway needs the anointing of God [oil: the anointing of God] (func);

bad knees [may indicate the need to pray—"get on your knees"—or to hold steadfast]; (char; see Themes/ Body Parts/Knees);

word of knowledge that there are bad knees that are anointed for healing.

Hiss: boo/threaten (see Ezekiel 27:36).

Holes:

way to get through (see Ezekiel 12:5);

areas in your life that are not upright or that give the enemy entrance, and from which you might reap bad results (see Psalm 7:15; Haggai 1:6);

place to hide (see Isaiah 2:19; Matthew 25:18).

Holiday: memorial to celebrate (see Exodus 12:14).

Hollow: without substance (see Colossians 2:8).

Holy Spirit: see Themes/People and Beings/Holy Spirit.

Hometown: prophet not accepted (see Luke 4:24).

Honey:

abundance/sweet things (see Exodus 3:8; 33:3; Numbers 13:27; 14:8; Judges 14:8; Psalm 19:10; 119:103; Jeremiah 11:5; 32:22);

revelation/Word of God (see Ezekiel 3:3);

food from God (see Matthew 3:4);

wisdom (see Proverbs 24:13–14);

pleasant words (see Proverbs 16:24; Song of Solomon 4:11);

rich and satisfying (see Psalm 81:16).

Honey, eat too much: have something in excess; something that is unbalanced and will cause sickness (see Proverbs 25:16).

Honeycomb: sweet and healing (see Proverbs 16:24); good things (see Proverbs 27:7).

Hood: hidden (see 1 Kings 19:12–14); power, authority and leadership (see 1 Kings 19:19).

Hoof: power (see Micah 4:13); ability to stamp down things (see Psalm 69:31).

Hook: capture (see Ezekiel 29:4; 38:4; Habakkuk 1:15); choosing to hold someone accountable [or not] for a past injury they did to you—or because you desire a particular action or outcome [as in "to let someone off the hook"].

Hordes: people (see Ezekiel 32:20).

Horizon: things you see ahead of you (see Job 26:10; Proverbs 8:27); the future (see Isaiah 13:5).

Horizontal: effects spreading outward to people (see Matthew 6:14–15; 28:19–20; Ephesians 1:15).

Horn:

authority (see Leviticus 16:18; Deuteronomy 33:17; 1 Samuel 2:1; 2:10; Psalm 89:24; 92:10; 132:17; 148:14; Ezekiel 29:21; Daniel 7:24; Revelation 5:6; 13:1; 17:12);

strength (see Psalm 89:17, 24; 92:10);

power (see 1 Kings 22:11; Psalm 18:2; 69:31; 75:4–5, 10; 89:24; 112:9; 132:17; Ezekiel 34:21; Daniel 7:24; Zechariah 1:18; Micah 4:13; Revelation 5:6).

Horn, black: dark authority (char; see General/Authority).

Horn, cut off: loss of power [horn: power] (see Jeremiah 48:25; Moab's [horn] power is cut off).

Hot: excited and proactive/come alive (see Judges 18:25; 1 Samuel 14:22;

Revelation 3:15); volatile (see Exodus 11:8; Psalm 78:49).

Hot tub: pressure and trials (to be "in hot water").

Hour: time (see John 12:23; 13:1; Revelation 3:10).

Hungry: force that drives a person on (see Proverbs 16:26); craving and able to receive the teachings of God/searching for God's Word (see Deuteronomy 8:3; 1 Samuel 2:5; Proverbs 13:25; Isaiah 65:13; Matthew 5:6; Luke 6:21; John 6:35).

Hurricane: scattered with a storm (see Zechariah 7:14).

Hurts: problems, areas of oppression (see Revelation 2:9–10).

Hymnal: praising the Lord (see Nehemiah 12:27; Psalm 40:3; Acts 16:25; Ephesians 5:19; Colossians 3:16); doctrinal way of worship (see Matthew 5:20).

Hyssop: cleansing (see Psalm 51:7); spreading the blood of Christ (see Exodus 12:1–36); getting rid of sin (see Psalm 51:7).

I

I Am: God (see Matthew 22:32); living in the now (see Matthew 22:32).

Ice:
slippery (see Job 6:16);
something saved for later (func);
a hard word/a harsh and cold word (see Job 37:10; 38:29; Psalm 147:17).

Ice cream: made cold by the sweet Word of God (char).

Icy road: slippery path (char).

Idol:
worthless (see Isaiah 44:10);
takes away from God (see Jeremiah 2:5);
fraud (see Psalm 24:4; Jeremiah 10:14);
detestable to God (see Deuteronomy 27:15).

Idolatry: arrogance (see 1 Samuel 15:23).

Ill-fitting:
not "fit"/not for you (see Judges 5:25; Acts 22:22 NIV; Ephesians 5:4);
not proper (see Ezra 4:14; Proverbs 19:10; 26:1);
not worthy of (see Matthew 3:11; Mark 1:7; Luke 3:16; 1 Corinthians 15:9).

Image:
visual impression (see Leviticus 26:1);
representing/likeness (see Genesis 5:3; Micah 1:7; 2 Corinthians 2:14–15);
fraud/worthless/object of mockery (see Jeremiah 51:17–18).

Imitate: follow (see Hebrews 6:12); striving to be like (see Hebrews 13:7).

Immortality: everlasting life/a beginning that will never end (see 2 Timothy 1:10); eternity/always has been and always will be/only God (see 1 Timothy 6:14–16).

Incense:
covering up (see Ezekiel 8:11–12);
prayers (see Psalm 141:2; Jeremiah 34:5; Revelation 5:8; 8:3–4);
paying homage to (see Jeremiah 44:8);
intercession (see Revelation 5:8);
accepted (see Ezekiel 20:41);
offering (see Ezekiel 16:18; Numbers 16);
worship (see Numbers 16:37; 2 Chronicles 26:16; Jeremiah 18:15; 32:29; 44:8);
atonement (see Exodus 30:7–10);
angry (see Nehemiah 4:1; Sanballat became angry and was greatly incensed);
memory (see Isaiah 66:3);
dead (see Jeremiah 34:5).

Indictment: accusations (see Job 31:35).

Indifference: the opposite of love (see General/Love).

Infertility: brought on by sin (see Genesis 20:18).

Inheritance:
promise of grace (see Genesis 21:10; Exodus 32:13; Ephesians 1:11);
children should share in (see Proverbs 17:2);
not a law (see Galatians 3:18);

your heritage (see Isaiah 54:17; Ephesians 1:11);

receiving is based on timing (see Galatians 4:1–5).

Iniquity: premeditated sin (see Exodus 34:6–9).

Instruction: life with God (see Proverbs 4:13); knowledge (see Proverbs 19).

Instrument: tool used by God (see Acts 9:15).

Insulation:

to isolate (see Leviticus 13:4–11; 2 Kings 15:5);

to separate out sin and infections (see Leviticus 13:4–11; 2 Kings 15:5);

to isolate self from wisdom (see Proverbs 18:1);

protection.

Intercession: bring two together (see Joshua 17:10; Isaiah 59:16; Romans 8:34; Hebrews 7:25).

Interest: no charges brought against your brother (see Deuteronomy 23:19–20).

Interest, excessive: wrong practices that put people into slavery/usury (see Nehemiah 5:6–11).

Intersection: intercession [Hebrew: met together] (see Joshua 17:10; Romans 8:34).

Interstate: highway to height [Holiness] (see Isaiah 35).

In time: eventually (see Genesis 4:3; Exodus 13:14); before it is too late (see Genesis 21:2; Galatians 6:9; Ephesians 1:10; 1 Peter 1:5).

Intoxicated:

full of the Holy Spirit (see Acts 2:15; Ephesians 5:18);

caught up in feelings (see Acts 2:15; Romans 13:13; Revelation 17:2; 17:6);

reeling to and fro/staggering in own vomit (see Psalm 107:27; Isaiah 19:14; 24:20);

overwhelmed by (see Deuteronomy 32:42);

one who hurts others (see Proverbs 26:9).

Invisible:

Jesus (see 1 Timothy 6:15–17);

unable to see through worldly eyes (see Romans 1:20; Colossians 1:15–16; 1 Timothy 1:17);

overlooked (see Acts 6:1).

Invitation: honor/trust (see Isaiah 55:1); snare/lure (see 2 Samuel 11:13).

Iron:

unfailing strength (see Genesis 4:22; Judges 1:19; Job 19:24; Jeremiah 1:18; 28:13–14; 15:12; 28:14; Micah 4:13; Revelation 9:9; 12:5);

empire (see Daniel 2:40);

substitute for silver [redemption] (see Isaiah 60:17);

strength that comes from trials (see Ezekiel 22:18);

bars or chains that need breaking (see Isaiah 45:2);

crushes and smashes everything (see Daniel 2:40);

stubborn, hard and unyielding (see Leviticus 26:19; Revelation 2:27);

corrupt (see Jeremiah 6:28).

Iron, neck: punishment (see Jeremiah 29:26).

Iron, sharpens iron: equal measures of strength sharpen each other (see Proverbs 27:17).

J

Jackal's haunt: bars/taverns (see Isaiah 35:7).

Jar:

vessel of God (see Isaiah 22:24; Hebrews 9:4);

power in simple, overlooked weapons (see Judges 7:15);

to contain (see Psalm 33:7).

Jar, broken: see General/Pottery, broken.

Jar, empty: of no worth (see Jeremiah 51:34).

Jasper: diamonds/wealth (see Ezekiel 28:13; Revelation 4:3).

Javelin, held out: conquer (see Joshua 8:18).

Jelly: preserved fruit (see General/Fruit); work will be lasting (char); sweet word [food] (char).

Jelly beans: preserved fruit and produce, lasting work.

Jewel, rare: knowledge (see Proverbs 20:15).

Jewelry:

adornment of mind, will, emotions [heart] (see Proverbs 25:12; 1 Peter 3:4);

out of mourning and repentance (see Exodus 33:4–6);

wisdom to one who needs it (see Proverbs 25:12).

Jewelry, without: in repentance and mourning (see Exodus 33:4–6); treasures (see Genesis 24:53; Exodus 32:24; Proverbs 20:15).

Jewels: beautiful (see Ezekiel 16:7).

Jewels, building with: good works erected on Jesus' foundation (see 1 Corinthians 3:12).

Job: one who endures afflictions (book of Job).

Journalism: journey (play on words).

Joy: upright in mind, will and emotions (see Psalm 97:11).

Judge: see Themes/People and Creatures/Judge.

Judgment:

wisdom (see Proverbs 17:18);

discipline that begins with God's own people and church (see 1 Peter 4:17);

condemnation, not to be given by us (see Matthew 7:1–2; Romans 2:1–4; 14:1–22).

Juice: energy, works, power [juice up] (see Isaiah 65:8).

Junk: a lot of worthless stuff (char).

Justice: right with the Lord (see Isaiah 56:1; Hebrews 6:10); of the Lord (see Matthew 22:16).

K

Kettle: vessel of offering (see 1 Samuel 2:13–14).

Key:

Jesus (see Revelation 3:7);

knowledge (see Matthew 16:19);

authority to open (see Revelation 1:18);

open choices/doors (see Matthew 16:19; Revelation 3:7–8; 20:1);

tool to do something (func).

Kimono:

Japanese culture;

the beauty of the "foreign" (char);

loose clothing [covering] (char);

not a good covering [because loose] (see General/Clothing);

foreign (see Themes/People and Beings/Foreigners).

Kindle: start with small quantity and cause to grow by nurturing (see 2 Timothy 1:6).

Kindling: something that sets off a "fire" about something (see Job 18:5; 20:26); fire-starter [see General/Fire] (func).

Kiss:

in agreement with (see 1 Samuel 10:1; 2 Samuel 15:5; Matthew 26:48–49);

affection (see 2 Samuel 14:33; 1 Thessalonians 5:26);

betrayal (see Proverbs 27:6; Luke 22:47–48).

Knife:

Word of God (see Matthew 10:34; Ephesians 6:17; Hebrews 4:12);

cut off (see Genesis 22:10; Exodus 4:25; Jeremiah 36:23);

cut up (see Judges 19:29);

attack of the enemy (char);

cutting words (see Revelation 2:16);

sharp words (see Psalm 57:4; Revelation 2:16; 19:15; 21);

see General/Sword.

Knife, holding the knife: holding onto and using the Word of God (see Ephesians 6:17; Hebrews 4:12).

Knit: bind together (see Ephesians 4:12; Colossians 2:2).

Knock: request to act for whoever hears (see Matthew 7:7–8; Revelation 3:20).

Knot: marriage [as in "tie the knot"]; a tie (see Psalm 18:4–5; 116:3).

Knowledge: often false understanding/worldly arguments (see 1 Timothy 6:20–21).

L

Labor:
repercussions of rebellion (see Psalm 107:12);
to work hard and diligently (see 1 Thessalonians 5:12);
preparing to birth/bring about (see Matthew 24:8; Galatians 4:19);
anguish/struggles (see Isaiah 55:2; Jeremiah 6:24).

Labor pains: come upon one suddenly (see 1 Thessalonians 5:3).

Labyrinth, bends: difficulties encountered (char).

Ladder:
steps to ambition (as in "climbing the ladder to success");
portal/tie between heaven and earth (see Genesis 28:11–19);
see General/Stairs.

Ladle: spooning [giving] out limited portions at a time (char).

Lair: dwelling place of an enemy/destroyer [lion] (see Jeremiah 4:7; Nahum 2:11).

Lake:
Word of God—the water is the Word of God (see Isaiah 55:1; Mark 4:1; John 4:10–15; Ephesians 5:26; Revelation 7:17; 19:20; 20:10);
church—offering the Word of God [water] to the people (func; see Mark 4:1; 6:49); providing teaching to the people of the Word of God (church); a small pond or lake might represent a small church (char); a larger lake might represent a larger church or ministry (char);
life (see Matthew 4:18; 13:47; Mark 1:16).

Lake, stagnant or polluted: large church or ministry polluted.

Lame: weak and unable to move quickly (see 2 Samuel 5:6).

Lamp:
light of God/Christ (see 2 Samuel 22:29; Psalm 104:2; Isaiah 2:5; Luke 8:16; 11:36; John 1:9; Revelation 1:12–13; 4:5; 11:4);
church (see Proverbs 6:23; Revelation 1:12–20);
God's power reflected (see 2 Kings 8:19; Proverbs 6:23; Zechariah 4:2);
direction (see 2 Samuel 21:17; Job 29:3; Psalm 119:105; 132:17).

Lamp, burning: ready and waiting (see Matthew 25:1–13; Luke 12:35).

Lamp stand:
church receiving oil (see Matthew 5:14–16);
anointing from a central source [Jesus] (func);
oil received to support (see Matthew 5:14–16);
servant, knowledge, counsel, wisdom, understanding, might, fear of the Lord [meaning of each branch and center] (see Exodus 37:18–19).

Land, dry: place without support (see Psalm 63:1; 143:6).

Land, tilled: prepared for new beginning (see Psalm 80:9).

Land, used up: place without continued support (see Psalm 63:1).

Language: say only what helps; each word a gift (see Ephesians 4:29).

Language, difficult: not God's people (see Ezekiel 3:6).

Language, native: lie (see John 8:44).

Lap: given to you (see Jeremiah 32:18); received (see Psalm 79:12).

Last: God/Jesus (see Revelation 1:17); will be first (see Matthew 19:30; 20:1–16).

Laughter: foolish (see Ecclesiastes 2:2), mockery (see Matthew 9:24).

Lava: effects of fallout (char).

Law:
God's law/perfect law (see Psalm 40:8; 119; 147:19; Isaiah 51:7; Matthew 14:4; James 1:25);
Bible/Christ's teachings (see Colossians 2:17; 1 Timothy 1:7–10);
words of God (see Joshua 1:8; Isaiah 2:3; Galatians 2:19);
law is good if used lawfully (see 1 Timothy 1:8);
treasures (see Matthew 13:52);

loaded down with burdens one cannot carry (see Galatians 3:10–13);

rules of religiosity/legalism/following the law, even though it is against what God is doing (see Daniel 6:4–16; Matthew 12:2–6; Galatians 2:16; 3:11; 4:4–5, 21;5; Ephesians 2:15; Colossians 2:13–15; 5:4, 20–23);

do not help (see Luke 11:46; Colossians 2:23);

take away knowledge (see Luke 11:52);

a tutor/a guardian (see Psalm 119; Galatians 3:23–24; 4:1–5);

careful to follow (see Deuteronomy 12:1);

copy and shadow of good things (see Hebrews 8:5; 10:1);

treat others as you want to be treated [God's law] (see Matthew 7:12);

self-importance (see Luke 20:45–47);

rules of mankind (see Galatians 2:19; 5:18; Colossians 2:8, 20–23; Hebrews 7:18–19);

made for those who are disobedient (see 1 Timothy 1:9–11).

Law, end: Christ (see Romans 10:4; Colossians 2:20–23).

Lawless:

rebellious (see 2 Samuel 3—Abner was rebellious, disobeying the law, and was punished with death; Matthew 7:23; 13:41; 2 Thessalonians 2:1–9);

sin (see Hebrews 1:9; 1 John 3:4);

antichrist (see 2 Thessalonians 2:7–9).

Lead:

part left inside furnace after silver is burnt (see Ezekiel 22:18);

heavy (see Exodus 15:10);

strong and enduring (see Job 19:24).

Leaf: shrivel up (see Psalm 1:3; Isaiah 64:6); easily goes with the wind (see Leviticus 26:36; Job 13:25).

Leaf, green: thrive (see Proverbs 11:28).

Leaf, wind-blown: tossed about sporadically (see Leviticus 26:36; Job 13:25).

Leak: beginning of strife or contention (see Proverbs 17:14).

Learned: arrogant in their own knowledge (see Matthew 11:25).

Leather: protective (func).

Leaven: a little thing that affects the whole matter/contamination (see Exodus 12:34; Matthew 13:33; Galatians 5:9); boasts (see 1 Corinthians 5:6).

Leaves:

protection (see Daniel 4:12, 21);

covering (see Genesis 3:7);

political healing (see Ezekiel 47:12; Revelation 22:2);

gifts [the leaves of the tree were for the healing of nation: gift healing] (see Revelation 22:2).

Leaves, fading: vulnerable; dying without strength (see Isaiah 1:30).

Leaves, new: summer is near (see Matthew 24:32; Mark 13:28; Luke 21:30).

Leaves, dropping: withering (see Jeremiah 8:13; Ezekiel 47:12).

Left:

things you are born to (see Leviticus 14:15, 26; Matthew 20:23);

left behind or rejected by Christ because the spiritual choice to reject Christ first (see Matthew 24:40–41; 25:33, 41);

foolishness (see Ecclesiastes 10:2);

sin (see Ecclesiastes 10:2; Ezekiel 4:4; Matthew 25:41);

those who are not His people/sheep; weakness of man (see Matthew 25:33);

turning aside (see Genesis 13:9; Exodus 11:8 NIV—in anger Moses turned aside and left Pharaoh; 2 Chronicles 34:2);

not accepted (see Matthew 25:33, 41);

remains (see Genesis 7:23; 32:8; Exodus 10:19).

Left turn: sharp spiritual change (see Matthew 24:40–41; 25:33, 41).

Legal documents: legalistic approach (char).

Legalism: following the law or religious traditions, even though it is against what God is doing (see Daniel 6:4–16; Matthew 27:20–24; Galatians 1:14; Colossians 2:13–17); see General/Law.

Length: method of appraisal (see 2 Samuel 8:2).

Lengthen: will spread out and grow (see Isaiah 54:2–3).

Leprosy:

covered in uncleanness (see Matthew 8:2–3; 11:5);

destroys ability to be sensitive to things that are harmful (char);

kills when you do not realize you are being hurt or are in danger (char);

repercussion against judging others [Miriam judged wrongly Moses' choice of wife] (see Numbers 12:1–16).

Lethargic: asleep or not paying attention to what is going on (see Psalm 121:3–4; Isaiah 5:27).

Letter: spiritual word (see Exodus 4:13); rules/laws of demands/legalism (see 2 Corinthians 3:6).

Levee: man-made hedge that hold trials [floods] back (func).

Level: path of righteousness (see Proverbs 4:26; Isaiah 26:7).

Libra: scaled balance of remission [valley] and atonement [mountain] (see Isaiah 40:1–12); astrology, not of God (see Deuteronomy 4:19).

Lick: consume with nothing left/overcome/beat (see Numbers 22:4).

Lick, dust: be humbled (see Psalm 72:9).

Lie: not of God (see John 8:44; Titus 1:2); hates those it crushes (see Proverbs 26:28).

Lie down: rest (see Isaiah 14:30).

Life:

God (see 1 Timothy 6:13);

Jesus (see John 14:6);

spiritual change (see 1 Samuel 2:6; 1 John 3:14);

spiritual revelation/communion/communication (see Proverbs 10:16; Jeremiah 8:3; John 1:4; Revelation 1:18; 2:7);

everlasting spiritual existence (see Isaiah 28:18; Jeremiah 8:3; Matthew 22:32; John 6:63; 2 Timothy 1:10; 1 John 5:11–13; Revelation 1:18; 3:5; 7:17; 20:12—22:6);

position and wealth (see Matthew 10:39).

Lifted: high in the Spirit (see Exodus 40:36–37; Numbers 9:21; 1 Samuel 2:1).

Light:

understand/able to "see" (see Psalm 36:9; 49:19; 97:11; Ephesians 3:9);

Word of God (see Isaiah 42:6; 49:6);

of God (see Psalm 18:28; 27:1; 36:9; 97:11; 104:2; Isaiah 50:10; 60:19–20; 104:1–2; John 8:12; 11:9; James 1:17; 1 Timothy 6:16; 1 John 1:5–7);

Jesus (see Matthew 4:16; 17:2; John 1:4–5; 8:12; 9:5; 11:9; 12:35–36, 46, 1 Timothy 6:16);

Lord (see 2 Samuel 22:29; Job 1:16; Ps 43:3; 97:11; 104:2; Proverbs 6:23; 1 Timothy 6:16);

Gospel (see 2 Corinthians 4:4);

protection/armor (see Romans 13:12);

things of the Lord (see Genesis 1:4; Isaiah 5:20; Matthew 4:16; John 1:4; 12:46; 2 Corinthians 4:4; Ephesians 5:8–13);

anointing; power of God (see Job 29:3; Psalm 118:27; Isaiah 60:1–2);

Christians (see Matthew 5:14);

one who shows the way (see 2 Samuel 21:17; Psalm 119:105; Isaiah 42:6; Matthew 5:16);

allows others to understand/"to see"/ teachings (see Proverbs 6:23; Matthew 5:14);

truth (see Proverbs 29:13).

Light, dark: not of God (see Psalm 118:27; Matthew 6:23; Luke 11:35); darkness (see Luke 11:35).

Lights, on: revelation of God (see John 11:9; James 1:17).

Lights, turned off: not being revealed (see Luke 11:35; John 11:9).

Light, unapproachable: dwelling of God (see 1 Tim 6:16).

Lightning:

God's judgment (see Psalm 18:12; 29:7);

power/presence of God (see 2 Samuel 22:13; Psalm 77:17; Matthew 3:16; Luke 10:18; Revelation 4:5);

Jesus' splendor (see Luke 9:29);

flash (see Ezekiel 21:28);
energy (see Revelation 4:5);
fall of Satan (see Luke 10:18);
attack from enemy (see Job 1:16).

Lily: capital (see 1 Kings 7:19–22); will
blossom greatly (see Hosea 14:5).

Lime: easy to burn (see Isaiah 33:12).

Line: family generations (see Psalm
89:4, 29).

Linen:
righteous actions of the saints (see
Revelation 19:8);
no perspiration (see Ezekiel 44:17–18);
adorned (see Ezekiel 16:13).

Lines: boundaries/plumb line (see Jeremiah 31:39; Zechariah 4:10).

Liquid: see General/Watery.

List: remember (see Psalm 56:8).

List, to do: religiosity/legalistic works (see
Matthew 7:21–23); our own efforts
(see Ephesians 2:8–9; 2 Timothy 1:9).

Live:
keep going through others' faith (see
1 Thessalonians 3:7–8);
stay in Christ (see Philippians 1:21;
2 Timothy 2:11);
alive in the flesh (see Philippians 1:22);
where you are emotionally (see John
15:6–10).

Livelihood: commitment not to go back
(see 1 Kings 20:21).

Liver: man-made decision (see Ezekiel
21:21); will eliminate past problems
[eliminates bile/bitterness] (func).

Liver, bad: will not eliminate past problems (func).

Living stone: Jesus (see 1 Peter 2:4).

Loaf: things that are able to nourish (see
Matthew 7:9).

Locker: secure place (func).

Locker room: place where clothes are
stored, place where one receives
"spiritual covering" (func: see
General/Clothing).

Lockers, gray: locked in compromise
(see Themes/Colors/Gray).

Log: large issue of the world (dead
issue) (see Matthew 7:3–5); of large
measure (see Matthew 7:1–5).

Loom: life (see Isaiah 38:12); work being
done/look at the pattern and colors
(func).

Loot: reward (see Ezekiel 29:19).

Lost: going the "wrong" direction (see
Numbers 17:12; Jeremiah 50:6);
separated from God (see Matthew
18:11–14; Luke 15:24).

Lots: division by God or by chance (see
Matthew 27:35).

Love:
God (see Psalm 62:12);
affection of Christ Jesus (see Philippians 1:8);
does no wrong (see Romans 13:10);
without hypocrisy (see Romans 12:9);
honored (see Romans 12:10);
grants favor (see 1 Corinthians 13:1);
seeks opportunity to help others (see
1 Corinthians 13:2);
causes proper motives (see 1 Corinthians 13:3);
patient (see 1 Corinthians 13:4);
kind (see 1 Corinthians 13:4);
not jealous (see 1 Corinthians 13:4);
chooses no self-glory (see 1 Corinthians 13:4);
careful in its response to others (see
1 Corinthians 13:5);
does not act out of revenge (see 1 Corinthians 13:5);
thrives in truth (see 1 Corinthians 13:6);
able to hear and react appropriately
to life situations (see 1 Corinthians
13:7);
consistent (see 1 Corinthians 13:8);
greater than faith and hope (see 1 Corinthians 13:13);
should be pursued (see 1 Corinthians
14:1);
sex (see Proverbs 7:18).

Low:
go lower (see Deuteronomy 28:43);
unimportant (see Psalm 49:2);
humbled (see Isaiah 23:9);
life is about self (see Matthew
10:37–39).

Lubricated: anointed by God (see Matthew 25:4–10; 1 John 2:20).

Lukewarm: just going along (see Revelation 3:16).

Lupus: attack from the enemy [wolf] (char); (see Themes/Animals and Creatures/Wolves).

Lyre:

prophesying (see 1 Samuel 10:5);

praise God (see Psalm 71:22; 81:2; 92:1–3; 150:3);

worship (see 2 Chronicles 29:25–28).

M

Magic:

ensnare/fool people (see Ezekiel 13:18–20; Acts 8:11; Revelation 18:23);

powers, not of God (see Deuteronomy 18:10; Ezekiel 13:18; Acts 19:19);

cause fear (see Isaiah 47:12).

Magnifier: God (see Psalm 138:2).

Mahogany: a tree that is dark or leaders of God [tree], who are not acting in a godly manner [dark]; see General/Tree.

Mail, overnight: prayer (see Exodus 4:13).

Mail, receive: spiritual word (see Exodus 4:13).

Make-up: need to "make up" or set things right with someone (play on words); putting on a face [mask] (char).

Manna: overwhelmed with awe and provision (see Exodus 16:31–35; Deuteronomy 8:16).

Manure: nasty stuff that will ultimately cause things to flourish (see Luke 14:35).

Margin: time between the bulk of one's commitments (char).

Mark: see General/Seal.

Marriage:

in a covenant (see Genesis 29:26; Judges 12:9; Malachi 2:14);

close agreement/ close intimacy to the point of committing oneself (see Exodus 2:21; Joshua 23:12; Malachi 2:11; Matthew 22:2);

come together/unite (see Daniel 11:17; Matthew 19:4–6).

Marrow: satisfied/plenty (see Job 21:24; Psalm 63:5; 65:11; 73:4).

Master: what is controlling you (see Genesis 4:7; 24:65; 1 Corinthians 6:12).

Math: calculations [life] (char).

Mature: attaining growth, understanding, obedience and faith in Christ (see Ephesians 4:13–15); spiritual maturity (see Colossians 4:12).

Measure: evaluate/determine/appraise (see Deuteronomy 25:13–15; 2 Samuel 8:2; Haggai 2:1–13; Matthew 7:1–2; Revelation 11:1–2); apportioned amount (see Jeremiah 31:37; Ecclesiastes 10:1; Ephesians 4:7).

Measure, uneven: unequal, God detests (see Proverbs 20:10, 23).

Measuring stick/tape: even, equal, evaluate (see 2 Kings 21:13; Haggai 2:1–13; Revelation 11:1–2).

Meat:

people of God (see Ezekiel 11:3);

mature spiritual learning (see Genesis 9:3; Hebrews 5:12–14);

good food (see Daniel 10:3; Job 31:31).

Medicine: something being received that affects the mind, body, will, emotions [heart] (see Proverbs 17:22).

Melt: slowly transformed (see Psalm 68:2; John 14:8); went away (see Job 6:16).

Members: parts of the body (see James 4:1).

Mementos: things of the past (char).

Menorah: seven lamps illuminated by one oil [Holy Spirit] (see Exodus 26–27). First lamp is knowledge; second lamp is counsel; third lamp is wisdom; center lamp is servant [*chamash*]—supplies light to all the other lamps; fifth lamp is understanding; sixth lamp is might; seventh lamp is fear of the Lord.

Menstrual pad/cloth: throw away (see Isaiah 30:22).

Menstruation: unclean conduct (see Leviticus 15:19; Ezekiel 22:10; 36:17); defiled (see Leviticus 12:7; Ezekiel 36:17).

Menstruation, on clothes: fallen and exposed/no comfort (see Lamentations 1:9).

Message: spiritual word (see Exodus 4:13).

Messy: needs cleaning (see Job 30:19; Psalm 18:42; 2 Peter 2:22).

Metaphor: figurative language (see Matthew 13:10–13; John 16:25); so that we might understand (see Matthew 13:10–17).

Metal: people (see Jeremiah 6:27).

Metal detector: finds God's people (see Jeremiah 6:27).

Metal tester: tests God's people/prophet (see Jeremiah 6:27).

Mildew:
the work of our hands judged by God (see Haggai 2:17);
uncleanness or sin that will spread (see Leviticus 14:33–53);
destructive contamination (see 2 Chronicles 6:28).

Milk:
Word of God (see 1 Peter 2:2);
foundation/truth (see 1 Peter 2:2— pure [without contamination or untruth]);
immature learning/spiritual food for babies in Christ (see Hebrews 5:12–14; 1 Peter 2:2);
elementary spiritual learning (see Joshua 5:6; Hebrews 5:12–14; 6:1–2);
good food (see Numbers 13:27; 14:8; Isaiah 55:1; Jeremiah 11:5; 32:22);
white (see Lamentations 4:7);
provision and good things (see Exodus 3:8; 33:3; Jeremiah 32:22).

Millstone: toil/work/labor (see Jeremiah 25:10; Lamentations 5:13); livelihood (see Deuteronomy 24:6).

Mind: focused on the main thing (see 1 Chronicles 12:38); understand (see Deuteronomy 29:4).

Mind, double: to vacillate; inconsistent thinking (see Psalm 119:113; James 1:8; 4:8).

Miracle:
God testifying to us of His goodness and will (see Psalm 145:5; Hebrews 2:4);
a means to bring about repentance (see Matthew 11:20–24);
requires belief (see Matthew 13:58).

Mirage: unfulfilled promises (see Isaiah 35:1–10).

Mire:
unable to find a good foothold (see Psalm 69:2);
despair (see Psalm 40:2); sin (see 2 Peter 2:21–22);
dungeon/trapped (see Jeremiah 38:6, 22).

Mirrors:
reflection of God (see 2 Corinthians 3:17–18);
what it looks like/reflection of what is going on in you (see 1 Corinthians 13:12);
dealing with your image of self (see 1 Corinthians 13:12);
able to see only temporarily (see James 1:23–24).

Mirror, rearview: hindsight (char).

Misfit: not fitting in the Lord (see Colossians 3:18).

Missing: lacking something (see Leviticus 6:4; Deuteronomy 22:3; 1 Samuel 9:3); not counted (see Ecclesiastes 1:15).

Mist: life/appearing a little while and vanishing (see James 4:14).

Mist, driven by a storm: those who follow their own course (see 2 Peter 2:17).

Mist, morning: fades away early (see Hosea 6:4).

Mix: not united (see Daniel 2:43).

Mock:
creates heavy chain (see Isaiah 28:22);
ridicule (see Psalm 69:11–12);
see Themes/People and Beings/ Mocker.

Mold: uncleanness or sin that will spread (see Leviticus 14:33–53); destructive contamination (see 2 Chronicles 6:28).

Molten image: falsehood (see Jeremiah 10:14).

Money:
God's favor and blessing (see Genesis 47:15; Isaiah 40:10);

favor/grace (see Genesis 47:15; Isaiah 40:10);

loss of favor (see Genesis 47:15; Isaiah 40:10);

payment/paycheck (see Genesis 42:35; 47:14–18; Exodus 21:11; 2 Kings 12:15; 2 Chronicles 34:14);

investments (see Deuteronomy 23:19; Nehemiah 5:10–11; Matthew 25:27);

belongs to the world (see Matthew 22:19–21).

Money, in hole: not investing (see Matthew 25:18); ignore gifts/squander gifts/abuse gifts (see Matthew 25:15–18).

Money, love of: root of all sorts of evil (see 1 Timothy 6:10).

Money, none: without ability to purchase (see Isaiah 55:1; Mark 6:8).

Monument: in honor of (see 1 Samuel 15:12; Isaiah 19:19).

Moon:

shine on darkness (see Job 26:9; 31:26; Psalm 136:9; Isaiah 60:19; Revelation 21:23);

faithful witness (see Psalm 89:37);

established forever (see Psalm 72:5–7; 89:37);

season (see Deuteronomy 33:14; Psalm 104:19);

mother (see Genesis 37:9–10);

one month (func);

reveal bad things (see Revelation 21:23–27);

occult/spiritual things that are not of the Lord (see Deuteronomy 4:18–20; 17:3; 2 Kings 23:5; Jeremiah 8:3).

Moon, new: beginning (see Isaiah 66:23); time of blessing and first fruits (see Numbers 10:10; 29:6; 1 Samuel 20:5, 18, 24; 2 Kings 4:23; 1 Chronicles 23:31).

Moon, no light: spiritually dead (see Ezekiel 32:7); die (see Ezekiel 32:7).

Morning: new/spring up (see Psalm 90:6); to begin to come out of a time of trials (see Psalm 65:8).

Mountain:

things high in the Spirit (see Genesis 49:26; Exodus 3:12; 19:23);

heaven (see Psalm 43:3);

place of safety (see Genesis 19:17–19; Luke 21:21);

place of God (see Exodus 3:1, 12; 19:3; Deuteronomy 33:2; Psalm 99:9);

places held high in your esteem (see Genesis 22:2, 14; Exodus 15:17; 19:12–13);

a difficult crossing (char).

Mortar, with pestle: a place/time wherein one receives a "pounding" (see Proverbs 27:22);

trials/work of the Lord that releases or reveals what is inside (see Proverbs 27:22).

Mud: dirty, messy things of the world/ worldly garbage (see Job 30:19; Psalm 18:42; 2 Peter 2:22).

Muddy trail: stress; sin; difficult/unable to find a good foothold (see Psalm 69:2); pounded and trampled down (see 2 Samuel 22:43; Psalm 40:2; Isaiah 10:6).

Murdered: causes old flesh to die and rise to a new way; see General/ Death.

Music: worship of God or idols (see Judges 5:3; 2 Samuel 6:5; 1 Chronicles 6:32; 13:8; 20:28; Psalm 57:7; 61:8; 62:5; 98:4; 108:1; Daniel 3:5–15; Ephesians 5:19); things of the Spirit in symbols; prophesying (see 2 Kings 3:15; 1 Chronicles 25:1–3).

Music box: place of worship (see General/Music).

Music, stopped: no joy (see Lamentations 5:16).

Musical instruments:

prophesying (see 1 Samuel 10:5);

worship (see 2 Chronicles 29:25–28);

praise (see Nehemiah 12:27, 36; Psalm 33:2; 149:3; 150:3–5; Isaiah 38:20).

Mustache: covering up what they are saying (see Ezekiel 24:17); unclean prophesy (see Leviticus 13:45); humanity (see 2 Samuel 19:24).

Mustard seed: a smaller than normal seed that grows to produce a larger than normal result (see Matthew 13:31–32).

Mute: unable to voice or speak out (see Psalm 38:13; Proverbs 31:8; Isaiah 56:10).

Myrrh: used for embalming/death (see Matthew 2:11).

Myrtle: sweet smelling (see Isaiah 55:13).

Mystery: unknown things (see Ephesians 3:4; 6:19).

N

Nail: keep from toppling (see Isaiah 41:7; Jeremiah 10:4).

Naked:
vulnerable/everyone can see what is going on (see Isaiah 57:8; Matthew 27:28);

nothing to hide/all revealed/expose what is hidden (see Genesis 2:25; 2 Samuel 6:20–22; Isaiah 57:8);

(if it is in a good dream): without covering (see Isaiah 20:2–6; Revelation 3:17–18);

without guile/innocent (see 1 Samuel 19:24);

bare (see Hosea 2:3; Matthew 27:28);

unprotected (see 2 Corinthians 5:3–4);

not cared for (see Ezekiel 16:7);

stripped by God (see Lamentation 4:21; Ezekiel 16:37; Revelation 17:16);

adultery (sée Isaiah 57:8);

shamefully exposed (see Revelation 16:15).

Naked, start putting on clothes in a dream: vulnerable, but will be covered by God (see Genesis 3:7); vulnerable, but is conforming to pressures of environment.

Naked, waist down: creating things/ability to birth and reproduce (func); humiliation (see Isaiah 20:4; Jeremiah 13:26–27).

Naked, waist up: visibly vulnerable (char), but no fruit being produced (reproductive area not vulnerable) (func).

Name: personalized (see Psalm 147:4).

Name of Jesus: weapon against enemy (see Mark 16:17).

Napkin:
protective covering [clothes] (see Isaiah 50:3; Job 8:22; Psalm 30:11);

cleansing of things spoken [mouth] (func);

trying to wipe off lusts of your own accord (see Proverbs 30:20).

Narrow: way of the Lord/way less traveled (see Matthew 7:13–14); leads to life (see Matthew 7:14).

Nazi: evil bondage (char); demonic enemy (char).

Necklace: laced with your will/your will is a factor [neck: your willfulness] (see Themes/Body Parts/Neck; see Exodus 32:9 NIV; 33:3–5 NIV; Deuteronomy 9:6 NIV); pride in adornments (see Psalm 73:6).

Needle, eye: small, well-defined entrance/gate (see Matthew 19:24).

Needle, injection: work of the Great Physician [God] (see Psalm 147:3; Matthew 8:7; Mark 2:7; Luke 4:23; 5:31).

Nest: holding wealth (see Isaiah 10:14); place to live/home (see Proverbs 27:8; Matthew 13:32).

Nest, uncomfortable with stuff in it: time to "fly."

Net:
kingdom of God (see Matthew 13:47–48);

ministry (see Ezekiel 47:10; Luke 5:4–11);

livelihood; disciples (see John 21:11);

snare/trap/fear of man (see Psalm 10:9; 57:6; Ezekiel 12:13; 17:20; 32:1–3; Hosea 5:1; Habakkuk 1:15; Micah 7:2);

caught up with others (see Psalm 66:11);

to bring down (see Psalm 140:5; 141:9).

Net, dragnet: catches both [good and bad] (see Matthew 13:47–48).

Nettles: see General/Thorns.

Network: interaction (see 1 Kings 7:17).

New:
something beginning (see Hebrews 8:8);

strong (see Judges 15:13–15);

makes the previous obsolete (see Hebrews 8:13);

will not remember the previous (see Isaiah 65:17).

New Year: soon (new: current, year: time).

News, good: Word of God (see Hebrews 4:2).

Night:

darkness of the world; the dream is the plans of the enemy (see Revelation 22:5);

when beasts prowl/time of evil (see Psalm 104:20);

time when you need help/time of trial (see Psalm 63:6–7);

without God (see 1 Samuel 2:9);

no work can be done (see John 9:4).

Nomad: waiting to plunder (see Jeremiah 3:2).

Nonsense: things of the Spirit to non-Christians (see 1 Corinthians 2:14).

Noodles: strips and pieces of the Word (bread).

Noose: constrict and choke the life out of (func); plots to hang you up so as to keep you from God's blessings (see Job 18:9–11).

North:

God comes (see Job 37:22; Ezekiel 1:4);

coldness (see Job 37:9);

disaster (see Jeremiah 4:6; 10:22);

evil (see Proverbs 25:23; Jeremiah 1:13; 6:1).

Nostrils, stuff coming out: things you loathe/reject (see Numbers 11:20).

Numbered: limited time (see Daniel 5:26).

O

Oak:

strength (see Isaiah 2:13; 57:5; Ezekiel 27:6; Amos 2:9);

righteous person of God (see Isaiah 61:3);

lofty/high/magnificent (see Isaiah 61:3).

Oak, sacred: strong idols (see Isaiah 1:29–30).

Oak, twisted: voice of Lord striking (see Psalm 29:9 NIV).

Oasis: fulfilled promises (see Isaiah 35:1–10).

Oath: commitment/binding forever (see Hebrews 7:20–22); greater than the law (see Hebrews 7:28).

Obey: better than sacrifice (see 1 Samuel 15:22).

Obstacle: things keep us from the truth (see Isaiah 57:14; Galatians 5:7–11); stumble (see Jeremiah 6:21).

Obstacle, getting over/around: sign of effective Christian living (see 1 Thessalonians 3:1–4).

Obstinate: rebellion against God (see Isaiah 30:1).

Oil:

anointing (see Leviticus 8:30; 21:12; 1 Sam 10:1; 16:13; 1 Kgs 1:39; 2 Kgs 9:3, 6; Ps 23:5; 45:7; 89:20; 92:10; Joel 2:24; Hebrews 1:9);

honor (see Judges 9:9);

soothing/healing (see Isaiah 1:6; James 5:14);

make holy (see Exodus 30:22–29);

cleansing (see Luke 10:34);

blessing (see 2 Kings 4:2–7; Haggai 1:11);

of Jesus/Holy Spirit (see Matthew 25:4–10; 1 John 2:20);

harmony (see Psalm 133:1–2);

make shine (see Psalm 104:15);

Holy Spirit (see Luke 10:34; Acts 10:38; 1 John 2:20);

lift up (see Hebrews 1:9);

smooth words, but not sincere (see Psalm 55:21; Proverbs 5:3);

cannot hold onto (see Proverbs 27:16).

Oiled: slips through fingers (see Proverbs 27:16).

Ointment: cause to heal (see Ecclesiastes 7:1; Ezekiel 16:9).

Old: will soon disappear (see Hebrews 8:13).

Old way: past (see Hebrews 8:13); way of living before Christ entered your life (see Ephesians 4:22).

Olive:

honor (see Judges 9:9);

healthy and blessing of the Lord (see Deuteronomy 8:8; Job 29:6; Isaiah 57:9; Revelation 11:4);

food (see Exodus 23:11);

fuel (see Exodus 23:11; 27:20; Leviticus 24:2);

peace [dove carried olive branch to Noah] (see Genesis 8:11).

Olive leaf: renewal (see Genesis 8:11).

Olive oil: prosperity (see Job 29:6; Isaiah 57:9); see General/Oil.

Olive shoots: many (see Psalm 128:3).

Olive tree: anointed to serve God (see Zechariah 4:12–14).

Omega:

God the Father (see Revelation 1:8);

last (see Revelation 1:8);

end (see Revelation 21:6; 22:13).

Omen: a sign, not of God (see Deuteronomy 18:10).

Omnipotent: God/all powerful (see Luke 1:35; Acts 1:8).

Omnipresent: God/everywhere (see Psalm 139:7–10).

Omniscient: God/all knowing (see John 14:26; 1 Corinthians 2:10–11).

Onyx: of great value (see Job 28:16–19); truth and wisdom (see Exodus 28:9).

Oops: transgression that is not premeditated (rel).

Open: openly visible to others (see Daniel 4:20; Acts 10:40).

Opinions: [pinions] claws (see Deuteronomy 32:11).

Order: using discernment to perform God's will (see Exodus 27:21).

Ore: God's people (see Jeremiah 6:27 NIV—"and my people the ore").

Organic: something that was once alive (char).

Ornaments:

children (see Isaiah 49:17–18);

jewelry (see Jeremiah 2:32);

not in repentance nor mourning (see Exodus 33:4–6).

Outer space: see General/Flying.

Oven: hot (see Lamentations 5:10).

Overflow: more than enough/abundance (see Psalm 65:12).

Overlay: not real/not pure/not solid (see Proverbs 26:23).

Overnight mail: "overnight" communication/dreams (see Job 33:15–16; Joel 2:28); prayers [communications] (char).

P

Paid: getting what is deserved [earned] (see Proverbs 14:14).

Pain: problems, areas of oppression (see Revelation 2:9–10).

Pale gas: acronym for the seven deadly sins: pride, anger, lust, envy, gluttony, avarice, sloth.

Palm branches: praise and worship (see John 12:13).

Pan: vessel of offering (see Judges 6:19; 1 Samuel 2:13–14; Isaiah 66:20).

Paper: will disintegrate and break down (char).

Paper towels: cleaning or using temporary weak things (char).

Parable: picture words so that it is easier to receive/understand (see Matthew 13:10–13, 34–35).

Parachute: preparing to leave/to bail out (func).

Parade: walking to display themselves (see 1 Samuel 25:13; Isaiah 3:9); following each other (char).

Party: fellowship with others (see Ecclesiastes 8:15; Jeremiah 15:17; Luke 12:19).

Passport: credentials to authorize you to go that direction (see 2 Corinthians 5:17—those who are ambassadors for Christ [their government] are authorized to go in a "new" direction).

Pasture: place of salvation (see Psalm 37:3); life (see John 10:9).

Path: the direction you are going in life (see Numbers 22:32; Proverb 14:12).

Path, crooked: trials (see Lamentations 3:9); not the way of the Lord (see Proverbs 2:13–15; 3:6; 4:27; 21:8; Hebrews 12:13).

Path, old: where evil men have trod (see Job 22:15).

Path, straight: the right way (see Proverbs 9:15; 14:12).

Pattern: guideline (see Exodus 25:9); something to be imitated (see Philippians 3:17; Hebrews 8:5); conformity (see Romans 12:1–2).

Pay: reaping the benefits/penalties of; receiving what is due you (see Isaiah 65:6–7).

Peace:

Word of God (see Ephesians 2:14–22);

worldliness reconciled to God through Christ's blood (see Ephesians 2:14–16);

not the absence of something, but the presence of Jesus (see Matthew 10:34; Luke 10:6).

Peach:

fruit [results] are orange [dangerous] and yellow [fear] (see General/Fruit, see Themes/Colors/Orange, Yellow);

give evidence against another/accusations [as in impeach—slander/gossip] (play on words);

thing well-liked (as in "he's a peach").

Pearl:

wisdom/things of worth (see Matthew 7:6; 13:45–46);

kingdom of heaven (see Matthew 7:6; 13:45–46);

licentiousness; greed (see Revelation 17:4).

Pedals: power (as in powering a bicycle or tricycle).

Pee: getting rid of toxins (func); unclean things (see Deuteronomy 22:12–14; 2 Kings 18:27; Isaiah 36:12).

Peer pressure: bring destruction (see Proverbs 1:10–19).

Peg: carries a load (see Isaiah 22:25); secure to foundation (see Exodus 27:19).

Pen, feather tip: anointing to write (func).

Perfume:

anointing (see Matthew 26:7; John 12:3);

fragrant memories (see Song of Solomon 4:10);

day of burial (see Matthew 26:7–12; John 12:7);

worldly pleasure (see Isaiah 57:9).

Permit: allow (see Exodus 3:19).

Person changing appearance: person at an unstable time (char).

Pestilence: trouble from Lord (see Jeremiah 34:17).

Phone: message from God (see Jeremiah 33:3); prayer (see Psalm 20:9).

Phone booth: private communication with God in a public place (func).

Photo: memories of (char).

Picture: about the person in the picture (char); memories of (char).

Picture, black and white:

work of mankind (see Themes/Colors/Black, White);

bigotry issue (as in "black vs. white");

without doubts (as in "it is black and white").

Picture, family: about the family (char).

Picture of self as child: a reminder, prepared from childhood, for this hour (char).

Piers:

peers/people in one's own age group/friends (play on words);

obstacles (func);

direction (func).

Pigeonhole: stuck away and forgotten about (char).

Pilfer: steal slowly and lightly (see Titus 2:10).

Pilgrimage: journey to find the Lord (see Psalm 84:5).

Pillar:

leader (see Deuteronomy 31:15; 2 Chronicles 3:17; 23:13; Psalm 144:12; Galatians 2:9; 1 Timothy 3:15; Revelation 3:12);

leaders or strong people in God's church (see Galatians 2:9);

he who overcomes (see Revelation 3:12); he who carries the name of God; leader (see Nehemiah 9:12).

Pillar, iron: extremely strong leader of God (see Jeremiah 1:18).

Pine: grieves (see 1 Samuel 2:5).

Pinions: claws (see Deuteronomy 32:11).

Pinnacle: on top where it is easy to fall (see Matthew 4:5–6).

Pipes: conduit (see Zechariah 4:12).

Pipes, gold: conduit of God to others (see Zechariah 4:12).

Pisces: the fishes/the Church (see Ezekiel 29:4–5; Habakkuk 1:14; Matthew 4:19; 7:10; 12:40; 13:48–49; Luke 5:10); astrology, not of God (see Deuteronomy 4:19).

Pit:

obstacle that hinders one from going forward (see Psalm 57:6);

trap (see Ezekiel 19:8; Psalm 119:85; Proverbs 26:27);

depression (see Ezekiel 28:8);

darkness/away from God (see Psalm 40:2; 88:6; 94:13);

grave (see Ezekiel 31:15);

hell (see Matthew 13:24–50; Ezekiel 31:14).

Pit, dig: will fall into the "pit" dug for others (see Psalm 7:15, 16; 9:15; 10:2; 57:6; Proverbs 26:27; 28:10).

Pitch:

cover over (see Genesis 6:14);

make atonement for (see Genesis 6:14);

resists Word of God [water] (see Genesis 6:14).

Pitcher: pouring out to others (see Exodus 25:29; 37:16); power in simple, overlooked weapons (see Judges 7:15).

Pitchfork: to separate out and clean up (see Matthew 3:12).

Plague: judgment by God to get our attention (see Numbers 16:46; 25:9; Jeremiah 14:12; 15:2; 29:17; Ezekiel 14:19–21; 38:22).

Plant:

own home (see 2 Samuel 7:10);

place (see Jeremiah 31:27);

people's roots (see Psalm 44:2; Jeremiah 24:6);

begin (see 2 Kings 19:26; Isaiah 40:24);

people (see 2 Kings 19:26).

Plants, healing: immersed in the works [water] of God (see Ezekiel 47:12; Revelation 22:2).

Plastic: man-made.

Plate:

vessel to hold good offerings (see Numbers 4:7);

giving to others (see Exodus 37:16);

vessel to hold bad offerings (see Matthew 14:8–11).

Platter: a lot of spiritual food.

Play: actions of life.

Plow:

work to be done (see Luke 9:62);

turn up or uncover things (func);

preparation (see Ezekiel 36:9);

only for a season (see Isaiah 28:24).

Plumb line: God's measuring line of righteousness (see Isaiah 28:17); God's measure (see Isaiah 34:11); taking measure of/judge (see 2 Kings 21:13; Zechariah 4:10).

Plunder: reward (see Ezekiel 29:19).

Pocket: hidden in covering (see Psalm 74:11); carry (see Proverbs 17:23); bribe (see Proverbs 17:23).

Points: favor (as in "having or making points").

Poison: evil talk about someone/things speaking out (see James 3:8).

Pole, with snake on it: power of Jesus on cross that overcomes the snake [enemy] (see Numbers 21:8–9; John 3:14–15).

Ponder: to realize (see Isaiah 57:1).

Ponds, individual: individual anointing (see General/Water); selfishness (as in "water not being poured out to others").

Pool table: games being played (func).

Poor: areas of need (see Revelation 2:9); without God's wisdom and grace (see Revelation 3:17).

Pop: sweet things (char).

Popeye: eyes on "papa" (God).

Portal:

a place where God speaks to you (func);

place where there is easier access to heaven (func);

gate to heaven [Jacob's ladder—angels ascending and descending] (see Genesis 28:11–13; Ezekiel 3:22–24; Matthew 3:16–17);

access to second or third heaven.

Position, high: fools (see Ecclesiastes 10:6).

Pot:

holy (see Zechariah 1; 14:21);

vessel of offering (see Judges 6:19; 1 Samuel 2:13–14);

man (see Jeremiah 22:28);

power in simple, overlooked weapons (see Judges 7:15);

used in service (see Jeremiah 52:18).

Pot, boiling: God's scalding judgment (see Job 41:20, 31); disaster (Jeremiah 1:13–14).

Pot, broken: despised/unwanted person (see Jeremiah 22:28).

Pot, cooking: common vessel (see 2 Kings 4:41; Zechariah 14:20); city (Ezekiel 11:3).

Pot, cracked: someone who is dealing with hurts from their past (see General/Pot, see General/Vessel).

Pot, seething: evil (see Jeremiah 1:13).

Potato: "apple of the earth" [French meaning]; fruit from the earth (see General/Fruit).

Potential: expectation (see Hebrews 11:11).

Pottery: easily dashed to pieces (see Psalm 2:9; Revelation 2:27).

Pottery, broken: worthless (see Psalm 31:12; Isaiah 45:9; Jeremiah 22:28; 48:38–39).

Poverty: areas of need (see Revelation 2:9); loss of job (char).

Praise: scepter (see Psalm 60:7); man is judged by what he praises (see Proverbs 27:21).

Prayer: transfer of a burden (see Romans 8:20); weapon against the enemy (see Psalm 149:6–8; Matthew 18:18–19; Revelation 12:11).

Precious stones:

gifts and abilities (see Matthew 6:19–20);

licentiousness, greed (see Revelation 17:4);

wall (see Isaiah 54:12).

Pregnant: a new seed growing/new idea or new work (see Isaiah 26:17–18; James 1:15; Revelation 12:2); preparing for the birthing of a new thing (see Psalm 7:14; Isaiah 42:14; Micah 4:10; John 16:21).

Prenatal: aware of what's going on outside the mom (see Luke 1:44).

Present:

gift (see Genesis 24:53; 25:6; Numbers 18:11; 1 Corinthians 12);

current time period (see 2 Samuel 14:20; 1 Chronicles 9:18);

offer (see 1 Samuel 10:19; 1 Kings 11:12).

Preserve: loving-kindness and truth (see Psalm 61:7).

Press: perseverance (see Hosea 6:1–3); being hard pressed [pressured] in order to conform (see Philippians 1:23).

Prime: best (see Job 29:4).

Print: written (see Exodus 17:14; Numbers 5:23).

Priority: seeking to put first in your life the kingdom of heaven and righteousness (see Matthew 6:33).

Prize: follow Christ (see Philippians 3:14); Christ in you, the hope of glory; peace and joy in the Holy Spirit and Kingdom of God (see Colossians 1:27).

Profanity: disobey (see Jeremiah 34:16).

Promise: things not under the law (see Galatians 3:18).

Prophecy: What has been told to them by God (see 2 Chronicles 9:29; Jeremiah 49:34; 50:1); what they have not heard, they will understand (see Isaiah 52:15).

Prophets: Abel to Zechariah (see Luke 11:51); to speak things from God (see Deuteronomy 18:21–22; Mark 10:37).

Prostrate: humbled (see 1 Chronicles 29:20).

Protocol: approach authority in a certain way (see Esther 4:11; 5:2; 8:4).

Prune: cut back to allow healthy growth (see Leviticus 25:3; Isaiah 5:6; John 15:2).

Pruning shears: Bible (see John 15:3).

Public spectacle: conflict for learning (see Hebrews 10:33).

Pump: brings water [Word of God] out of the well [deep places of Word of God] (char).

Purchase: see General/Buy.

Purse:
life/identity (as in "identification cards");
finances/financial support (see Proverbs 1:14; Matthew 10:9; Luke 10:4; 22:35–36);
favor (see Proverbs 1:14; Matthew 10:9);
treasures (see Luke 12:33).

Q

Quality: compassionate, gracious, forgiving, slow to anger, faithful, just, abounding in love (see Nehemiah 9:17–33; 1 Corinthians 3:13; 1 Peter 3:4).

Quarry: parents (see Isaiah 51:1–2); source; origin (see Isaiah 51:1).

Quench: stopped (see 2 Chronicles 34:25).

Question, hard: period of testing (see 1 Kings 10:1).

Quicksand: the more you struggle, the more stuck and entangled you are (char); getting in over your head (char).

Quiet: inactive (see Psalm 83:1).

Quiver: where God keeps His people until He needs us (see Isaiah 49:2); where the gift of children are kept (see Psalm 127:3–3).

R

Rabble: craving things not of God (see Numbers 11:4).

Race:
competition (see 1 Corinthians 9:24; 2 Timothy 2:5);
one's endurance throughout life; life's struggles (see Ecclesiastes 9:11; Acts 20:24; 2 Timothy 4:7);
fast-paced life (see Job 39:24; Nahum 2:4).

Race, on sand: life endurance on a poor foundation (see General/Race).

Radiant: glory of God (see Psalm 50:2; Ezekiel 43:2).

Radio: unceasing message (func).

Rafter, sagging: laziness (see Ecclesiastes 10:18).

Rags, filthy: actions (see Isaiah 64:6).

Rail: support (func); stay on course (func); boundary (see Deuteronomy 19:14; 27:17).

Railroad: being "railroaded"/to act certain way (play on words); see Themes/Transportation/Trains.

Rain:
teaching of righteousness (see Deuteronomy 32:2; Psalm 19:2; Hosea 6:3);
God's blessing (see 2 Samuel 1:21; Psalm 68:8–9; Jeremiah 3:3; Haggai 1:11; Zechariah 14:17–18; Matthew 5:45);
presence of God (see Psalm 68:8–9; 72:6; Hosea 6:3);
sustenance from the Lord (see Psalm 72:6; 147:8; Isaiah 55:10);
trials/difficulties (see Matthew 5:45; 7:24–27).

Rain, barrel: life's difficulties that can be drawn upon to help others (see Proverbs 20:5)

Rain, gray: trials (see Matthew 7:25–27); plans of the enemy.

Rain, hard: hard trials (see Matthew 5:45; 7:24–27); judgment of God's wrath (see Judges 5:4–5; Ezekiel 13:11; Isaiah 28:2; 29:6; 30:30).

Rain, in harvest: not fitting (see Proverbs 26:1).

Rain, in spring: God's favor (see Proverbs 16:15).

205

Rain, white: blessing from Lord (see 2 Samuel 1:21; Psalm 68:8–9; Jeremiah 3:3; Matthew 5:45).

Rainbow:

Lord's covenant (see Genesis 9:9–17);

calling (see Genesis 9:9–17; Ezekiel 1:28);

encircling the Lord (see Revelation 4:3; 10:1).

Raisins: strength/sustenance (see Song of Solomon 2:5).

Rampart: faithfulness (see Psalm 91:4); strength (see Psalm 48:12).

Rank: greater measure (see 1 Samuel 18:5).

Ransom: to redeem out of the hands of those stronger than the ransomed ones (see Jeremiah 31:11); payment for bad choices [yours or theirs] (see Matthew 20:28; 1 Timothy 2:6).

Rape: exert power over (see 2 Samuel 13:14; Zechariah 14:2).

Rash: actions or words that are hasty and without forethought (see Psalm 106:33).

Rat race: a choice made each morning (as in "working in the rat race").

Rations: preparation (see Jeremiah 40:5).

Raw: unprepared (see 1 Samuel 2:15); without trial by fire (see Exodus 12:9); rubbed sore (see Ezekiel 29:18).

Rays, flashing: power of God (see Habakkuk 3:4).

Razor: plotting (see Psalm 52:2); humiliating (see Isaiah 7:20).

Reap: harvest/receive general results (see 1 Samuel 8:12; John 4:36; Revelation 14:15).

Reap, what you sow: to receive a result because of a deed done (see 2 Samuel 3:39; 12:10–11; Job 42:7–9; Jeremiah 50:29; Ecclesiastes 10:8; Ephesians 6:8); to bring upon yourself the judgment you planned for others (see Psalm 7:15–16; 9:15; 10:2; 57:6; Proverbs 26:27; 28:10; Matthew 7:1–2; Galatians 6:7–8; 2 Thessalonians 1:6).

Rebuke: loving correction (see Revelation 3:19).

Reception: interface and communion (see 1 Thessalonians 1:9).

Recoil: ready to strike (see Psalm 54:5).

Recompense: get what you lost and also what you missed (see Isaiah 35:4).

Redeem: to pay what is due (see 2 Samuel 7:23).

Red light: stop (func); revealing anointing (char [red may represent anointing; light may represent something being revealed]); (see Exodus 29:21—blood [red]; 1 Samuel 16:12—"he was ruddy [red] . . . and the Lord said, "Arise, anoint him"; Zechariah 4:2–14—lampstands show the anointed).

Reed: individual/one (see Matthew 11:7; 12:20); see General/Stick.

Reed, battered: one who is hurt by life (see Matthew 12:20).

Reed, in water: to sway/to go back and forth/to be inconsistent (see 1 Kings 14:15).

Reed, shaken by wind: one who is led by teachings that come and go (see Matthew 11:7).

Reeds:

hiding place (see Psalm 68:30); splinters when grabbed (see Isaiah 36:6);

disciplines or hurts others (see Proverbs 13:24);

when leaned on, it breaks; therefore, it will hurt those who depend on it (see Ezekiel 29:6–7);

to bow before/to submit (see Isaiah 58:5);

see General/Stick.

Reef: hidden danger (see Jude 12).

Reel: to stagger (see Psalm 107:27; Isaiah 24:20).

Refined: a process that brings out impurities (see Proverbs 27:21); being put through trials that will teach us things (see Psalm 66:10).

Reflector: a person who reflects (see Ecclesiastes 9:1; 2 Timothy 2:7); Christian leader (char).

Register: list of those assigned to partake in the activity (see Psalm 87:6); to record events (see Numbers 1:18; Psalm 87:6; Luke 2:5).

Registration: census (see Luke 2:1).

Reincarnation: false belief (see Hebrews 9:23–28).

Reins: control (see James 1:26); to allow movement (see Job 10:1).

Religion:
try to *approve* the will of God (see Acts 25:19);
try to *improve on* the will of God (see Acts 26:5);
keep oneself from being polluted by the world and look after distressed widows and orphans (see James 1:27).

Remember: grant favor toward (see 1 Samuel 1:19).

Remnant:
those saved by grace/God's people (see Jeremiah 31:7; Romans 9:27; 11:5);
will take root and grow (see 2 Kings 19:30);
those remaining after (see Isaiah 10:21).

Remote-controlled: manipulation from a distance (func).

Remove: die (see 1 Kings 9:7).

Repay: to give good for evil (see 2 Samuel 16:12).

Repent: a change of mind that leads to a turning away from (see Acts 3:19; Revelation 3:19); replacing an old way of thinking with a better way of thinking (see Acts 20:21).

Requirements: a process of abandonment to the Lord (see 1 Peter 1:13–14).

Rest: to die and be buried (see 1 Kings 11:21; 2 Chronicles 32:33); peace that comes from knowing you are in God's care (see Matthew 11:28–30; Hebrews 3:11; 4:3–5).

Revelation:
the visible appearance of Jesus (see Revelation 1:1);
to understand the words/thoughts of God through Jesus and the Holy Spirit (see Ephesians 3:5; Revelation 1:1);
belongs to us and our children (see Deuteronomy 29:29; Matthew 11:25).

Reward: getting what is given by grace [not works] (see Proverbs 14:14); result (see 2 Samuel 4:10; Psalm 62:12).

Ribbon: reminder (see Numbers 15:37–40; Deuteronomy 6:8); tied around [notice what the ribbon is tied around, as well as the color] (see Themes/Colors).

Ribbon, scarlet: lips (see Song of Solomon 4:3).

Riches:
needs are met in an overabundant manner (see Revelation 2:9);
full of God and His grace and wisdom (see Ephesians 1:18; 3:8; Colossians 1:27; Hebrews 11:26; Revelation 3:17–18);
financial plenty (see Revelation 3:17).

Riddle: question (see Psalm 49:4).

Ridge: dangerous divider (see Jeremiah 48:28); on the edge (see Luke 16:26).

Right:
wisdom: (see Ecclesiastes 10:2);
authority (see Genesis 48:18; Hebrews 9:1; 10:12; 12:2);
power (see Exodus 15:6);
right with God (see Matthew 25:33);
turning aside (see 2 Chronicles 34:2).

Righteous:
see God in His beauty (see Isaiah 33:17);
is beautiful (see Isaiah 62:3);
provides others with health, nourishment, oil (see Hosea 14:6).

Right, hand:
the "right hand of fellowship"/to be in good fellowship with another (see Matthew 20:20–23; Colossians 3:1);
approval (see Galatians 2:9; Hebrews 8:1);
Jesus (see Mark 14:62; Ephesians 1:20);
God's works (see Exodus 15:6);
offensive (see 2 Corinthians 6:7).

Ring:
covenant (see Genesis 41:42; Haggai 2:23; Luke 15:20–23);

chosen one/promise (see Genesis 41:42; Haggai 2:23);

sin (*Lord of the Rings*).

Ring, nose: finery (see Isaiah 3:21).

Ring, signet: important and valuable person (see Genesis 41:42; Jeremiah 22:24); favor (see Genesis 41:42; Jeremiah 22:24).

Risk: faith (see Matthew 14:28–30).

River:

movement of God (see Psalm 46:4; Revelation 22:1);

sustenance of God (see Psalm 36:7–8; 46:4);

going to the lowest place (char);

being swept away by the enemy (Revelation 12:15).

River, frozen: the Word of God—cold/ does not flow [e.g., a legalistic/ religious setting where the Word of God is being restricted and without enforcement of the second greatest commandment—love others as yourself] (see Matthew 22:30; Psalm 147:17).

Road: pathway of life; the direction your life is going (see Isaiah 57:14; Jeremiah 31:21).

Road, crooked: life's bends (see Luke 3:4–5).

Road, rough: life's roughness (see Luke 3:5).

Road, signs: directions (see Jeremiah 31:21); directions toward God (see Jeremiah 31:21).

Road, smooth: way of the Lord (see Isaiah 26: 7–8; Luke 3:5).

Road, straight: way of the Lord (see Isaiah 40:3; Matthew 3:3; Luke 3:5; Hebrews 12:13).

Roaming charges: repercussions of sin (char; play on words).

Roar, lion: a king's command (see Proverbs 20:2); has prey (see Amos 3:4).

Roar, of rushing waters: voice of God (see Ezekiel 43:2).

Rob: to pounce with evil intent on the unsuspecting (see Judges 9:25).

Robe:

ruling/authority (see Psalm 93:1; Ezekiel 26:16);

royalty (see 2 Chronicles 18:9; Matthew 27:28–31);

to grab hold of (see Zechariah 8:23);

to be immersed in (see Psalm 93:1; 104:1–2).

Rock:

Jesus (see Deuteronomy 32:4; Psalm 28:1; 92:15; 94:22; Isaiah 51:1–2; Daniel 2:45; Matthew 7:24–28; Luke 20:17; 1 Corinthians 10:4; 1 Peter 2:7–8);

God (see 1 Samuel 2:2; 6:18; 2 Samuel 22:2, 32, 47; 23:3; Psalm 18:2; 31:2–3; 62:2–7; 78:35; 92:15);

belief in the Word of God (see Luke 8:13);

strong safety (see Numbers 24:21);

things dependent upon (see Deuteronomy 32:31, 37; Job 19:24; Psalm 40:2);

refuge (see Judges 15:13; Psalm 61:2–3);

common (see 2 Chronicles 9:27);

your origin, parentage, source (see Isaiah 51:1);

unable to nourish you (see Matthew 7:9);

offense (see Psalm 91:12; 1 Peter 2:8);

hard place (see Jeremiah 23:29);

hard and cold (see Jeremiah 5:3; Ezekiel 11:19; 36:26);

gods and idols (see Deuteronomy 32:37).

Rocks, pile: barred the way (see Lamentations 3:9).

Rocky: no root (see Matthew 13:20–21).

Rod:

strength (see Psalm 23:4);

strength of God (see Psalm 23:4);

to comfort/to watch over (see Psalm 23:4; Jeremiah 1:11);

inheritance (see Jeremiah 10:16);

good results (see Isaiah 28:27);

punishment of sin (see Psalm 89:32);

violence (see Ezekiel 7:11).

Rod, budded: fresh, new violence (see Ezekiel 7:10).

Roller coaster:

the ups and downs of life (char);

emotional instability (char);

unfaithfulness (char);

wavering/double-minded thinking (see Psalm 119:113; James 1:8; 4:8);

unstable life and spirit (see James 1:8; 4:8);

manic-depressive (char);

trials (char).

Roof, hidden: something hidden that will wreck you (see Jude 12).

Roof, leaks: laziness (see Ecclesiastes 10:18); a contentious woman (see Proverbs 19:13; 27:15).

Root:

foundation/beginning (see Psalm 80:9; Isaiah 11:1; 40:24; 53:12; Matthew 3:10; Ephesians 3:17; Colossians 2:7; 1 Timothy 6:10; Hebrews 12:15);

Jesus (see Colossians 2:6–7; Revelation 22:16);

standing firm in times of testing (see Mark 4:17; Luke 8:13; Colossians 2:6);

ancestors (see Job 18:16–19);

support system (char).

Root, pulled up: removed (see Matthew 15:13); uprooted (see Deuteronomy 28:63) without a support system (char).

Root, rot: where wicked people get their support (see Isaiah 5:24).

Roots of trees: trees are God's Church; the root is Jesus.

Roots, shallow soil: easily forgotten when gone (see Job 8:16–18).

Roots, spread: to reach out for sustenance (see Job 29:19).

Rope: in service to/committed to (see Numbers 4:26; Psalm 119:61; Ezekiel 3:25); not quickly broken (see Ecclesiastes 4:12; Ezekiel 4:8).

Rose: glory of God (see Song of Solomon 2:1; Isaiah 35:1–2).

Rot: wrath of God (see Hosea 5:12); decaying (char).

Round: see General/Circle.

Royal: of God/of Jesus Christ (see Isaiah 28:5; Hebrews 2:9).

Rubber: man-made things of the world (char); will bounce right back (func).

Rubble: destruction (see 2 Kings 19:25; Jeremiah 26:18; Ezekiel 26:4; Daniel 2:5; Micah 1:6; 3:12).

Ruby: red/ruddy (see Lamentations 4:7); a fine jewel; of great value (see Job 28:18–19).

Rudder:

steers a large vessel (see James 3:4);

something small controlling something large (see James 3:3–4);

Holy Spirit.

Ruins:

breaks in the walls (see Ezekiel 13:5);

the judgment of God (see Jeremiah 9:11; Ezekiel 35:4; Matthew 24:2);

destruction from the enemy (see Psalm 74:3; Micah 3:12).

Ruler:

leader (see 1 Chronicles 11:2; Psalm 76:12; Matthew 2:6);

from God (see Zechariah 10:4);

Christ (see Isaiah 28:5; Revelation 3:14);

one who controls (see Daniel 9:25);

taking measure of or judging (see 1 Samuel 5:8; 2 Kings 21:13; Isaiah 28:17; Haggai 2:1–13; Revelation 11:1–2);

those who exert strong, negative control; bad spirit (see Ephesians 6:12).

Rumor: things said that are often not true (see John 21:21–23).

Rust: destroys (see Matthew 6:19); will consume (see Matthew 6:19–20; James 5:3).

Rusty gate, oil hinges: rusty in prayer [knees: hinges] to open the gate to reach God; need for practice [oiling the hinges] in prayer.

S

Sackcloth: repent (see Matthew 11:21; Luke 10:13); in mourning (see Genesis 37:34; 2 Samuel 3:31; Lamentations 2:10); humbled (see 1 Kings 20:31–32; 2 Kings 19:2; 1 Chronicles 21:16).

Sage: wise (see Jeremiah 18:18).

Sagittarius: archer (char); Jesus Christ (see Psalm 45:5–6; Revelation 6:2); astrology, not of God (see Deuteronomy 4:19).

Saints: people of God (see Daniel 7:27).

Salt:

Christians who bring out the flavor of God's Word (see Matthew 5:13; Colossians 4:6);

grace—speaking or doing things tastefully (see Colossians 4:6);

a little here and there to flavor, but not too much (char);

a covenant or contract (see Leviticus 2:13; 2 Chronicles 13:5);

cleansing (see 2 Kings 2:19–22);

fiery trials (see Mark 9:49);

without future growth (see Judges 9:45).

Salt, land: an area laid waste (see Jeremiah 17:6; 48:9 NIV).

Salt, pillar: looking back to old ways; unwilling to let go (see Genesis 19:26).

Salt, pit: wasteland (see Zephaniah 2:9).

Salt, rubbed: preserved; tended to (see Ezekiel 16:4).

Salt, without flavor: of no use (see Matthew 5:13).

Salvation:

redeemed by the Lord (see Isaiah 56:1; Ephesians 1:13; 2:1–9);

saved by the washing of regeneration through Jesus (see Titus 3:5);

reserved and beyond the reach of change [salvation cannot be lost] (see 1 Peter 1:3–4).

Salve: healing (see Revelation 3:18).

Sanctuary: Christ (see Isaiah 8:14).

Sand:

numerous/countless (see Joshua 11:4; Judges 7:12; 2 Samuel 17:11; 1 Kings 4:20, 29; Job 29:18; Psalm 78:27; Jeremiah 15:8; Habakkuk 1:9; 11:12; Revelation 20:8);

numerous people (see Genesis 22:17; 1 Samuel 13:5; Isaiah 10:22; Hosea 1:10; Revelation 20:8);

place without measure (see Hosea 1:10);

improper foundation; shifts with [the tides] public demand or popularity (see Matthew 7:24–27);

boundary/shores (see Jeremiah 5:22);

heavy/weighty (see Job 6:3; Proverbs 27:3);

burden (see Proverbs 27:3).

Sand grains: multiplication (see Romans 9:27).

Sandal, given to another: a contractual agreement (see Ruth 4:7).

Sapphire: brilliance (see Lamentations 4:7); of great value (see Job 28:16–19); held back (see Acts 5:2).

Sash: profitable for nothing (see Jeremiah 13:10–11).

Saved: brought out of death and into life; brought out of sin and into righteousness (see Ephesians 2:8).

Saw: something seen; to cut through ambiguity (char).

Scales:

to look honestly at (see Job 31:6);

to evaluate (see Job 6:2; Daniel 5:27);

staying balanced; without excess (see Proverbs 16:11);

no favoritism/just (see Proverbs 16:11; Colossians 3:25);

pride (see Job 41:15–17).

Scales, uneven: unequal (char); God detests (see Proverbs 20:10, 23).

Scarecrow: cannot speak (see Jeremiah 10:5); must be carried (char).

Scars: previous wounds that are healed, but still remembered (see Leviticus 13:23, 28).

Scatter: judgment for not obeying God's laws (see Ezekiel 20:33–34); to spread in all directions (see Ezekiel 12:14–15).

Scepter:

of royalty (see Numbers 21:18; Esther 4:11);

of the Lord (see Genesis 49:10; Numbers 24:17; Hebrews 1:8);

to rule others (see Psalm 60:7; Hebrews 1:8; Revelation 12:5; 19:15).

Scepter, broken: loss of control (see Jeremiah 48:17).

Scepter, iron: to rule with strength (see Psalm 2:9).

School, cannot unlock locker: something that is trying to stop you from getting spiritual tools (char); see Themes/Places/School.

Scissors: Bible/Word of God (see John 15:3).

Scorpio: the scorpion (rel); conflict with the lawless one/Antichrist (see Psalm 144:1 [speaks of our battles with the enemies of the Lord]; Revelation 19); astrology, not of God (see Deuteronomy 4:19).

Scream, and nothing comes out: circumstances choking off passion for prayer (char); not praying enough (char).

Scripture: not given by a writer (mankind), but by God (see Colossians 2:17; 1 Timothy 1:7–10; 2 Peter 1:20–21).

Scroll: remembrance (see Malachi 3:16); tough Word of God (see Ezekiel 2:9).

Scroll, flying: judgment against thieves and liars (see Zechariah 5:1–4).

Sea:
humanity/people (see Psalm 78:53; Matthew 13:47–49; Revelation 20:13);
deep (see Lamentations 2:13; Revelation 4:6);
restless, upheaval (see Revelation 21:1);
oceans (see Revelation 16:3);
wide (see Job 11:9);
earth (see Matthew 12:40);
roars (see Jeremiah 6:23);
rage (see Isaiah 17:12);
rebellion against God (see Revelation 21).

Sea level: level where you can "see what's going on around you" (play on words); level of tumultuousness; being rocked by waves (char).

Sea of glass: throne of God (see Revelation 4:6; 15:2).

Seal:
identify (see Ephesians 1:13; Song of Solomon 8:6–7);
set apart (see Ephesians 1:13–14; Revelation 7:3);

binding agreement (see Nehemiah 9:38; Ephesians 4:30).

Season:
when the time is right (see Ecclesiastes 3:1–8; 9:12; 2 Timothy 4:2);
time period in which you have grace to do something (see Ezekiel 34:26; 2 Timothy 4:2);
indicates an end and a beginning (see Ecclesiastes 3:1–8; 9:12).

Seat: see General/Chair.

Secret: false teaching (see Revelation 2:24).

Secret service: service to the Lord that is behind the scenes (rel).

See: to understand (see Numbers 24:3; Isaiah 6:9; Luke 10:23; Revelation 3:18); to perceive (see Isaiah 6:9; Matthew 13:14).

Seed(s):
Christ (see Genesis 3:15; Jeremiah 2:21; Galatians 3:16–19);
descendants (see Genesis 3:15; Galatians 3:16);
faith (see Matthew 13; 17:20);
Word of God (see Isaiah 55:11; Matthew 12:1–23; 13:3–11; 17; Mark 4:14; Luke 8:11);
will take root and grow; results in a harvest (see 2 Kings 19:30; Proverbs 14:12; Jeremiah 2:19);
the beginning point (see Isaiah 55:10; James 3:18).

Seed, enemy: weeds/messages of Satan (see Matthew 13:25).

Seed, good: children of God (see Matthew 13:38).

Seed, grow: blessing (see Zechariah 8:23).

Seed, mustard: small beginning blessed by God that grows to a big harvest (see Mark 4:31).

Seed, pounded: crushed to prepare for feeding others (see Isaiah 28:27–28); making ready for use (func).

Seek: crave, pursue and go after (see Deuteronomy 4:29; 2 Chronicles 7:14; Matthew 6:33).

Senseless: without knowledge (see Jeremiah 10:14).

Sensor: to censor; tools of worship (see 2 Chronicles 26:19); taking measure of (func).

Sentence: written against (see Psalm 149:9).

Serum: whey of milk (char); watery healing fluid; word that is healing (func).

Seven years: to cancel the debts of fellow Christians (see Deuteronomy 15:1–3).

Sew, piece: to sow in peace [raising a harvest of righteousness] (play on words) (see James 3:18).

Sex:

to join self with; to be in union with (see Numbers 25:1–3; Song of Solomon 7:10);

to understand (old form of "*knew* his wife"); to come into close agreement with; to be united (see Genesis 4:1, 17; Revelation 2:22);

a covenant of intimacy; to share a close or personal thing with (see Ezekiel 16:8);

sexual intimacy (see Genesis 4:1);

to degrade oneself (see Ezekiel 16:25–26);

an abuse of authority [as in rape] (func);

sinful indulgence (see Ephesians 4:19).

Sex, abuse: abuse of authority; control [as in rape] (func).

Sex, relation with husband in church: intimacy with Holy Spirit (rel).

Shackles: bound (see Psalm 149:8; Nahum 1:13).

Shade: the Lord (see Isaiah 25:4); under the protection of whatever or whoever the tree represents (see Isaiah 30:3; see General/Tree).

Shadow:

to vaguely point toward or foretell something (see Colossians 2:17; Hebrews 8:5; 10:1);

covering ("I have covered you with the shadow of My hand," see Isaiah 51:16); to overshadow (see Psalm 63:7; Matthew 17:5);

denominations and splinter groups (see Colossians 2:16–17);

healing (see Acts 5:15);

protection (see Psalm 17:8; 57:1; 62:7; 91:1–2; Isaiah 51:16; Lamentations 4:20; Hosea 14:7);

in the vicinity of (see Psalm 23:4);

without hope (see 1 Chronicles 29:15; Isaiah 59:9);

concealed (see Job 40:22; Psalm 11:2; 57:1; Isaiah 16:3; 49:2);

fleeting (see Psalm 144:4; Ecclesiastes 6:12);

time to rest (see Job 7:2);

unable to see clearly (see Ecclesiastes 6:12);

time of darkness (see Nehemiah 13:19).

Shadow, evening: soon to be dark (see Psalm 102:11); time to rest (see Job 7:2).

Shadow, no: there is no darkness in them (char).

Shadow, people: people without the Lord (see Luke 1:79); wicked people/demonic (see Job 34:22; Psalm 11:2).

Shadow, shifting: change (see Job 8:9; 14:2; James 1:17).

Shadow box: an unknown issue [box—an area of interest; (char of shadow)]; shadowy things, possibly not of the Lord (char; see General/Shadow).

Shake: judgment of God (see Haggai 2:6, 21); to remove things that can be removed (see Hebrews 12:26–29).

Shalom: harmony, peace, abundance, delight, fulfillment, completeness (see Psalm 133:1).

Shamrock: Ireland/Irish (cultural or national issue—rel); pretending to be of Christ [sham—fake, rock—Christ] (play on words).

Shave: cleanse (see Numbers 8:7).

Shears: the Lord's Word and ways (see John 15:1–3).

Sheaves: people (see Genesis 37:7); sustenance (see Ruth 2:7–15; Job 24:10; Amos 2:13).

Sheet: death, salvation (see Isaiah 25:6–9); cover (see Isaiah 25:7).

Shell: protection (func); empty (char).

Shield:

Jesus/God (see Genesis 15:1; Deuteronomy 33:29; 2 Samuel 22:31; Psalm 18:2; 18:30; 28:7; 59:11; 119:114);

faith (see Psalm 91:4; Ephesians 6:16); protect (see Genesis 15:1; Psalm 89:18); hide or cover up (see Exodus 40:21; Deuteronomy 13:8 NIV).

Shine: of Christ (see Exodus 34:29; Ephesians 5:14).

Shipwreck: damaged by things that come against your faith (see 1 Timothy 1:19).

Shirt:

covering over one's heart (func; see Ephesians 6:14; 1 Thessalonians 5:8);

sin or righteousness (see Psalm 109:17–19, 29; Isaiah 59:17);

personal items (see Matthew 5:40; Luke 6:29).

Shoe, remove another's: basic service to another (see Mathew 3:11); causing another to lose their peace (see Ephesians 6:15).

Shoe, given to another: contractual agreement (see Ruth 4:7).

Shoe, heel: betrayal by someone (see Genesis 25:26–34).

Shoe, heavy boots: spiritual warfare (see Ephesians 6:12–17); Gospel (see Ephesians 6:12–17).

Shoe, missing sole: soul exposed (play on words); losing coverings (func).

Shoe, off:

lost peace/without peace or harmony (see Jeremiah 2:25; Ephesians 6:12–17);

upset (see Deuteronomy 25:9–10); unprepared (func).

Shoe, throw: to cause property to be yours; ownership (see Psalm 60:8).

Shoes:

your individual peacefulness (see Ephesians 6:15);

preparation (see Ephesians 6:13–15);

comfort zone (see Exodus 3:5);

protection in your "walk" [way of living] (see Exodus 3:5; Ephesians 6:15).

Shooting star: rises or is promoted quickly but does not last (char).

Shoots, plant: people (see Isaiah 60:21); that from which growth comes (see Isaiah 11:1; 53:2).

Shore: place of decision (see Matthew 13:48).

Shortsighted: see General/Blind.

Shorts: being casual (func); not taking things seriously (char).

Shovel: used in service (see Jeremiah 52:18); to clean out (see Matthew 3:12).

Shower:

blessings (see Jeremiah 3:3);

cleansing rain (see Ezekiel 34:26);

place of cleansing before God (see Exodus 40:30–32; Jeremiah 3:3).

Shrine: high place (see Leviticus 26:30; 1 Kings 14:23; 2 Kings 23:13–16; 2 Chronicles 20:33; Isaiah 2:14; 40:4; Jeremiah 7:31–32; 32:35; Ezekiel 6:3–4; 43:7); spiritual region (see Ezekiel 16:24).

Shroud:

salvation (see Isaiah 25:6–9);

to enfold (see Isaiah 25:7);

in darkness (see Job 19:8; Ecclesiastes 6:4);

curse of death (see Job 40:13).

Shuttle: swift (see Job 7:6).

Sick:

sick in the spirit [not having the Holy Spirit within your personal spirit] (see Psalm 149:4; Matthew 9:1–12);

the judgment of God (see Numbers 14:11–12; 16:46; 2 Samuel 12:15);

the result of bad choices (see 2 Samuel 12:15; 13:2; Psalm 107:17);

in need of healing [spiritual healing] (see Exodus 23:25; Ezekiel 34:4; Matthew 4:23; 8:16; Mark 6:13; Luke 9:2).

Sickle:

results/harvest (see Mark 4:29; Revelation 14:14–19);

used to bring about or harvest (see Deuteronomy 16:9);

separation (see Revelation 14:14–16);

Russia or relating to Russian culture (rel to nation).

Side: a happening occurring at the same time (rel); adjacent to you (see 1 Samuel 20:21).

Sift: to sort or separate (see Luke 22:31).

Sight: to see physically (see 2 Corinthians 5:7).

Sign:

a message/communication (see Genesis 1:14; Luke 1:22);

remembrance of direction (see Exodus 3:12; Numbers 16:38; Joshua 4:6–7; Psalm 74:4);

to convince//bear a message; proof of something (see Genesis 1:14–16; Exodus 4:8–9; Judges 6:17; Isaiah 7:10–11; Matthew 2:38–39; 12:38–39);

claim authorship (see Job 31:35);

symbol; God testifying to us of His will (see Ezekiel 12:6; Hebrews 2:4);

warning (see Numbers 17:10).

Silent: inactive (see Psalm 83:1).

Silver:

offering (see Numbers 7:13, 19, 25, 31);

has come through refinement/trials (see Psalm 66:10);

money/wealth/great value (see Exodus 12:35; Job 28:15–19; Proverbs 2:4; Isaiah 60:9; Matthew 10:9);

kingdom/leadership/royalty (see Daniel 2:39);

redemption (see Psalm 68:13; Matthew 27:6);

legalism (see Psalm 115:4; 135:15; Jeremiah 6:30; Acts 19:24);

betrayal/blood money (see Matthew 27:6–9).

Silver, building with: good works erected on Jesus' foundation (see 1 Corinthians 3:12).

Silver, corroded: your wealth is diminishing or where you have placed your priorities is not healthy (see James 5:3).

Silver, metal:

ruling crown (see Psalm 68:13; Zechariah 6:10–11);

wealth (see Genesis 13:2; 24:35);

redemption (see Genesis 20:16);

salvation (see Malachi 3:3; Acts 3:6);

spiritual adultery/idolatry (see Psalm 115:4; 135:15; Acts 19:24);

reasons for betrayal (see Matthew 26:15; 27:3).

Silver, rejected: people the Lord rejected (see Jeremiah 6:30).

Sin: walk in wilderness/trials (see Leviticus 16:20–22); understands and knows the right thing to do and does not do it (see John 9:41; James 4:17).

Sin, generational: fallout to the third and fourth generation (see Exodus 34:7).

Singing: praise or worship (see Judges 5:3; Psalm 57:7; 61:8; 71:22; 92:4–5).

Sink: place of cleansing before God (see Exodus 40:30–32; Psalm 60:8); no foothold (see Psalm 69:2).

Sitting:

rest in the presence of God (see 2 Samuel 7:18; 1 Chronicles 17:16; Luke 10:39);

peace (see Zechariah 3:10);

in relationship with (see Judges 6:11; 19:6; Jeremiah 15:17);

place of authority (see Exodus 6:12–29 [the head/authority of a group may be represented in a dream by one seated at the head of a table]; 1 Kings 2:12–19);

weariness (see Nehemiah 1:4).

Skateboard: risky, individual, self-propelled work on tiny tires [little spirituality] (char; see General/Tire).

Skeleton: dry bones/dried up (see Jeremiah 8:1–2); without God's life/dead (see Ezekiel 37:1).

Skill: acquired understanding received as a gift (see Daniel 9:22).

Skin, shriveled on bones: emaciated (see Lamentations 4:8).

Skin, soft and renewed: restored (see Job 33:25).

Skirt: responsible for others/allowing others to obtain a hold (see Jeremiah 2:34; Zechariah 8:23); to avoid an issue (play on words: "to skirt an issue").

Skirt, lifted up: to expose oneself (see Nahum 3:5).

Skirt, over face: shame (see Jeremiah 13:26).

Sky:

things high in the Spirit (see Matthew 11:23; Luke 10:15);

God's arena (see Matthew 11:23; Luke 10:15);

first heaven—nature's arena around earth that will keep changing (see Hebrews 1:10–13; Revelation 20:11).

Sky, red at evening: fair weather/good things ahead (see Matthew 16:2).

Sky, red at morning: stormy weather/rough times ahead (see Matthew 16:3).

Sky roof: covering of the Holy Spirit (see Luke 10:15).

Sledge hammer: too harsh for getting good results (see Isaiah 28:27); false testimony against someone (see Proverbs 25:18).

Sleeping:

rest (see Psalm 127:2; 132:4);

not paying attention (see Psalm 121:3–4; Isaiah 5:27; Matthew 13:25; Ephesians 5:14; 1 Thessalonians 5:6);

not praying (see Luke 22:46);

has died and is in the Spirit (see John 11:11; 1 Thessalonians 4:15–16; 5:10; 2 Peter 3:4);

see Themes/Actions/Sleep.

Sleepless: meditating on God's promise (see Psalm 119:148).

Sleet: destroy sustenance (see Psalm 78:47).

Slime: worldly garbage (char).

Slip: fall away from (see Psalm 66:9); go into sin (see Psalm 17:5; 73:2–3; 121:3).

Slippery: easy to fall (see Psalm 35:6); fail (see Jeremiah 20:10).

Sluggish: slow to act (see Hebrews 6:12).

Small: of no worth/not valuable (see 1 Samuel 15:17; Jeremiah 49:15).

Smell: memory (see Isaiah 66:3 NIV [burning memorial incense]); offering and sacrifice (see Ephesians 5:2).

Smelter: place of intense trial (see 1 Kings 8:51).

Smoke:

Holy Spirit; glory of God (see Exodus 19:18; 20:18; Isaiah 6:1–4; Revelation 15:8);

will vanish (see Psalm 37:20; 68:2; 102:3; Isaiah 51:6);

lies; things concealed/a ruse to disguise intentions [smokescreen] (see Leviticus 16:13 NIV ["the smoke of incense will conceal"]; Proverbs 10:26; Revelation 9:17);

proof and effects of destruction (see Isaiah 14:31; Revelation 18:9, 18; 19:3);

see General/Smoke; in nostril for cigarettes.

Smoke, column: Jesus appears (see Song of Solomon 3:6; Isaiah 6:4).

Smoke, drifting upward: prayers going to God (see Luke 1:9).

Smoke, in nostril: pride/arrogance/people who say, "Keep away; do not come near me, for I am too sacred for you" (see Isaiah 65:5).

Smokescreen:

concealed work of the Holy Spirit (see Leviticus 16:13; Revelation 9:17);

sacred (see Isaiah 65:5);

lies/strongholds; things concealed (see Leviticus 16:13; Revelation 9:17).

Smooth: path of righteousness (see Isaiah 26:7).

Snakeskin: covering of lies and painful words (see Genesis 3:4; Psalm 140:3; Matthew 10:16; Revelation 12:9).

Snakeskin, shed: removing a covering of lies (see Themes/Animals and Creatures/Snakes).

Snare:

bring down (see Psalm 140:5);

unforeseen trap (see Job 18:9–11; Psalm 18:5; 64:5; 91:3; Jeremiah 18:22; Ezekiel 12:13; Daniel 6:4–16);

enemy ways (see Psalm 25:15; 91:3, Proverbs 5:22; 6:2; 22:5; Isaiah 8:14–15);

see General/Trap.

Sniper: deceives others and says, "I was only joking" (see Proverbs 26:18–19); shoots power from afar and unexpectedly (func).

Snow:

blessing from Lord/favor/grace of God (see Isaiah 55:10; Revelation 1:14);

bright (see Lamentations 4:7);

spread around (see Psalm 68:14; 147:16);

pure/clean/sin-free (see Psalm 51:7; Isaiah 1:18);

times that are cold (char);

leprous (see Exodus 4:6; Numbers 12:10; 2 Kings 5:27).

Snow, in summer: not fitting (see Proverbs 26:1).

Snuff out: die (see Ezekiel 32:7).

Soap: cleansing (see Jeremiah 2:22); works of the Lord (see Malachi 3:2).

Soaring: high spiritual activity that God is taking you to (see General/Flying).

Sober:

our wits about us (see 1 Thessalonians 5:6–8; 2 Timothy 4:5; 1 Peter 1:13);

circumspect/morally alert (see 1 Peter 1:13–14);

not partaking in spiritual [spirits: intoxication] activities or words (char).

Soccer ball: peace in life (see General/Sports game: actions in life; feet: individual peace; see Ephesians 6:12–17).

Soda: cleansing (see Jeremiah 2:22).

Soil: see General/Dirt.

Soil, good:

noble and good hearts who persevere (see Luke 8:15);

understanding the Word (see Matthew 13:23);

will bear good results (see Matthew 13:23).

Solarium: place where growth should occur (func).

Song: worship (see 2 Samuel 6:5; 2 Chronicles 29:25–28; Psalm 40:3; 98:1–4; Ezekiel 33:32; Matthew 26:30); witness for the Lord (see Deuteronomy 31:19).

Soot: blackness (see Lamentations 4:8).

Sorcery: not of God (see Deuteronomy 18:10–14); power gained from spirits; not of the Lord; from wickedness (see Deuteronomy 18:10–14; 2 Chronicles 33:6).

Sore: sin (see Jeremiah 30:13, 15).

Soul: personal will; mind [own inspiration] (see Jeremiah 14:14–16); emotion (see 1 Chronicles 11:19).

Soup: partaking thinly of God's Word (see General/Food); God's teachings (see Nehemiah 9:15; Proverbs 18:20; Isaiah 3:1; Hebrews 5:12–14).

Sound: words of Jesus Christ and doctrine conforming to godliness (see 1 Timothy 6:3; 2 Timothy 1:13).

South: storm (see Job 37:9; Zechariah 9:14); warm wind (see Song of Solomon 4:16; Luke 12:55).

Sow:

action that will result in something; a beginning (see Isaiah 40:24; Ezekiel 28:25; 36:9; Galatians 6:7–9);

seeking God (see Hosea 10:12);

follows breaking up; harrowing (see Isaiah 28:25; Hosea 10:12);

causes an equal reaction (see Galatians 6:7–8; Colossians 3:25).

Sow, in tears: harvest joy (see Psalm 126:4–6).

Speak: give direction to (see Hebrews 1:1).

Speak the truth in love: grow in Christ (see Ephesians 4:15); hear loving discipline (see Ephesians 4:15).

Spear: ready for battle (see Jeremiah 46:4); sharp attack (see 1 Samuel 13:19–22).

Speck: of little measure (see Matthew 7:3–5).

Speckled: undesirable/weak/wounded (see Genesis 30:25–43; 31:5–9).

Speech, foreign: not God's people (see Ezekiel 3:6).

Speed, high: thrilling (char); fast and scary (char; see Ezekiel 1:14).

Spells: trying to control others or things—this is not of God [as in witchcraft] (see Deuteronomy 18:11).

Sphere: area (see 2 Corinthians 10:13, 15–16).

Spices: mixed ways (see Psalm 75:8; Proverbs 23:30).

Spigot: ability to pour out Holy Spirit (water) to others (func; see General/Water).

Spin spider web: useless and evil (see Isaiah 59:5–6).

Spirit:

Holy Spirit of God (see Matthew 3:11; 4:1; 10:20; 12:18, 31–32; Acts 1:8; Galatians 5:25; Revelation 2:11);

wisdom/communion/conscience (see Matthew 5:3; 27:50; Philippians 2:20; Colossians 2:5; Philemon 1:25; Revelation 1:10; 4:2; 17:3; 21:10);

one's own human spirit [own wisdom] (see Ezekiel 13:3);

receiving communion of a spiritual nature (see Matthew 22:43);

see Themes/People and Beings/Spirit, good;

see Themes/People and Beings/Spirit, bad.

Spirit, broken: a breaking of the world view and an acquiring of God's design for wisdom, communion and conscience [spirit consists of wisdom, communion and conscience] (see Psalm 51:17).

Spirit, fruit:

acts of [love, joy, peace, patience, kindness, goodness, faithfulness, gentleness, self-control] (see Galatians 5:22–23);

wine (see Esther 1:10);

demons (see Matthew 8:16; 12:45).

Spirit, in us: deposit (see 2 Corinthians 5:5).

Spirit, lowly: humble (see Isaiah 57:15).

Spirit, seven: before the throne of God (see Revelation 1:4); seven times more evil than before (see Matthew 12:45).

Spit: scorn (see Matthew 26:67); reject (see Revelation 3:16).

Spit, in face: ultimate insult (see Numbers 12:14; Matthew 26:67).

Splendor: of God (see Exodus 15:11; Psalm 29:2; 96:6; 145:5); caught up in things of the world (char).

Splint: healing to become strong (see Ezekiel 30:21).

Spoiler: enemy (see Jeremiah 6:26).

Spoils: reward for aggression (see Hebrews 7:2–4).

Sponge: absorbs (see Matthew 27:48; John 19:29); filled (see Mark 15:36).

Sports game: actions of life (see Genesis 39:17; Job 21:31; Ecclesiastes 9:11; 1 Corinthians 9:24); competitions/relationships (see 2 Timothy 2:5).

Spot:

set apart (see Genesis 30:32–43);

disease (see Leviticus 13);

defect (see Numbers 19:2; 28:3–26; Song of Solomon 4:7);

shame (see Job 11:15);

stain (see Ephesians 5:27);

sin (see 1 Timothy 6:14; Hebrews 9:14; 1 Peter 1:19).

Spotted: undesirable [weak/wounded/weary] (see Genesis 30:25–43; 31:5–9).

Spring: Lord (see Jeremiah 17:13).

Spring: new beginning (see Psalm 132:17; Isaiah 42:9; 43:19).

Spring, dry: individuals who follow their own course (see 2 Peter 2:17).

Spring, water: God's ways (see Psalm 84:6; Jeremiah 2:13; 17:13).

Sprinkle: spread around (see Isaiah 52:15).

Sprout: take root and grow (see Numbers 17:5); chosen of God (see Numbers 17:5).

Spur: digs into, causing an immediate response; to encourage (see Hebrews 10:24).

Stable: stay firm in Christ (see Philippians 1:27–28).

Staff:

comfort; something or someone to lean on (see Genesis 32:10; Hebrews 11:21);

tool to do God's work (see Genesis 32:10; Exodus 4:17, 20; 8:5; Numbers 20:8–11; 2 Kings 4:29; Psalm 23:4);

support system (see Genesis 32:10; Matthew 10:10);

favor (see Genesis 38:25; Zechariah 11:7);

union/brotherhood (see Zechariah 11:7, 10, 14);

tool to do livelihood/employment (see Exodus 4:2–4);

those who work for you to get your work done (see Exodus 7:19);

tool to do wrong work (see Numbers 22:27).

Staff, broken: fall (see Jeremiah 48:17).

Staff, in splinters: wounds you if you lean on it (see 2 Kings 18:21).

Staff, reeds: splinters when grabbed (see 2 Kings 18:21; Isaiah 36:6); hurt others (see 2 Kings 18:21; Isaiah 36:6); when leaned on, you break (see Ezekiel 29:6–7).

Stain: remains of guilt or sin (see 2 Samuel 21:1; Isaiah 4:4; 59:3; Jeremiah 2:22; 1 Timothy 6:14; James 1:27; 2 Peter 2:13).

Stained glass: tainted/stained way of looking at things (char).

Stainless steel: powerful strength without stain (char; play on words).

Stairs, down: going to lower level for a purpose, possibly to help others (see Genesis 28:12; John 1:51); transition time of backsliding (func).

Stairs, up: transition time of going upward to a higher level (see Genesis 28:12; 1 Kings 10:4–6; 2 Chronicles 9:4; John 1:51).

Stalk: lie in wait in order to come against (see Psalm 59:3); receiving unwanted and obsessive attention at every step so that you cannot go forward (see Lamentations 4:18).

Stalks: stocks (play on words).

Staple: things that bind (func).

Star(s):

shining one (see Numbers 24:17);

Jesus (see Genesis 15:5 [seed of Abraham is singular, not plural as in Galatians 3:16; therefore, *seed* here means Jesus who is represented by the constellations] (see Psalm 19:1–6; 147:4; Matthew 2:2–10; 4:16; John 1:5; 8:12);

numerous/immeasurable (see Genesis 15:5; 22:17; 26:4; Deuteronomy 1:10; 28:62; 1 Chronicles 27:23; Nehemiah 9:23; Psalm 147:4; Jeremiah 31:37; 33:22; Hebrews 11:12);

points to Jesus (see Psalm 19:1–6; Matthew 2:2–11);

leader (see Matthew 2:9; Revelation 1:20);

hero (see Daniel 11:33–35; 12:3; Revelation 3:1);

angels (see Judges 5:20; Job 38:7; Isaiah 14:13);

brothers (see Genesis 37:9–10);

constellations named and ordered [listed] by God (see Genesis 15:5; Psalm 147:4; Isaiah 40:26);

practice of demonic astrology/demonic star gazing (see Leviticus 20:6; Deuteronomy 4:15; 2 Kings 23:5; Isaiah 47:11–14; Amos 5:25–27; Acts 7:41–43; Romans 1:21–23);

enemy, spiritual forces (see Judges 5:20; Isaiah 14:13; Daniel 8:10).

Star, falling/shooting:

meteors (see Revelation 6:13);

goes up fast, but does not last (char; see Revelation 6:13);

wandering in the blackest darkness (see Jude 13);

fallen angels (see Jude 13).

Star, hidden and dark: to die (see Ezekiel 32:7).

Star, morning:

Christ (see Revelation 2:28; 22:16);

forerunner of light to come or coming out of a dark place (see 2 Peter 1:19; Revelation 2:28; 22:16);

angels (see Job 38:7);

Satan (see Isaiah 14:11–13).

Starry hosts: angels (see 2 Chronicles 33:3–5; called gods).

Starve: without strength (see 1 Samuel 28:20).

Statue: fraud/no breath/worthless (see Jeremiah 51:17–18).

Statue, cast: falsehood (see Jeremiah 10:14).

Statute: rules of the Lord (see Psalm 119).

Steep hill: difficult challenge (char; see Judges 7:24; Hebrews 12:1).

Steering: control (see James 3:4).

Steering wheel: work/ministry you have some control of (see James 3:4; see Themes/Transportation/Car).

Stench: without favor (see 2 Samuel 10:6); repulsive (see Exodus 5:21; 2 Samuel 16:21; 1 Chronicles 19:6).

Stepping stool: an enemy God uses to take you higher.

Stick:

broken branch of people/kingdoms (see Ezekiel 37:15–17);

dry (see Lamentations 4:8);

ineffective weapon (see 1 Samuel 17:43);

tool to inflict injury onto others (see Matthew 27:30).

Stink: repulsive (see 2 Samuel 16:21; 1 Chronicles 19:6).

Still: inactive (see Psalm 83:1).

Stilts: high minded (char); neglecting basic things of life (as in "not on solid ground").

Stock: personal wealth (see Job 5:24; Jeremiah 2:21); doctrines of vanities (see Isaiah 40:23–25; Jeremiah 9:8).

Stocks: punishment (see Jeremiah 20:2; 29:26); boundaries (see Job 13:27; 33:11).

Stomach: vulnerable (see Habakkuk 3:16).

Stone(s):

Christ (see Joshua 24:27; 2 Samuel 22:47; Psalm 118:22; Isaiah 28:16; Matthew 21:42–44; Luke 20:17; Ephesians 2:20; 1 Peter 2:6);

people (see 2 Samuel 22:2, 32; Psalm 31:3; 94:22; Isaiah 28:16; Matthew 4:3; 16:18; Luke 20:17; Romans 9:33; 1 Peter 2:4–5);

common (see 2 Chronicles 9:27);

hard and cold (see Jeremiah 5:3; Ezekiel 11:19; 36:26);

things of earth that are cold and hard (see Jeremiah 2:27; Ezekiel 36:26);

witness (see Genesis 31:44–54; Joshua 24:27);

unable to move; heavy (see Proverbs 27:3; Habakkuk 2:19);

without life (see Deuteronomy 28:64; Matthew 3:9);

weighty force when set in motion (see Genesis 49:24; Daniel 2:34–44);

heavy (see Proverbs 27:3);

substitute for iron; strength (see Isaiah 60:17; Job 6:12);

things that are unable to nourish (see Matthew 7:9);

see General/Rock.

Stone, block: barred the way (see Lamentations 3:9).

Stone, builders rejected: Jesus (see Matthew 21:42; 1 Peter 2:7).

Stone, capstone: Jesus (see Matthew 21:42; Ephesians 2:20).

Stone, cause to stumble: disobey message of God (see Romans 9:33; 1 Peter 2:8).

Stone, cornerstone: Jesus (see Matthew 21:42; Ephesians 2:20; 1 Peter 2:6).

Stone, in mighty waters: hurled to the depth (see Nehemiah 9:11).

Stone, living: Jesus (see 1 Peter 2:4); Christians (see 1 Peter 2:5).

Stone, piles: fortified cities that have been demolished (see 2 Kings 19:25); barred the way (see Lamentations 3:9).

Stone, quarry: where we are shaped [hewn] (see Isaiah 51:1); digging up cold, hard, earthly things (see 1 Kings 5:17).

Stone, wall: hard barrier (see Numbers 22:25).

Stone, white: permanently of God (see Revelation 2:17).

Stoning: condemning and lashing out (see Numbers 14:10).

Storm:

divine chaos [tearing down to build up] (see Jeremiah 25:30–32);

intense trouble (see Psalm 55:8; 57:1; Isaiah 25:4; Jeremiah 30:23; Matthew 7:24–27);

undeserved trouble (see Matthew 7:24–27; 8:24–27).

Straight:

Jesus (see Deuteronomy 32:4; Matthew 3:3);

way of the Lord (see Psalm 107:7; Proverbs 4:27; Matthew 3:3);

the correct way (see Ecclesiastes 1:15).

Straight, way: moral character (see Proverbs 11:5); way of the Lord (see 2 Kings 22:2; Psalm 107: 7; Proverbs 4:25–27; Ecclesiastes 1:15).

Strange:

different from the world (see Jeremiah 2:21; Hebrews 11:13; 1 Peter 4:3);

plunging into righteousness (see 1 Peter 4:12–13);

things not right/not of God (see Proverbs 2:16; 1 Timothy 1:3).

Straw:

mixed with mud [earthly trials]; it creates strength (see Exodus 5:7);

unproductive products (see Isaiah 33:11);

words of man (see Jeremiah 23:28).

Straw, building with: inferior works erected on Jesus' foundation (see 1 Corinthians 3:12).

Straw, in manure: trampled down (see Isaiah 25:10).

Stray: falling into sinful ways/not of the Lord (see Matthew 18:11–15).

Streaked: undesirable [weak, wounded, weary] (see Genesis 30:25–43; 31:5–9).

Stream: ministry/life filled with God (see Psalm 65:9); see General/River.

Stream, flooding: wealth (see Isaiah 66:12).

Stretch: to spread out and grow (see Isaiah 54:2–3).

Stripe(s):

wound that scours away evil (see Proverbs 20:30);

to receive injury due to other's sin (see Matthew 27:26);

punishment (see Deuteronomy 25:2, Psalm 89:32);

undesirable (see Genesis 31:5–9).

Stripe, white: a little bit of God (see Matthew 27:26).

Strong: God (see Psalm 62:11; 96:7); enemy/Satan (see Matthew 12:25–29).

Stronghold:

place/structure of protection [good or bad] (see 1 Chronicles 11:16; Psalm 89:40);

information and wisdom accumulated over time; thought patterns based on prejudices;

religion; philosophies; a hopeless mindset that convinces us that thought patterns are unchangeable; human reasoning (see Proverbs 14:12; 2 Corinthians 10:3–7; James 3:15);

to overcome one must first understand and acknowledge the stronghold and not conform (see Romans 12:1–2);

causes instability as we attempt to balance opposing agendas (see James 1:5–8).

Stubble: evildoer (see Malachi 4:1; Isaiah 47:14); arrogant (see Malachi 4:1); insufficient equipping (see Exodus 5:11–13).

Stubble, dry: easy to consume or destroy (see Exodus 15:7; Nahum 1:10).

Stumbling block:

ways of God that hinder transgressors (see Hosea 14:9);

obstacles (see Hosea 14:9; Romans 14:13, 21);

things of the world that cause you to make wrong decisions; hindrances, e.g., anger, offense, negative thinking, sins (see Hosea 14:1–2; Matthew 18:7–10; John 11:9; Romans 14:13–23; Jude 24);

someone/something the enemy is using to cause you to make bad choices (see Matthew 4:6; 13:41; 16:23).

Stump:

holy seed (see Isaiah 6:13);

something that can be restored (see Job 14:7–9; Daniel 4:26);

where seeds are deposited and may sprout again (see Job 14:7–9);

stubbornness (see Daniel 4:26);

roots (see Isaiah 11:1);

stronghold/bitter roots (see Daniel 4:26);

something chopped down (see Isaiah 11:1).

Stupid: hates correction (see Proverbs 12:1).

Submission: under the same purpose [sub (under), mission (purpose)] (see 1 Corinthians 15:28).

Success: comes when seeking the Lord (see Joshua 1:1–11; 2 Chronicles 26:5; 31:20–21).

Sugar:

Holy Spirit (see Psalm 119:103; Proverbs 25:16);

good things (see Deuteronomy 26:15; 27:3; Joshua 5:6; Judges 14:18);

choosing the right way (see Isaiah 7:14–16);

not good if in excess (see Proverbs 25:16, 27);

see General/Honey.

Suicide: self-destruction (see 1 Samuel 31:4–5; Matthew 27:5).

Suitcase: prepare for leaving on a personal basis; being prepared (see Ezekiel 12:3); baggage/issues from the past in which we hide (see 1 Samuel 10:21–22).

Sulfur: stinking and putrid (see Revelation 9:18).

Sulfur, burning: Lord's vengeance (see Isaiah 34:9).

Sun:

Jesus (see Psalm 19:4–6; Malachi 4; Luke 1:79; Ephesians 5; Revelation 21);

righteousness/things of the Lord (see Psalm 19:4–5; Isaiah 60:20; Malachi 4:2; Matthew 5:45; 13:43; 17:2; Luke 1:76–79; Revelation 21:23–24);

endurance/a long time (see Psalm 72:5, 17);

father (see Genesis 37:9–10);

time on earth (see Ecclesiastes 8:9; 9:9–13; 10:5);

beat down and scorch (see Matthew 13:6; Revelation 7:16);

burn/hurt (see Psalm 121:6; Song of Solomon 1:6; Isaiah 49:10);

false god (see Jeremiah 8:2).

Sun, rising:

Jesus (see Luke 1:79);

follower of Christ (see Judges 5:31);

becoming strong (see Judges 5:31).

Sun, scorch: persecution from the world (see Matthew 13:6).

Sun, shining brilliance: face/heart of God (see Revelation 1:16).

Sunlight: radiance of God (see Habakkuk 3:4).

Superhuman power: power of God (see 2 Thessalonians 1:11–12).

Support: Lord (see 2 Samuel 22:19; 2 Chronicles 16:9; Job 8:20).

Surf: doubt (see James 1:6).

Swallow: overcome (see Numbers 14:9; Psalm 35:25; 124:3; Isaiah 25:8);

destroyed by others (see 2 Samuel 20:19–20; Psalm 124:3; Lamentations 2:16).

Swear: an oath sworn on someone greater than oneself to end a dispute (see Hebrews 6:16); not to be entered into falsely or thoughtlessly (see Leviticus 5:4; 19:12).

Sweat: one's own efforts (see Genesis 3:19); agony (see Luke 22:44).

Sweet: see General/Food, candy; General/Honey.

Swimming pool, clear:

refresh (see Psalm 84:6; 107:35; 114:8; Isaiah 41:18);

immersed in Holy Spirit (see 2 Kings 3:16; John 5:1–8; 9:7);

Lord's healing (see John 9:7).

Swing, gentle: relaxing (char).

Swing, park: danger (see Deuteronomy 19:5).

Sword:

Word of God (see Psalm 55:21; 64:3; Isaiah 16:16; Matthew 10:34; Ephesians 6:17; Hebrews 4:12; Revelation 1:16);

same as knife (see Isaiah 49:2);

verbal abuse/sharp words (see Psalm 57:4; 59:7; 64:3; Proverbs 12:18; 25:18; Revelation 19:15, 21);

judgment (see Isaiah 66:16; Jeremiah 14:12; 15:2; Ezekiel 21:3–16; 29:8; 30:4; Haggai 2:22; Revelation 2:16);

cut off righteous/wicked (see Jeremiah 29:17);

going through trials (see Genesis 27:40; Jeremiah 34:17);

death (see Job 1:17; Psalm 63:10; Jeremiah 2:30; Lamentations 4:9; 5:9; Ezekiel 14:17–18);

ready for battle (see 1 Samuel 13:19–22; Psalm 44:3; Song of Solomon 3:8; Matthew 26:52);

false testimony against another (see Proverbs 25:18);

violence/struggles against each other (see Genesis 49:5; Ezekiel 30:4; Matthew 10:34).

Sword, double-edged:

sharp coming and going (see Revelation 1:16);

sharp, hard word (see Hebrews 4:12; Revelation 19:15);

complete judgment (see Psalm 149:6).

Sword, extended: ready to destroy (see 1 Chronicles 21:16); effective in battle (see Genesis 34:25).

Sword, flaming: blocks the way to eternal life (see Genesis 3:24).

Sword, in sheath: not going to destroy (see 1 Chronicles 21:27; Ezekiel 21:3–5; John 18:11); ineffective (char).

Sword, on necks: slain (see Ezekiel 21:29).

Sword, sharp: sharp, painful words (see Psalm 64:3; Proverbs 25:18; Isaiah 49:2; Revelation 1:16, 19:15); vengeance (see Deuteronomy 32:41).

Symbol: metaphor for; representing (see Exodus 13:15–17; Numbers 6:7; Deuteronomy 6:8; 11:18; Isaiah 8:18; Hebrews 9:9).

T

Tabernacle: picture of how to approach God [inner court—soul: mind, will, emotion] (see Psalm 27:5; 76:2; Hebrews 8:2; 9:2–21; Revelation 15:5).

Table:

fortune (see Genesis 43:34; Isaiah 65:11);

communion and fellowship (see Exodus 26:35; Psalm 23:5; Matthew 8:11; 9:10–12; 26:20–29);

feeding on the same thing/embracing the same thing (see Matthew 8:11; 9:11);

place of negotiation (see Ezekiel 40:39; Matthew 9:10; 21:12; Mark 11:15; John 2:5).

Table and chairs: provision (see Psalm 78:19); communion/fellowship/who you are receiving teachings from (see Psalm 69:22; Matthew 15:27; 26:20–29).

Table of showbread:

candlestick: mind [place of illumination] (see 2 Chronicles 13:11);

bread: will [needs fresh bread weekly] (see 1 Chronicles 23:29; Nehemiah 10:33);

altar of incense: emotions (see 2 Chronicles 2:4; Ezekiel 40:42–43).

Tail: follower (see Deuteronomy 28:13); end (see Exodus 4:4; Deuteronomy 28:44; Isaiah 9:14).

Take: pick it up/take it/receive it (see Isaiah 35:4).

Talent:

gift that is supposed to be invested (see Matthew 25:14–30);

to be used for lighting the way (see Exodus 25:39);

those who have already, will receive more (see Matthew 25:21–29);

given in proportion to one's ability to use (see Matthew 25:15, 21–29);

money (see Matthew 25:18).

Tall:

high up in position (see 1 Samuel 9:2; 10:23);

of great stature (see Deuteronomy 1:28; 2:10, 21; 9:2);

high in the Spirit (see Deuteronomy 33:2; Psalm 43:3);

lofty (see Isaiah 10:33).

Tambourine:

prophesying (see 1 Samuel 10:5);

praise (see Judges 11:34; Psalm 68:25; 150:4);

joy (see Exodus 15:20; Psalm 81:2; Jeremiah 31:4);

holiday (see 1 Samuel 18:6; 2 Samuel 6:5).

Tangled: in bondage to (see Hebrews 12:1–3; 2 Peter 2:20); caught up in (see 2 Timothy 2:4; Hebrews 12:1).

Tape measure:
Lord (see Isaiah 28:16–17);
evaluation (see Revelation 11:1–2);
justice (see Isaiah 28:17).

Tare: those of the evil one (see Matthew 13:38); weed that resembles good things (see Matthew 13:25).

Tarot cards: see General/Sorcery.

Tassel: to remember and obey Lord's commands (see Numbers 15:37–40); an outward sign/a show of deeds (see Matthew 23:5).

Taste: experience (see Luke 9:27; Hebrews 2:9; 6:4–5).

Tattered appearance: neglected (see Proverbs 23:21).

Tattoo: permanent label of who they follow (see Galatians 6:17; Revelation 13:16–17; 14:1); mark of disobedience (see Leviticus 19:28).

Taurus: see Themes/Animals and Creatures/Bull.

Taurus: the bull who gores His enemies [Jesus at Second Coming] (see Deuteronomy 33:17); astrology, not of God (see Deuteronomy 4:19).

Tea: soothing (func).

Teachable: willing to try again; ready to flourish (see Luke 5:4–5).

Tear:
sadness/grief (see Job 1:20; 2:12; Ecclesiastes 4:1; Matthew 25:30; Revelation 7:17; 21:4);
sincerity (see Hebrews 5:7; 12:17).

Tear, torn: damaged (see Exodus 28:32; Leviticus 10:6); flaw (see John 21:11).

Telephone: message from God (func).

Television:
message delivered through humanistic means (func);
prophecy [tell a vision] (play on words)—caution: humanistic means are used; therefore, it may not be of God (func);
public/open knowledge (char).

Temptation: drawn to lust or things not of God (see James 1:13–14).

Tent:
house (see Isaiah 54:2; Malachi 2:12);

temporary place you are in (see Exodus 33:7–11; 2 Samuel 7:2; Isaiah, 5:1–4; 38:12; Hebrews 11:9);
being stretched (see Psalm 104:2);
temporary body/life on earth (see 2 Corinthians 5:1–10; 2 Peter 1:13);
easily destroyed (see 2 Corinthians 5:1–8);
where you are emotionally (see Exodus 33:7; Psalm 91:10).

Tent, peg: support for your area of life (see Zechariah 10:4 NIV—Jesus referred to as the tent peg, i.e., support system for a tent [room]).

Terrain, steep: difficult going upward; hindrances (see Judges 7:24; Galatians 5:7; Hebrews 12:1).

Territory, reduced: judgment of God (see Ezekiel 16:27).

Test:
test by God to bring out our character (see Judges 2:22; 3:4; 2 Chronicles 32:31; Psalm 26:2; Proverbs 17:3; 1 Timothy 3:10; Hebrews 11:17; Revelation 3:10);
test by God so we might know ourselves (see 2 Chronicles 32:31; Proverbs 17:3; Ecclesiastes 3:18–21; 2 Corinthians 13:5);
process God uses to teach us something (see Judges 3:1; 1 Kings 10:1; Psalm 105:19);
seeking proof in lieu of faith (see Matthew 4:7);
test by enemy to encourage bad choices (see Matthew 16:1; 22:16–21; John 8:6; Revelation 2:10);
to discern the truth (see Genesis 42:16; 1 Kings 10:1; 2 Chronicles 9:1; Job 12:11; 34:3; Proverbs 30:5; 2 Corinthians 13:5–6; 1 Thessalonians 5:21; 1 Timothy 3:10).

Testimony: words of validation (see Matthew 10:18); sharing test experiences to help others because God is not a respecter of persons and will do it for others also (see Acts 10:34).

Thermometer: test (func).

Thickets: place where one stumbles (see Jeremiah 12:5); neglected (see Micah 3:12).

Thirsty: craving "real" life (see Revelation 21:6); craving the Word of the Lord (see Isaiah 65:13; Matthew 5:6; John 6:35).

Thistle:

Scotland [or of the Scottish nation or culture] (rel);

small and annoying hindrance (see 2 Chronicles 25:18);

reaching small heights (see 2 Kings 14:9).

Thorn:

torment or weakness that keeps you from exalting yourself (see 2 Corinthians 12:7–9);

persecution (see Judges 2:3; Ezekiel 2:6; Matthew 13:7–22; 27:29; Luke 8:14; 2 Corinthians 12:7–10);

recurring problems often brought on by disobedience (see Judges 2:3; 8:7–17; Ezekiel 2:6; Matthew 7:16; 13:9–22; Hebrews 6:8);

obstacles/hindrances; trouble doing God's will (see Exodus 22:6; Numbers 33:55; Isaiah 7:23; 34:13; 2 Corinthians 12:7–10);

rejected (see Hebrews 6:8); cast aside; not gathered or touched (see 2 Samuel 23:6–7);

life's worries/choking/deceitfulness of wealth (see Genesis 3:18; Nahum 1:10; Matthew 13:9–22);

life's sins (see Matthew 13:22);

riches and pleasures (see Luke 8:14);

not good for sowing (see Isaiah 7:23; Jeremiah 4:3; 12:13);

uncultivated/without the Lord (see Isaiah 5:6; Matthew 13:7);

malicious or undermining people (see Numbers 33:55; Joshua 23:12–13; Judges 2:3; Isaiah 27:4–5; Ezekiel 28:24);

places of no discipline/of discord and fear (see Isaiah 7:25; Hebrews 6:8);

suitable for hunting (see Isaiah 7:24).

Thornbush:

created fire (trouble) (see Judges 9:15);

little growth toward the Lord (see Matthew 7:16);

full of [stickers] hurtful ways (see Isaiah 55:13).

Thorn hedge: protection of God; blocked by God (see Hosea 2:6); lazy (see Proverbs 15:19).

Thorn, removed: not sufficient in itself—only God is sufficient (see 2 Corinthians 12:7–10).

Threshing floor: place where separation of good from bad occurs (see 2 Samuel 24:18–25; Isaiah 27:12; Matthew 3:12).

Threshing sledge: [new and sharp with many teeth] many ways to understand or cut down (see Isaiah 41:15).

Throne:

of God (see Isaiah 66:1; Revelation 4:2);

ruling place of authority (see Ezekiel 26:16; 1 Samuel 2:8; Jeremiah 1:15; Matthew 25:31–46; Hebrews 1:8; Revelation 4:4; 20:4);

authority to judge (see Psalm 47:8; Matthew 25:31–46; Revelation 20:4).

Throne, overturn: God changing rulers and control (see Haggai 2:22).

Throne, white: God's holy judgment (see Matthew 25:31–46; Revelation 20:12).

Thunder:

change, without an understanding of what the Spirit is saying (see John 12:28–29);

loud (see Job 37:2–4; 40:9; Revelation 6:1; 14:2; 16:18; 19:6);

voice/glory of God (see 1 Samuel 2:10; 7:10; 2 Samuel 22:14; Job 37:5; 40:9; Psalm 18:13; 29:3–4; 104:7; Isaiah 33:3; Revelation 4:2–6; 14:2; 19:1–6);

mighty (see Psalm 93:4).

Tickets: given grace and mercy; encouragement to enter.

Tickled: meaningless good feelings (see 2 Timothy 4:3).

Tied: unable to move (see 1 Samuel 14:24).

Time(s):

life (see Ecclesiastes 3:1–8; 9:12; Ephesians 5:16);

time period, year(s) (see Genesis 4:3; Daniel 4:25, 32; 7:25; Revelation 12:14);

life/death (see Job 14:13, Ecclesiastes 3:1–8; 9:12).

Time, wrong: going through a difficult time (see Ecclesiastes 3:1–8); not prepared (see Matthew 25:9–11).

Tin: part left inside furnace after silver is burnt (see Ezekiel 22:18).

Tire: moving forward and held up by spiritual activity [air] (char); see General/Air.

Tissue: cleansing comfort received while dealing with issues.

Tithe: portion to church [priests and Levites] (see 2 Chronicles 31:4).

Tomahawk: doubt that destroys or kills (play on words: [Tom: doubt (see John 20:25)] [hawk: predator (see Job 39:26)]); blade (see General/Knife).

Tomato: acidic fruit/bad results (char); attractive young woman (as in "she's one juicy tomato").

Tone: attitude (see Galatians 4:20).

Tongues, speaking in: spiritual gift (see Acts 10:46; 1 Corinthians 12:10, 28; 14:39).

Tool: equipped with good things to work (see Hebrews 13:21); useful to the extent that God allows (see Isaiah 10:15).

Top: on top of things (see Deuteronomy 28:13).

Topaz: of great value (see Job 28:18–19).

Torch, flaming:

your own fire; your own light (see Isaiah 50:11);

salvation (see Isaiah 62:1);

consumes (see Zechariah 12:6).

Tornado:

what is the color?

white/brilliant: a storm from God that tears down or takes up (see Proverbs 10:25; Isaiah 40:24; 66:15; Jeremiah 4:13; 23:19; Ezekiel 1:4; 13:13–15; Nahum 1:3);

black: destructive, from the enemy (see Proverbs 1:27; Isaiah 5:28; 21:1);

sent to uproot/invade (see Isaiah 21:1).

Tower:

to watch over (see Matthew 21:33);

look out (see Lamentations 4:17);

Lord (see Proverbs 18:10);

proud (see Ezekiel 31:14).

Town, a previous town of your residence: dealing with an issue from an area of your past (rel).

Town, current town of your residence: going home [either earthly home or heavenly home] (see Jeremiah 31:21–22).

Toy:

childish ways/immature thinking (see 1 Corinthians 13:10–12);

plaything (see 1 Corinthians 13:11);

immature way (see 1 Corinthians 13:11);

of little importance (char);

not real (char).

Traction: friction/stress (see 1 Timothy 6:5).

Tradition: old teachings (see Galatians 1:14; 2 Thessalonians 3:6); hollow rituals/hollow understandings/without substance (see Matthew 15:2–6; Colossians 2:8).

Trample: beat down (see Hebrews 10:29; Revelation 11:2).

Trance: a day vision (see Acts 10:10; 11:5; 22:17).

Transformer: under the authority of a higher power [God] who has the ability to change [transform] your life (see Romans 12:2; 2 Corinthians 3:18; Philippians 3:21); changes (see Job 28:5).

Transfusion: giving a renewal of life; needing the same "type" of blood (Jesus).

Transport: to move supernaturally from one location to another (see Ezekiel 3:12–15; 8:3; 11:1, 24; 37:1; 40:17; Acts 16:9).

Trap:

catch (see Job 18:9–11; Matthew 26:4);

pride (see 1 Timothy 3:7);

sin (see John 8:20; Galatians 6:1–5);

snare of the enemy (see Psalm 25:15; Proverbs 5:22; 6:2; Isaiah 8:14–15; Jeremiah 5:26; Daniel 6:4–16; Amos 3:5; Matthew 22:15; 2 Timothy 2:26).

Trap-like passages: hindrances and snares of the enemy/difficulties (see Psalm 141:9).

Treasure:

relationship with Christ and following His will; the kingdom of heaven (see Matthew 6:19–21; 13:44–45);

wisdom and knowledge; sound words (see Colossians 2:3; 2 Timothy 1:13–14);

followers of Christ (see Exodus 19:5);

good foundation for the future (see 1 Timothy 6:19);

financial institution/banks (see Jeremiah 50:37).

Treasure, location: location of the heart (see Matthew 6:21; Mark 10:21).

Tree(s):

God's people (see Judges 9:8; Psalm 1:3; Isaiah 10:19, 33–34; 11:10–19; 55:12; 65:22; Jeremiah 11:16–19; 17:5–8; Ezekiel 20:46–47; Matthew 3:10);

people of the world (see Judges 9:8; Jeremiah 11:19; Ezekiel 17:24; Matthew 7:17–20);

person (see Job 14:7–9; Matthew 7:15–20);

leadership (see Zechariah 4:3; Daniel 4:10–22);

structure/manner of organization, i.e., business, church, plan of salvation (see Proverbs 15:4—plan of salvation [structure] is called tree of life; Revelation 2:7; 22:2);

nation (see Ezekiel 31:8–9).

Tree, apple [among other trees]: one who has fruit (see Song of Solomon 2:3).

Tree, autumn: past fruit-bearing time/dead (see Jude 12).

Tree, bad:

bears no fruit (see Jude 12);

unbelievers (see Matthew 7:18; 12:33);

will be cut down (see Matthew 7:19);

Tree, barren: no harvest (see Jeremiah 8:13; Jude 12).

Tree, by the water:

roots in God's Word; leadership in God's church;

will always bear fruit; prospers and yields fruit (see Psalm 1:3);

will not fear when heat comes (see Jeremiah 17:8).

Tree, cedar:

the envy of the other trees (see Ezekiel 31:1–9);

flourish (see Psalm 92:12);

still bears fruit in old age (see Psalm 92:14).

Tree, cut: dead (see Jeremiah 11:19).

Tree, dry: God will make flourish (see Ezekiel 17:24); leaders not receiving water ("life") of God (see Luke 23:31).

Tree, fig: provides fruit or results (see Judges 9:11).

Tree, fruit: products of person's life (see Jeremiah 11:19; 12:2; Matthew 3:10; Colossians 1:6; Jude 12).

Tree, good: bears good fruit (see Matthew 3:10; 7:18; 12:33).

Tree, green:

flourish (see Psalm 37:35; Proverbs 11:28);

people who have access to water ("life") of God (see Luke 23:31);

God will dry up (see Ezekiel 17:24).

Tree, green olive: fair and of good fruit (see Psalm 52:8; Jeremiah 11:16).

Tree, lost its leaves: a person who has lost his covering (see Matthew 21:19; Mark 11:13).

Tree, low: God will make it grow tall (see Ezekiel 17:24).

Tree, myrtle: place of angels (see Zechariah 1:11).

Tree, new leaves: things about to happen (see Luke 21:29–31).

Tree, of Knowledge of Good and Evil: man's will and intelligence/emotions (see Genesis 2:9; 3:17); of the enemy (see Genesis 3:1–5).

Tree, of Life: life everlasting in Jesus Christ (see Genesis 2:9; Revelation 22:19).

Tree, olive: priestly and royal office; bringing forth oil (see Psalm 52:8; Zechariah 4:3; Revelation 11:4); provider of honor (see Judges 9:9).

Tree, palm: provision (see 1 Kings 6:32); flourish and have long life (see Psalm 92:12; Jeremiah 11:16).

Tree, pine: tall growth toward the Lord (see Isaiah 55:13).

Tree, shade: under the protection and nourishment of (see Ezekiel 31:6, 12).

Tree, shaken by the wind: people shaken (see Isaiah 7:2).

Tree, shoot: part of the kingdom, family (see Ezekiel 17:22).

Tree, spreading: growth and protection (see Isaiah 57:5).

Tree, stump: holy seed (see Isaiah 6:13); stubborn/will sprout again (see Job 14:7).

Tremble: God's presence (see Ezekiel 38:20); fearful (see Exodus 15:14–15; Hebrews 12:21).

Trench: in battle mode (as in "in the trenches"); contains water to provide life (see 1 Kings 18:32–38; 2 Kings 3:16).

Trials:
acts of discipline from God (see Psalm 60:3; Isaiah 45:2–7; 1 Peter 1:6);
acts of learning from God/enables one to hear (see Deuteronomy 7:19; 1 Peter 1:6);
attacks of the enemy (see Luke 22:28; 2 Thessalonians 1:4; 1 Peter 1:6);
hard times (see 2 Peter 2:9).

Trick or treat: not trustful (see Matthew 26:4).

Trip: bring down (see Psalm 140:4).

Troop: many enemies (see 2 Samuel 22:30).

Troops, of women: weak (see Nahum 3:13).

True: of God (see Philippians 3:3).

Trumpet:
conquering (see Zephaniah 1:16);
announcement (see Hebrews 12:19);
call out (see Isaiah 27:13; 58:1; Matthew 6:2; 1 Thessalonians 4:16; Revelation 4:1; 11:15);
gather together (see Numbers 10:1–2; Judges 6:34; Jeremiah 4:5, 19; Matthew 24:31);
remembered and rescued (see Numbers 10:9);
praise (see Psalm 98:6; 150:3);
joyful promise (see Psalm 47:5; 98:6);
God's voice/preach (see Exodus 20:18; Revelation 1:10; 4:1);
start/stop (see 2 Samuel 2:28);
raised voice (see Isaiah 58:1).

Trumpet, one sounding: leaders come together (see Numbers 10:4).

Trumpet, two sounding: whole community assemble (see Numbers 10:3).

Truth:
Holy Spirit (see 1 John 5:6);
of God (see Psalm 43:3; John 1:14; 14:6; Philippians 3:3);
messages of God (see Ephesians 1:13);
Gospel (see John 1:14, 17; 14:6; 17:17; 18:37; Colossians 1:5);
set free (see John 8:31–32).

Truth, hard: hold others accountable (see Matthew 26:34).

Truthy/truthiness: approximately the truth but not the real truth (rel).

Twin(s):
not alone (see Song of Solomon 4:2);
double blessing (see Song of Solomon 4:2);
double trouble (see Song of Solomon 4:2);
see Themes/Numbers/2.

Twist: twisted/not straight (see Psalm 56:5; Ecclesiastes 1:15); not spoken correctly (see Deuteronomy 16:19); to manipulate things (see Exodus 23:8).

Tumbleweed: tossed about by things and without roots (see Psalm 83:13; Isaiah 17:13).

Tumor: kill (see 1 Samuel 6:4–5); judgment of God (see 1 Samuel 5:6, 9).

Tunnel: transition (see 2 Kings 20:20; Job 28:10).

Tunnel vision: vision of a covered [protected] transition (play on words).

Turban: justice (see Job 29:14).

Turban, removed: without justice (see Job 29); brought low from a higher position (see Ezekiel 21:26).

U

Unchanging: God (see Hebrews 1:10–12).

Uncircumcised: not a follower of Christ (see 2 Samuel 1:20; Isaiah 52:1; Ezekiel 32:19–31); keeping a sinful nature (see Colossians 2:11–12).

Unclean: with sin (see Leviticus 22:3; 2 Chronicles 29:16); not spiritually clean (see Leviticus 11:47; Isaiah 6:5; 52:11).

Underground:
things below the surface (char);
not in the light (as in "in the dark");
things that spurn the Lord (see Numbers 16:30–32).

Understanding: knowledge in how to do things (see Proverbs 3:19).

United: stand [as in "united we stand; divided we fall"] (see Matthew 12:25–26); to come together (see Judges 20:11; Romans 6:5).

Unpolished: needs a little polishing (char).

Unruly: needs correction (see 1 Thessalonians 5:14).

Upright: those who are of the Lord (see Psalm 49:14).

Uproot: move (see Psalm 52:5); without possibility for growth (see Jude 12).

Urine: getting rid of bad things [toxins] (func).

Usury: wrong practices (see Nehemiah 5:6–11).

V

Vapor: there for a while, then gone (see Proverbs 21:6; James 4:14); without substance (char).

Vassal: vessel of supply (see 2 Samuel 10:19).

Vegetation: blessings (see Hebrews 6:7).

Veil:
cover or tone down the radiance of God/Christ (see Exodus 34:29–35; Matthew 27:50–51; Mark 15:37–38; Luke 23:45; Hebrews 10:19–20);
concealed behind the law or legalism (see Song of Solomon 4:1—eyes behind the veil [old tradition and cultural law stated that women should wear veils to conceal their face]);
hidden from those who are not of God (see 2 Corinthians 3:4–18);
the fading of the old system and the veiling of people's minds by pride (see 2 Corinthians 3:13–18);
to ensnare; to fool people (see Ezekiel 13:18–20);
barrier (see Hebrews 10:20).

Velvet: soft covering (char).

Veneer: not solid/not real (see Proverbs 26:23).

Vengeance: might be trouble, but God will save you (see Isaiah 35:4).

Venom: poison (see Psalm 58:4).

Vent:
to display (see Lamentations 4:11);
poured out anger (see Lamentations 4:11);
to unleash (see Job 15:13).

Vertical: actions that reach upward toward heaven; prayer (see Ephesians 1:16; Matthew 6:9–13).

Vessel:
people (see Isaiah 22:24);
conduit of offering (see Judges 6:19; Isaiah 52:11; 66:20);
vassals, carrying the things of others (see 1 Chronicles 19:19);
where God pours in so that we can pour out to others (see Matthew 20:22; Mark 10:38–39; Luke 22:20);
our body (see 1 Thessalonians 4:4);
see General/Bowl.

Vest: covering/protection (see Isaiah 50:3; Psalm 30:11; Jeremiah 52:33); teaches God's people [nobility] thriftiness (per Wikipedia: this sleeveless garment worn by men beneath a coat may have been first popularized by King Charles II of England, since a diary entry by Pepys (October 8, 1666) records that "the King hath yesterday, in Council, declared his resolution of setting a fashion for clothes . . . It will be a vest, I know not well how; *but it is to teach the nobility thrift"*).

Veteran: post battle (char).

Vine:

people/lineage of people (see Genesis 49:22; Psalm 80:8);

peace (see Zechariah 3:10);

Jesus (see Jeremiah 2:21; John 15:1, 5);

life source/source (see Genesis 49:22; Deuteronomy 32:32);

provides wine (communion) (see Exodus 22:5; Judges 9:13);

producing branches (see Genesis 40:10; Ezekiel 17:6);

fuel for fire (see Ezekiel 15:6).

Vine, choice: sound and reliable stock (see Jeremiah 2:21).

Vine, cut down: people rebuked by the Lord (see Psalm 80:16).

Vine, false: other ways to live without tapping into Jesus; producing fruit ourselves (see Deuteronomy 32:32).

Vine, fruitful: able to produce (see Psalm 128:3).

Vine, no grapes: no harvest/no results (see Jeremiah 8:13).

Vine, true: Jesus/Christianity (see John 15:1); one with no excuse (see Isaiah 5).

Vine, wild: corrupt (see Jeremiah 2:21); against God (see Jeremiah 2:21).

Vineyard:

place of production (see Jeremiah 31:5; Matthew 20:1–16);

church (see Jeremiah 12:10; Matthew 20:1–16);

wealth (see Numbers 16:14).

Vinegar: appears to meet thirst [desire] but will not and makes it worse (see Psalm 69:21; Luke 23:36); something that messes with understanding/sets your teeth on edge (see Proverbs 10:26).

Vinegar, on soda: an inappropriate action (see Proverbs 25:20).

Violin: prophesying (see Habakkuk 3:19); worshipping in the Spirit; gifts of God (see Psalm 4:1; 6:1; 54:1; 55:1; Isaiah 38:20; Habakkuk 3:19).

Virgo: the virgin (symbolic of birth of Christ) (see Isaiah 7:14); astrology, not of God (see Deuteronomy 4:19).

Vision: a scene that appears to be—or is—a real happening (see Genesis 15:1; 46:2; Numbers 12:6; 24:4, 16; 1 Samuel 3:1, 15; 2 Chronicles 9:29; 32:32; Job 7:14; 20:8; 33:15; Psalm 89:19; Isaiah 1:1; 21:2; 28:7; 29:7, 11; 30:10; Jeremiah 14:14; 23:16; Lamentations 2:9, 14; Ezekiel 1:1; 7:26; 8:3–4; 11:24; 12:23, 27; 40:2; 43:3; Daniel 1:17; 2:19, 28; 2:45; 4:5, 10–13; 7:1–15; 8:1–19, 26–27; 9:21–24; 10:1–16; 11:14; Hosea 12:10; Joel 2:28; Obadiah 1:1; Micah 1:1; 3:6; book of Nahum; Zechariah 1:8; 13:4; Matthew 17:9; Luke 1:22; 24:23; Acts 2:17; 9:10–12; 10:3, 9, 17–19; 11:5; 12:9; 16:6, 9–10; 18:9; 26:19; 2 Corinthians 12:1–2; Revelation 9:17); redemptive revelation of God (see Proverbs 29:18).

Vision, false: not true (see Ezekiel 12:24; 13:6–9, 16, 23; 21:29; 22:28; Zechariah 10:2).

Vision, of death: metaphoric death (change in life); literal death (see General/Vision).

Vision, purpose: expose sin to ward off captivity (see Lamentations 2:14).

Voice, recognize: God/Jesus (see John 10:3–6).

Volcano: land touched by the Lord (see Psalm 144:5).

Vomit:

getting rid of bad things (see Job 20:15);

expunging sin (see Leviticus 18:28; 20:22; Isaiah 28:8; 2 Peter 2:20–22);

individual is sick (see Proverbs 23:8).

Vow: must be paid (see Deuteronomy 23:21); fulfilled day after day (see Psalm 61:8).

W

Wages: reward (see Job 7:2).

Waist, covered with black/sackcloth: mourning (see Jeremiah 48:37).

Wake up: be aware and change what you are doing (see Revelation 3:3); pay attention (see Revelation 3:2).

Walk:

direction in life (see Deuteronomy 8:6; Jeremiah 9:13–14; Psalm 23:4; Ephesians 5:2; 1 Thessalonians 2:12);

way of living (see Joshua 22:5; 1 Samuel 8:3–5; Isaiah 35:9–10; Zechariah 3:6–10; Ephesians 2:10; 4:1; 5:2–15; Colossians 2:6; 1 John 2:6);

daily life/actions/your conduct (see Judges 2:22; John 13:8–10; Ephesians 2:2; 4:1; 5:2; 1 Thessalonians 4:1);

spiritual way of behaving (see Ephesians 4:17; Colossians 2:6).

Walking, together: one-on-one interaction with others (see Judges 2:22).

Wall:

protection (see 2 Chronicles 14:7; Psalm 80:12; Isaiah 5:5; Jeremiah 1:15–18);

faithful people united in their effort to resist evil (see Ezekiel 22:30);

barrier (see Numbers 35:4; Lamentations 3:7; Ezekiel 12:5–7; Haggai 2:3–5; Ephesians 2:14);

no escaping (see 1 Samuel 19:10);

fortified (see Deuteronomy 3:5–6; Psalm 78:13);

division (see Ephesians 2:14).

Wall, break:

ability to see inside (see Ezekiel 8:7);

unable to stand firm (see Ezekiel 13:5);

broken foundation (see Isaiah 58:12);

tearing down a stronghold (see Ecclesiastes 10:8).

Wall, fire: God's protection (see Jeremiah 49:26–27 [God is silencing men of war]; punishment allowed by God (see Amos 1:6–7).

Wall, leaning: ready to fall from high position (see Psalm 62:3); man in his weakness (see Psalm 62:3).

Wall, scale: get past or over a barrier (see 2 Samuel 22:30; Psalm 18:29; Jeremiah 51:58).

Wall, thick: deep, wide protection (see Jeremiah 51:58).

Wall, whitewashed:

barrier (see Matthew 21:33);

a barrier that appears to be doing right, but in fact is against God (see Matthew 23:27; Acts 23:3);

blocked by God (see Hosea 2:6).

Wall, without a: unsuspecting and peaceful (see Ezekiel 38:11).

Wallet:

life/identity; finances (see Proverbs 1:14; Matthew 10:9; Luke 10:4; 22:35–36);

financial support/favor (see Matthew 10:9);

treasures (see Luke 12:33).

War club: weapon for battle (see Jeremiah 51:20).

Warehouse: see Themes/Places/Warehouse.

Warning: told of things not yet seen in order to be prepared (see Hebrews 11:7).

Warped: not of the Lord; not right (see Deuteronomy 32:5).

Wash: cleansing of sin (see Numbers 8:7; 19:9, 20; Deuteronomy 21:6; Psalm 24:4; Proverbs 30:12; Jeremiah 2:22; 33:8; Ezekiel 16:4–9; 1 Corinthians 6:9–11; 2 Timothy 2:21; Hebrews 10:22; James 4:8); spiritual cleansing (see Exodus 30:21; Jeremiah 4:14; Luke 11:38–41; 1 Corinthians 6:9–11; Hebrews 10:2; Revelation 22:14).

Wash basin: place of cleansing before God (see Exodus 40:30–32; Psalm 60:8).

Wash, body: total cleansing of all sin (see John 13:8–10).

Wash, feet: service to others (see John 13:5); daily walk should be washed before service (see Genesis 19:2; Exodus 30:19; John 13:8–10, 14; 15:3).

Watch:

time on earth (see Exodus 14:24; Judges 7:19; 1 Samuel 11:11);

life span (see Matthew 14:25; Mark 6:48);

note who the watch belongs to (rel);

watch over (see Genesis 28:15, 20);

study (see Genesis 24:21);

protect (see Genesis 21:16).

Water: look at the color and size of the water

Word of God (see Isaiah 55:1; John 4:10–15; Ephesians 5:26; Revelation 7:17);

Holy Spirit (see Matthew 3:11–16; John 7:37–39; Revelation 22:17);

baptism (see Matthew 3:11; 1 Peter 3:21);

to cleanse spiritually or repent from sin/repentance (see Leviticus 11:31–32; 1 Samuel 7:6; Psalm 66:12; Matthew 3:11);

drink up something; enter into something (see Psalm 109:18);

living water [spiritual life through Jesus] (see John 4:14);

refresh (see Psalm 23:2);

sustenance (see Song of Solomon 4:15);

humanity [especially if the body of water is the sea] (see Psalm 78:53; Matthew 13:47–49; Revelation 20:13);

overwhelming trials (see Genesis 6:17; Job 20:28; Matthew 7:24–27).

Water, boiled in: changing something (as in "watering it down," see Exodus 12:9).

Water, clean: make clean (see Ezekiel 36:25; Hebrews 10:22).

Water, current: the "now" or current movement of God (see John 7:37–39).

Water, deep:

wisdom/deep things of the Lord (see Nehemiah 9:15; Psalm 73:10; Proverbs 18:4; Isaiah 55:1; Luke 5:4–6; John 4; Ephesians 5:26; Revelation 7:17);

deep issues (see Luke 5:4–6);

words of man (see Proverbs 18:4, 16);

a plan (see Proverbs 20:5);

where one may receive a large quantity (see Luke 5:1–7);

unable to reach (see Proverbs 20:5);

overwhelming trials; feet cannot touch the ground, and you are not in control (see Psalm 18:16; 69:2, 14).

Water, dirty, muddy or polluted: compromising integrity (see Proverbs 25:26; Micah 2:10).

Water, dried up: without blessings of God/without God's Word in your life (see Psalm 32:4).

Water, floor covered: the Word of God affecting the foundation and flowing into the situation (char).

Water, flow: movement of God (see John 7:37–39).

Water, flow away: vanish (see Psalm 58:7); wrath of God (see Job 20:28 NIV).

Water, living: God/Holy Spirit (see Jeremiah 2:13; 17:13; John 7:37–39).

Waters, many: voice of God (see Ezekiel 43:2 NIV; Revelation 1:15 NIV); angels of God (see Ezekiel 1:24 NIV; Revelation 14:2 NIV).

Water of life: eternal message (see Revelation 21:6); Word of Jesus; Jesus (see Jeremiah 2:13; John 4:10).

Water, over: voice of Lord (see Psalm 29:3).

Water, poisoned: doomed to perish (see Jeremiah 8:14); punishment (see Jeremiah 9:15).

Water, poured on dry ground: God's Word [water] in areas without the Lord [dry ground] (see Job 8:11); will be life-giving [blood] (see Exodus 4:9).

Water, quiet: easy place to be filled (see Psalm 23:2).

Water, spilled on ground: cannot be recovered (see 2 Samuel 14:14).

Water, stream: refresh (see Jeremiah 31:9).

Water, underwater things: deep things of the Spirit; the purposes of a man's heart (see Proverbs 20:5).

Watery: compromise (as in "watering things down"); political correctness (char).

Wave:

to the Lord and back to you (see Leviticus 7:30);

offering (see Numbers 8:15);

sweep over (see Psalm 42:7);

doubt (see James 1:6–7);

a negative impact that causes you to lose balance (see Psalm 42:7; Ephesians 4:12–14).

Waves, muddy: cannot rest from bringing up dirty things (see Isaiah 57:20).

Waves, of sea:

power (see Job 9:8; 38:11; Psalm 88:7; 89:9; 93:4; 104:7–9);

doubts (see James 1:6);

current trends/tossing and blown around (see Ephesians 4:14; James 1:6–7; Jude 13);

double-minded (see James 1:6–7);

different movements (see Ephesians 4:14);

foe (see Ephesians 4:14);

judgment from God;

fear/swept over (see Matthew 8:24);

overwhelmed/something coming constantly against you (see Psalm 88:7; Jeremiah 5:22; Ezekiel 26:3; Matthew 14:24);

God's enemy (see Isaiah 57:20).

Wax: falls apart [melts] in a trial by fire (see Psalm 22:14; 68:2; 97:5; Micah 1:4).

Wax/blockage, in ears: a soulish nature that keeps one from listening/hearing (see Psalm 58:2–5; Isaiah 59:1).

Wayside: no understanding (see Psalm 110:7; 140:5).

Weak: needs help (see 1 Thessalonians 5:14).

Wealth:

full assurance of wisdom (see Ecclesiastes 9:11);

knowledge and understanding the truth (see Colossians 2:2–3);

financial reward (see Exodus 3:22);

a master we serve (see Matthew 6:24).

Wealth, lost: because of sin (see Psalm 39:11).

Weapon: something forged to be used against you (see Isaiah 54:16–17).

Weapons, not working: lost power (see Isaiah 54:17).

Weary: discouraged (see Hebrews 12:3).

Weather: change in the atmosphere (char).

Weather, storms:

difficult time (see Psalm 55:8; 57:1; Isaiah 25:4; Jeremiah 30:23; Matthew 7:24–27);

white, red, blue and green are of God; black is of enemy;

see Themes/Colors/(color of the storm).

Weaver's rod: very long (see 1 Chronicles 20:5).

Weaving:

life (see Isaiah 38:12);

things put together (see Psalm 139:15);

network (see 1 Kings 7:17);

interaction with others (see 1 Kings 7:17).

Web, spider: fragile and easily gives way (see Job 8:14–15; Isaiah 59:6).

Webbing: netlike structure that is strong/tough (see Job 18:7–9); interwoven (see Judges 16:13–15).

Wedding: come into intimate covenant/agreement with (see Matthew 22:2, 25:1–12; Revelation 19:7).

Weed:

followers of the enemy (see Matthew 13:25–30, 38);

wasteland (see Zephaniah 2:9);

message of the enemy (see Matthew 13:25);

bad result (see Job 31:40);

bad results mixed with good results due to the enemy (see Matthew 13:24–30).

Weep:

no one to bring comfort; no one to restore spirit (see Lamentations 1:16);

sorrow (see Matthew 13:48);

regret (see Matthew 22:13).

Weigh: judge/evaluate (see Job 6:2; Proverbs 21:2; Daniel 5:27; 1 Corinthians 14:29).

Weight, dead: burden of humanism (char).

Weights:

equal/fair (see Proverbs 11:1);

comparisons (see Deuteronomy 25:13–15);

works (see Proverbs 16:11).

Weights, uneven: unequal (see Leviticus 19:36; Proverbs 16:11); God detests (see Proverbs 20:10, 23).

Well:

direction/plans that can be drawn upon (see Proverbs 20:5);

life (see John 4:12–14);

counsel within a man (see Proverbs 20:5).

West: wild/unruly/without discipline (char).

Wet: Word of God on you (see General/Water).

Wheat:

people (see Matthew 13:24–30);

those who follow Jesus (see Matthew 3:12; 13:25–30; Luke 3:17);

good food/nourishment/sustenance (see Psalm 81:16);

results/harvest (see Joel 2:24; Jeremiah 12:13).

Wheat, sift: fall to temptation (see Luke 22:31); allow enemy into your life (see Luke 22:31).

Wheat, tops clipped: discipline and teaching (as in "clip the top and leave the roots," see Isaiah 28:23–26).

Wheel cart: Holy Spirit (air is the Spirit: Spirit holding things up (func; see General/Tire).

Wheel chair: chariots of the most powerful of God's army (see General/Chair).

Whip, lashing: strike down (see Isaiah 10:26).

Whirlwind:

movement of the Spirit, causing upheaval (see 2 Kings 2:2, 11; Isaiah 40:24; 66:15; Jeremiah 4:13; Hebrews 12:18);

scatter (see Zechariah 7:14);

fast and furious (see Isaiah 5:28; Jeremiah 4:13);

see Themes/Transportation/Chariots, Cars (see Jeremiah 4:13).

Whistle:

ministering in the Spirit (see Isaiah 7:18);

call for/call out to (see Isaiah 5:26; 7:18; Zechariah 10:8).

White cloth: what is it used for? If cleaning: cleansing process of God.

White stone: acquitted (see Revelation 2:17).

Whitewash:

cover up/looks good on the outside, but is bad on the inside (see Matthew 23:27; Ezekiel 13:10–12; 22:28; 23:3);

lie (see Ezekiel 22:28);

hide (see Ezekiel 13:10; 22:28).

Whisper: voice of God (see 1 Kings 19:12); word given privately (see Matthew 10:27).

Whispers: gossip (see Proverbs 18:8).

Wick, smoldering: will not be extinguished (see Matthew 12:20).

Wide: way of the world (see Matthew 7:13).

Wilderness: trials and difficulties (see Jeremiah 2:2; Ezekiel 29:5; Revelation 12:6; 17:3); place of trials (see Matthew 3:1–3).

Wind:

message from God/prophecy (see 1 Kings 19:11; Psalm 104:4; Jeremiah 5:13);

Holy Spirit (see Isaiah 66:15; Ezekiel 37:9–10; John 3:8);

angels (see Hebrews 1:7);

prophecy without God's Word in it; the enemy (see Jeremiah 5:13; Ephesians 2:2);

cleanse/winnow and cleanse (see Job 37:21; Jeremiah 4:11);

changes (see Matthew 11:7);

tossed about (see James 1:6);

sweep away/sweep us away (see Ecclesiastes 5:16; Isaiah 64:6; Matthew 11:7);

sweeps through/unrestrained/cannot be caught (see Ecclesiastes 1:14–17; Job 6:26; 8:2; 30:15; Proverbs 27:16; Isaiah 41:29; 57:13; Habakkuk 1:11; Ephesians 4:14).

Wind, blown around by:

winds of teaching (see Jude 12);

233

cunning and craftiness of deceitful men (see Ecclesiastes 1:14–17; 2:11, 17, 26; Ephesians 4:14);

scattered all different directions (see Jeremiah 49:32);

doubt causing trouble (see James 1:6; Isaiah 7:2).

Wind, scorching: judgment (see Jeremiah 4:11–12).

Wind, storm:

judgment of the Lord (see Jeremiah 30:23; Ezekiel 1:4; 13:11; Revelation 7:2);

things battering you (see Matthew 14:24);

trials/temptations (see Matthew 7:25–27).

Wind, strong/violent: judgment from God (see Isaiah 28:2; 29:6; 30:30; Jeremiah 4:12; Ezekiel 13:11; Revelation 7:2); voice of the Lord (see 1 Kings 19:10–13; Ezekiel 10:5; Acts 2:1–2).

Winding: not straightforward (see Judges 5:6; 1 Kings 6:8); much bending or compromise (char).

Window:

ability to receive revelation (see Proverbs 7:6–23; Isaiah 24:18);

revelation/seeing beyond (see Genesis 7:11; 8:2; 26:8; 2 Kings 7:2, 19; Proverbs 7:6–23; Isaiah 24:18);

an area where the enemy or evil can gain entrance (see Genesis 8:6; Joshua 2:15–21; 1 Samuel 19:12; 2 Kings 9:32; Jeremiah 9:21; Joel 2:9; Malachi 3:10; 2 Corinthians 11:33).

Wine:

Gospel (see Matthew 9:16–17);

Holy Spirit (see Ephesians 5:18);

spiritual communion (see Isaiah 25:6; 55:1);

good blessings (see Psalm 104:15; Isaiah 62:8–9; Micah 2:11);

new covenant with God (see Luke 22:20);

strong, emotional feelings [joy, anger, hate, sorrow] (see Psalm 104:15; Ecclesiastes 10:19; Song of Solomon 1:2; Zechariah 10:7);

cleansing (see Luke 10:34);

Word of God (see Matthew 9:16–17);

being merry (see Ecclesiastes 10:19);

earthly appetites (see Ephesians 5:18);

mocker (see Proverbs 20:1);

venom of evil; poison (see Deuteronomy 32:33);

brings lack of judgment and sin (see Proverbs 20:1; 31:5; Isaiah 28:1; Revelation 14:8);

to make intoxicated or cause one to stagger (see Psalm 60:3; Revelation 17:2, 6).

Wine, cup:

communion/promise of relationship (see Jeremiah 35:5);

covenant in Jesus' blood (see Luke 22:20);

partake in (see Isaiah 51:17; Jeremiah 49:12; Matthew 20:22; Mark 10:38–39);

destiny (see Matthew 26:39; 20:22–23; Luke 22:42; John 18:11);

same fate (see Lamentations 4:21; Isaiah 51:22; Jeremiah 49:12; Matthew 20:22; Mark 10:38–39; Revelation 18:6);

suffering/trials (see Matthew 26:39–42; Luke 22:42);

God's wrath (see Jeremiah 25:15; Revelation 14:10; 16:19);

wrath (containment of the cup of His wrath; see Psalm 116:13; Isaiah 51:17);

to make stagger (see Isaiah 51:22);

isolation and death (see Matthew 26:39–42);

to bring ruin, horror, curses (see Jeremiah 25:15–17).

Wine, in barrel/in wine cellar: at rest and waiting to be used (see Jeremiah 48:11).

Wine, in bottle not open: at rest (see Jeremiah 48:11); ready to burst open (see Job 32:19).

Wine, drink: makes the heart glad (see Zechariah 10:7); caught up in the world (see Isaiah 56:12).

Wine, mixed: destiny (see Isaiah 65:11).

Wine, poured on table/altar: drink offering (see 2 Timothy 4:6).

Wine, new: thrive (see Haggai 1:11; Zechariah 9:17).

Wine, with spices: judgment given by God (see Psalm 75:8).

Wine press: pressure that will release the goodness (see Isaiah 63:3–6; Lamentations 1:15); God's judgment (see Joel 3:12–13; Revelation 14:19–20; 19:15).

Wineskin: man's way of thinking/paradigm; man's way of living; the ability to expand/to be flexible (see Matthew 9:16–17); religious system (see Matthew 9:16–17).

Wineskin, new:

not stretched yet (see Matthew 9:16–17);

is flexible (see Matthew 9:17);

the way Christians should be (see Matthew 9:16–17; Luke 5:37).

Wineskin, old: already stretched to capacity (see Matthew 9:16–17); inflexible.

Wing:

refuge (see Ruth 2:12; Psalm 36:7; 57:1; 61:4; 91:4);

protective (see Psalm 91:4; Matthew 23:37);

healing (see Malachi 4:2);

lift/holding it up/rise up (see Isaiah 40:31);

a part or a section (see Daniel 9:27);

will fly away/disappear (see Psalm 55:6; Jeremiah 48:9).

Wink: devise perverse things (see Proverbs 6:13; 16:30).

Winter, season: time of coldness (char).

Wire: current power.

Wisdom:

of God (see Proverbs 3:19; Isaiah 28:29; Ephesians 1:17);

gift for the asking (see James 1:5);

building life on Jesus Christ (see Matthew 7:24–27);

respect and obedience to the Lord (see Job 28:28);

humility (see James 3:13);

using discernment (see Proverbs 16:21);

patience (see Proverbs 19:11);

will cause promotion (see Proverbs 16:3).

Wisdom, of this age: foolishness (see 1 Corinthians 3:19).

Wise:

understanding the truth of Christ (see Colossians 2:2);

building on a good foundation (see Matthew 7:24–25);

arrogant in their own knowledge (see Matthew 11:25).

Witchcraft: things not of God (see Deuteronomy 18:10); forced control (see 2 Kings 9:22).

Witness:

Lord (see Genesis 31:50);

bond (see Genesis 21:30; 31:44, 48);

tie (see 1 Samuel 20:23, 42).

Witness, expert: relies on his authoritative learning (see Genesis 31:50; Exodus 20:16; 23:1).

Witness, personal: has personal experience.

Womb:

ability to bring forth life (see Genesis 20:18; 25:23–24);

sea/mankind (see Job 38:8, Jeremiah 20:17);

earth (see Proverbs 30:16).

Wonderful: Jesus (see Isaiah 9:6).

Wonders:

miraculous testimony from God to point to His Word and power (see Exodus 7:3; 11:9; Psalm 72:18; Daniel 4:2–3; Hebrews 2:4);

took place by followers of the Lord and by His power (see Acts 5:12; 6:8; 2 Corinthians 12:12);

false miraculous testimony to misdirect others toward Satan (see Matthew 24:24; Mark 13:22; 2 Thessalonians 2:9).

Wood:

humanity (see Jeremiah 5:14; 2 Timothy 2:20–21);

worldly things/humanism (Deuteronomy 28:64; Jeremiah 2:27; Isaiah 45:20; 2 Timothy 2:20–21);

life; without life (see Habakkuk 2:19);

consumable (see Jeremiah 5:14; 28:14); substitute for bronze (see Isaiah 60:17).

Wood, building with: inferior works erected on Jesus' foundation (see 1 Corinthians 3:12).

Wood, carved:
man-made (see Isaiah 44:14–20);
human works (see Ezekiel 41:25);
legalism (char).

Wooden:
of man (see Deuteronomy 28:64; Jeremiah 2:27; 5:14; 2 Timothy 2:20–21);
less strength (see Jeremiah 28:13–14);
worthless (see Jeremiah 10:8).

Wool:
white purity (see Isaiah 1:18; Revelation 1:14);
spreads around (see Psalm 147:16);
able to be devoured by worms (see Isaiah 51:8).

Word: Jesus (see John 1:1–3, 14; 1 John 1:1; Revelation 19:13); a weapon (see Psalm 149:5–9; Ephesians 6:17; Hebrews 4:12).

Words: weapon to kill (see Hosea 6:5); defiles men (see Matthew 15:11).

Work:
actions driven by faith are good (see Matthew 7:21–23; James 2:14–26);
actions driven by our own efforts, rather than God, which is not good (see Matthew 7:21–23; Ephesians 2:8–9; 2 Timothy 1:9);
service/what you do (see Genesis 5:29; Exodus 3:20; Deuteronomy 21:7; 28:8; 30:9; 31:29; 33:11; Ruth 1:13; 1 Samuel 5:6; 10:7; 2 Samuel 22:21; 2 Chronicles 32:14 19; Psalm 8:3–6; 9:16; 19:1; 90:17; 92:4; 138:8; Ecclesiastes 2:11; 9:1–10; Isaiah 44:2; 56:2; Jeremiah 32:21; 44:25; Haggai 1:11; 2:17; Matthew 17:12; 23:4; James 4:8);
service to the Lord (see Ephesians 4:12);
direction (see Genesis 19:16);
to assist (see Genesis 21:18; Deuteronomy 2:15; John 10:12);
relationship (see Genesis 16:12; 1 Chronicles 4:10);

in control of (see Genesis 9:2; 14:20; 16:6; Deuteronomy 2:24; Judges 2:23; 8:3; 1 Samuel 17:47; Proverbs 6:3; Jeremiah 34:3; 38:5);
touch (see Colossians 2:21);
actions of humans (see Ephesians 2:8–10);
labor to receive sustenance (see 2 Thessalonians 3:10);
winnowing fork, gathering His wheat [God's people] and burning the chaff [people not of God] (see Matthew 3:12);
things done on earth [not by God] [e.g., worshipping spirits, idolizing wealth, destroying each other, practicing spiritual art not of God, sexual openness, theft] (see Jeremiah 38:4; Colossians 2:11; Hebrews 9:11, 24; Revelation 9:20–21);
to deprive self of pleasure (see Ecclesiastes 4:8).

World: see General/Worldly; see Themes/Places/World.

Worldly:
not of God (see John 8:23; 15:19; 17:16; 18:36; Romans 12:2; 1 Corinthians 2:12; James 4:4; 1 John 2:15–17);
things of the earth (see John 16:33, Ephesians 2:2; James 4:4).

World, friend: enemy to God (see James 4:4).

World War I, II: in a war situation [possibly spiritual warfare] (rel); fighting (rel).

Wormwood: bitterness and poison (see Revelation 8:11).

Worship: set up as "most important" (see Judges 2:19).

Worthy: one who follows Christ amidst their trials (see Matthew 10:37–38).

Wound: sin (see Psalm 38:5; Jeremiah 30:12, 15).

Woven: something twisted together (see Matthew 27:29).

Wrap around you: the same as a coat (see Psalm 109:19).

Wrapping paper: motive (func; "wrapped up in it").

Wreath: crown of the Lord (see Isaiah 28:5–6); pride (see Isaiah 28:3).

Wretched: without God (see Revelation 3:17).

Writings:

remembrance (see Malachi 3:16; Revelation 21:5);

make permanent (see Ezra 1:1);

teaching (see 1 Thessalonians 4:9; 5:1);

binding agreement (see Nehemiah 9:38; Daniel 6:8–9).

Wrong time:

going through a bad time (char);

see General/Time, wrong.

Y

Yardstick: taking measure of; to judge (see 2 Kings 21:13).

Year: time era or period (see Revelation 12:14).

Yeast:

growth that permeates all (see Matthew 13:33);

hypocrisy (see Luke 12:1);

sin (see Exodus 12:15; 13:7; Leviticus 2:11; 23:6; Matthew 16:6; Mark 8:15; 1 Corinthians 5:8);

boasts (see 1 Corinthians 5:6);

contamination (see Exodus 12:17–20);

corrupt teaching (see Matthew 16:5–12);

one wrong person affects all the others (see Galatians 5:9);

malice; wickedness (see Mark 8:15; 1 Corinthians 5:8);

sin in members of the church (see 1 Corinthians 5:6).

Yeast, old: sins of the past (see 1 Corinthians 5:7); malice; wickedness (see 1 Corinthians 5:8).

Yoke:

servanthood (see Jeremiah 2:20; 27:12; 28:2; Philippians 4:3);

willing to come under God's discipline to learn (see Lamentations 3:27; Matthew 11:29–30);

strength (see Ezekiel 30:18);

used to obeying (see 1 Samuel 6:7; Jeremiah 5:5);

attach to (see Galatians 5:1);

work (see Deuteronomy 21:3; Matthew 11:29–30);

burden (see 2 Chronicles 10:4; Jeremiah 2:20; Nahum 1:13);

bondage/oppression (see Exodus 6:6; 1 Kings 12:4; Isaiah 10:27; Ezekiel 34:27);

sins (see Lamentations 1:14).

Young: without wisdom and maturity (see 1 Kings 3:7; 12:6–15; Jeremiah 4:22; Matthew 11:25).

Z

Zodiac:

Mazzaroth; signs and order of the constellations (see Job 38:32; 147:4);

proclaims the work of God's hands (see Psalm 19:1–5; Romans 10:18);

created and named by God to proclaim His work (see Genesis 1:14–16; Psalm 89:37; Isaiah 40:26)

not to be used for horoscope or false god worship (see Leviticus 20:6; Deuteronomy 4:15; 2 Kings 23:5; Isaiah 47:11–14; Amos 5:26–27; Acts 7:41–43; Romans 1:21–23).

7

Dictionary of Theme Symbols

Like the "Dictionary of General Symbols," these meanings come from biblical application; characteristics; relationship; function of an item, building, area or being. Other meanings may come from modern culture.

These symbols are listed with some positive meanings first, followed by some negative meanings. To determine whether to apply a positive or negative meaning, look at the dream context.

Warning: To determine the correct definition of symbols in a dream, first seek the Holy Spirit's guidance (see Genesis 41:16). One symbol may have many different meanings. The meanings in this dictionary may not be the accurate meanings for your dream.

This "Dictionary of Theme Symbols" section includes the following:

a. Places
b. Body Parts
c. Animals and Creatures
d. Transportation
e. Colors
f. People and Beings

g. Numbers

h. Actions

Terms for deriving dream symbolic meanings:

- Char—This denotes the characteristic of the item or animal (based on Proverbs 6:6–8; 2 Samuel 2:18).
- Rel—This denotes a relationship inference (based on Hebrews 2:11; Matthew 12:46–50).
- Func—This denotes the function, or use, of the item, building, area or being (based on Nehemiah 12:44; Isaiah 39:2).
- General—This references "Dictionary of General Symbols."
- Themes—This references the "Dictionary of Theme Symbols" section for the named category.

Places

A

Airport:
waiting while being made ready for ministry or work (func);
crossroads (func);
place of coming and going (func);
way of getting somewhere (func);
spiritual portal (char).

Alaska, or place with similar characteristics: for example, a place that is cold; full of adventure; associated with gold mining or pioneers (char).

Alley: pathway (char); behind the scenes (char).

Amphitheater:
game of life (char);
pretense (char);
something magnified (char).

Apartment: place where you are "living" or where you are emotionally/spiritually (see Themes/Places/House).

Apartment, brick: a hard, man-made place you are at (see Themes/Places/House).

Assembly: council of holy ones [councils consisting of angels and/or Christians] (see Psalm 35:18; 40:9–10; 89:5–7; Proverbs 26:26; Ephesians 1:20 [Jesus at the right hand of God in heavenly places—plural]).

Assembly, great: great court of God [an assembly probably in the Second Heaven where the Lord holds court as Supreme Judge and Commanding General to make known and discuss His plans for the earth] (see Psalm 82:1; 89:5–7; Ephesians 1:20 [Jesus at the right hand of God in heavenly places—plural]).

Atrium: growth from heaven (func; the sun—see General/Sun).

Attic:
past (char);
old memories (char);
accumulated things (rel);
past history (char);
gifts of God left unused (func).

Auditorium:
life (see General/Games);
place where one lives and understands [sees and hears] things (see 1 Corinthians 9:24–26).

Avenue, number: path of (see Themes/Numbers, e.g., Second Avenue may be a path of discernment or a path of division).

B

Babylon:
land of merchants/commerce (see Ezekiel 16:29; Revelation 18);
man's organized rebellion (see Genesis 10:8–9; 11:1–9; Isaiah 14:4 12–14; 47:13–15);
political (see Daniel 2; Revelation 19);
false religion (see Revelation 17).

Balcony: high places [God or idols]; going to be displayed for everyone to see.

Bank: place of great wealth (func); divine favor (char); resources (char).

Bar: new wine (see Genesis 27:28; Numbers 18:12); haunt of predators [jackals] who hang out in dark places (see Isaiah 35:7).

Barn:

storing up things (see Matthew 3:12, 30; Luke 12:18);

place for harvest (see Matthew 13:30);

place of provision (see Psalm 144:13; Matthew 3:12, 30);

place where animals [unclean things] reside (as in "raised in a barn").

Base: support/foundation (see Exodus 26:18–20).

Basement:

foundation (func; see Matthew 7:24–27; foundational issue (func; see Matthew 7:24–27);

below the surface issues; beneath the surface (char);

underground (char);

hidden; unseen issues, good or bad (rel).

Bathroom:

place of cleansing (func; see Numbers 8:7; 19:9; Hebrews 10:22);

see General/Wash;

place to get rid of spiritual toxins [confession and repentance] (see Exodus 30:21; 1 Samuel 7:6; 2 Kings 10:27; Matthew 3:11);

see General/Pee;

place to get rid of wastes [confession and repentance] (see 2 Kings 10:27);

see General/Excrement;

deliverance issues (func).

Bathroom, cannot get to toilet: environment is not good for cleansing (char).

Bathroom, exposed: cleansing will be exposed to others (char); getting cleaned out [good dream] (func).

Bathroom, going into the wrong one: submission issue (char).

Bathroom, need to go: under pressure (char); needing cleansing (char).

Bathroom, not clean: not a good place to receive cleansing (char).

Bathroom, place of refuge: confession [getting rid of spiritual toxins and wastes] helps to disarm the enemy (func).

Beach: place of decision (see Matthew 13:48); where you meet the enemy (see Revelation 13:1).

Bedroom:

place of intimacy (see Genesis 49:33; Exodus 8:3; Deuteronomy 22:30);

private (see 1 Samuel 19:13; 2 Samuel 13:10);

place of rest (see Genesis 19:4; 48:2; Deuteronomy 3:11);

sex (see Genesis 39:7–12; 49:4);

sickness (see Exodus 21:18; Leviticus 15:4–5).

Bedroom, dark, elegant, cold feeling: place where intimacy occurs (rel); looks good, but is not healthy (char).

Bedrooms, many: lots of intimacy (see Genesis 49:33; Exodus 8:3; Deuteronomy 22:30).

Bleachers: high in the Spirit (char).

Booth: boxed-in area (func).

Borough: stubborn (burro: play on words).

Bowling alley:

path of bowls [vessels] (see General/Vessel);

place of being fed (see General/Vessel);

place of being bowled down/over (func);

path of doctrine [i.e., a church not necessarily doing it God's way] (func);

various religions—most lead into the gutter, which is hard to get out of. The right way is straight without deviation (char).

Bridge:

Jesus as a go-between [bridge] between us and God (see Romans 14:9; 1 Corinthians 15:3, 1 Peter 3:18);

transition [as in "bridge the gap"];

in a temporary area while going a new direction (func);

one choosing to avoid walking in the "flow" of the Holy Spirit [making a bad choice to not be included in what God is doing] (see 1 Corinthians 2).

Broad place: good area for growth (see Psalm 18:19).

Brook: wisdom (see Proverbs 18:4).

Building:

think of the function of the building; self (see Jeremiah 22:23);

corporation/structure (see 2 Kings 25:9; Jeremiah 52:13; Ezekiel 40:2);

church (see 1 Kings 6:5; 1 Chronicles 29:1; Mark 13:2; Ephesians 2:21);

church people (see 1 Corinthians 3:9; Ephesians 2:21).

Building, burning or burned down: destruction or trials coming to whatever the building represents (rel); look at the building's function.

Building, commercial: commercial structure (func); corporation (func); place of work (rel).

Building, granite: workplace of Jesus (the Rock); a beautiful, but cold, hard place to work (char).

Building, old and regal: old church (as in the original church); church people (see 1 Corinthians 3:9).

Building, tall: high [high in the Spirit] place of work (char).

Bunker: safe place (func).

Burning building:

the fire of God is there (see Deuteronomy 4:24; Isaiah 66:15; Hebrews 12:29; Revelation 20:9); see General/Fire;

revival (see Deuteronomy 4:24; Isaiah 66:15; Hebrews 12:29; Revelation 20:9);

destruction (char).

Burrow, pit: hole or pit that exists due to stubbornness (burro: play on words).

C

Café: see Themes/Places/Restaurant.

Cafeteria: see Themes/Places/Restaurant.

Camp:

"camping out" or staying in the same place (play on words);

spending time with (char);

staying on something for a while; staying in a temporary place (see Exodus 15:27; Hebrews 13:11–13; Revelation 20:9);

place of transition (char).

Campus: place of learning (see Themes/Places/High School).

Casino: place of chance (char); gambling with something (func).

Castle:

fortress/place of protection (func);

in defense mode (char);

place of authority (func);

fairy tale (rel);

stoicism(rel);

unchanging (char);

a stronghold (func).

Cave:

shelter (see Exodus 33:21–23; Judges 6:2; Isaiah 2:21);

protection (see Judges 15:8; 1 Samuel 22:1; Isaiah 2:21; Ezekiel 33:27; Revelation 6:15);

introspection (char);

to be hard on oneself (char);

depression (char).

Ceiling: covering (func); there is a limit to going higher (char).

Cemetery: place where there are people without life [without God] (see Genesis 25:10; 35:4; 47:30; Romans 6:4).

Church:

God's people (see 2 Corinthians 11:28–29; Ephesians 2:22);

where God's judgment always begins (see Ezekiel 9:6);

visible kingdom of God on this earth; God's earthly following (see Revelation 2:9; 21:22).

Chute: a steep slide (func); a trough for conveying water or the Word of God (func).

Citadel: place of safety (see Psalm 48:3, 13).

City:

circumstance in life (see Matthew 10:23);

inheritance (Note: Is this a previous town? If so, then the dream might be dealing with issues from the past.);

look at the town's name (see a Christian name reference book).

City, broken into and without walls: person with no control over his spirit (see Proverbs 25:28).

City, strong: wealth (see Proverbs 18:11).

Classroom: place of learning; place where tests are taken; see Themes/Places/High School.

Cliff: a dangerous area that could lead to falling; a precarious time/difficult (see 1 Samuel 14:4).

Closet: something hidden; private; personal (see Matthew 6:6).

College: see Themes/Places/High School.

Concrete city: hard circumstances in life (char).

Construction site: process of being built up or torn down (char).

Counters: place of preparation (func); someone who counts (func).

Counters, full: a place of preparation that is cluttered (func).

Country, lit up: God will display (char).

Course: spiritual journey (see 2 Timothy 4:7).

Court:

resolve dispute (see Deuteronomy 25:1; Psalm 37:33; 84:2; James 2:6);

access to (see Psalm 65:4);

confront others; dissension and argument (see Job 9:32; Matthew 10:17).

Court, inner: decisions made on the inside (see Ezekiel 8:16).

Courtyard: a place of judgment (func; play on words).

Crossroad: a place where one must decide which way to go (see Proverbs 8:2; Jeremiah 6:16).

time of purification; place of death (see Numbers 16:13);

place of trials (see Jeremiah 2:2; Ezekiel 29:5; Revelation 12:6; 17:3);

dry, thirsty place; place without God (see Psalm 107:4; Ezekiel 19:13; 29:5; Matthew 3:3);

an unsown land (see Jeremiah 2:2);

unproductive place/unfulfilled promises/mirage (see Isaiah 33:9; 35:1–10; Jeremiah 9:12).

Door: choice (see Psalm 118:19–20; 141:3; Song of Solomon 8:8–9; John 10:7; Colossians 4:3); ability to enter (see Ezekiel 8:8).

Door, back: not the way things are usually done (func).

Door, behind: hidden (see Isaiah 57:8).

Diner: see Themes/Places/Restaurant.

Dining room: place of spiritual food/spiritual nourishment (see Ezekiel 2:8; Matthew 15:27; John 4:34); teach [feed] others (see Leviticus 10:14–19).

Disneyland:

place of rest and enjoyment (func);

place to refresh (char);

place of hearing God (big ears: Mickey Mouse—"he who has ears, let him hear"; see Matthew 13:9–16).

Dungeon:

those who sit in the darkness of the mind (see Psalm 142:7);

those in the darkness of not understanding the light of God (see Isaiah 42:7; John 1:5);

those who are oppressed (see Psalm 146:7; Isaiah 42:22).

D

Darkroom: exposes the negative (func).

Desert:

place where there is nothing but God (see Isaiah 35:1–10; Hosea 2:14);

where God speaks tenderly (see Hosea 2:14);

E

Elevator:

going up/rising quickly (char);

an increase in anointing (char);

an increase in influence (char);

to lift out of a situation (char);

a falling/decrease of anointing (char);

going down to a lower level (char).

Europe: foreign (char).

Excavation site: in the process of being built up or torn down (func).

F

Far country: a place where God does not reside (see Luke 15:13).

Fargo: going far [look at the name of the city/town].

Fence:

hedging (play on words);

barriers/hindrances (see Psalm 62:3; Acts 17:26);

see General/Wall.

Field:

working/living area (see Judges 9:27; Daniel 4:30–33; Matthew 12:1; 21:28–43);

wealth (see Micah 2:2);

world (see Psalm 23:2; Isaiah 55:12; 56:9; Matthew 13:37);

in the open [abandoned and despised] (see Ezekiel 16:5);

things/areas "plowed under" (see Jeremiah 26:18);

people (see 1 Corinthians 3:9).

Floor:

foundation/foundational issues [look at the color of the floor; see Themes/Colors] (char);

destiny (the floor number indicates the level);

floor number: indicates the level of anointing or work (see Themes/Numbers);

first floor: if ground level—foundational issues;

second floor: in progress—or, if this is the top floor, where one wants to be;

third floor: Father, Son and Holy Spirit [3: Trinity].

Floor, black:

a foundation based on soul [mind, will and emotions] (see General/Floor; see Themes/Colors/Black);

a foundation based on ignorance (see General/Floor; see Themes/Colors/Black);

a foundation based on evil (see General/Floor; see Themes/Colors/Black).

Floor, bottom/basement: the foundation (char); basic teachings (see Ephesians 2:20).

Floor, brown:

a foundation spread with compassion (see General/Floor; see Themes/Colors/Brown);

foundation speckled with humanism (see General/Floor; see Themes/Colors/Brown).

Floor, first: lower level (char).

Floor, shiny and well-polished:

foundation that is well taken care of (char);

firm (char);

polished (char).

Floor, wood: man-made foundation (see General/Floor; see General/Wood).

Forest: God's people (see Isaiah 10:34).

Fort: shelter (see Judges 6:2).

Fortress:

place of Christians (see 2 Samuel 5:7–9);

safety (see 2 Samuel 5:7; 1 Chronicles 11:7; Psalm 48:3; 91:1);

Lord (see 2 Samuel 22:2, 32, 47; 23:3; Psalm 18:2; 31:2–3; 46:11; 62:2–7; 91:2, 9; 94:22; Isaiah 17:10; Jeremiah 16:19);

a stronghold (func).

Foundation:

primary issues (see Ephesians 2:20);

solid enough to build upon (see Ephesians 1:4; 1 Timothy 6:19);

God (see Isaiah 33:6; Hebrews 11:10);

source (see Psalm 87:1; Ephesians 1:4);

established by (see Psalm 87:1–5).

Front porch: see Themes/Places/Porch, front.

G

Garage: a place where a ministry or work might be "stalled" or not going forward (func; see Themes/Transportation/Cars); a place where a work or ministry might receive help [servicing] (func; see Themes/Transportation/Cars).

Garden:

intimacy (see Song of Solomon 4:12–15; 5:1);

love (see Song of Solomon 4:12–15; 5:1);

places of growth and sustenance (see Song of Solomon 4:12–15; 5:1; Isaiah 58:11; 61:11);

place where God's guidance can be found (see Song of Solomon 4:12–15; 5:1; Isaiah 58:11);

romance (see Song of Solomon 4:12–15; 5:1).

Gate:

protection (see 2 Chronicles 14:7; Ezekiel 26:2);

church (see Psalm 24:7);

a choice one may enter into (see Psalm 118:19–20; Jeremiah 37:13; 38:7; Ezekiel 38:11; Matthew 7:13);

a way to escape (see Jeremiah 39:4);

captivity (see Micah 2:13).

Gate, open: the enemy is able to come in (see Nahum 3:13).

Good soil: an area that is ready to thrive (see Matthew 13:8).

Grave:

place where things are dead (without God);

death (see Job 10:19);

captivity (see Ezekiel 37).

Greenhouse: place where plants are grown; a safe place; nurturing/flourishing (see Proverbs 11:28).

Ground floor: getting grounded (func); foundation (func).

Gymnasium:

place to exercise faith (see Genesis 39:17; Ecclesiastes 9:11);

place to work out salvation/your life (see Genesis 39:17; Ecclesiastes 9:11);

exercising self-discipline, competitions and struggles (func; see 1 Corinthians 9:24–27; 2 Timothy 2:5).

H

Hall: transition period; passageway (see 2 Samuel 5:8).

Hallways: transition period (see 2 Samuel 5:8).

Harlot's house: churches that are not of God (see Jeremiah 5:7).

Heaven:

high up (see Deuteronomy 30:12; 1 Samuel 5:12; Chronicles 28:9; Job 11:8);

things of God (see 2 Kings 1:10; 2:1; Colossians 3:2);

too high to ascend (see Deuteronomy 9:1; 30:12);

more than one heaven (see Ephesians 1:3, 10, 20; 2:6; 6:12).

Heavens: more than one heaven (see Ephesians 1:3, 10; 2:6; 6:12).

Heaven, first: area above the earth (see Genesis 15:5; Psalm 147:4; Isaiah 40:26; Habakkuk 3:11; Revelation 6:13).

Heaven, second: area where dark spirits reign (see Isaiah 24:21; Galatians 1:8; Ephesians 6:12).

Heaven, third: heaven of the Almighty God (see 2 Corinthians 5:6–8 [dwelling place for those who die in the faith of Jesus Christ]; 12:2–4).

High places:

altar; things we have placed high in our esteem (see Leviticus 26:30; 1 Kings 14:23; Isaiah 2:14; Jeremiah 32:35; Ezekiel 43:7; Matthew 4:8);

idols (see 2 Kings 23:13–16; 2 Chronicles 20:33; Psalm 78:58; Jeremiah 7:31–32; Ezekiel 6:3–4);

of the Lord (see Psalm 48:2; Isaiah 52:13; Ephesians 4:8–10; Colossians 3:1–2).

High rise:

high spiritual calling (play on words);

work (func; see Themes/Places/Buildings);

status (func);

level of calling (char; look at the floor level);

where you are going (char);

where you are (char).

High school:

higher level of learning (see 2 Timothy 2:15);

no longer elementary teachings (char; see Themes/Places/School);

past educational experience; things learned in the past (func).

Highway:

"high" way or high path of God (see Proverbs 15:19);

path of holiness (see Proverbs 16:17; Isaiah 2:3; 35:8; Jeremiah 31:21);

see Themes/Places/Road;

see General/Highway;

see General/Road.

Hill:

safety (see Matthew 17:1);

place of the Lord (see Psalm 24:3);

high place (see Isaiah 55:12);

spiritual region (see Ezekiel 16:24);

difficulty (char).

Hill, high:

place of the Lord (see Psalm 24:3);

seeking high things not of God (see Numbers 14:40; Jeremiah 2:20; 3:23);

things men hold up high (see Isaiah 57:7).

Hill, rocky: going through an "uphill" or "downhill" difficult [rocky] time (char).

Hill, rugged: place where it is easy to go wrong (see Song of Solomon 2:17).

Hill, steep: a precarious downward or upward path (char).

Home: place where one's belief system is (see Matthew 13:57); see Themes/Places/House.

Hometown: where prophecy is not believed (see Matthew 13:57–58).

Hospital: place of healing; church (see Ezekiel 34).

Hotel:

temporary place; place of transition (see Luke 2:7);

high spiritual calling (see Jeremiah 35:2–9);

rising high (high-rise apartment) (char).

House: Note: who is in the house with you? What color is the house? What is the address of the house? What is the condition of the house? These are all clues as to what the house represents.

you/your personal life and relationships (see 2 Samuel 13:7–8; 14:24; 17:23; 18:17; 19:8; 23:5; Proverbs 15:25; Isaiah 38:12; Jeremiah 35:2–9; 37:15; Matthew 7:24–27; 10:11–13; Hebrews 3:6; 2 Timothy 2:20–21);

individual (see Haggai 1:3–9; Matthew 7:24–27; 10:11–13; 12:43–44; 2 Timothy 2:20–21);

church (see references for God's universal Church);

God's universal Church without denomination; total church (see 2 Samuel 7:5–10, 13, 25–29; 1 Kings 8:13; 1 Chronicles 22:7, 19; Psalm 23:6; 31:20; 65:4; 66:13; Isaiah 2:3; Jeremiah 26:2–7; 29:26; Haggai 1:2–8; 2:3; Matthew 15:24; 21:13; John 14:2; Ephesians 2:19–22; Philemon 1:2; Hebrews 3:6; 10:21; 1 Timothy 3:5–15; 1 Peter 2:5; 4:17). Note: are there other indications in the dream that this is a house? Is it white? Are there church people in the dream? Are there other church-related things in the dream?

one's life and relationships (see 2 Samuel 13:7–8; 14:24; 17:23; 18:17; 19:8; Isaiah 38:12; Jeremiah 35:2–9; 37:15; Hebrews 3:3–6);

family [Note: are other family members in the house with you? Are there family issues in the dream?] (see Jeremiah 35:3; Amos 1:4; Zechariah 12:10–13; 13:1; 1 Timothy 3:5–15);

generational family line [Note: are other family members in the house with you, especially grandparent(s)? Are there family issues in the dream?] (see 2 Samuel 7:11–12, 19; 21:1; 1 Kings 14:10; 16:3; 2 Kings 8:27; 9:7–9; 10:1; Isaiah 7:2, 13; 33:11; Jeremiah 2:4);

group of like-minded individuals/community [Note: who is in the house with you?] (see 1 Kings 20:31);

heritage/nation (see Jeremiah 31:27; 33:14; Ezekiel 8:10–11; Matthew 10:6);

mindset of person [where you reside/ how you feel about things] [Note: is this about emotional issues, i.e., where you are "living"?] (see 2 Samuel 18:17, 19:8; 1 Kings 14:17; 1 John 2:6);

note the color of house. What significance might it have? Is the house brick? If so, is your workplace brick?

House, big:

Lord's house/temple (see 2 Samuel 7:5–10, 13, 25–29; 1 Kings 8:13; 1 Chronicles 22:7, 19; Psalm 23:6; 31:20; 65:4; 66:13; Isaiah 2:3; Jeremiah 26:2–7; 29:26);

church (see Haggai 1:2–8; 2:3; Matthew 15:24; 21:13; John 14:2; Ephesians 2:19–22; Philemon 1:2; 1 Timothy 3:5–15; Hebrews 3:6; 10:21; 1 Peter 2:5; 4:17);

see Themes/Places/House.

House, buy someone else's: you have the same calling as the owner of the house (rel).

House, burned out: enemy has ravaged whatever the house represents [person, church, life, family, generational family] (func).

House, childhood: dealing with old issues (see Isaiah 7:17).

House, clean: person is clean (see Matthew 12:44).

House, decorated with: look at the decoration and this may tell you where you are emotionally and that what you are dealing with may have this quality [e.g.: if your house is decorated with antiques (that is not normal) then this may indicate you are dwelling with issues from the past] (see Psalm 93:5).

House, divided: will not stand (see Matthew 12:25).

House, farm: where teachings (food) are developed for feeding people (func).

House, full of antiques: dealing with things of the past (rel).

House, grandma's: safety/security (char); calming (char).

House, haunted:

past family issues (rel);

ghost's house (func);

Holy Spirit abode (func).

House, inner room: done on the inside (see Ezekiel 8:16).

House, in order: affairs in order (see Isaiah 38:1).

House, large:

church (see Jeremiah 7:1–11, 14, 30; 32:34; 34:15; 35:2; Hebrews 3:6; 1 Peter 2:5);

large family (see Themes/Places/House);

person (see Themes/Places/Persons and Beings/Person).

House, large atrium: healthy place to grow and mature [an atrium is a large, open-air [Holy Spirit] area with light [God's light] and air [Holy Spirit] (func).

House, mobile: move on (func).

House, mom: church (see Themes/Places/House; see Themes/People and Beings/Mom); family (see Themes/Places/Church).

House, neglected and in disrepair: indolence and slackness (see Ecclesiastes 10:18).

House, old, gray, neglected and in disrepair: a neglected blood line (see Themes/Places/House).

House, someone else's, living in another person's house: similar anointing (see Themes/Places/House).

House, small: you (see Themes/Places/House); person (see Themes/Places/House).

Housetop: place to proclaim loudly (see Matthew 10:27).

House, two-story: double anointing (char).

House, up high: place where God resides (see Isaiah 57:15).

House, wealthy:

influence (char);

favor (rel);

inheritance (rel);

rewards (rel).

House, white:

holiness (see Themes/Colors/White);

purity (see Themes/Colors/White);

clean (see Themes/Colors/White); church (see Themes/Places/House; see Themes/Colors/White).

Hut, in wind: sways/vacillates (see Isaiah 24:20).

I

Island: about yourself (see Isaiah 60:9).

J

Jerusalem: city of truth (see Zechariah 8:3); God's full Church (see Revelation 21:9–14).

Jungle:

area of rich diversity and fertility (char);

area of dense growth, but tangled and without cultivation (char);

difficult to see/dense (char);

noisy strife (char);

abode of spiders, snakes and other dangerous predators (func);

demonic/not a healthy environment (char).

K

Kitchen:

place of preparing spiritual food (see Nehemiah 9:15; Proverbs 18:20; see General/Eat);

teach (see Leviticus 10:14–19);

heart (the kitchen is the heart of the home);

plans (see Nehemiah 9:15; Proverbs 18:20).

L

Lake:

Word of God (see Mark 4:1; Revelation 19:20; 20:10);

larger church or ministry (see Mark 4:1; 6:49);

life (see Matthew 4:18; 13:47; Mark 1:16).

Land, desert/sun scorched: where the rebellious [jackals, wolves] live (see Isaiah 35:7; Jeremiah 5:6).

Land, desolate: because they have forsaken God's laws (see Jeremiah 9:12–14); without God (see Psalm 68:7; Jeremiah 23:10).

Land, drought: not good for growth (see Ezekiel 36:34); God not blessing (see Jeremiah 2:5; 17:6).

Lawn: people (see 2 Kings 19:26; Psalm 37:2; 90:5; Isaiah 40:6–8; 51:12; 1 Peter 1:24).

Library: place to receive knowledge (func).

Lighthouse: place to receive direction (func).

Living room: public place (char); situation one is living in (func).

Locker room: place where your covering is stored (see General/Clothes); areas that are locked up (func).

Lodge: place where you are (see Philippians 1:22).

Loft:

lofty/high places (see Psalm 48:2);

things higher up (see Isaiah 57:7);

Lord (see Isaiah 57:15);

idolatry/not of the Lord (see Isaiah 57:7).

Log cabin: tranquil time of hearing (living in a "past era").

Lumberyard: place where people have been refined (func).

M

Mall: place of provision/church; egotism (see Matthew 11:16); trying to get everything one needs or wants (see Matthew 11:16).

Market: life/materialism (see Matthew 11:16).

Marsh: see Themes/Places/Swamp.

Mesa, flat area with mountains: portals/ heaven opening up (char).

Mobile home: temporary state of being [emotionally or physically] (char).

Moon: established forever (see Psalm 89:37); faithful witness (see Psalm 89:37).

Motel: see Themes/Places/Hotel.

Mountain:

places that are most high; heaven/holy place of God (see Deuteronomy 33:2; Psalm 43:3; 48:1; 68:16; Isaiah 2:2–3; 25:10; 52:7; 55:12; 65:11; 66:20; Ezekiel 20:40; 28:14; 38:21; Micah 4:1–2; Hebrews 8:5; 12:18, 22);

closeness to Jesus (see Matthew 28:16; John 6:3);

high in the Spirit (see Psalm 76:4; Matthew 17:1–3);

things held in high esteem (see Psalm 76:4; Matthew 4:8);

safety (see Matthew 17:1);

haughty/high period (see Isaiah 40:4);

high places that are not of God (see Deuteronomy 12:2; 1 Kings 11:7; 2 Chronicles 21:11; Ezra 6:13; Jeremiah 3:6, 23).

Mountain, burnt: no growth from there (see Jeremiah 51:25–26).

Mountain, green trees: high places where God's people flourish (see Proverbs 11:28).

Mountain, red rocks: dangerous high places (char).

N

Narrow hall: narrow is the way (see Matthew 7:13).

North: disaster (see Jeremiah 4:6).

Nursing home: place to receive care from [injuries] of the past (func).

O

Office building:

place of calling (see Themes/Places/Building);

work (func);

administration (func);

performance (func);

function (see type of business run out of office).

Office, new building: new anointing (char).

Open area: an area that is open to new, worldly ideas (see Revelation 22:15).

Outside: open to the Spirit of God [air] (see Ephesians 2:2); an area that is open to new, worldly ideas (see Revelation 22:15).

P

Park: restful place (func); God's provision (char); not going forward (char).

Parking lot: people [ministry/work] who are not going forward (see Themes/ Transportation/Car).

Pasture: peace (see Isaiah 14:30); plenty (see Psalm 23:2); life/world (see Psalm 23:2; Ezekiel 34:31).

Path: direction you are going in life (see Numbers 22:32; Proverbs 14:12; Isaiah 57:14).

Path, ancient: good way (see Jeremiah 6:16).

Path, crooked: not the way of the Lord (see Psalm 27:11; Proverbs 2:13–15; 3:6; 9:15; Ecclesiastes 1:15; Isaiah 2:3; 40:3; Jeremiah 31:9; Matthew 3:3).

Path, dark and slippery: hard life/walk (see Psalm 35:6); difficult to live without making errors (see Jeremiah 23:12; Zechariah 3:6–10).

Path, level: life without obvious hindrances (see Hebrews 12:13).

Path, narrow: way to spiritual life (see Matthew 7:13–14); way least traveled (see Matthew 7:13–14).

Path, sandy: hard place to walk; difficult living conditions (char).

Path, straight: correct way/way of the Lord (see Psalm 27:11; Proverbs 2:13–15; 3:6; 9:15; Ecclesiastes 1:15; Isaiah 2:3; 40:3; Jeremiah 31:9;

Matthew 3:3); see Themes/Places/
Road, Straight.

Path, thorny: way of the sluggard (see
Proverbs 15:19).

Penthouse: lots of revelation [high in the
Spirit] (char).

Pit: hell (see Isaiah 24:18; Ezekiel 31:14;
32:18, 23–25); grave (see Ezekiel
31:15).

Place of honor: for a more distinguished
person (see Luke 14:8).

Pool, clear and clean: resources of God/
Word of God (see Psalm 84:6).

Pool, contaminated, dirty or bloody: resources of God/Word of God that are
contaminated and not correct (see
Exodus 7:18–20).

Porch, back: history/past (rel); things
done behind the scene (char).

Porch, front:
revealed/open for viewing (func);
welcome (func);
clarity to see (char);
focus (char).

Prison:
in bondage (see Isaiah 42:7, 22);
legalistic custody (see Galatians 3:23);
caught up in bad things/tribulation
(see Revelation 2:10).

Property, belonging to you: your responsibility (char).

Q

Quarry: where you originate [are hewn];
your source (see Isaiah 51:1).

R

Ravines: low areas that are hard to get
out of (see Isaiah 57:5–6).

Refuge: Lord (see 2 Samuel 22:2, 32,
47; 23:3; Psalm 46:1; 91:2, 9; 94:22;
119:114; Jeremiah 16:19).

Restaurant: prepares teachings (food) for
people (see Nehemiah 9:15; Proverbs

18:20); place where one is "fed" or
taught (see Nehemiah 9:15; Proverbs
18:20).

Restaurant, fast food: learning things fast
(see Nehemiah 9:15; Proverbs 18:20);
learning that is not good/healthy for
you (see Nehemiah 9:15; Proverbs
18:20).

Ridge: cliff (char); a dangerous area that
could lead to falls (func).

River:
movement/way of God (see Psalm
36:8; Isaiah 48:18; 66:12; John
7:38–39);
flowing in the Spirit; difficulty (see Isaiah 43:2);
life (see Ezekiel 47:9).

River, frozen: Word of God that is cold;
does not flow (char).

Riverbed: a channel that the flow of God
may flow through (see Isaiah 66:12;
Jeremiah 17:7–8).

Riverbed, dry: a hard, dry period of life
(see Isaiah 19:5; Jeremiah 50:38);
Lord's provision and works have
dried up (see Isaiah 19:5; Jeremiah
50:38).

Road:
life's pathway (see Isaiah 57:14; Matthew 7:13);
the direction you are going (see Numbers 22:32; Psalm 23:3; Proverbs
14:12);
see Themes/Places/Highway.

Road, crooked: veering off from the correct course (see Ecclesiastes 1:15).

Road, dirt: man's pathway/not God's
way (see Isaiah 57:14).

Road, ends: point at which you need
to review the way you are going or
what you are doing (rel).

Road, narrow: leads to life (see Matthew
7:13).

Road, straight: of the Lord (see Psalm
27:11; Proverbs 2:13–15; Ecclesiastes
1:15; Isaiah 40:3; Matthew 3:3).

Road, wide: leads to destruction (see
Matthew 7:14).

Rock: Lord (see Deuteronomy 32:4, 15,
18; Psalm 31:2–3; Isaiah 17:10); a hard,

unprofitable area (see Deuteronomy 32:13; Matthew 13:5).

Rock, cleft: protection (see Exodus 33:21–23; Jeremiah 16:16).

Roof: spiritual or worldly covering over what's under the roof (func); look at who/what is protecting or controlling things (char).

Roof, caved in: lost protection (func).

Roof, on top of:

outside protection (func);

control (covering) (char);

place from which to proclaim loudly (see Matthew 10:27).

Room: area/where you are emotionally, etc. (char).

Rooms with closed doors: unknown things going on (char).

Ruins: not fortified/desolate (see Ezekiel 35:4; 36:35).

Runway: to go your own way (func); run away (play on words).

S

Salem: peace (see Hebrews 7:2).

Sanctuary: place of peace (see Psalm 63:2); place to find God (see Psalm 96:6; 150:1; Isaiah 8:14).

Sand:

[shores] place of decision (func);

false; bad foundation (see Matthew 7:26);

will not withstand trials (see Matthew 7:27);

numerous (see 2 Samuel 17:11, Isaiah 48:19).

School:

teaching [spiritual learning] (see Matthew 9:13; Hebrews 5:12; 6:1);

spiritual education process/learning spiritual things (see 2 Timothy 2:15, 3:7; Hebrews 5:12; 6:1);

learning to do good (see Isaiah 1:17).

School, classroom: an area of learning or training (see 2 Timothy 2:15; 3:7; Hebrews 5:12; 6:1).

School, college or high school: place of a higher (godly) level of learning (see Hebrews 5:12—6:2).

School, elementary: place of an elementary level of learning (see Hebrews 5:12—6:2).

School building, upper floor: higher level of learning (see 2 Timothy 2:15; 3:7; Hebrews 5:12; 6:1).

Sea:

multitudes of people/humanity (see Psalm 68:22; Hebrews 11:12; Revelation 13:1);

deep (see Lamentations 2:13);

trouble (see Isaiah 57:20; Jeremiah 49:23; Zechariah 10:11);

spiritual impact; too far to cross (see Deuteronomy 30:13);

immeasurable (see Jeremiah 33:22).

Seashore: numerous people (see Joshua 11:4); [shores] place of decision (char).

Shack: vacation (rel); where you are living now (char).

Shaft: transition/passageway (see 2 Samuel 5:8).

Shelter: protection (see Psalm 91:1); the Lord (see Isaiah 25:4).

Shopping center: place of provision (func); able to receive provisions from several sources (func).

Shore, distant: other nations (see Psalm 97:1).

Shoreline: line of decision (char).

Shower, clogged: cleansing cannot occur until you get rid of plugged-up stuff (func).

Shower, plugged: communication plugged (func).

Shrine: idol (see 2 Kings 23:19).

Sidewalk: daily action; life on the side [away from main place of dream] (char).

Sink: to sink low (char).

Sky: very high (see Psalm 71:19).

Skyscraper: high revelation (char).

Sky roof: covering of the Holy Spirit (see General/Roof, see General/Sky).

Slippery places: areas where it is easy to slide downward to destruction (see Psalm 73:18).

Solarium: place where growth should occur (func).

Spring, muddied: righteousness infected by evil (see Proverbs 25:26).

Stadium: tremendous impact (func).

Stage: in public (func); being watched (char); life in public (char).

Stairs:

transitioning up to a higher level (char);

improving (char);

transitioning down to a lower level (char);

regression (char);

portal to heaven (see Genesis 28:12–17).

Stairs, down:

loss of anointing (char);

downward transition (char);

lower level of living (char);

to dark night of the soul (char).

Stairs, narrow, upward: narrow way to life (see Matthew 7:13); portal (see Genesis 28:12–17); transition to a higher level (char).

Stairs, steep: difficult transition (char).

Steps: passageway (char); short time (see 1 Samuel 20:3).

Storage area: storing things you are no longer using (func); see Themes/Places/Warehouse.

Store:

place of provision for receiving teachings [food]/church (see 1 Kings 9:19; 1 Chronicles 27:25; Nehemiah 12:44–47; Psalm 33:7; 144:13; Isaiah 33:6; 39:2–9; Jeremiah 10:13; 51:16; Matthew 11:16; 20:3);

church (see Malachi 3:10);

materialism/trying to get everything one needs or wants/materialism (see 1 Kings 9:19; 1 Chronicles 27:25; Nehemiah 12:44–47; Psalm 33:7; 144:13; Isaiah 33:6; 39:2–9; Jeremiah 10:13; 51:16; Matthew 11:16);

egotism (see Matthew 11:16).

Store, convenience:

convenient materialism (char);

convenient provision (char);

work or church (char).

Store, country: serene (rel).

Store, nationwide:

nationwide center of distribution (func);

nationwide provision (func; see Matthew 11:16);

large church (char; see Matthew 11:16);

look at the name of the store.

Storehouse: place of storage/place of provision (see Jeremiah 10:13); see Themes/Places/Stores; see Themes/Places/Warehouse.

Story: phase (char).

Stream, intermittent: undependable (see Job 6:15–17).

Stream:

ministry;

life filled with God (see Psalm 65:9);

God's sustaining care and gentleness; movement of God (see Psalm 1:3; Isaiah 8:6; 66:12);

see Themes/Places/River.

Streams, dry:

without God's direction and Word (char);

judgment of God (see Ezekiel 30:12);

without life (char).

Streams, from spring runoff, dry at other times: undependable (see Job 6:15–17).

Street, broad: fleshly ways (see Jeremiah 5:1).

Street, in the middle of the city: marketplace (func); government (rel); business (rel).

Street, muddy: places that are dirty and not of God (see Zechariah 10:5).

Street: no home (see Lamentations 4:5); see Themes/Places/Road.

Street, of dust: without water of God (see Lamentations 2:2; 3:16).

Streets, with houses: where people live; where you are emotionally (see Isaiah 58:12).

Stronghold:

place of protection [good or bad] (see Judges 6:2; 1 Samuel 22:3–5; 23:14–19; 2 Samuel 5:17; 1 Chronicles 11:16; Psalm 18:2);

area of behavior (see 1 Samuel 22:3–4; 23:14–19);

Lord (see 2 Samuel 22:2, 32, 47; 23:3; Psalm 9:9; 18:2; 27:1; 46:11; 48:3; 59:9; Nahum 1:7).

Swamp: trials/easy to get bogged down; not fresh; left for salt (see Ezekiel 47:6–11); not a good foundation (char).

Swimming pool:

immersed in the Word [see General/ Water] of God;

place of healing (see John 5:7, 9:7);

place of favor, blessing and refreshment (see Psalm 107:35; 114:8; Isaiah 35:7; 41:18; Nahum 2:8).

Swimming pool, draining away: losing God's favor or the Word of God (see Nahum 2:8); losing immersion in the Word of God (see General/Water).

Synagogue: earthly place of following (see Revelation 2:9; 21:22).

T

Table: see General/Table.

Temple:

God's children (see Revelation 3:12);

church people (see 1 Corinthians 3:16);

earthly place of following (see Revelation 2:9; 21:22).

Tent:

temporary situation you are in (see 1 Chronicles 17:1–6; Psalm 52:5, 76:2);

house where you are living (see Hebrews 11:9–10);

church in a temporary position (see 1 Chronicles 9:23);

temporary state of being (see Jeremiah 35:7–10; Hebrews 11:9–10);

easily removed (see Isaiah 38:12).

Tent, covering: priest (as in covering over a church).

Theater: life (see Acts 19:28–32).

Theater, playhouse: acting out roles in life (func).

Threshing floor:

churches (see Joel 2:24);

lifted higher [floor raised] (see 2 Chronicles 18:9);

place where the separation of good from bad occurs (see 2 Samuel 24:18–25; Isaiah 27:12; Matthew 3:12);

trampled (see Jeremiah 51:33);

harvest will come later (see Jeremiah 51:33).

Tomb: place where the spiritually dead are (see Genesis 23:6; Mark 5:2–5; Luke 11:48); death (see Genesis 50:5; Judges 16:31).

Tomb, white: looks beautiful on the outside, but on the inside is unclean and full of dead bones (see Matthew 23:27).

Tower:

protection (see 2 Chronicles 14:7);

strength (see Psalm 48:12);

leader (see Judges 9:46–47, 51);

name of the Lord (see Proverbs 18:10);

things held high (see Isaiah 2:15);

looking out for you (see Ezekiel 27:11);

proud (see Ezekiel 31:14).

Town, empty: because of violence (see Ezekiel 12:20).

Town, home: dealing with issues from the past (char); place without honor (see Matthew 13:57).

Train station:

waiting while being made ready for ministry or work (func);

on track [doing it right] (func);

being railroaded (play on words).

Tunnel:

transition/passageway (see 2 Samuel 5:8; 2 Kings 20:20; 2 Chronicles 32:30);

trial (see Job 28:10);

dark, troubling experience (char);

unable to understand or see clearly the things around you (as in "tunnel vision").

U

Unfamiliar places: future issues (see Isaiah 42:16); unknown (see Isaiah 42:16); fear (char).

University: called to learn at a higher level (func).

V

Valley: low period (see 2 Kings 3:16; Job 30:6; Isaiah 40:4; Ezekiel 32:5).

Vineyard:

church/a place where one may enjoy the fruit from the work of the Holy Spirit (see Jeremiah 31:5; Micah 1:6; Matthew 21:28–43);

nation/people (see Isaiah 5:1–7);

workplace (see Matthew 21:28, 33–43).

W

Wall:

protection (see 1 Samuel 25:16; 2 Chronicles 14:7; Psalm 80:12; 89:40; 144:13; Isaiah 5:5; Jeremiah 1:15, 18; Ezekiel 26:4; Matthew 21:33);

barrier (see Numbers 35:4; 1 Samuel 25:16; Lamentations 3:7; Song of Solomon 8:8–9; Isaiah 2:15; Jeremiah 39:4; Ezekiel 12:5–7; Haggai 2:3–5; Ephesians 2:14);

faithful people united in their efforts to resist evil (see Ezekiel 13:5; 22:30);

something to get through/fortified (see Deuteronomy 3:5–6; 1 Samuel 25:16; 2 Chronicles 14:7; Psalm 78:13; 89:40; 144:13; Jeremiah 1:15, 18; Ezekiel 26:4; Matthew 21:33);

no escape (see 1 Samuel 19:10);

division (see Ephesians 2:14).

Wall, break down:

removing barriers (see Ephesians 2:14);

may be bitten by evil as a result (see Ecclesiastes 10:8);

no self-control (see Proverbs 25:28);

unable to stand firm (see Ezekiel 13:5);

foundation is broken (see Isaiah 58:12).

Wall, disrepair/gap: no one to lead people back to God (see Ezekiel 22:30).

Wall, fire: God's protection (see Zechariah 2:5).

Wall, gap repaired by the feeble: rituals or messages of opinion rather than God's will (see Ezekiel 22:30).

Wall, high: pride (see Isaiah 25:11–12).

Wall, hole: area where you can get out (see Ezekiel 12:5); area where bad things can get in (see Nehemiah 4:1–23; 6:1–6; Ezekiel 8:7).

Wall, leaning: ready to fall from a high position (see Psalm 62:3); man in his weakness (see Psalm 62:3).

Wall, scale: to get past or go over a barrier (see 2 Samuel 22:30; Psalm 18:29).

Wall, thick: deep, wide protection (see Jeremiah 51:58).

Wall, whitewashed:

barrier (see Matthew 21:33);

barrier that appears to be doing right but in fact is against God (see Acts 23:3);

blocked by God (see Hosea 2:6).

Wall, without: unsuspecting and peaceful (see Ezekiel 38:11).

Warehouse:

place of storage [storehouse]/place of provision (see 1 Chronicles 27:25; Nehemiah 12:44–47; Psalm 33:7; Jeremiah 51:16; Matthew 13:52);

treasure/to place great store [as in storehouse] on something/wealth (see Psalm 144:13; Isaiah 39:2; Matthew 13:52);

inheritance (see Isaiah 39:6).

Waters, deep: see General/Waters, deep.

Well: where one gets refreshed (see Genesis 13:10; 21:19; 24:20; Proverbs 5:15).

Well, polluted: righteousness that is infected by evil (see Proverbs 25:26).

Whorehouse: churches that are not of God (see Leviticus 19:29; 20:5–6; Jeremiah 5:7).

Wilderness: place of trials (see Matthew 3:3; 4:1); see Themes/Places/Desert.

Wooden structure: man-made (see 2 Samuel 5:11; 7:7; 2 Timothy 2:20).

World: not of God (see John 8:23; 15:19; 17:16; 18:36; Romans 12:2; 1 Corinthians 2:12; James 4:4; 1 John 2:15–17); things of the earth (see John 16:33; Ephesians 2:2; James 4:4).

Y

Yard: area you have authority over (see 2 Kings 9:27); domain (see 1 Kings 21:2; 2 Kings 21:18).

Z

Zion: city of God (see Hebrews 12:22).
Zoo: caged in (func).

Body Parts

A

Accent: designates where they "live" or whom they represent (see Judges 12:5–6; Matthew 26:73).

Ankle:

stability (see 2 Samuel 22:37; Psalm 18:36; Acts 3:7);

faithful following (see Ezekiel 47:1–3);

easy to turn (see 2 Samuel 22:37; Psalm 18:36).

Arm:

strength (see Genesis 49:24; Deuteronomy 7:19; 2 Chronicles 32:8; Psalm 44:3; 78:11; 89:10, 21; Isaiah 44:12; 51:9; 62:8; Ezekiel 30:21–25; Zechariah 11:17);

power (see Numbers 11:23 NIV; Psalm 89:13; Isaiah 40:10; 63:12; Jeremiah 32:17, 21);

justice (see Exodus 6:6; Isaiah 51:5);

strength of God (see Exodus 6:6–8; Deuteronomy 4:34; 33:27; Isaiah 52–53);

works (see Deuteronomy 7:19; John 12:38);

embrace (see Genesis 33:4; 45:14; 46:29; Numbers 11:12);

weapon (see Numbers 31:5; 32:17–20).

Arm, bare: holy salvation of God (see Isaiah 52:10); show strength (see Isaiah 52:10; 53:1).

Arm, broken: loss of strength (see Jeremiah 48:25; Ezekiel 30:21).

Arm, broken, without a cast or splint: not strong enough to cause pain to others (see Ezekiel 30:21); to take away strength (see Ezekiel 30:22–24).

Arm, left: things you are born to do (see Leviticus 14:15, 26; Matthew 20:23).

Arm, long: lots of ability (see Numbers 11:23; Isaiah 59:1).

Arm, outstretched:

redeem (see Exodus 6:6; Deuteronomy 7:19);

save (see Isaiah 59:2);

judgment against (see Deuteronomy 4:34; Ezekiel 20:33–34).

Arm, right: things you have an anointing to do (see Genesis 48:18; Hebrews 10:12; 12:2).

Arm, tensed: forced (see Exodus 13:18; 15:16; Psalm 89:13; Isaiah 40:10; 63:12; Jeremiah 32:17, 21).

Arm, too short:

not able to ransom (see Isaiah 50:2);

obtain (see Isaiah 50:2);

limited ability (see Numbers 11:23; Isaiah 59:1).

Arm, will not work: something in the Spirit not fully operating yet (see Hebrews 12:13).

B

Back:

support/burden (see Psalm 66:11 NIV);

hidden from (see Exodus 33:23; Joshua 8:4);

to turn one's back on (see 1 Kings 14:9; Isaiah 38:17; Jeremiah 18:17; Ezekiel 8:16);

away from (see Exodus 33:23; Jeremiah 2:27; 32:33; Mark 8:33).

Back, behind: not paying attention to (see 1 Kings 14:9).

Back, bent: burdened (see Psalm 69:23 NIV).

Back, pain: see General/Burden (see Psalm 38:7 NIV).

Back, turned: to flee (see Psalm 18:40).

Beard: maturity (see Job 15:10; Proverbs 20:29; Joel 2:28; Acts 2:17).

Beard, cut off: mourning (see Jeremiah 48:37).

Beard, half-shaved: to ridicule; humiliate (see 2 Samuel 10:4–5).

Belly:

heart (see Matthew 12:40);

exposure [a good thing]; to be vulnerable (see Judges 3:21; 2 Samuel 2:23; 3:27; 4:6; 20:10);

appetites/desires (see 1 John 2:17);

inner man (see Job 40:16; Matthew 12:40);

humility (see 1 Chronicles 29:20).

Belly, fat or obese [in the dream only because the person in real life is not overweight]: operating out of "fleshly" motives [in the flesh] (see Deuteronomy 32:15; Job 15:25–27); dealing with appetites/desires (see Job 20:23).

Belly, full: an unbalanced soulish issue that does not allow rest (see Ecclesiastes 5:12).

Blemish: sin (see Leviticus 22:21; Ephesians 5:27; 1 Peter 1:19).

Blood:

covenant (see Exodus 29:12–20; 1 Kings 18:28; Ezekiel 45:19; Hebrews 12:24);

salvation/redemption/allows entrance to God (see Ephesians 2:13; Hebrews 10:19);

life (see Genesis 49:11; Deuteronomy 12:23; 1 Samuel 14:32–34; Matthew 27:24–25);

family (see Genesis 29:14; 37:27; Isaiah 58:7);

Passover (see Exodus 12:23);

injury (see Deuteronomy 19:6; Ezekiel 16:6; 32:6);

defiled (see Isaiah 59:3);

murder (see Genesis 4:10–11; 42:22; 2 Samuel 21:1; Isaiah 59:3; Matthew 27:24–25).

Blood, you caused to be shed: guilty (see Genesis 4:10–11; Ezekiel 22:3–4).

Body:

true church of God; church's individual parts (see Ephesians 1:20–23; 4:12–16; 5:30; Colossians 1:24; Hebrews 13:3);

followers of Christ (see 1 Corinthians 12:20);

true church as a whole (see Ephesians 1:22–23);

human body (see Colossians 2:5).

Body, without spirit: dead (see James 2:26).

Body parts immobilized: could be spiritual hindrance—see the Body Part.

Bones:

dried up (see Jeremiah 8:1–2);

things that are dead (see Ezekiel 37:1);

garbage/refuse (see Ezekiel 24:5; Psalm 141:7);

core of humanness (see Proverbs 12:4; 14:30; Isaiah 38:13; 66:14).

Bones, dry:

scattered and dead (see Ezekiel 37:1–12; Matthew 23:27);

no hope (see Ezekiel 37:11);

spiritually dead (see Ezekiel 37:4–5).

Bones, exposed: things that should be honored are exposed and dishonored (see Jeremiah 8:1–2).

Bone, rot: envy (see Proverbs 14:30); shame (see Proverbs 12:4); fear (see Habakkuk 3:16).

Bottom: on the bottom of things (see Exodus 15:5; 26:24; Deuteronomy 28:13).

Brace, on body part: human efforts to compensate (func).

Brains, two: see Themes/Body Parts/Doubleminded.

Breasts:

nurturing (see Isaiah 60:16; 66:11; Lamentations 4:3; Song of Solomon 8:1; 1 Thessalonians 2:7);

safety/comfort (see Job 24:9; Psalm 22:9; Song of Solomon 8:10);

emotions and the heart of life (see Job
3:12; Ephesians 6:14);

female sexuality (see Proverbs 5:19;
Song of Solomon 1:13; 4:5; 7:3, 8);

adultery (see Ezekiel 23:21).

Breasts, false: false front (char).

Buttocks, bare: in shame (see 2 Samuel
10:4; 1 Chronicles 19:4; Isaiah 20:4).

C

Callous: giving oneself over to sensual-
ity for impurity and greediness (see
Psalm 73:7; Acts 28:27; Ephesians
4:19); unfeeling (see Psalm 17:10;
119:70; Isaiah 6:10; Matthew 13:15).

Cheek:
vulnerability (see Job 16:10; Psalm 3:7);

place of attack (see 1 Kings 22:24;
2 Chronicles 18:23; Job 16:10; Isaiah
50:6; Lamentations 3:30; Micah 5:1;
Luke 6:29);

to offer to one who would strike you
(see Lamentations 3:30; Isaiah 50:6;
Matthew 5:39);

beauty (see Song of Solomon 1:10;
5:13).

Chin: confidence/arrogance/pride (char;
as in "chin is set").

D

Doubleminded: to be unstable in all
one's ways and lacking faith (see
James 1:8); people who cannot make
up their mind between good and
evil; to balance competing agendas
in one's thinking; duplicity (see
Psalm 119:113; James 1:8; 4:8).

E

Ears:
hearing God's Word (see Job 12:11;
Proverbs 5:13; Matthew 13:43);

the ability to listen/understand (see
Deuteronomy 29:4; 2 Chronicles
6:40; 17:20; Psalm 5:1; 115:6; 116:1–2;
135:17; Proverbs 5:1; Isaiah 55:3; Jeremiah 5:21; 34:14; Ezekiel 12:2; 40:4;
Matthew 13:9–19; 15:10; 2 Timothy
4:4; Revelation 3:22);

those who can "hear" [understand]
(see Deuteronomy 29:4; 2 Chronicles 6:40; 17:20; Psalm 5:1; 115:6;
116:1–2; 135:17; Proverbs 5:1; Isaiah
55:3; Jeremiah 5:21; 34:14; Ezekiel
12:2; 40:4; Matthew 13:9–19; 15:10;
2 Timothy 4:4; Revelation 3:22);

attentiveness (see 2 Chronicles 6:40;
7:15; Nehemiah 1:6, 11; 8:3; Psalm
130:2);

to be discerning (see Job 12:11).

Ears, dull: not going to listen/hear well
(see Psalm 58:4–5; Isaiah 59:1).

Ears, full of wax: not going to listen/hear
as well (see Psalm 58:4–5; Isaiah 59:1).

Ears, marked: designated for cleansing
(see Leviticus 14:14, 17, 25).

Ears, pierced: belonging to (see Exodus
21:6); made to "hear" or understand
(see Psalm 40:6); forced to serve
(see Exodus 21:6).

Ears, tickled: to hear meaningless, "good
feeling," but unsound things (see
2 Timothy 4:3).

Elbow:
joint power/the power of many (see
Job 31:22);

closeness to others (holding onto the
elbow of another);

to make room for [as in "elbow in"]
(see 2 Kings 6:1; Esther 1:8).

Eye, picked out: one who mocks and dis-
obeys (see Proverbs 20:20; 30:17).

Eye, right: intellect (see Zechariah 11:17).

Eyebrows raised: arrogant (see Proverbs
30:13).

Eyelids raised: arrogant (see Proverbs
30:13).

Eyes:
prophetic (see Isaiah 29:10; Matthew
6:22);

to understand/see (see Deuteronomy
11:7; 29:4; Psalm 115:5; 135:16;

Jeremiah 5:21; Ezekiel 12:2; 40:4; Matthew 13:13; Ephesians 1:18); insight (see Judges 8:7; Revelation 1:14; 4:6);

those who can see [understand] (see Psalm 119:18; Revelation 1:14; 4:6);

to keep watch over (see Psalm 33:18; 91:8; Ezekiel 5:5; 1 Peter 3:12);

the way you are seeing life (see Matthew 6:22–23; Ephesians 1:18);

flirting with sin/lust (see Isaiah 3:16);

fountain of tears (see Jeremiah 9:1).

Eyes, bad: not looking at things correctly (see Matthew 7:5); fixed on darkness (see Matthew 6:23; Luke 11:34).

Eyes, blazing fire: God/Jesus (see Revelation 1:14; 2:18; 19:12); angel (see Daniel 10:6).

Eyes, blind:

not able to see the light of the Gospel/God (see Isaiah 59:10; Matthew 15:14);

unable to understand (see Psalm 69:3; Isaiah 29:18);

refusing to act justly (see Deuteronomy 16:19; 1 Samuel 12:3).

Eyes, closed: sleep/unaware (see Psalm 77:4; Matthew 13:15).

Eyes, dark: unable to understand/see (see Psalm 69:23; 1 John 2:11).

Eyes, dark circles underneath: seeing things darkly; depressed (see Job 16:16).

Eyes, dim: unable to understand/see clearly/unbelief (see Psalm 88:9).

Eyes, flashing: anger (see Job 15:12–13).

Eyes, good: spiritual vision fixed on God (see Matthew 6:22).

Eyes, green: envy (as in "green with envy"); see Themes/Colors/Green.

Eyes, haughty: pride (see 2 Samuel 22:28; Psalm 18:26–27; 101:5).

Eyes, hollow: unable to see (func); empty inside (char); no substance (char).

Eyes, of a person: a person's opinion (see 2 Chronicles 28:1; 29:2–8; 33:2).

Eyes, open: understands (see Genesis 3:5–7; Numbers 24:4; 1 Kings 8:52).

Eyes, piercing: opponent (see Job 16:9).

Eyes, red: sorrow (see Proverbs 23:29); anger (as in "to see red"); demon (char).

Eyes, someone closing another's: to see their death (see Genesis 46:4).

F

Face:

man's heart (see Leviticus 26:17; 1 Chronicles 16:11; Nehemiah 2:2; Proverbs 27:19);

reflection of the inner heart (see Daniel 3:19);

going in the direction of (see Ezekiel 8:16; 10:11; Habakkuk 1:9);

draw near to (see Genesis 32:30; Jeremiah 2:27);

look at clearly (see Genesis 33:10; Numbers 12:8; Deuteronomy 31:17);

outer covering (see Genesis 1:2, 29);

glory and majesty (see Revelation 1:16).

Face, against: to come against/oppose (see Ezekiel 35:2; 38:2).

Face, covered: so that you cannot see (see Genesis 9:23; Ezekiel 12:6–13).

Face, hard: without wisdom (see Ecclesiastes 8:1); refusing to receive correction (see Proverbs 21:29; Jeremiah 5:3).

Face, hidden: Holy Spirit (see Isaiah 59:2).

Face, hide: to alienate from others and curse (see Psalm 13:1; 30:7; 44:23–26; 88:13–14).

Face, lit up:

love (see Psalm 44:3);

blessing (see Psalm 67:1);

look upon the Lord/Lord (see Psalm 34:5; Revelation 1:16).

Face, on the ground: to pay honor (see Genesis 19:1; 2 Samuel 14:22); repentant (func); humility (see Lamentations 3:29).

Face, pale: frightened/alarmed (see Isaiah 29:22; Jeremiah 30:6; Daniel 5:6–10).

Face, red: weeping (see Job 16:16).

Face, revealed: blessing (see Psalm 4:6–7; 31:15–16; 67:1; 80:3).

Face, wash: to clean up outer covering; to hide what you are doing (see Matthew 6:17–18).

Faces, four (one on each side): a watchdog—looking in all four directions (see Daniel 7:6).

Fangs, broken: unable to be effective in wickedness (see Job 29:17).

Fatness: satisfied/plenty (see Job 15:27; Psalm 63:5; 65:11; 73:4).

Feet:
individual peace (see Ephesians 6:15);
humbleness and closeness (see Luke 10:39);
Word of God (see Ephesians 6:15);
direction you choose to go/what you stand for/the path chosen (see Psalm 35:15; 40:2; Hebrews 12:13);
to have dominion over (see Ephesians 1:22);
human power (see Acts 9:1–22);
to travel to foreign places (see Matthew 28:19–20).

Feet, bare:
without peace or harmony/upset (see Jeremiah 2:25; Ephesians 6:15);
vulnerable to pain/upset (see Deuteronomy 25:9–10);
servant/humility (see Exodus 3:5; Deuteronomy 33:3);
tired/exhausted (see Jeremiah 2:25);
on holy ground (see Exodus 3:5).

Feet, cleansing:
servitude (see Genesis 24:32; 1 Samuel 25:40–42; John 13:5);
rest (see Genesis 18:4; 43:24);
daily walk; cleansing walk (see John 13:6–10).

Feet, dust: a remnant of where you have been (see Mark 6:11; Luke 8:5); problems picked up from life (see Isaiah 49:23; Matthew 10:14).

Feet, glowing bronze: God (see Revelation 1:14; 2:18).

Feet, kick: disdain for (see 1 Samuel 2:29; Acts 26:14); to fight against (see Acts 26:14).

Feet, lame: disabled; something affecting your walk (see Acts 14:8; Hebrews 12:13); something affecting the direction you choose to go (see Acts 14:8; Hebrews 12:13).

Feet, soles: where you live or what you are doing (see 2 Kings 19:24; Ezekiel 43:7).

Feet, underneath: standing; under control (see 1 Kings 5:3; Matthew 22:44); overcome (see Matthew 22:44; Romans 16:20).

Finger: a very small work (see Matthew 23:4; Luke 11:46); into details (see Exodus 8:19).

Finger, cut off: losing work (see Exodus 8:19; Matthew 23:4).

Finger, little: teaching (direction or relationship of fivefold ministry); the least of me (see 1 Kings 12:10; 2 Chronicles 10:10).

Finger, longest: evangelist (direction or relationship of fivefold ministry).

Finger, middle: evangelist (direction or relationship of fivefold ministry).

Finger, motion: stirs up dissension (see Proverbs 6:13).

Finger, pointer:
intercession; discernment (see John 8:6–10);
prophet (see Exodus 8:19; John 8:6–10; direction or relationship of fivefold ministry);
works (see Isaiah 2:8);
conviction/accusation (see Proverbs 6:13; Isaiah 58:9; Daniel 5:5–28; Luke 11:20; John 8:7).

Finger, thumb: apostolic; organization/administration; able to hold others securely;

Finger, ring: pastoral (direction or relationship of fivefold ministry).

Fist, shake: anger (see Job 15:25).

Fist, tight: stingy (see Deuteronomy 15:7).

Flesh:
tenderhearted and open (see Ezekiel 11:19; 36:26);
life (see Judges 8:7; Ephesians 2:15);
worldly/carnal (see 2 Chronicles 32:8; Romans 8:1–13; 2 Corinthians 10:3–4; Ephesians 2:11, 22; 6:12);

temporary (see Psalm 78:39);

weak/man (see Jeremiah 17:5; 2 Corinthians 10:3–4; Ephesians 2:11; 6:12);

desires/craving of man (see Ephesians 2:3; 1 John 2:17).

Foot: go to (see Joshua 1:3; Proverbs 25:17).

Foot, bare: without peace (see Isaiah 20:2); stressed (see 2 Samuel 15:30).

Foot, lame: unreliable (see Proverbs 25:19).

Foot, out of joint: relying on an unreliable person (see Proverbs 25:19).

Foot, slip: to make a mistake (see Deuteronomy 32:35).

Foot, unsteady: receiving wrong counsel (see Proverbs 25:19).

Forehead:

remember (see Deuteronomy 6:8);

for distinct viewing (see Revelation 7:3; 13:16; 22:4);

unyielding and hardened (see Jeremiah 3:3; Ezekiel 3:8–9).

Forearm: armed [prepared] ahead of time (play on words); strength and faith (see Exodus 6:6–8; Isaiah 52:10).

Foreskin: fleshly covering (see Jeremiah 4:4); covenantal relationship (see Genesis 17:11, 14; Deuteronomy 10:16).

G

Gall bladder: place where you hold bitterness (see Hebrews 12:15).

Genitals:

being productive (see Genesis 4:1);

a secret/private matter (see Genesis 3:21);

shame (see Genesis 2:25; Ezekiel 23:17);

lust (see Ezekiel 23:20).

H

Hair:

covenant authority over you (see Numbers 6:9; Ezekiel 44:20; Acts 18:18);

covenant of love (see John 12:3);

covering/who you are/anointing (see Song of Solomon 7:5; 1 Corinthians 11:14–15; Revelation 1:14);

strength (see Judges 16:19–22);

many in number (see Psalm 40:12; 69:4; Matthew 10:30; Luke 12:7).

Hair, braid: thinking that ties your covering in knots (see 1 Timothy 2:9; 2 Timothy 2:4; Hebrews 12:1–3; 1 Peter 3:3); covering that is twisted (see Matthew 27:29).

Hair, clumped baldness: the result of haughtiness (see Isaiah 3:16–24).

Hair, curly: bending toward (char); flexible covenants (char).

Hair, cut: grieve (see Jeremiah 7:29).

Hair, gelled back: a covenant covered up to look like something else or controlled (func).

Hair, gray:

old (see Deuteronomy 32:25; Job 15:10; Proverbs 20:29; Isaiah 46:4);

crown of splendor/glory (see Proverbs 16:31; 20:29);

righteous person (see Proverbs 16:31);

honor (see Proverbs 20:29).

Hair, groomed: a covenant that is correct and taken care of (char).

Hair, kinky: thinking that entangles (see 2 Timothy 2:4; Hebrews 12:1–3).

Hair, light: covered by the light of God (char; see General/Light).

Hair, long on a man: strength (see Judges 16:17–19); vow (see Judges 13:4–5); rebellion/dishonor (see Ezekiel 44:20; 1 Corinthians 11:14).

Hair, long on a woman: honor/glory (see 1 Corinthians 11:15).

Hair, messy: unwilling to submit to disentanglement (see 2 Timothy 2:4; Hebrews 12:1–3).

Hair, shaved: in mourning (see Jeremiah 47:5; 48:37; Micah 1:16); consecrated (see Numbers 6:19).

Hair, tangled: covering you are in bondage to (see Leviticus 10:6; Psalm 68:21; Hebrews 12:1–3).

Hair, thin: thin covering (char).

Hair, white: holy (see Daniel 7:9; Revelation 1:14); occult [if you feel uneasy about the person] (see Matthew 23:27).

Hair, yellow: a covenant or covering of God (see Ezekiel 1:4, 27; 8:2); a covering of hope (as in "tie a yellow ribbon: hope, faith and expectation").

Hair, yellow and thin: unclean (see Leviticus 13:30–36); sick (see Leviticus 13:30–36).

Hand(s):

work/service/what you do (see Genesis 5:29; Exodus 3:20; Deuteronomy 21:7; 28:8; 30:9; 31:29; 33:11; Ruth 1:13; 1 Samuel 5:6; 10:7; 2 Samuel 22:21; 2 Chronicles 32:14, 19; Psalm 8:3–6; 9:16; 19:1; 90:17; 92:4; 138:8; Ecclesiastes 2:11; 9:1–10; Isaiah 56:2; Jeremiah 32:21; 44:25; Haggai 1:11; 2:17; Matthew 17:12; 23:4; James 4:8);

direction (see Genesis 19:16; Hebrews 8:9);

to assist (see Genesis 21:18; Deuteronomy 2:15; John 10:12; Hebrews 8:9);

relationship (see Genesis 16:12; 1 Chronicles 4:10);

in control of; ready to be taken (see Genesis 9:2; 14:20; 16:6; Deuteronomy 2:24; Judges 2:23; 8:3; 1 Samuel 17:47; Proverbs 6:3; Jeremiah 34:3; 38:5; Matthew 3:2; 4:17; Hebrews 8:9);

strength (see Psalm 89:13);

winnowing fork; gathering His wheat [God's people] and burning the chaff [people not of God] (see Matthew 3:12);

things done on earth [not by God], i.e., worshipping spirits, idolizing wealth, destroying each other, practicing spiritual art not of God, sexual openness, theft (see Colossians 2:11; Hebrews 9:11, 24; Revelation 9:20–21);

touch (see Colossians 2:21).

Hands, bloody: guilty, sinful (see Genesis 4:11; Isaiah 1:15; 59:3).

Hands, clapping: approval (char); joy (see Psalm 47:1; 98:8).

Hands, clean: clean work/clean conscience (see Genesis 20:5; 2 Samuel 22:21; Psalm 18:20–24).

Hands, dirty: dirty/bad work (see 2 Samuel 22:21; Psalm 18:20–24; Mark 7:5).

Hands, empty: without possessions (see Exodus 3:21).

Hands, feeble: works without strength/power (see Isaiah 35:3).

Hands, fist: ready to fight/anger (see Isaiah 9:17).

Hands, folded: not working (see Proverbs 6:10).

Hands, heavy: pressure on you (see Job 23:2; Psalm 32:4); bad or hard work (see Exodus 17:12; 1 Samuel 5:11); hard on others (see Psalm 32:4); judgement of the Lord (see 1 Samuel 5:6).

Hands, lay on: to impart to another (see 2 Timothy 1:6); blessing (see Matthew 19:15).

Hands, left:

things you were born for; your spiritual gifts (see Leviticus 14:15, 26; Matthew 20:23);

man (see Acts 2:25);

riches and honor (see Proverbs 3:16);

defensive (see 2 Corinthians 6:7).

Hands, left-handed: cunning and effective warrior/deliverer (see Judges 3:15; 20:16).

Hands, lifted:

worship (see Nehemiah 8:6; Psalm 28:2; 63:4; 91:12; 1 Timothy 2:8);

beg (see Lamentations 2:19);

sacrifice (see Psalm 141:2);

come against (see 2 Samuel 18:28; 20:21; Micah 5:9).

Hands, limp: unable to work (see Isaiah 13:7; Jeremiah 6:24).

Hands, on head: anguish (see Jeremiah 2:37).

Hands, open: freely offered (see Deuteronomy 15:8; Matthew 10:7).

Hands, raised: see Themes/Body Parts/Hands, lifted.

Hands, reached out: to take (see Genesis 3:22; 8:9).

Hands, right:

things you have strength of faith or skill to do now (see Psalm 63:8; 137:5; 138:7; 2 Corinthians 6:7);

of the Lord (see Psalm 98:1; Mark 16:19; Acts 2:25; Ephesians 1:20; Colossians 3:1; Revelation 1:16);

long life (see Proverbs 3:16; Hebrew 1:13; 10:12);

good works/purification (see Psalm 44:3; 78:54; 89:13, 25; 98:1; 108:6; 118:15–16; Hebrews 1:3).

Hands, shake: show of good intentions and good relationship (see Isaiah 33:15).

Hands, shriveled: powerless (see 1 Kings 13:4).

Hands, slashed: mourning (see Jeremiah 48:37).

Hands, stretched out: work extends outward widely (see Exodus 3:20; 1 Kings 8:38); help coming (see Matthew 14:31).

Hands, uplifted palm out: a promise (see 1 Kings 8:22; Ezekiel 44:12 NIV; 47:14 NIV) receiving/imparting (char).

Hands, upraised: ready to strike (see Isaiah 9:17, 21; 10:4; 19:16).

Hands, washing: sanctification (see Exodus 30:17–21; James 4:8); trying to obtain innocence/disassociate self from (see Psalm 73:13; Matthew 27:24).

Head:

power (see Daniel 2:36–38; Psalm 18:43; Isaiah 7:9; 9:14; Colossians 1:18; 2:10; Revelation 9:19; 17:9–10);

Christ (see Psalm 18:43; Isaiah 7:9; 9:14; Ephesians 4:15; 5:23; Colossians 1:18; 2:10);

leader (see Numbers 10:4; Psalm 18:43; Isaiah 7:9; 9:14; Ephesians 1:22; Colossians 1:18; 2:10);

authority (see Numbers 17:3; Deuteronomy 28:13; 1 Samuel 10:1; 15:17; 2 Chronicles 23:2; Ephesians 1:22; Revelation 1:14; 13:3);

judge (see Micah 3:11);

source (see Colossians 2:19; Philemon);

seer (see Isaiah 29:10);

beginning (see Colossians 1:18);

see Themes/Body Parts/Head, two-headed.

Head, bald: powerful man of God (see 2 Kings 2:23–24).

Head, covered: dismayed/despairing (see Jeremiah 14:4).

Head, cut off:

without leadership (see Numbers 10:4; Colossians 1:18);

without authority (see Numbers 17:3; Deuteronomy 28:13);

without Christ (see Psalm 18:43; Colossians 1:18; 2:10).

Head, dust on:

in mourning (see Lamentations 2:10);

humbled (see Genesis 18:27);

grief (see Lamentations 2:10);

stress (see 2 Samuel 15:32).

Head, of gold: human government (see Daniel 2:36–38).

Head, rubbed bare: hard campaign (see Ezekiel 29:18).

Head, shaking: disapproval/mockery/ scorn (see Job 16:4; Psalm 64:8; Matthew 27:39–41).

Head, shaved: cleansed of past life (see Deuteronomy 21:12); in mourning (see Isaiah 15:2; Jeremiah 16:6).

Head, two-headed: two main leaders involved (see Numbers 10:4; Isaiah 7:9; Colossians 1:18).

Head, white: holy (see Revelation 1:14); occult [if not a good thing] (see Matthew 23:27).

Heart:

mind, will and emotions (see Isaiah 6:10);

courage (see Joshua 7:7; Ephesians 3:13; Hebrews 12:3);

loyalty (see 2 Samuel 15:6, 13; 1 Kings 8:61; 11:4; 15:3; 1 Chronicles 29:9);

will/emotions/feelings (see 2 Chronicles 36:13; 36:22; Nehemiah 4:6; Psalm 62:8; Proverbs 15:13; 17:22; Jeremiah 17:9; Matthew 5:8, 28; 6:21; 9:4; 12:34; 15:8, 18–19; Luke 6:45; Ephesians 1:18; 6:22; Colossians 2:2; 3:12, 23; Philemon 12; Hebrews 3:8–10; 8:10; 10:22; James 4:8; 1 Peter 1:22; 3:15; 1 John 3:19–22);

evil thoughts (see Jeremiah 3:17; Matthew 15:19; Hebrews 10:22);

center (see Ezekiel 27:25);

stubborn (see Psalm 78:8; 81:12; Jeremiah 9:14; Isaiah 46:12);

compassionate (see Isaiah 6:10).

Heart, broken:

God will heal (see Psalm 147:3; Isaiah 61:1–3);

God wants from us (see Psalm 51:17);

God is near (see Psalm 34:18).

Heart, fail: unable to function because of sin (see Psalm 40:12).

Heart, flesh: soft heart (see Ezekiel 36:26).

Heart, guard: do not hang onto offenses; protect your willful actions, emotions and feelings (see 2 Chronicles 36:13; Matthew 5:8).

Heart, hard:

without compassion (see Deuteronomy 15:7; 2 Chronicles 36:13);

mind, will and emotions are so strong the Holy Spirit is unable to penetrate; unteachable (see Ephesians 4:17–20);

hard emotions; unbelief (see Hebrews 3:15–19).

Heart, moved: desire (see 2 Chronicles 36:22); led by God (see Ezra 1:1–5).

Heart, stone: hardhearted/hard emotions (see Ezekiel 36:26).

Heart, uncircumcised: those who do not believe (see Ezekiel 44:8).

Heel:

betrayal (see Psalm 41:9; John 13:18);

following closely/pursuing (see Job 18:9; Lamentations 5:5; Hosea 12:3);

injury that affects your walk; hurts that affect your way of living (see Genesis 3:15; 49:17);

bruising done by the enemy (see Genesis 3:15).

Hip: stubborn/tenacious [Jacob wrestled with angel and was struck on the hip] (see Genesis 32:25).

I

Immobilization of body parts: a spiritual hindrance to going forward (see the body part, e.g., foot: peace; hip: stubbornness, etc.).

J

Jaw: stubborn/tenacious and effective (see Judges 15:15–17); in the clutches of (see Job 36:16; Isaiah 30:28; Ezekiel 29:4; 38:4).

K

Kidney: way of cleansing toxins (see Exodus 29:13, 22; Lev 3:4; 4:9; 7:4; 8:16).

Knees:

pay homage to/bow before (see 1 Kings 1:31; 8:54; 19:18; Esther 3:2; Isaiah 45:23; Romans 11:4; 14:11; Ephesians 3:14; Philippians 2:10);

humble (see 1 Kings 18:42; Ezra 9:5; Mark 5:6);

niece (play on words);

ability to hold steady (see Job 4:4; Isaiah 35:3; Ezekiel 7:17; 21:7; Daniel 5:6; Hebrews 12:12);

beg (see Matthew 20:20; Mark 1:40; 5:6; Luke 5:8).

Knees, give way: without steadiness/fearful (see Job 4:4; Isaiah 35:3; Ezekiel 7:17; 21:7; Daniel 5:6; Hebrews 12:12).

Knees, knocked together: fearful (see Daniel 5:6).

Knees, on: bending one's will (see 1 Kings 18:42; Mark 5:6).

L

Lap: place of honor and love (see Genesis 48:12; 50:23; Job 3:12; Isaiah 66:12).

Leg:

foundation (see Exodus 25:26; Song of Solomon 5:15; Daniel 2:33; Revelation 10:1);

standing on (see Song of Solomon 5:15; Daniel 5:6);

ability to go forward (see Psalm 147:10; Proverbs 26:7; Habakkuk 3:16);

your "walk" or way of living (see Hebrews 12:13).

Leg, give way: fearful (see Daniel 5:6).

Leg, will not work: something not working completely (see Proverbs 26:7; Hebrews 12:13).

Ligament: built of love (see Ephesians 4:16).

Light: God (see 1 John 1:5).

Lips:

words spoken (see Exodus 13:9; 23:13; Numbers 30:6; Deuteronomy 23:23; 1 Samuel 1:13; Psalm 59:12; Proverbs 10:32; 16:13; Isaiah 6:5; 59:3; Matthew 15:8);

glorify (see Psalm 34:1; 51:15; 63:3);

grace (see Song of Solomon 2:5–15);

to preserve knowledge (see Proverbs 20:15; Malachi 2:7);

door (see Job 41:14; Psalm 141:3);

lies (see Isaiah 59:3).

Lips, burning: uttering insincere words of love (see Proverbs 26:23).

Lips, falter: speak ineffectively (see Exodus 6:12, 30).

Lips, pursed: bent on evil (see Proverbs 16:30).

Lips, unclean: speaking out wrongly (see Isaiah 6:5–7).

Liver: man-made decision/to tear down (see Ezekiel 21:21); purify/eliminate past problems (see Leviticus 8:16).

M

Marrow: satisfied/plenty (see Job 21:24).

Mind: focused on the main thing (see 1 Chronicles 12:38).

Mind, righteous: studies how to answer (see Proverbs 15:28; 1 Peter 3:15).

Mouth:

ability to prophesy (see Exodus 4:10–12; Numbers 22:28, 38; 23:5, 12, 16; Deuteronomy 18:18);

speaks of the heart (see Matthew 12:34; 15:18; Luke 6:45);

speak/things spoken (see 2 Chronicles 18:21–22; Joshua 1:8; Psalm 59:12;

63:5, 11; Proverbs 2:6; 10:32; 31:26; Isaiah 40:5; Jeremiah 1:9; 9:8; 115:5; 135:16);

seek instruction (see Proverbs 16:10; Malachi 2:7);

pastors; those who speak out (see Matthew 5:2);

teaching (see Matthew 5:2);

words (see Jeremiah 1:9–10; Psalm 62:4; Revelation 1:16; 9:17, 19);

emits hurtful things (see 2 Chronicles 18:21–22; Psalm 18:8; 19:15; 59:7; 149:6);

entrance (see Joshua 10:18–27; 15:5; 18:19; 1 Kings 19:13).

Mouth, cannot speak: ability to speak out is hindered (see Psalm 135:16); unable to talk to God/unable to pray (see Matthew 22:12).

Mouth, full of gravel: fraud (see Proverbs 20:17).

Mouth, open: able to speak (see Numbers 22:28).

Mouth, wicked: spews out evil things (see Proverbs 15:28).

Mustache: covering of the mouth; needs to be trimmed [watch what you speak] (see 2 Samuel 19:24).

Mustache, long, curling: villain (as in cartoon villains).

N

Nails: like claws/weapon (see Daniel 4:33).

Neck:

beauty (see Proverbs 1:9; 3:22; Song of Solomon 1:10; 4:4; 7:4);

warrior (see Song of Solomon 4:4);

will (see Exodus 32:9; 33:3, 5; Deuteronomy 9:6; Proverbs 29:1);

humility (see Exodus 32:9; 33:3, 5; Deuteronomy 9:6);

strength/tenacious (see Job 41:22);

support for the pastor [the head] (func).

Neck, brace: human efforts to compensate for stubbornness (see Nehemiah 9:16–19; 2 Kings 17:14).

Neck, outstretched: haughty; prideful (see Psalm 73:6; 75:5; Isaiah 3:16).

Neck, restrained: being controlled (see Psalm 105:18; Lamentations 1:14); bound to (see Proverbs 6:21; 105:18).

Neck, stiff:

not listening (see Nehemiah 9:29; Jeremiah 7:26; 17:23; 19:15);

stubborn (see Nehemiah 9:16–19; 2 Kings 17:14);

unyielding/not listening (see Exodus 32:9; Proverbs 29:1 NIV; Jeremiah 17:23; 19:15);

self-willed/disobedient (see Exodus 33:3–5; 34:9; Deuteronomy 9:6–13; 2 Chronicles 30:8; 36:13; Proverbs 29:1).

Neck, water comes up to: overwhelmed (see Psalm 69:1–2; Isaiah 30:28).

Nose: discernment/to sniff things out (see 2 Samuel 10:6; 22:9; 1 Chronicles 19:6; Psalm 115:6; Isaiah 65:5); smell (see Psalm 115:61; Amos 4:10).

Nose, bloody: covenantal discernment; unclean/defiled/blocking discernment.

Nose, ring: to stake a claim (see Genesis 24:47; 2 Chronicles 33:11; Job 40:24); to control (see Isaiah 37:29).

Nose, smoke in:

anger (see Psalm 18:8);

pride/arrogance/people who say; "Keep away, do not come near me, for I am too sacred for you" (see Isaiah 65:5);

see General/Smoke.

Nose, stick out: nosy (func).

P

Palate: tastes food/what you enjoy or dislike learning (see Job 12:11).

Palms: where God has engraved us (see Isaiah 49:16).

R

Ribs: close relationship (see Genesis 2:21–23); church; protector of the heart (see Hosea 13:8).

S

Shoulder:

burden (see Genesis 49:15; Numbers 7:9; Joshua 4:5; Isaiah 9:4–6; 10:27; Matthew 23:4);

ability to bear weight/be responsible (see Genesis 49:15; Exodus 12:34; Isaiah 9:6; Luke 15:5);

carry (see Numbers 7:9; Joshua 4:5; Ezekiel 12:6);

shove (see Ezekiel 34:21).

Shoulder, raw: hard campaign (see Ezekiel 29:18).

Shoulder, riding: being responsible for someone (see Deuteronomy 33:12).

Side: place of friendship/alongside of (see Genesis 31:52; Exodus 17:12); relationship/new relationship (see 1 Samuel 12:11; 22:17).

Skin:

outer covering (see Genesis 3:21–22; Leviticus 13:20; Numbers 6:4);

appearances (see Genesis 27:11);

container (see Judges 4:19; 1 Samuel 1:24; 10:3; Matthew 9:17).

Skin, broken and festering: problems coming against self (see Job 7:5).

Skin, ram: atonement (see Genesis 15:9; 22:13–14).

Skin, shriveled on bones: emaciated (see Lamentations 4:8).

Skin, soft and renewed: restored (see Job 33:25).

Skin, white [unpleasant]: occult covering (see Leviticus 13:3–19).

Skull: where Christ is crucified (see Luke 23:33).

Stomach: see Themes/Body Parts/Belly.

T

Tail:

follower (see Deuteronomy 28:13);

power (as in fish);

a story (char);

tale or lies (see Revelation 9:19);

ending (char);

torment (see Revelation 9:10);
prophets who lie (see Isaiah 9:15);
destroys (see Revelation 12:4).

Teeth:

understanding ["chew" on something] (see Proverbs 25:19);

ability to think (see Proverbs 25:19);

instrument of destruction/chew on others (see Psalm 57:4; 58:6; 124:6; Proverbs 30:14; Revelation 9:8).

Teeth, aching: difficulty in understanding (see Proverbs 25:19; see Themes/Body Parts/Teeth).

Teeth, baby: immature understanding (see Proverbs 25:19; see Themes/Body Parts/Teeth).

Teeth, bad:

brushing up your understanding(see Proverbs 25:19; see Themes/Body Parts/Teeth);

thinking things through (see Proverbs 25:19);

incorrect/wrong understanding (see Proverbs 25:19; see Themes/Body Parts/Teeth);

receiving wrong counsel (see Proverbs 25:19).

Teeth, broken: ineffective/to cause to be powerless (see Job 4:10); having confidence in undeserving people (see Proverbs 25:19).

Teeth, brush: understanding (see Proverbs 3:5; see Themes/Body Parts/Teeth—to "chew on something" is to try to understand; to brush the teeth is to "brush up on your understanding).

Teeth, canine or lions: the capacity to tear apart in an attempt to understand (see Revelation 9:8).

Teeth, eye tooth: ability to see and understand prophetic things (see Proverbs 25:19; see Themes/Body Parts/Teeth); see Themes/Body Parts/Eye.

Teeth, false: wrong understanding (see Proverbs 25:19; see Themes/Body Parts/Teeth); not looking at things correctly and clearly (see Proverbs 25:19; see Themes/Body Parts/Teeth).

Teeth, gnashing:

grief (see Matthew 22:13);

extreme anxiety or pain (see Psalm 112:10; Matthew 13:42; 22:13);

threatened (see Job 16:9; Psalm 35:16; 37:12; Acts 7:54).

Teeth, incisor tooth: ability to be decisive; to tear off things in order to understand them (see Proverbs 25:19; see Themes/Body Parts/Teeth).

Teeth, losing teeth:

lost ability to think something through (see Themes/Body Parts/Teeth).

lost understanding/something you need to understand (see Proverbs 25:19; see Themes/Body Parts/Teeth);

removing your own wisdom [lost wisdom teeth] (play on words).

Teeth, on edge: repercussions of past sins (see Jeremiah 31:29–30).

Teeth, snatched from: unable to keep from hurting others (see Job 29:17).

Teeth, wisdom tooth: ability to understand wisely (play on words).

Thigh:

faith (see Genesis 47:29);

strongest part of the body (see Genesis 32:25);

covenantal promise (see Genesis 24:2–9; 47:29);

stubbornness (see Genesis 32:25).

Thigh, right: contribution (see Leviticus 7:32).

Throat: ready to kill (see Jeremiah 4:10); sound (see Psalm 115:7).

Throat, dry: needing [water] God's words and ways (see Jeremiah 2:25); unable to pray well (see Psalm 69:3).

Thumb: apostle/church founding (direction or relationship of fivefold ministry); ability to work (see Judges 1:6–7); able to hold others.

Toe, big: balance (see Judges 1:6–7).

Toes: balance/stability (see Judges 1:6–7).

Tongue:

words/speak out (see Exodus 4:10; 2 Samuel 23:2; Job 15:5; 20:12; Psalm

45:1; 64:3; 71:24; Proverbs 31:26; Isaiah 59:3; Philippians 2:11; 1 Peter 3:10; 1 John 3:18);

choice silver/speaks rightly/understanding/powerful (see Proverbs 10:20; 11:12; 25:15);

language (see Esther 1:22; Psalm 114:1; Acts 2:4, 11; 1 Corinthians 12:10, 28; 14:21);

praise and cursing both (see Psalm 35:28; 51:14; Jeremiah 18:18; James 3:10);

sword/hurtful things (see Psalm 64:3; Jeremiah 18:18);

bow from which to shoot lies/deadly arrow/lies (see Job 5:21; Psalm 120:2; Proverbs 26:28; Jeremiah 9:3, 8);

untamed/tamed only by God, not by man (see James 1:26; 3:8);

a small thing that starts big things (see James 3:5–6);

restless evil (see Psalm 34:13; 1 Peter 3:10);

fire from hell (see Isaiah 5:24; James 3:6);

defiles entire body; poison (see Psalm 5:9; 15:3; 140:3; James 3:6–8).

Tongue, hold: wise (see Proverbs 10:19).

Tongue, silver: righteous (see Proverbs 10:20).

Tongue, stick out: sneer/mock (see Isaiah 57:4).

Tongue, stick to roof of mouth: thirsty/needing the Word of God (see Lamentations 4:4); caused to be silent/unable to rebuke (see Job 29:10; Ezekiel 3:26).

V

Voice: power and strength (see Revelation 1:15).

W

Womb: ability to bring forth life (see Genesis 20:18; 25:23–24); sea/mankind (see Job 38:8, Jeremiah 20:17).

Wrist: upper hand; to get the upper hand on someone; to gain control over (see Jeremiah 40:4; Acts 12:7).

Animals and Creatures

The Bible tells us to look at the characteristics of the animal and draw from them (see Proverbs 30:25).

A

Adder:

will kill (see Job 20:16);

will destroy spiritually (see Job 20:16);

will hurt you (see Jeremiah 8:17; Psalm 73:21; Proverbs 23:32).

Alligator:

someone opening their big mouth (char);

a big mouth intent on doing harm (func);

biting things that are under the surface (char);

looks religious, but is not (char; see Psalm 104:26); lies in the water [Word] waiting to bite with a big mouth; legalism; Pharisee (see Ezekiel 29:3; 32:2);

see Themes/Animals and Creatures/ Leviathan;

speaking twisted things (see Job 41; Psalm 74:14);

using a big mouth to twist things in a "sea" of people (see Job 3:8; 41:1; Psalm 74:14; Isaiah 27:1).

Animal: unreasoning; creature of instinct (see 2 Peter 2:12).

Animal, blind: bad sacrifice (see Malachi 1:8).

Animal, crippled: bad sacrifice (see Malachi 1:8).

Animal, cut in half: split apart (see Genesis 15:9–14; Jeremiah 34:18–20); to ratify a contract (see Genesis 15:9–10).

Animal, deceased: bad sacrifice (see Malachi 1:8).

Animal, wild: will devour (see Ezekiel 33:27).

Ant:

wisdom (see Proverbs 6:6);

industrious (see Proverbs 30:25);

team work; busy (see Proverbs 6:6–8; 30:25);

people who are not strong but work together (char);

annoyances from earthly situations and endeavors that you are facing (rel);

unwanted guests (rel);

demonic attack (rel).

Anteater: will consume industrious people (see Proverbs 30:25).

Ape: to imitate (play on words).

Armadillo: destruction; harasser/destroyer (char).

Ass:

an all-purpose vehicle for transportation (see Numbers 22:22, 30);

carries burdens (func);

dependable and used by God (see Numbers 22:22–33);

to be subdued (see Judges 15:16; Proverbs 26:3);

self-indulgent and contrary (see Numbers 22:32);

makes mockery of you (see Numbers 22:29).

B

Badger: wise, but without power; lives in crags (see Proverbs 30:26); hides in crags (see Psalm 104:18); to pester; to ask repeatedly (play on words).

Bat:

satanic tormentors (char);

of the dark realm (char);

spiritual annoyance (char);

feeds on garbage (see Leviticus 11:19; Isaiah 2:20).

Bear:

powerful force (see Proverbs 17:12; 28:15);

destructive (see Proverbs 17:12);

a great fear or unexpected attack that you feel helpless against (see 1 Samuel 17:34; Proverbs 28:15);

appears docile but is a destroyer; destroyer (see 1 Samuel 17:34; 2 Samuel 17:8; 2 Kings 2:23–24; Proverbs 17:12; 28:15; Lamentations 3:10–11; Daniel 7:5; Amos 5:19; Revelation 13:2);

the fierce attack of a volatile issue (see Proverbs 17:12; Revelation 13:1);

economic downturn (bear market);

Russia [Russian bear] (see Daniel 7:5);

wicked ruler/wicked authority (see Proverbs 28:15).

Bear, charging: strong attack coming at you (char); wicked with power over others (see Proverbs 28:15).

Bear, feet: destroys peace (see Revelation 13:2).

Bear, grizzly: destroyer (see 1 Samuel 17:34; 2 Samuel 17:8; 2 Kings 2:23–24; Proverbs 17:12; 28:15; Lamentations 3:10–11; Daniel 7:5; Amos 5:19;

Revelation 13:2); the fierce attack of a volatile issue (see Proverbs 17:12; Revelation 13:1).

Bear, growl: to complain loudly (see Isaiah 59:11).

Bear, lying in wait: to drag from the path and mangle (see Lamentations 3:10–11).

Bear, with cubs: fierce destroyer (see 2 Samuel 17:8).

Beast:

danger; predators (see Ezekiel 34; Psalm 25, 28; Isaiah 56:9);

judgment of God (see Ezekiel 14:15, 21);

kingdoms (see Daniel 7:17).

Beast, from earth: miraculous/religious power of enemy (see Revelation 13:11–17; 16:13; 19:19–20).

Beast, from sea: the political power of the enemy (see Matthew 4:1–11; Revelation 13:1–10).

Beaver: busy (as in "busy as a beaver"); hard worker (char); damming up things (func).

Bee:

produces sweet things (see Judges 14:8);

busy (as in "busy as a bee");

stinging attack; demonic attack (see Deuteronomy 1:44);

swarm around, ready to attack (see Psalm 118:12);

judgment (see Exodus 23:28).

Bee, honey: sweet revelatory promise; to produce sweet [or revelatory] things (see Judges 14:8).

Bird:

leaders/messengers/people (see Proverbs 1:17; Revelation 19:17);

women (see Isaiah 16:2);

prey of others (see Psalm 124:7; Proverbs 7:23; Lamentations 3:52);

Lord's defense (see Genesis 1:21; Psalm 50:11);

free (see Leviticus 14:7; as in "free as a bird");

coming your way (see Job 41:5);

coming to steal and eat off of the dead (see Jeremiah 15:3; 16:4; Ezekiel

32:4; Matthew 13:4–19; Revelation 18:2; 19:17–21);

bad/evil spirit (see Ecclesiastes 10:20; Matthew 13:4–19; Mark 4:3–15; Luke 8:5–11);

deceit (see Jeremiah 5:26–27);

fearful (see Psalm 11:1; Isaiah 16:2).

Bird, alone on a roof: loneliness and desolation (see Psalm 102:6).

Bird, baby: child of God (see Matthew 23:37).

Bird, cage: house full of deceit (see Jeremiah 5:27).

Bird, caged: leader; someone trapped in something (see Psalm 124:7).

Bird, colorful: God's leader (multiple colors: of God; see 1 Chronicles 29:2; Isaiah 63:1).

Bird, flock: flock of God's children/people of God (see 1 Peter 5:2–3).

Bird, fly away from the nest: leaving home (see Proverbs 27:8).

Bird, hatches eggs it did not lay: to gain riches that are not deserved; riches will leave when life is half gone (see Jeremiah 17:11).

Bird, overhead: hovering near (see Isaiah 31:5).

Bird, prey: will try to eat sacrifices (see Genesis 15:11).

Bird, speckled: those whom others are against (see Jeremiah 12:9).

Bird, swift: cry out (see Isaiah 38:14).

Bird, types: (Look at characteristics and stories/myths of the bird).

blue jay: false prophet (char); arrogant (char).

chick: children of God (see Luke 13:34); girl (as in slang for a girl).

chicken: see Themes/Animals and Creatures/Chicken or Hen.

crane: does not seek deep things of God (stays in shallow water).

crows, black: mocker, harasser (see Proverbs 30:17).

dove: innocent (see Song of Solomon 1:15); Holy Spirit/God's Word (see Matthew 3:16; John 1:32–33); moaning (see Isaiah 38:14; Ezekiel 7:16).

eagle: see Themes/Animals and Creatures/Eagle.

falcon: ability to see/understand (see Job 28:7); minister/priest/leader (see Job 39:26); false revelation (not an eagle); minister/priest/leader who is a predator (see Job 28:7); someone who may use the ability to see/understand as a predator (see Job 28:7).

hawk: false revelation (not an eagle [true prophets are eagles; see Exodus 19:4; Isaiah 40:31]); see Themes/Animals and Creatures/Hawk.

hen: see Themes/Animals and Creatures/Hen.

hummingbird: peace (as in "humming indicates peacefulness"); harassing (as in "always flitting around").

loon: something/someone loony or crazy (play on words).

magpie: speaking loud and falsely [legalism, control, witchcraft] (char); grabbing at shiny things (char).

owl: wisdom (as in "wise as an owl"); false (see Psalm 102:6; Isaiah 34:11); creature of the night (char).

pigeon: sometimes represents a dove (see Genesis 15:9; Leviticus 1:14; dove: peace), carrier (char—carrier pigeon); unclean scavenger (func).

quail: provision from God (see Exodus 16:13; Psalm 105:40); provision from man [sea] (see Numbers 11:31); provision taken away before it can be consumed (see Exodus 11:33; Matthew 13:4).

raven: provision from God (see 1 Kings 17:4–6); will peck out the eye that mocks and scorns (see Proverbs 30:17).

robin: perseverance; compassion/a good nurturer (char—of most birds, including robins; see Deuteronomy 22:6); the promise of spring or a new beginning (char).

rooster: pride (see Luke 22:59–62; Peter's pride in himself fell when he heard the cock crow); to dominate (see Proverbs 30:31).

sparrow: God's care/provision to those who feel unworthy (see Matthew 10:29–31).

sparrow, fluttering: will not rest (see Proverbs 26:2); a curse without cause will not alight (see Proverbs 26:2).

swallow, darting: will not rest (see Proverbs 26:2); a curse without cause will not alight (see Proverbs 26:2).

swan: grace (char); lifelong relationship (char).

thrush: cry out (see Isaiah 38:14).

vulture: see Themes/Animals and Creatures/Vulture.

Bird nest, at mouth of cave: ready to flee (see Jeremiah 48:28).

Bison: stubbornness (char).

Boar: ravager (see Psalm 80:13).

Buck:

wise and capable (see Song of Solomon 2:9, 17; 8:14);

blame (to "pass the buck");

see Themes/Animals and Creatures/ Deer, stag.

Buffalo: being deceived (as in "to buffalo someone").

Bug:

has a problem (as in "it has a bug in it");

irritants/harassers (as in things that "bug" you; see Exodus 8:18);

unclean things (see Leviticus 11:20–23);

will destroy (see Exodus 8:16).

Bull:

Christ [as He will gore His enemies at the Second Coming] (see Deuteronomy 33:17);

to consecrate self (see Exodus 29:1; 2 Chronicles 13:9);

sin offering (see Exodus 29:10–14, 36; Leviticus 1:1–9);

financial upswing (as in "bull market");

reproduction (see Genesis 32:15);

intimidating (char);

not true (see 2 Chronicles 13:9);

leaders, not of God (see 2 Chronicles 13:9; Isaiah 34:7);

a controlling faction (see Psalm 68:30; 69:31);

false god/idol (see Numbers 25:3; Psalm 22:12);

to trample underfoot the redemptive/ silver things (see Psalm 68:30; Jeremiah 31:18);

destroys or hurts people (see 1 Kings 22:11; Psalm 22:12; 106:20–21; Jeremiah 46:21)

Bull, fat: mercenary (see Jeremiah 46:21).

Bull, firstborn: majesty (see Deuteronomy 33:17).

Bull, head: stubborn (as in "he is bullheaded").

Bull, killed: murder (see Isaiah 66:3).

Bullfrog: Jeremiah anointing; prophetic anointing ["Jeremiah Was a Bullfrog"]; see Themes/Animals and Creatures/Frog.

Burro:

stubborn (char);

burden-bearer (see Genesis 42:26; Exodus 4:20);

see Themes/Animals and Creatures/ Ass.

Butterfly:

opening out from oppression (char);

transition coming to an end (char);

flitting from one to another (char).

Buzzard:

cleans up dead issues (func);

unclean (see Leviticus 11:13);

watching for reward from others' death/spiritual death (func).

C

Calf: in need of training (see Jeremiah 31:18; Hosea 4:16); idolatry (Exodus 32:4, 8, 19; 2 Chronicles 11:15; Nehemiah 9:18; Hosea 8:5).

Calf, cut in two: vow (see Jeremiah 34:18).

Calf, leap: joy (see Psalm 29:6; Malachi 4:2).

Calf, unruly: needs discipline (see Jeremiah 31:18).

Calves: those who are easily led (char).

Camel:

ungraceful strength and endurance (char);

provision (see Isaiah 66:20);

significant (see Matthew 23:24);

running here and there (see Jeremiah 2:23);

bearing burdens through trials (see Genesis 24:32; 37:25; 1 Kings 10:2; 1 Chronicles 12:40; 2 Chronicles 9:1; Isaiah 30:6);

takes you where you want to go, but causes you to go up and down in the process (see Genesis 24:61–64; 31:17);

kneels to a task master (see Genesis 24:11);

not good to learn from (consume) (see Leviticus 11:4; Deuteronomy 14:7).

Camel's hair: provisions from God (see Matthew 3:4; Mark 1:6).

Cancer crab: Gospel of two folds becoming one [the two folds, Jew and Gentile, of the Good Shepherd Jesus are brought into one fold—just as the cancer crab's two claws bring in two groups to the one/Jesus] (see John 10:16; Ephesians 2:14); astrology, not of God (see Deuteronomy 4:19).

Cat:

your own pet: it may refer to something close to you [a pet issue] (rel); area of thinking you like and want to hang on to (char);

an unknown cat: negative independent thinking (char); the occult (rel).

Cat, eyes: used for witchcraft (rel); the occult watching you (rel).

Caterpillar: preparing for better change (char); preparing for transition (char).

Cattle: stupid/without understanding (see Job 18:3); God's people (see Amos 4:1).

Cattle, on a plain: rest and plenty (see Isaiah 63:14).

Centaur:

creature of two natures (char);

e.g., God and man (char);

e.g., bad spirit and man (char).

see Themes/Transportation/Car.

Chick: children of God (see Luke 13:34); girl [slang]

Chick, under wing: Jesus/God protecting (see Matthew 23:37; Luke 13:34).

Chicken: protective (see Matthew 23:37; Luke 13:34); fearful/scared (as in "you are a chicken").

Chipmunk: pet issue (seemingly innocent, but destructive); something the dreamer likes that is destructive.

Cockatrices: will bite you (see Jeremiah 8:17).

Cockroaches: something that feeds off of garbage left unattended (char).

Colt: the offspring of one who carries burdens (see Matthew 21:5).

Cougar: vicious attack (char).

Cow:

women (see Amos 4:1);

slow wait (as in "wait 'til the cows come home"; see 1 Samuel 6:7–14);

stubborn (see Hosea 4:16);

years (see Genesis 41:27).

Cow, has calved: a natural desire not to travel from home (see 1 Samuel 6:7).

Crab: irritable person (slang); see Themes/Animals/Cancer crab.

Cricket: noisy during dark times, but soothing; mythically: represents good luck.

Crocodile:

lies in the water [Word, the church] with a big mouth [speaking out things to people] waiting to bite [hurt people]; [e.g.: this could be someone at church who speaks harmful words to others] (char; see Ezekiel 29:3; 32:2);

legalism/Pharisees (func);

see Themes/Animals and Creatures/Alligator.

D

Deer:

sure-footed (see 2 Samuel 2:18; Song of Solomon 2:9, 17; Habakkuk 3:19);

able to negotiate rough terrain; able to handle hard times (see 2 Samuel 2:18; 22:34; Habakkuk 3:19);

no misstep (see Psalm 17:5; 18:33);

your walk with God (see Psalm 18:33; 42:1; Isaiah 35:4–6);

good to listen to (consume) (see Deuteronomy 12:15, 22; 15:22);

swift (see 2 Samuel 2:18; 1 Chronicles 12:8; Isaiah 35:6);

loving and graceful (see Proverbs 5:19);

timid (see Lamentations 1:6);

see Themes/Animals and Creatures/ Doe.

Deer, hungry: in weakness, flees before a pursuer (see Lamentations 1:6).

Doe: wife (see Proverbs 5:19).

Dog:

friend, protector, servant (see 2 Samuel 9:8);

servant of the master (see Matthew 15:27);

assistant to the shepherd (Jesus);

priest/preacher/protector of the sheep—God's children (see Job 30:1);

man (see 2 Kings 8:13; Isaiah 66:3);

things you care about; pet things (func; Mark 7:27);

one who follows (see Job 18:11);

of no worth (see 1 Samuel 17:43; 2 Samuel 3:8; 2 Kings 8:13);

strife; dangerous people (see Psalm 22:16; Matthew 7:6; Philippians 3:2; Revelation 22:15);

unbelievers (see Psalm 22:16; Isaiah 56:10; Matthew 7:6; 15:26–27; 2 Peter 2:22; Revelation 22:15);

one who feeds off dead things; one who thrives on things not of God (see 1 Kings 14:11; 16:4; 21:23–24);

ready to devour the injured (see Psalm 68:23; Matthew 7:6; Philippians 3:2).

Dog, dead: inability to bite or fight (see 1 Samuel 24:14); of no worth (see 2 Samuel 9:8; 16:9).

Dog, dragging something: someone [whoever the dog represents—possibly an unbeliever] is pulling you or something away [look at what is being dragged in the dream] (see Themes/ Animals and Creatures/Dog).

Dog, friendly: a friend (rel).

Dog, head: traitor (see 2 Samuel 3:8).

Dog, with its neck broken: pervert, e.g., a pedophile [whoever the dog represents—possibly an unbeliever] is suffering from a damaged (broken) willfulness (neck—see Themes/Body Parts/Neck), thus wanting something perverted (see Isaiah 66:3).

Dog, pet: friendly protector (see Psalm 68:23); a favorite [pet] issue or project (rel).

Dog, snarling: ready to attack (see Psalm 59:6).

Dog, vomit: going back to old ways; repeating one's folly (see Proverbs 26:11; 2 Peter 2:21–22).

Dog, types:

beagle: hounded by something with a short foundation (hound with short legs); hounded (char).

Chihuahua: friend talking all the time (char).

German shepherd: pastor/leader/priest (see Job 30:1); protector of the herd who is into rules (char).

golden retriever: angel (see General/ Gold); friend from God that will bring you back to God (play on words, see General/Gold).

hound: torment/harass/bother (see Job 19:28); pursued (see Ezekiel 36:3).

pit bull: ferocious and will not let go (char).

sheepdog: protector of God's children (see Job 30:1).

Dolphin: moves with the things of the Spirit [living water: spiritual life in Jesus] (see John 4:14); is helpful (char).

Donkey:

peace/humility (see Judges 15:16);

trusting totally in God and not in horses or chariots (see Matthew 21:2–5);

dependably used by God (see Numbers 22:27; Matthew 21:2–7; 2 Peter 2:15–16);

accustomed to the desert/places of abandonment (see Jeremiah 2:24);

all-purpose vehicle for transportation (see Matthew 21:5);

carries burdens (see Matthew 21:5);

controlled by a bridle (see Proverbs 26:3);

rebuked from God (see 2 Peter 2:15);

against everyone (see Genesis 16:12).

Donkey, wild:

craving dry things (see Jeremiah 2:24);

prostituting self; sinful (see Jeremiah 2:24);

used to trials and ways that are not of God (see Jeremiah 2:24; 2 Peter 2:15).

Dove:

Holy Spirit (see Matthew 3:16; Luke 3:21);

presence of God (see Psalm 68:13; Isaiah 60:8; Matthew 3:16–17);

rest/peace (see Psalm 55:6);

innocent (see Matthew 10:16);

easily deceived (see Hosea 7:11);

without sense (see Hosea 7:11);

carrier (see Hosea 12:11);

sacrifice/offering (see Genesis 15:9–14; Leviticus 1:14–17; 5:7).

Dove, coo: a call for peace (see Themes/Dove); moan mournfully—implication that someone is grieving (see Isaiah 59:11).

Dragon:

no hope of subduing; fierce (see Job 41:1–34);

enemy (see Isaiah 27:1; Revelation 12:1–9; 13:2; 20:2);

Satan (see Isaiah 27:1; Revelation 12:3–9, 17).

Duck:

moving quickly (as in "ducking to avoid something");

evade (as in "to duck out");

a quack (play on words).

swift (see 2 Samuel 1:23; Jeremiah 4:13; Lamentations 4:19);

enemy of the serpent/snake (see Job 9:26);

ready to consume the easily deceived and senseless (see Hosea 8:1);

the young feast on blood [good—to embrace the teachings of the blood of Jesus] (see Job 39:30);

the young feast on blood [bad—to embrace the teachings of dead/destructive things] (see Job 39:30).

Eagle, flying high:

the higher we go in the Spirit, the more we can see (see Isaiah 40:31);

soaring high (see Exodus 19:4; Obadiah 4);

swooping down to devour (see Job 9:26; Habakkuk 1:8).

Eagle, golden head: prophetic from God (see Psalm 103:5).

Eaglets with golden heads: new revelatory people rising up (see Exodus 19:4; Isaiah 40:31).

Elephant:

wisdom (as in "elephants never forget");

strength (see Job 40:15–24);

big impact/intimidating (char);

attack of the mind (char; memory);

historical issues (char; of ancient times);

old memories (as in "elephants never forget");

religious spirits (the elephant plays a role in various religious cultures around the world);

a large church (elephant plays a role in various religious cultures around the world).

Elephant, small and staked to ground:

children abused (people who were abused as children and still respond to memories of the abuse).

E

Eagle:

followers of Christ (see Psalm 103:5);

prophetic (see Exodus 19:4; Isaiah 40:31);

F

Fish:

good, clean nourishment (see Matthew 7:10);

followers of Christ (see Matthew 7:10; 13:48; Luke 5:10);

people seeking a leader or ruler (see Ezekiel 29:4–5; Habakkuk 1:14; Matthew 4:19; 13:48–49; Luke 5:10);

nations/earth (see Matthew 12:40);

to try to obtain information (play on words);

fishy (as in "something's fishy").

Fish, decaying and rotting: people decaying and rotting (see Matthew 4:19; 13:48–49).

Fish, good: God's people (see Matthew 13:48–49).

Fish, rotting and dead: lack of Holy Spirit [water] (see Isaiah 50:2); people who are not of God (see Matthew 13:48–49).

Fish, tail: power (func).

Flamingos: instruments carrying out God's purpose (walking in movement [water] of God).

Flea: small and harmless (see 1 Samuel 24:14; 26:20); warning to flee (play on words).

Flies:

will die (see Isaiah 51:6 NIV);

God's judgment (see Exodus 23:28);

devoured (see Psalm 78:45);

contaminates teachings [food] (char).

Flock: God's people (see Psalm 77:20; 78:52; Isaiah 40:11); easily led (see Psalm 80:1).

Fly, dead: to give things a "bad smell" (see Ecclesiastes 10:1).

Fox:

sly/witty (see Luke 13:32);

steal from and prey on the weak (see Ezekiel 13:4);

cunning but good-looking (see Psalm 63:10);

evil (see Luke 13:32);

doing damage (see Psalm 63:10; Song of Solomon 2:15).

Frog: demon of lust/destroying; to make foul; devastating (see Exodus 8:3–14; Psalm 78:45; Revelation 16:13); materialism (see Revelation 16:13).

G

Gazelle:

swift (see 1 Chronicles 12:8);

surefooted (see Song of Solomon 2:17);

good to learn from [eat] (see Deuteronomy 12:15, 22; 15:22).

Gemini: [twins] two strongmen joined together (see Acts 28:11).

Giraffe: to stick one's neck out; to take a risk (char); high-minded (char).

Gnat: insignificant (see Matthew 23:24); affliction (see Exodus 8:16–18).

Goat:

sacrifice/offering (see Genesis 15:9; Leviticus 1:10–13; 16:5–10);

stately (see Proverbs 30:31);

things of the world (see Numbers 31:20; Matthew 25:32–33);

person who is not of God (see Ezekiel 34:17; Matthew 25:32–33);

self-willed (see 2 Chronicles 29:23–24; Isaiah 34:14);

full of sin (see Leviticus 16:22; Numbers 15:24).

Goat, with horn: mighty power to ram and destroy (see Daniel 8:21).

Gopher: destructive pest that hides underground (char).

Gorilla: heavy bully (char); strong hidden attack (guerrilla warfare—play on words).

Grasshopper:

people (see Isaiah 40:22);

numerous/multiply (see Jeremiah 46:23; Nahum 3:15);

small and ineffective (see Numbers 13:33);

destroying pests (see 2 Chronicles 6:28; Psalm 78:46; 105:34; Nahum 3:15).

H

Hamster: running in circles and getting nowhere (char).

Hawk:

fast-moving spiritual warrior who is able to "see" far (see Job 39:26);

soars, searching and stretching his wings (see Job 39:26);

good ability to see (see Job 39:26);

predator that soars high and searches (see Job 39:26);

false revelation [not an eagle, therefore, not a true prophet].

Heifer:

peace (see Leviticus 3:1);

wife (see Judges 14:18);

sacrifice (see Genesis 15:9).

Heifer, stubborn: stubborn (see Hosea 4:16).

Hen:

Jesus (see Matthew 23:37; Luke 13:34);

protective (see Matthew 23:37);

mothers (see Matthew 23:37);

gathers followers [children] together (see Matthew 23:37; Luke 13:34).

Hen, wing: protective (see Matthew 23:37).

Hippopotamus: someone opening a big mouth (char).

Hind: see Themes/Animals and Creatures/Deer.

Hog: selfishness/greed (as in "hog the food"); see Themes/Animals and Creatures/Pig.

Hog, in mud: going back to old ways (see 2 Peter 2:21–22); rooting in muddy things (char).

Horn on an animal:

leaders of nations (see Deuteronomy 33:17; 1 Samuel 2:10);

protection (func);

strength (see Revelation 5:6);

evil power (see Genesis 49:17);

see General/Horn.

Hornet:

seek out to inflict injury (see Deuteronomy 7:20);

God's judgment (see Exodus 23:28);

see Themes/Animals and Creatures/Bee.

Hornets, swarming: large harassment (see Exodus 23:28); demonic attack; larger demonic power (see Deuteronomy 7:20).

Horse:

military might/great power/great strength (see Judges 5:22; Job 39:19–25; Psalm 33:17; 147:10; Jeremiah 8:16; Revelation 9:7, 17);

authority (look at color; see Revelation 6:8);

work of the flesh (see 1 Kings 18:5; Psalm 32:9; Proverbs 21:31; Isaiah 31:3);

work of the Lord going throughout the world (see Zechariah 1:8–10);

controlled by a bit (see Psalm 32:9–10);

controlled by a whip (see Proverbs 26:3).

Horse, black:

go north (see Zechariah 6:6);

judgment (see Zechariah 6:6–8; Revelation 6:5);

famine (see Revelation 6:6).

Horse, brown: powerful compassion (see Themes/Animals and Creatures/Horse; Themes/Colors/Brown); power; making a way to go forward (see Exodus 14:23; Judges 5:22).

Horse, charging into battle: each is pursuing his own course (see Jeremiah 8:6).

Horse, dappled: go south (see Zechariah 6:6).

Horse, mouth: power (see Revelation 9:19).

Horse, mouth with bit: obey (see James 3:3).

Horse, open country: do not stumble (see Isaiah 63:13).

Horse, pale:

death, Hades (see Revelation 6:8);

plagues [as in HIV, AIDS, pestilence, famine, etc.] (see Revelation 6:8);

to let them live with the consequences of their abuse of freedom (see Revelation 6:7–8).

Horse, proud: strong and confident (see Job 39:19–25; Zechariah 10:3).

Horse, racing forward: pursuing one's own course (see Jeremiah 8:6).

Horse, red:

war (see Zechariah 1:8; 6:6);

killing each other (see Revelation 6:4);

consequences of sin (see Revelation 6:4).

Horse, tail: power to inflict injury (see Revelation 9:19).

Horse, white: victory (see Zechariah 1:8; 6:6; Revelation 6:2; 19:11); go west (see Zechariah 6:6).

Hyena: powerful mouth; powerful, destructive words (see Isaiah 13:22); lives in a desert place (without life) (see Isaiah 34:14; Jeremiah 50:39).

I

Insects: things detestable (see Leviticus 11:20–23); plague (see Exodus 8:16–24); demonic attack (bites that suck the life [blood] out of you).

J

Jackal:
live among ruins (see Job 30:29; Isaiah 35:7; Jeremiah 9:11; 49:33; 51:37; Ezekiel 13:1–4 NIV);

prophet who speaks out of his own imagination (see Ezekiel 13:2–3);

predators; those who are cruel and haunt dark places (see Isaiah 35:7);

those who feed on the spiritual death of others (see Psalm 63:10).

K

Kangaroo:
someone with "deep pockets" [lots of money] (char);

someone jumping all around/not staying on task (char);

someone jumping to conclusions (as in "Kangaroo Court").

Kitten: see Themes/Animals and Creatures/Cat.

L

Ladybug: God will send something to help (char); eats harassers (func).

Lamb:
Jesus (see John 1:29; Revelation 5:6–12; 6:1; 17:14; 19:7);

Christ as a sacrifice (see 1 Corinthians 5:7; 1 Peter 1:19; Revelation 5:12);

those who are weak (see Isaiah 53:7; Luke 10:3);

children of God (see Isaiah 40:11; John 21:15);

innocent (see Isaiah 53:7),

easily led to the slaughter (see Jeremiah 11:19);

sacrifice for repentance (see Exodus 12:1–13; 1 Samuel 7:9; Isaiah 53:7; Hebrews 10:1–12);

offering (see Isaiah 53:7; Hebrews 10:1–12, 18);

skips youthfully (see Psalm 114:6).

Leech:
demands to be given to; taker (see Proverbs 30:15);

someone/something sucking life from you (see Proverbs 30:15);

something/someone living parasitically off of you (see Proverbs 30:15).

Leo: Lion of Judah/Jesus (see Genesis 49:9; Numbers 24:8–9; Proverbs 28:1; Revelation 5:5); astrology, not of God (see Deuteronomy 4:19).

Leopard:
swift (Habakkuk 1:8);

warfare; beast or tool of the enemy (see Revelation 13:1–4);

lies in wait to destroy (see Jeremiah 5:6);

cruel (see Revelation 13:1).

Leviathan:
large, active sea creature/Satan/enemy (see Psalm 104:26; Isaiah 27:1);

bad assumptions; demon that twists communications (see Psalm 74:14; Isaiah 27:1).

Lice: things getting under your skin; things harassing you (see Exodus 8:15–18; Psalm 105:31).

Lion:
Judah authority (see Revelation 5:5);

Jesus Christ (see Genesis 49:9; Revelation 5:5);

followers of Christ (see Proverbs 28:1);

strong (see Judges 14:18; 2 Samuel 1:23);

bold/intense/courageous (see 1 Samuel 17:34; 1 Chronicles 12:8; Proverbs 28:1);

uncompromisingly righteous (see Proverbs 28:1);

strong warrior and stately (see Numbers 23:24; Proverbs 30:30);

king (see Proverbs 20:2);

carries off sheep to destroy; beast of the enemy (see 1 Samuel 17:34; 1 Kings 13:24; 2 Kings 17:25; Psalm 91:13; Jeremiah 2:30; 4:7; Isaiah 35:9; 38:13; Ezekiel 22:25; Nahum 2:11–12; 2 Timothy 4:17; 1 Peter 5:8; Revelation 9:17; 13:1–2);

dare not disturb (see Numbers 24:9);

tears things apart (see Psalm 35:17; Jeremiah 2:15, 30);

attack (see Psalm 35:17; 104:21; Jeremiah 5:6; 49:19; Lamentations 3:10–11; Ezekiel 19:3);

destroys nations (see Jeremiah 2:15);

bad past/bad heritage (see Jeremiah 12:8).

Lion, heart: strong loyalty (see 2 Samuel 17:10); bold (see Proverbs 28:1).

Lion, many: pride [group of lions] that attacks (see Psalm 57:4).

Lion, roar:

ruler's intimidation (see Zephaniah 3:3);

ruler's anger (see Proverbs 19:12);

aroused (see Jeremiah 51:38).

Lioness:

rises up in might (see Numbers 23:24);

lies among lions raising her children (see Ezekiel 19:2);

dare not disturb (see Genesis 49:9; Numbers 24:9; Nahum 2:11–12);

church (mate of the Lion, Jesus).

Living creatures: a form like a man, with four faces and four wings, straight legs, feet hooved like a calf, gleaming bronze under their wings on four sides and the hands of a man; all four had faces and wings. The wings spread out and touched one another, and each one went straight ahead;

they did not turn as they moved (see Ezekiel 1:4–28).

Lizard: unclean (see Leviticus 11:29–31); unclean found everywhere (see Proverbs 30:28).

Lobster: food from [the sea] humanity; teachings of mankind (see General/Food, see General/Sea).

Locusts:

food (see Matthew 3:4);

invasion to ravage/damage (see Judges 6:5; Psalm 78:46; Nahum 3:16);

leap(see Job 39:20);

advance together in ranks (see Proverbs 30:27; Jeremiah 51:27);

thick or high density/multiply (see Judges 7:12; Nahum 3:15);

things that devour (see 2 Chronicles 6:28; 7:13; Psalm 105:34; Isaiah 33:4; Joel 1:4; 2:25; Revelation 9:3–11);

things held in high esteem that torment people (see Revelation 9:1–11);

strip the land, then leave (see Nahum 3:16).

M

Maggot: dead (see Isaiah 14:11).

Mice:

larger demons that feed off of garbage you gave permission to be there (see Isaiah 2:20);

problems that appear because of something left unattended (char);

ravages things (see 1 Samuel 6:3–5);

detestable things (see Isaiah 66:17).

Mole: tattletale; feeds on garbage (see Isaiah 2:20).

Monkey:

harassers (as in "monkey around with");

mockers (as in "ape someone");

fool (as in "make a monkey out of");

addiction (as in a "monkey on my back").

Monster: something to guard against (see Job 7:12; Isaiah 27:1; 34:14); evil (see Psalm 74:13; Isaiah 27:1; Jeremiah 51:34).

Moose: huge teachings [meat] native to the USA and Canada (see General/Meat; see Genesis 9:3; Daniel 10:3; Hebrews 5:12–14).

Mosquito: a small attack that causes larger pain and swollenness (char).

Moth:

eats and destroys valuable things (see Job 13:28; Psalm 39:11; Isaiah 50:9; 51:8; Matthew 6:19–21; Luke 12:33);

wrath of God (see Hosea 5:12);

lightly touched (see Job 4:19).

Mule:

strength and stamina (see 1 Kings 18:5; 2 Kings 5:17; 1 Chronicles 12:40);

stubborn (see Psalm 32:9);

forced to obey without understanding (see Psalm 32:9–10);

inability to be productive (as in "mules cannot reproduce").

N

Nanny: (as in nanny [female] goat) sin atonement (see Numbers 15:27–29).

O

Opossum:

travel or work at night (hiddenness);

rodent (can work and see in the darkness);

needs deliverance (lives in darkness).

Ostrich:

joyful without good sense (see Job 39:13–18);

careless (see Job 39:13–18);

fast (see Job 39:18);

to keep one's head in the sand; to be unwilling to see what is going on (char);

not to be learned from (eaten) (see Leviticus 11:13–16; Deuteronomy 14:12–15);

harsh; neglects her children harshly (see Job 39:13–18);

cruel (see Lamentations 4:3).

Otter: playful (char).

Owl:

wise (as in a "wise old owl");

lives in waste and desolation as a predator (see Psalm 102:6; Isaiah 34:11);

alone/loneliness (see Psalm 102:6).

Ox: see Themes/Animals and Creatures/Oxen.

Ox, muzzled: denied benefits while working (see Deuteronomy 25:4).

Oxen:

those who serve/worker (see Deuteronomy 25:4; 1 Samuel 11:5; Job 39:9; 1 Timothy 5:18);

slow, laborious change (see Psalm 69:31);

strength (see Numbers 23:22; Psalm 92:10; 144:14; Proverbs 14:4);

sacrificed for others (see Matthew 22:4);

pulls heavy loads (Psalm 144:14);

dumb (as in "dumb as an ox").

P

Panther, black: enemy sneaking; cunning predator; see Themes/Animals and Creatures/Leopard.

Parrot: repeating things (char); gossip (play on words).

Partridge:

to be hunted (char);

prosperity/influence (see 1 Samuel 26:20; Jeremiah 17:11);

temptation (see Jeremiah 17:11).

Partridge, on nest not her own: person who gains riches by unjust means (see Jeremiah 17:11); will forsake (see Jeremiah 17:11).

Peacock: boastful and aggressive (char); vain (char).

Penguin: looking at things in a very black and white manner; straight-laced (char); lives in a cold place (char).

Pig:

has no discretion (see Proverbs 11:22);

has poor eyesight, therefore, he must taste something in order to identify what it is; being unable to see things correctly until you experience the result (see Matthew 7:6);

fleshly with big appetites (see Matthew 8:30, as in "pigging out on food");

unclean/messy (see Isaiah 65:4; 66:17; Matthew 7:6);

will turn on you and devour you (see Matthew 7:6);

defile others (see Deuteronomy 14:8).

Pig, blood: hypocrisy (see Isaiah 66:3).

Pig, ring in snout: person with no discretion (see Proverbs 11:22).

Pigeon: sacrifice/offering (see Genesis 15:9–14; Leviticus 1:14–17; 5:7; 12:6); sacrificing self for others (char).

Pigeonhole: stuck away and forgotten about (func).

Polar bear: appears good (white), but is a destroyer; see Themes/Animals and Creatures/Bear.

Porcupine: feeds on things of the earth (char); hurts others if touched (char).

Porpoise: purpose (play on words).

Praying mantis: someone preying on weakness; bad relationship.

Q

Quail: favor/provision from God (see Exodus 16:13; Numbers 11:31–32; Psalm 105:40).

R

Rabbit:

multiplication and fertility (char);

harmless (char);

destructive (char);

timid (char);

fast growth (char);

sexual torment (char).

Raccoon:

obsessive with cleanness; OCD (char; obsessive compulsive disorder);

comes during dark times (char);

is masked and destructive (char);

a thief (char);

deceitful (char).

Ram:

to consecrate self (see Genesis 22:13; 2 Chronicles 13:9);

sacrifice (see Genesis 15:9; 22:13–14);

guilt (see Leviticus 5:16–18);

person of God (see Ezekiel 34:17);

not true (see 2 Chronicles 13:9);

leaders/priests who are not of God (see 2 Chronicles 13:9);

mighty power to ram and destroy (see Daniel 8:21);

skips (see Psalm 114:6).

Ram, battering: slaughter (see Ezekiel 21:22).

Ram, with two horns: power of two leaders/two kings (see Daniel 8:1–20; Zechariah 1:18–21).

Rat:

large, ungodly leader (see 1 Samuel 6:4);

larger demons; destruction (see 1 Samuel 6:4–5);

feeds off of garbage you gave permission to be there (char);

lies/gossip/deceit; you have left something unattended that feeds on garbage (see Isaiah 2:20);

generational issue needs cleansing (rel);

spreads disease (func);

unclean (see Leviticus 11:29; Isaiah 66:17);

desensitizes others in order to do harm (char).

Raven:

provision from God (see 1 Kings 17:4–6; Matthew 6:25–27; Luke 12:24);

those who do not sow or reap (see Luke 12:24);

no storeroom (see Job 38:41; Luke 12:24).

Rhinoceros: a lot of power (char); intimidating (char).

Roach:

unclean things that entered possibly because of things left unattended;

unclean things that try to stay hidden (in the dark);

see Themes/Animals and Creatures/ Bug, Insects.

Rodent: needs deliverance; feeds on garbage (see Isaiah 2:20).

Rooster:

to become aware (see Matthew 26:74–75);

strutting and stately (see Proverbs 30:31);

to disown; deny (see Matthew 26:74–75; 26:75; Luke 22:61; John 13:38);

betrayal (see Matthew 26:74–75; 26:34, 75; Mark 14:72).

S

Scorpion:

will sting (see Ezekiel 2:6; Revelation 9:5–10);

black magic; white magic (see Revelation 9:3);

enemy/lawless one (Hebrew word); antichrist (see Luke 10:19).

Seal: stamp of God (see John 6:27); binding (see Deuteronomy 6:8; 11:18; Nehemiah 9:8); Mormon (as in the *Book of Mormon*, the seal of Mulek).

Serpent: see Themes/Animals and Creatures/Snake.

Shark: anger (char); cutting down (char); enemy with sharp teeth or a big bite (char).

Sheep:

people (see 2 Chronicles 18:16; Psalm 49:14; 107:41; Ezekiel 34:11–16, 31; Zechariah 10:2; Micah 2:12; Matthew 12:11; 15:24; 18:11–14);

followers of Jesus (see Psalm 74:1; 78:52; Jeremiah 23:1–4; Matthew 18:12–14; 25:32; 26:31; John 21:16–17);

those under your protection (see Psalm 44:11, 22; Isaiah 53:7; Luke 15:6);

those without defense who are easily led; passive and gentle (see Matthew 7:15; 10:16);

sinners (see Luke 15:6);

people who are following others blindly (see 2 Samuel 24:17; 1 Chronicles 21:17; John 10:26);

people of God (see Psalm 78:52; 79:13; 100:3; Jeremiah 13:17; 50:6; John 10:16; Hebrews 13:20);

those who tend to stray (see Psalm 119:176; Isaiah 53:6; Matthew 10:6; 1 Peter 2:25);

offering/sacrifice (see Leviticus 1:10–13).

Sheep, fat: those who take (see Ezekiel 34:20).

Sheep, lean: those who do not get enough (see Ezekiel 34:20).

Sheep, lost: people without a shepherd (the Lord) to attend to them (see Matthew 10:6).

Sheep, with shepherd: those who are saved (see Matthew 9:36; 10:6).

Sheep, without shepherd: the lost (see Matthew 9:36); dispirited and distressed (see Matthew 9:36).

Shrimp: food from [the sea] people (char; see General/Sea).

Skunk: smells bad (char).

Slug: melts away as it moves along (see Psalm 58:8); refuses to work/sluggard (see Proverbs 21:25).

Snail:

carrying a load (func);

with baggage (char);

afraid to leave shelter (char);

melts away as it goes (see Psalm 58:8).

Snake:

shrewd/wise (see Genesis 3:1–5; Matthew 10:16);

comes on quietly (see Jeremiah 46:22);

lie [long tale] (see Revelation 9:19); gossip (see Genesis 3:4; Revelation 12:9);

sharp tongue that is deadly with poison; saying painful, hurtful things (see Psalm 140:3; Matthew 10:16);

enemy (see Genesis 3:1–5, 13–15; Psalm 91:13; Isaiah 14:29; Matthew 12:34; 23:33; Luke 10:19; Revelation 12:9);

devil (see Genesis 3; Revelation 12:9);

will swallow up (see Jeremiah 51:34);

will bite/will hurt you; subtle but dangerous (see Jeremiah 8:17; Matthew 7:10);

guilty of hurting the righteous (see Matthew 23:35);

person who is doing evil (see Matthew 23:33);

Satan (see Genesis 3:1–15; Psalm 91:13; Revelation 12:9; 20:2).

Snake, becomes a staff/stick in your hand:

so that others may believe God has appeared to you (see Exodus 4:4);

there is a way to use its lie for good (see Exodus 4:4);

grab hold of its lie (tail); do not run from it (see Exodus 4:3–4).

Snake, bitten: lie has already been told, so "pray to break the power [poison] of the lie" (see Genesis 3:4; Revelation 12:9).

Snake, bronze: healed by God (see 2 Kings 18:4).

Snake, cobra: king of snakes; Jezebel spirit; major control and manipulation problem; the enemy (see Psalm 91:13; Isaiah 11:8).

Snake, egg: creates lies and wickedness (see Isaiah 59:5).

Snake, huge: spirit of control and manipulation attacking [Jezebel spirit] (see Psalm 91:13; Isaiah 11:8).

Snake, nest: ready to strike (see Isaiah 11:8).

Snake, old: Satan (see Psalm 91:13; Isaiah 11:8; Revelation 20:2).

Snake, python:

biggest form of a lie [a lie appearing as a revelation] (see Genesis 3:4; Revelation 12:9);

will squeeze and put pressure on you; divination (see Genesis 3:1–5; Deuteronomy 18:10; Psalm 91:13; Revelation 12:9).

Snake, rattler: noisemaking lie.

Snake, skin: covering of lies and hurtful words (see Genesis 3:4; Psalm 140:3; Matthew 10:16; Revelation 12:9).

Snake, white: religious spirit (char; see Genesis 3:4; Revelation 12:9); occult (see Deuteronomy 18:10).

Snakes, lots of small: gossip [lots of small "tales"] (see Matthew 12:34–35).

Sow: after being washed, she returns to wallow in the mud (see 2 Peter 2:22).

Sparrow: worthwhile and not forgotten by God (see Luke 12:6); small and of little worth by worldly standards (see Matthew 10:29).

Spider:

new age (see Job 8:14; Isaiah 59:5);

people trying to harm you; step on it with the peace of God—shoes (see Ephesians 6:13–15);

the occult (see Job 8:14; Isaiah 59:5);

demonic activity; uses entrapment; evil (see Job 8:14; Isaiah 59:5).

Spider, black widow: causes death; spiritual death to mate (char).

Squirrel:

those who push their way into places (char);

those who store up (char);

those who live among the (trees) church people and eat away the (eggs) new work of the (flock) (char);

people who are destructive, but appear harmless (char).

Stag: surefooted, strong (see Song of Solomon 2:17); see Themes/Animals and Creatures/Buck, Deer.

Stallion: well-fed and lusty; neighing for another man's wife (see Jeremiah 5:8).

Swallow, flying: a curse that does not alight (see Proverbs 26:2).

Swan: begins ugly, but ends with grace and beauty (char).

Swine: see Themes/Animals and Creatures/Pig.

T

Tick: something unhealthy that is attached to you without your knowledge; unhealthy relationship (func).

Tiger: evil/dangerous (char); false authority [not the Lion (of Judah)]; fierce attack (char).

Toad:
dry, without water [without the Word] (char);
witchcraft/control (as in traditional witchcraft familiar); see Themes/Animals and Creatures/Frog.

Tortoise: see Themes/Animals and Creatures/Turtle.

Transparent animal: [able to see through the animal like it is a ghost]: the dream is dealing with a spiritual issue—look at the animal; what does that symbol represent? (char).

Turkey: wisdom (char); foolish (char).

Turkey, dragging his wing tips: getting the attention of many females (func).

Turkey, fluffing out his feathers: attempt to appear more masculine (func).

Turkey, strutting: getting the attention of many females (func).

Turtle:
peace (char);
slow (char);
carrying a load/baggage (func);
afraid to leave shelter (char);
withdraws internally (char).

U

Unicorn: power and authority that is based on untruth (char); see General/Horn.

V

Viper:
guilty of hurting the righteous (see Matthew 23:33–35);
Pharisees/religious spirit (see Matthew 3:7; 12:34);
Sadducees/religious spirit (see Matthew 3:7);
of evil (see Matthew 12:34; 23:33);
cannot be charmed; will bite (see Jeremiah 8:17);
see Themes/Animals and Creatures/Snake.

Vixen:
malicious (char);
will breed more maliciousness (char);
see Themes/Animals and Creatures/Fox.

Vulture:
gather around the dead (see Jeremiah 34:20; Matthew 24:28; Luke 17:37);
will eat the eye that mocks and scorns (see Proverbs 30:17);
feeds off of dead things, thrives on things that are not of God (see 1 Kings 14:11; 16:4).

W

Wasp: stinging words (char).

Weasel: sneaky/deceitful (char); manipulative (char).

Weevil: concealed, but causing unhealthy teachings (char).

Whale: deep in the Spirit [in water]; large impact (char); able to overwhelm and swallow up others (see Jonah 1:17; 2:10; Matthew 12:40).

White monsters: appears to be holy, but is destructive and deadly (see Leviticus 13:3–4; 13:16–26; 2 Kings 5:27; Matthew 23:27).

Wild beasts/wild animal:
untamed (char);
danger (see Genesis 31:39);
predators (see Exodus 22:13; Leviticus 26:6, 22; Ezekiel 34:25, 28);
antichrist and false prophet.

Wolf/wolves:
ravenous (see Jeremiah 5:6);
evil that comes in the darkness (see Jeremiah 5:6; Habakkuk 1:8);
operates in packs (char);
turns without warning (char);
officials that tear people and kill for gain (see Ezekiel 22:27);
those who come against God's people [the sheep] (see Matthew 10:16; John 10:12; Acts 20:29);
devours prey in a day; divides plunder at night (see Genesis 49:27; Matthew 7:15; 10:16; Luke 10:3).

Wolves, at night: those who prey on others in darkness (see Zephaniah 3:3; Matthew 10:16).

Woodchuck: feeds on and destroys earthly things (char); cuts down (func).

Worm:
enriching the soil (func);
gets into things (as in "to worm your way in");
weak and fearful (see Isaiah 41:14);
tainted/unclean (see Job 21:26);
devours (see Isaiah 51:8);
constant torment (see Isaiah 66:24);
despised (see Psalm 22:6).

Worms, covering: dead (see Isaiah 14:11).

Worms, in earth: humility (char).

Transportation

Transportation may represent a work or ministry, or it may denote your life or family. It is a "vehicle" by which to get something done (see Psalm 104:3; Matthew 13:2).

A

Air balloon: ministry, work, or life of peaceful rising in the Spirit (see General/Wind).

Airplane: spiritual heights;
work, ministry, or your life that is high in spiritual things (see 1 Kings 19:11; Psalm 104:4; Jeremiah 5:13);
church/ministry (see Psalm 104:3; Matthew 13:2);
large corporation or business (see Psalm 104:3; Matthew 13:2);
flying: high spiritual activity God is taking you to; spiritual giftedness;
high in the Spirit/spiritual heights/in the spiritual realm (see 1 Kings 19:11; Psalm 104:4; Jeremiah 5:13).

Airplane, 747: ministry; a great movement; climbing spiritual heights.

Airplane, C4 Transport: God wants us to foresee; to take a ministry somewhere; spiritual heights.

Airplane, hang gliders: a ministry dependent on the Holy Spirit [wind] that reaches great spiritual heights.

Airplane, in air: already influenced; spiritual heights.

Airplane, on ground: not yet taken off to spiritual heights.

Ambulance: vehicle to receive healing.

B

Bike:
level of ministry or work; the type of call of God on your life (func);
work under your own efforts (char);
work of the flesh (char; pedaling);
slow, steady progress (char).

Boat/ship:
earthly and spiritual movement/ministry (see Matthew 13:2; 1 Timothy 1:19);
saved from drowning [through Jesus' salvation] (see 1 Peter 3:20–21).

Boat, types: (Look at characteristics.)
ark: movement in which God resides (see 1 Chronicles 13:5–6).
Navy destroyer: deliverance ministry (func); warfare (func).
riverboat: joy (see Jeremiah 31:9); life (see Revelation 22:1); slow (char); carries lots of people (func); long stretch [being swept away] (see Psalm 58:7; Revelation 12:15).

rowboat: ministry under our power (see Matthew 13:2).

sailboat: ministry empowered by the Holy Spirit; see General/Wind.

schooner: speedy movement or ministry (char).

ship: large movement (see Matthew 13:2); very large church (see Matthew 13:2); mission-minded church (char).

ship, three-masted schooner: Trinity with speed; see Themes/Numbers/3.

speedboat: short-lived (char); exciting (char).

submarine: intercessory (char); stealth/covert (func).

Titanic: big plan that is not going to work out (char).

tugboat: ability to guide people (char); help ministries (func); support for "leadership" (func).

wooden raft: things made (char); brings safety but leaves gaps (char).

Box car: work/ministry that is boxed in (char).

Bus:

Christian movement (see Psalm 104:3; Matthew 13:2);

ministry (see Psalm 104:3; Matthew 13:2);

large family (func);

church with great influence (char);

working together with others (char);

pressured by a lot of people (char).

C

Cars/Trucks: earthly travel or journey through life

ministry (see Matthew 13:2);

work [secular or spiritual]; (see 1 Samuel 6:7; Matthew 13:2);

you (see Judges 5:28);

your life (see Judges 5:28);

your family (see Judges 5:28);

earthly travel (see 1 Samuel 6:7; Psalm 104:3).

Car, being repaired: work, ministry or your life is in the process of being

healed (char; see Psalm 104:3; Matthew 13:2).

Car, black: ministry that is not of God (see Matthew 13:2; see Themes/Colors/Black); under your own efforts; humanistic work (see 1 Samuel 6:7; see Themes/Colors/Black).

Car, braking: a warning to slow down work, ministry, or your life (func).

Car, convertible: work, ministry or your life is open to the Lord (char); work or ministry where everything is revealed (char).

Car, gas station: where work, ministry or your life receives support and sustenance (func).

Car, limousine: call of God on work or ministry (see 1 Samuel 6:7; Matthew 13:2); alluring work (see 1 Samuel 6:7; Matthew 13:2).

Car, muscle car:

powerful work, ministry or your life (see 1 Samuel 6:7; Matthew 13:2);

high-performance work, ministry or your life (char);

a temptation to go too fast and lose control (char).

Car, parked: work, ministry or your life is on the sidelines (char).

Car, reversing: work, ministry or your life is not going the direction it should be with the anointing you have (char).

Car, rumble seat: work, ministry or your life without covering and susceptible to a rumble (char).

Car, shiny: work, ministry or your life that's the newest thing going (char).

Car, taxi: work, ministry or your life that helps others get where they want to go (char).

Car, van:

church/larger ministry (see 1 Samuel 6:7; Matthew 13:2);

whole family (see Judges 5:28);

larger work (see 1 Samuel 6:7).

Cart: transport (see 1 Samuel 6:7).

Chariot:

a major heaven-to-earth encounter (see 2 Kings 2:11–12; Psalm 104:3);

a vehicle to work (see 2 Samuel 15:1;
1 Kings 10:26);

a vehicle to minister (see 2 Kings 2:11);

a vehicle of life (see 1 Kings 22:35–38;
2 Kings 5:26);

see Themes/Transportation/Car.

Covered wagon: a powerful movement of work/ministry with roots in the past/ traditions (char); slow progress due to old ways (char).

H

Helicopter:

small home groups (char);

work/ministry that gets off the ground quickly (char);

rescue behind enemy lines (func).

Hummer: ministry that makes music (char); music that worships (char).

J

Jet, private: a private work or ministry that is going high and fast (func).

K

Kayak: private work or ministry carried by the flow of God (char).

M

Motorcycle: individual work or ministry (char).

Motor bike: see Themes/Transportation/ Motorcycle.

R

Roller coaster: temporary thrill (char); ups and downs (char); going round

and round and up and down, but getting nowhere (func).

Roller skates: individual ministry (char).

S

Ship/boat: earthly and spiritual travel; church of God/large ministry/faith (see Matthew 13:2; 1 Timothy 1:19); ministry or work steered by something very small [rudder] (see James 3:4).

Ship, merchant: brings sustenance [teachings] from afar (see Proverbs 31:14).

Ship, rudder: obey (see James 3:4); Holy Spirit (func).

Shipwreck: faith is damaged (see 1 Timothy 1:19); public ministry is damaged (char).

Sidecar: you will mentor someone or impact someone (func).

Sidecar, empty: someone on the side is not there (char).

Soaring: high spiritual activity God is taking you to (see Isaiah 40:31; Zechariah 5:1–2).

Spaceships: mystical realms; high in the unknown (char; see Isaiah 40:31; Zechariah 5:1–2).

Stagecoach:

rough ride to get where you are going (char);

going in stages (play on words);

doing it the "old" way (char);

see Theme/Transportation/Covered Wagon.

Stilts, on: high-minded; neglecting the basic things of life.

Street car: local church/local ministry (char; see Themes/Transportation/ Car).

Subway: in the "rat race" of humanity (char); something below the surface moving things around (func).

Subway strap: Jesus is the subway strap you hang on to during transitions (func).

T

Taxi: see Themes/Transportation/Cars/ Trucks/Taxi.

Train:

powerful movement/great power (see Isaiah 6:1);

large church (play on words; see Isaiah 6:1);

denomination (see Isaiah 6:1);

training facility/time of training (see Psalm 68:18).

Tricycle: life, work or ministry that is well grounded (char); life, work or ministry that is in a less spiritually mature phase (char).

Trucks/cars: earthly travel (see Themes/ Transportation/Cars).

Truck, armored car: major protection from God (func).

Truck, blazer: ministry blazing a new trail (play on words).

Truck, large tractor or semitruck:

carrying a load to deliver (char);

blessing (func);

transport for someone else (func);

what you are called to do, in part (play on words: semi).

Truck, pickup: personal ministry or natural work (char); see Themes/ Transportation/Car.

Truck, refrigerator truck: storehouse (char).

Truck, semi chasing you: something trying to take you away/transport you (char).

Truck, utility truck: delivery (char); things to take to people (func).

Truck, 4-wheel drive: ministry held up by the Holy Spirit [see General/Tires] under God's creative works.

U

Unicycle: individual ministry or calling that requires perseverance, human effort, commitment and extreme balance (char).

V

Vehicle, ATV/SUV: ministry or work in city (char); ministry or work out of the city (char).

Vehicle, larger vehicle: more about the church (char).

Vehicle, RV: transition time (func).

Vehicle, smaller vehicle: more about your ministry (char).

W

Walking: direction you are going (char); reaching others one on one (func).

Colors

A

Amber: God (see Ezekiel 1:4, 27; 8:2).

Ashen: pestilence and famine (see Revelation 6:8).

B

Beige: humanistic issues or humanism (char); fleshly (char); unassuming (char).

Black:

black skin—regardless of race, people tend to dream of "unknown others" in their own race color, or in cases of bi-racial families, either race may equally be displayed. The color of the skin is neutral and means nothing. However, if the dream tends to *accent* the color of a person's skin [e.g., the dreamer is saying: "some *white* lady" or "a *brown-skinned* man" or "a *black* lady," etc.], then the color of the skin *may be* an indication of the "authority" the person (or whoever they represent) is operating out of—then see Themes/Colors for a clue to the identity of their authority. To determine whether the "unknown other" person is good or bad, look to the dreamers' reaction. Are they freaked out about the person? If so, the meaning attached to the color is probably on the negative side. If they are embracing the person, then the meaning of the color is positive. If they have no negative or positive feelings about the person, the person is probably neutral. Remember, *if the dreamer* is making a point of stating the skin color, then it might be relevant to the interpretation of the dream. If there is no mention of the skin color, then it is of no consequence. *Do not ask the skin color as we do not want to "lead" the dreamer into saying the color may be relevant.* The omission of the skin color is enough to disregard it (see Song of Solomon 1:5);

darkness may indicate dealing with a normal soul [mind, will or emotions] or a humanity issue (see Job 3:5; 30:28–30; Micah 7:8);

darkness may indicate ignorance/ being "in the dark" as opposed to being "in the light" (see Job 12:22; Hebrews 12:17–19);

darkness may indicate mourning/ calamity/distress [going through a "dark night of the soul" or emotional struggles] (see Isaiah 50:3; Jeremiah 4:28; Revelation 6:12);

darkness in the setting of the dream often indicates the dream is outlining the plans of the enemy for you or others (see Job 18:5–6; 24:13; 30:26–27; Proverbs 7:9);

black may indicate being under the authority of the evil one (see Isaiah 59:9; 1 Thessalonians 5:5; 2 Peter 2:17; Jude 13).

Blue:

heavenly spiritual communion [as in the color of the heaven above the earth] (see Exodus 26:1–36; 27:15–17; 28:5–15, 31–38; Numbers 4:11–12);

revelation/carrying God's presence forth to yourself and others (see Exodus 39:1, 22; Numbers 4: 1–15 [to carry God's presence forth it is covered in blue cloth]; 15:37–39);

depression/anxiety/emotional woes (as in "I've got the blues").

Brown:

compassion (see Genesis 30:32–35, 40 [dark colored (brown) and multicolored animals—that were previously considered undesirable—were chosen]);

tradition (see Ezekiel 47:12);

humanism/things of the earth and flesh [shades of brown];

things of man, good and bad;

man-made/coming from the efforts of mankind instead of the divine;

false compassion [compassion from the mind not from the spirit];

without spirit (see Ezekiel 47:12);

withered/dried out (see Ezekiel 47:12).

Buff: shining/polished; new (char).

C

Crimson: sin (see Isaiah 1:18); see Themes/Colors/Red.

Cyan [blue green]:

will;

fasting;

strong-willed;

soulish will;

will (reference: Streamsministries.com, John Paul Jackson, "Understanding Dreams and Visions").

G

Gold, amber:

God (see Ezekiel 1:4, 27; 8:2; Haggai 2:8; Revelation 4:2–6);

holy (see Ezekiel 1:4, 27; 8:2; Haggai 2:8; Revelation 4:2–6);

purity (see Ezekiel 1:4, 27; 8:2; Haggai 2:8);

test (see Zechariah 13:9);

ruling authority (see Daniel 5:29; Zechariah 6:10–11);

greed (see Isaiah 2:20);

contamination (see Isaiah 2:20);

licentiousness/idolatry (see Isaiah 2:20);

luster (see Lamentations 4:1; Revelation 17:4).

Gray:

old (see Genesis 42:38; 44:29–31; Leviticus 19:32; Deuteronomy 32:25; 1 Samuel 12:2; Job 15:10; Psalm 71:18; Proverbs 20:29);

hair color: wisdom (see Themes/People and Beings/Old Man);

weak/compromise (something is gray);

vacillating/wishy-washy (as in "it is a gray area").

Green:

conscience (see Job 8:16);

growth/prosperity; to flourish (see Genesis 1:30; 9:3; Exodus 10:15; Deuteronomy 12:2; Job 8:12, 16; 15:32; Psalm 23:2; Proverbs 11:28; Luke 23:31);

immature (see Genesis 30:37; Leviticus 2:14);

moldy and spreading destruction (see Leviticus 13:49; 14:37–38);

pride/envy/jealousy (as in "green with envy").

Green, emerald: rest/refreshment (see Psalm 23:2; Ezekiel 28:13; Revelation 4:3).

Colors

M

Magenta [red blue]: emotions

wisdom (see Ephesians 3:10: the Hebrew word for *manifold* [multi] means "wisdom");

miracles, gifts (the Hebrew word for *various* also means "multi-colored");

emotions (reference: Streamsministries .com, John Paul Jackson, "Understanding Dreams and Visions");

look at the colors.

O

Orange:

perseverance (fire has relentless consumption);

power (see Proverbs 6:27);

warning/harmful/danger (orange is a color used for caution and danger);

strong-willed/stubbornness (char).

P

Pale: death (see Jeremiah 30:6; Daniel 10:8; Revelation 6:8).

Pink: childlike; faith; childish.

Pink, hot: faith that is heating things up; childish behavior that is heating things up.

Purple:

authority (see 2 Chronicles 2:7, 14; Daniel 5:29);

majesty/royalty (see Esther 8:15; Song of Solomon 3:10; Mark 15:17; John 19:5);

honor (see Daniel 5:29; Proverbs 31:22);

privilege (see Lamentations 4:5);

imperial luxury (see Song of Solomon 3:10; Revelation 17:4; 18:12, 16);

priesthood (see Revelation 17:1–6);

religious system (see Revelation 17:1–6);

false authority (see Revelation 17:4).

R

Red:

wisdom (see 2 Chronicles 2:7, 14; Psalm 75:8; Proverbs 31:21);

power (see 2 Samuel 1:24);

anointing (see 2 Samuel 1:24; Psalm 75:8);

redemption/sacrifice/covenantal blood of Jesus (see Matthew 27:28–31; Hebrews 9:19–22);

Pentecost (see Acts 2:3);

purification (see Hebrews 9:22);

not to go forward (red light; red flag);

anger (see Revelation 12:3);

war destruction (see Nahum 2:3; Revelation 6:4; 9:17);

bloodshed; dangerous (see Proverbs 23:31; Revelation 12:3);

sin (see Isaiah 1:18; Jeremiah 4:30; Revelation 12:3–4).

S

Sapphire: holding back (see Acts 5:2).

Scarlet: see Themes/Colors/Red.

Silver:

redemption (see Exodus 21:32; 35:24; Zechariah 13:9);

belonging to God (see Job 22:25; Haggai 2:8);

salvation (see Genesis 20:16; Jeremiah 6:30);

ruling crown (see Genesis 44:2; Zechariah 6:10–11);

riches (see Genesis 13:2; 23:15–17; Deuteronomy 8:13; Joshua 22:8);

purified/refined (see Psalm 66:10; Proverbs 27:21; Isaiah 48:10; Ezekiel 22:22; Zechariah 13:9; Malachi 3:3);

smooth words; "silver-tongued"; good word/righteous word (see Proverbs 10:20; 25:11);

daily money/wages (see Matthew 10:9; 26:15; Luke 15:8);

legalism (see Isaiah 2:20);

idolatry (see Isaiah 2:20; 30:22; 31:7; Daniel 5:4, 23; Hosea 8:4; Habakkuk 2:19; Revelation 18:12).

Colors

T

Turquoise: slightly greenish tone of light blue; valuable mineral; color is ancient.

bending your will toward your conscience [listening more to God];

listening to God is affected greatly by your will.

W

White:

holy (see Isaiah 1:18; Daniel 7:9; Matthew 28:3; Mark 9:3; 16:5; Luke 9:29; John 20:12; Revelation 2:17; 3:4; 4:4; 6:11; 14:14);

purity (see Ecclesiastes 9:8; Isaiah 1:18; Daniel 11:35; 12:10; Revelation 2:17; 1:14; 3:18; 7:9–14);

ancient/God (see Daniel 7:9; Matthew 17:2; Revelation 1:14; 20:11);

Jesus (see Matthew 17:2; 28:3; Mark 9:3; Luke 9:29);

with Christ (see Matthew 28:3; Mark 9:3; Revelation 3:4–5; 4:4; 19:11);

occult (see Matthew 23:27);

leprous (see Leviticus 13:3–4, 16–26; 2 Kings 5:27).

Y

Yellow:

mind [intellect/logic] (reference: Streamsministries.com, John Paul Jackson, "Understanding Dreams and Visions");

fear of the mind/fear (as in "he's yellow");

gift (gift of the magi—gold);

contaminated; sickness (see Leviticus 13:30, 32, 36).

Colors Addendum

Bright colors: often indicate the things of the Lord (see 1 Chronicles 29:2; Isaiah 63:1).

Dull/muted colors: often indicate things that are not of the Lord (see 1 Chronicles 29:2; Isaiah 63:1).

Multi-colored:

look at the colors;

being tolerant with differences and change (char);

altered/different (as in "it's a horse of a different color");

tinted or marked by exaggeration (as in "that story has been colored");

relating to persons of different races.

Without color: could mean that it is not relevant (char).

People and Beings

I t is important to remember that people in a dream often represent someone, or something, other than the actual person you recognize. Do not assume the person in the dream is actually that particular person. Instead, analyze the dream. They may represent any one of the following.

- May represent someone else with a pointed similarity [Joan the nurse may actually represent Gale the nurse; or orange-haired Francie may represent orange-haired Brittany];
- May represent someone in a similar relationship with you [Michelle who is your niece may actually represent Alisa who is your other niece] (see Matthew 16:13; 17:10–13; 25:31–45);
- May represent someone else of the same first name or same last name [Doug Jones may represent Doug Sheffield];
- May represent the meaning or symbolism of the person's *name*— and not a person at all [Nan may represent *gracious* or *grace*; Philadelphia in a dream may not represent the city but may be a symbol to the dreamer of going to an "area of brotherly love"];
- May represent the person's profession [your pastor in a dream may represent Father God—remember this is a symbol and not a statement that you are "worshipping" your pastor; likewise, your sister in a dream may represent your sister-in-law or a sister in Christ/a Christian friend];
- May represent the person [of course, people in the dream may represent themselves, but often they do not. Assuming that they represent themselves is the most common mistake interpreters make].

A

Accountant: keeps watch over (see Ecclesiastes 3:15; Ezekiel 3:19–21; Hebrews 13:17);

must give an accounting (see 2 Kings 12:15; 22:7; Romans 14:12–13).

Accuser:

plaintiff (see John 8:10; Acts 23:35; 25:18);

enemy/devil/Satan (see Zechariah 3:1–2; Revelation 12:10–11);

wicked one (see Psalm 109:6).

Actor:

look at the meaning and symbolism of the person's name;

look at the actor's character;

someone is "acting" (play on words).

Actress: see Themes/People and Beings/Actor.

Adam, first: effects of being an earthly person (see Genesis 1:26–27).

Adam, second: effects of Jesus' life (see Romans 5:12–21; 1 Corinthians 15:22).

Adulterer:

fleshly evil (see Psalm 50:18; Isaiah 57:3; Jeremiah 3:9; 7:9; Galatians 5:19);

betrayer (see Leviticus 20:10; Jeremiah 3:8);

infidelity (see Exodus 20:14; Leviticus 20:10; John 8:3).

Alcoholic: not a good steward (see Titus 1:7); will receive woe (see Proverbs 20:1; Isaiah 5:22).

Alien:

foreign to current ways or culture (see Psalm 105:23);

not belonging to those around you (see Hebrews 11:9; 1 Peter 1:1; 2:11);

foreign to God's people and household (see Judges 19:12; 2 Samuel 1:13; Psalm 39:12; 69:8; 81:9; Isaiah 61:5; Ephesians 2:19);

those away from Christ (see Numbers 19:10; 1 Chronicles 29:15; Galatians 5:4; Colossians 1:21);

not of God or not belonging (see 2 Samuel 4:3; Lamentations 5:2);

see Themes/People and Beings/Stranger.

Ambassador: fellow Christian (see Proverbs 13:17; Jeremiah 49:14; 2 Corinthians 5:20; Ephesians 6:20); representatives (see Joshua 9:4; Isaiah 18:2; Ephesians 6:20).

Ancestors: inheritance (see Genesis 49:26; Leviticus 26:45); where you will be; what you will reap (see Deuteronomy 32:50; 1 Kings 19:4).

Angel:

spiritual messenger from God (see Daniel 4:13; Mark 8:38; 12:25; Luke 1:19, 26–28; Hebrews 1:14; Revelation 1:1); only testifies to the Word of God (see Revelation 1:2);

spiritual guardians who protected Jesus (see Matthew 4:6; Luke 4:10–11);

spiritual guardians who protect humans that will inherit salvation (see Psalm 91:9–12; Hebrews 1:14);

God's ministering spiritual beings (see Psalm 91:11–12; Matthew 4:11; Luke 22:43);

speak things that are unalterable (see Hebrews 2:2);

spiritual messenger from the enemy (see Daniel 10:13; Matthew 25:41; Galatians 1:8; 1 John 4:1–6).

Angel, not representing God:

dark angels (see Jude 6);

speaks falsely and is cursed (see Galatians 1:8);

evil spirit (see 2 Chronicles 18:20–22; 2 Corinthians 11:14–15);

will be sent to lower reaches of hell [*Tartarus*] (see 2 Peter 2:4).

Antichrist: one who appears godly but does not remain under God's laws (see 1 John 2:18–22; 4:1–3; 2 John 1:7).

Apostle: Jesus (see Hebrews 3:1); those who go out to teach of Jesus and are accountable to Him (see Matthew 10:2; Mark 6:30; Luke 6:13; 9:10; 11:49).

Archer:

Jesus (see Revelation 6:2);

those who are equipped for battle (see Psalm 78:9);

those who harass others (see Genesis 49:23);

those who wound others (see 1 Samuel 31:3; 2 Samuel 11:24; 1 Chronicles 10:3; Proverbs 26:10).

Architect: God (see Genesis 1:1; 2:7; Hebrews 11:10; Psalm 136:6; Isaiah 48:13; 51:13); designer/planner (see Exodus 31:1–4; 35:30–32; Psalm 136:6; Isaiah 48:13).

Army:

angels (see Joshua 5:13–15; 1 Chronicles 12:22; Isaiah 6:1–4; 28:29);

protector (see Exodus 14:9; Deuteronomy 11:4);

military force (see Exodus 14:9; Deuteronomy 11:4).

Asian: foreigner/alien [if this is not your racial identification]; see Themes/People and Beings/Aliens.

Athlete: those who compete to win; life's competition and relationships (see 2 Timothy 2:5).

Attendants of the Bridegroom: disciples of Christ (see Matthew 9:15).

Attorney:

Lord (see Job 16:19–21; Psalm 68:5; Hebrews 7:25; 1 John 2:1);

those who make a defense for others (see Job 16:19–21; Romans 8:27; 1 Peter 3:15; 1 John 2:1);

those who practice the law (see Matthew 22:35; Luke 11:46–53);

those who are legalistic (play on words); Pharisees/Sadducees (see Matthew 21:33–46; 22:35–46; 23:13–15; Luke 11:46–53).

Aunt: ant (wisdom); prepares for the future (char); wise (char); diligent (char).

Author: originator (see Hebrews 2:10; 5:9; 12:2).

Authority: Lord (see Matthew 21:23–27).

Avenger: Lord (see 1 Samuel 24:12; 1 Thessalonians 4:6); revengeful (see Numbers 35:12–27; Deuteronomy 19:12; Psalm 8:2).

B

Baby:

new ministry/new work/new beginning (see Isaiah 53:10; 54:1);

immature Christian (see Matthew 11:25; 21:16; 1 Corinthians 14:20; Ephesians 4:14; Hebrews 5:13);

immature (see Psalm 8:2; Matthew 11:25; 21:16; 1 Corinthians 14:20; Ephesians 4:14; Hebrews 5:13);

in need of care and teaching (see Numbers 11:12; Job 8:9; Matthew 11:25);

baby (see Exodus 2:6).

Balak: evil doctrine to lead people away from God.

Band:

group of ministers (music: may be a ministry);

group of false leaders;

identifies who the dreamer represents (see Exodus 28:8; 29:5).

Best man: see Themes/People and Beings/Attendants of the Bridegroom.

Blacksmith: a starter (see Isaiah 54:16); someone who fans coals into flames; troublemaker (see Isaiah 54:16).

Blind guide: guide to those who are in darkness (see Romans 2:19); those who lead others into spiritual darkness (see Matthew 15:14; 23:16, 24).

Bond-servant: see Themes/People and Beings/Slave.

Boss: see Themes/People and Beings/Employer.

Boy: those without wisdom (see Isaiah 3:4); those still learning (see Judges 13:12).

Bride: God's pure Church (see Psalm 45:13–15; Jeremiah 2:1–2; John 3:25–31; Ephesians 5:23–26; Revelation 19:7; 21:2, 9–14; 22); to be in an intimate and covenantal relationship with (see Jeremiah 2:2).

Bridegroom:

Jesus (see Matthew 9:15; 25:10; Mark 2:19; John 3:25–31; Revelation 19:7; 21:2; 22);

God (see Isaiah 62:5);

spouse (see Isaiah 62:5; Matthew 1:16; Colossians 3:18–19);

someone coming into a committed covenantal relationship (see Exodus 4:25–26).

Brother:

brother in Christ (see 2 Samuel 20:9; Matthew 5:47; 12:46–50; 18:15; 23:8–10; 28:10; Ephesians 6:21; Philippians 1:12; 2:25; 1 Timothy 6:2; Hebrews 2:11–12; Revelation 19:10; 22:9);

Christian (see Romans 12:1–2; 1 Corinthians 16:12; 2 Corinthians 12:18; 1 Timothy 6:2);

natural brother (see Proverbs 27:10; Matthew 4:21; 10:21; Galatians 1:19);

brother-in-law (rel);

friend close to you (see 2 Samuel 1:26 [David and Jonathan]; 2 Samuel 20:9; 1 Chronicles 20:7; Proverbs 18:24);

fellow human (see Matthew 7:3–5; Hebrews 2:17; 2 Thessalonians 3:15; 1 Timothy 5:1).

Brother-in-law: a fellow Christian who is legalistic (play on words—law, legalistic).

Builder:

God (see Psalm 136:6; Isaiah 48:13; 51:13; Matthew 7:24–27; Hebrews 3:3–4; 11:10);

Jesus (see Hebrews 3:3–4);

building on God's Word; building on a foundation (func);

servant of the Lord (see 1 Corinthians 3:10);

designer/planner (see Exodus 31:1–4; 35:30–32; Psalm 136:6; Isaiah 48:13);

laying a foundation (see 1 Corinthians 3:10);

see Themes/People and Beings/Architect.

Builder, expert: laying God's foundation (see 1 Corinthians 3:10; Hebrews 3:4; 11:10).

Bus driver: leader in a large church; authority in ministry or church (func); see Themes/Transportation/Bus.

C

Captive: trapped into serving (Colossians 2:8; 2 Timothy 2:24); in bondage/not free (see Psalm 68:18; 69:33; Isaiah 61:1).

Carpenter: Jesus (see Matthew 13:55); one who builds (func).

Cashier: one who is trustworthy (see Genesis 47:14); one who controls the funds (func).

Charmer: one who controls others (see Psalm 58:5; Isaiah 19:3); a manipulator (char).

Child: see Themes/People and Beings/Children.

Children:

your descendants/your children (see Exodus 1:1–5; Matthew 10:21; Colossians 3:20–21);

fruit; prosperous (see Jeremiah 22:30; Revelation 2:23);

results (see Isaiah 53:10; 54:1; Matthew 11:16; Luke 7:35);

followers of God/Christ (see Deuteronomy 8:5; Matthew 18:3–6; John 16:33; Romans 8:16–17; Ephesians 5:1; Titus 1:4; Hebrews 1:13; 1 John 2:1; Revelation 12:17; 21:7);

those who are in need of teaching (see Isaiah 3:4; Mark 7:27; Galatians 4:19; Titus 1:4; Hebrews 2:13–14; 1 John 2:1, 12; 3:1–2);

humbly open to receiving the truth of God (see Matthew 11:25; 18:1–5; 21:15–16);

immature in Christ (see Matthew 11:16, 25; Ephesians 4:13–15; 5:1; 1 Peter 1:14);

followers (see Ephesians 5:1, 8; Philippians 2:15, 22; 1 Timothy 1:2; Titus 1:4; Philemon 10);

imitators of their father (see Ephesians 5:1);

heirs (see Genesis 15:2; Matthew 21:38; Romans 8:17; Galatians 4:1, 7);

dependence (see Galatians 4:3);

unwise (see 1 Kings 3:7; Jeremiah 4:22);

do not know how to speak (see Jeremiah 1:6);

held in bondage by elemental things (see Galatians 4:3).

Children, illegitimate: works not ordained by God (see Hosea 5:7; John 8:41; Hebrews 12:8).

Children, small:
those you are mentoring (char);
dependent and lacking in learning (see 1 Timothy 3:4);
immature/immature Christian (see 1 Corinthians 14:20; Ephesians 4:14).

Children, stillborn: a new beginning that gets cut off prematurely (see Psalm 58:8).

Chiropractor: one who does adjustments on others (func).

Christ: see Themes/People and Beings/ Jesus (see Matthew 22:42).

Christ, false: will mislead many (see Matthew 24:4–5, 24; Mark 13:22).

Christian women:
God's angels (see Hebrews 1:14 [ministering spirits]; Zechariah 5:9 [some angels are women]]);
who are the women? Are they members of your church? If so, this might be a clue that the dream is about your church or a group within your church;
other Christian women;
may represent another Christian woman in a similar relationship to you.

Citizen: one who belongs to the group (see Luke 15:15; Acts 21:39; 22:28; Ephesians 2:19); one who belongs to the Lord (see Isaiah 48:2; Ephesians 2:19; Philippians 3:20).

Common-law wife: wife of the world (char); worldly spirit (char); false wife (char).

Construction worker: servant of the Lord (see 1 Corinthians 3:10).

Counselor: God (see Psalm 73:24); Holy Spirit (see Luke 4:1; John 14:16, 26); Jesus (see Isaiah 9:6).

Cowboy:
one who does things without proper forethought or consideration (char; as in "he shoots from the hip");
doing things by oneself without proper authority (char);
nontraditional (char).

Co-worker: fellow Christian (see Philippians 2:25; 1 Thessalonians 3:2; 3 John 1:8).

Craftsmen: nations or people God uses to overthrow enemies (see Zechariah 1:21).

Creator: God/Jesus (see Genesis 1:1, 2:7; Colossians 1:16; Hebrews 1:2, 10); Holy Spirit (see Psalm 104:30).

Criminal: one who is guilty (see Exodus 22:2, 7; Psalm 50:18; John 12:6); the enemy's forces; one who does evil (see Luke 23:32–39; John 18:30; 1 Peter 4:15).

D

Dad: see Themes/People and Beings/ Father.

Daughter: child of God/follower of Christ (see Deuteronomy 32:19; Jeremiah 14:17; Matthew 9:22; Ephesians 2:19); see Themes/People and Beings/Son.

Deacon: see Themes/People and Beings/Elder.

Dead person, alive and giving a message:
message from God (see Mark 6:15; 8:28; Luke 9:30; Hebrews 11:4);
actual visitation from that person (see Mark 9:4; Luke 9:30);
someone or something that person represents (see Mark 6:15; 8:28);
an evil impersonation to give a false message (see 1 John 4:1).

Dead person, someone dying or dead in the dream:
change from old spiritual ways to new spiritual ways [often is wonderful] (see John 3:3–7);
their name is not written in the Book of Life (see Revelation 20:11–15);
dying to an "old way of life" (see John 3:3, 7; Colossians 3:3; 1 Peter 1:23);
without action (see Romans 4:18–20);
spiritually dead (see Psalm 88:5; Ephesians 2:1–5; Colossians 2:12–13; 1 Timothy 5:6; 1 Peter 4:6; 1 John 3:14; Revelation 3:1);
physically dead (see Genesis 44:20; Exodus 4:19).

Death angel: one who brings us home (func); threat (char).

Defender: see Themes/People and Beings/Attorney.

Deliverer: Lord (see Job 16:19–21; Psalm 18:2; 68:5; Hebrews 7:25; 1 John 2:1).

Delivery person: Lord (see 2 Samuel 22:2, 51).

Dentist:

keeps understanding (teeth) sharp and healthy (func);

corrects or removes wrong understanding (see Jeremiah 8:22);

God (see Psalm 147:3; Matthew 8:7, 13–15; 9:12–13, 22, 28–30, 35; 12:15; 14:14; 15:30; Mark 2:7; Luke 4:23; 5:31);

see General/Teeth.

Director: directing life (func); Lord (see 1 Thessalonians 3:11; 2 Thessalonians 3:5).

Disciple: follower (see Matthew 10:24–25; 11:1–2).

Doctor: Lord (see Psalm 147:3; Matthew 8:7, 13–15; 9:12–13, 22, 28–30, 35; 12:15; 14:14; 15:30; Mark 2:7; Luke 4:23; 5:31); one who heals (see Jeremiah 8:22).

Driver: in control of (see Exodus 5:13).

Drunkard:

full of the Holy Spirit (see 1 Samuel 25:36; Isaiah 29:9; Jeremiah 23:9; Ephesians 5:18);

caught up in one's feelings (see Revelation 17:2, 6);

overwhelmed by (see Deuteronomy 32:42; Psalm 107:27);

unable to fight or think clearly (see Isaiah 24:20; 63:6; Jeremiah 51:39, 57);

drunkenness (see Isaiah 5:11).

E

Elder:

respect (see Lamentations 5:12);

wise (see 1 Kings 12:6–15);

appointed regional leaders; authority (see Exodus 19:5–7; Philippians 1:1; Titus 1:5; 2 John 1:1; 3 John 1:1);

see Themes/People and Beings/Leader.

Employer:

authority over you/one in power over you (see Leviticus 25:6, 40, 53; Nehemiah 5:5; Ephesians 6:5–9);

represents God/Christ (see Ephesians 6:5–9);

one to be honored and respected (see 1 Timothy 6:1–2);

those we must serve (see 1 Timothy 6:2).

Enemy:

devil (see Matthew 13:25–28, 39; Luke 10:19; Acts 13:10);

those who oppose you (see Exodus 15:9; 1 Samuel 24:19; 26:8; 28:16);

death (see 1 Corinthians 15:26).

Enemy, oppressing you: you are not being obedient, and the Lord is teaching you (see Nehemiah 9:26–31; Isaiah 63:10; Jeremiah 18:17; Lamentations 2:5; James 4:4); attacks of the devil (see Matthew 13:25–28, 39).

Eunuch: unable to be productive (see Esther 2:15 [the king's eunuchs were in charge of the women because they were unable to have sex with the women and were considered safe]).

Evil workers: people who cause strife, pain, or death (see Psalm 28:3; 37:1; 94:16; Philippians 3:2).

Ex-family (ex-husband, ex-wife, etc.):

family you do not get along with (rel);

church family you do not get along with (rel);

past family issues (char).

Ex-spouse:

old love that was not good for you [Has the dreamer gone back to old destructive patterns or behaviors that might be harmful?] (rel);

Jesus [Have you moved away from Him?] (rel);

could it actually be about your ex?

old, comfortable ways (char);

see Themes/People and Beings/Old Love.

Eyewitness: insight; one who understands or "sees" (char); what you see (char).

F

Faceless people you cannot identify:
Holy Spirit (see Exodus 33:23);
angels (see Genesis 19:1, 15; Numbers 22:22–27; Psalm 91:11–12; Hebrews 13:2);
symbol of someone (rel);
demonic force (see Galatians 1:8).

Familiar, but unidentified woman or man:
angel (see Genesis 19:1, 15; Numbers 22:22–27; Hebrews 13:2).

Familiar person, bad: attacks reoccurring from the past (char); demonic activity (func).

Familiar person, good: from the Lord (char); angel (see Galatians 1:8).

Family:
one who belongs (see Genesis 12:1; Ephesians 2:19);
lineage (see Genesis 24:4, 38; 2 Samuel 16:5);
those who follow their leader (see Matthew 10:25);
can be our worst enemies (see Matthew 10:36).

Farmer:
Jesus/God (see Matthew 13:37; John 15:1);
those who plant (see 2 Chronicles 26:10; Jeremiah 31:24; 51:23; Joel 1:11; Matthew 13:3; Mark 4:3);
those who sow and harvest the Word of God in others (see Matthew 9:37–38; 13:3; Mark 4:14; Luke 8:5);
those who toil and work hard (see 2 Timothy 2:6);
devil (see Matthew 13:39).

Father:
God (see Psalm 68:5; Jeremiah 3:19; Matthew 10:33; 11:25–27; 23:9; 28:19; Luke 2:49; 10:22; John 8:42; 10:14–38; 14:6–9, 23; Romans 4:16; 8:15; Philippians 1:2; Titus 1:4; Hebrews 12:9; 1 Peter 1:2, 17; 1 John 2:1);
source; who you imitate (see Joshua 24:15; 2 Kings 17:41; Philippians 2:22);
Jesus (see Isaiah 9:6);
grandfather/forefathers (see Deuteronomy 5:9; 2 Kings 14:3; 2 Chronicles 28:1, 6, 9; Hebrews 1:1; 3:9);
natural father (see Matthew 1:2–16; 10:21; Colossians 3:21; Hebrews 12:9);
mentor/exhorter/one who encourages you to go in a good direction (see Proverbs 1:8; 1 Thessalonians 2:11; 1 John 2:14);
older man (see 1 Timothy 5:1);
Satan (see John 8:44).

Fighter: one with faith who effectively stays the course until the end (see Exodus 14:14; 1 Corinthians 9:26; 1 Timothy 6:12; 2 Timothy 4:7).

Firstborn: Jesus (see Colossians 1:18; Hebrews 1:6); preeminence (char); supremacy (see Colossians 1:18).

Fisherman: evangelists (see Jeremiah 16:16; Matthew 4:19–22; Mark 1:17); angel of God (see Matthew 13:47).

Fool:
does not understand (see Psalm 92:6; 94:8; Proverbs 9:6);
does not build on good foundation (see Matthew 7:24–27);
commits many errors (see 1 Samuel 13:13; 26:21; Psalm 107:17);
despises wisdom and instruction (see Proverbs 1:7, 22; 10:21; 12:15).

Football players:
those who compete to win (see 2 Timothy 2:5);
people messing around with your peace (see "shoes" in Ephesians 6:15);
life messing with your peace (see "shoes" in Ephesians 6:15).

Foreigners:
foreign to God's people and household (see 1 Kings 8:41; Nehemiah 9:2; 13:3, 23–30; Psalm 81:9; Isaiah 25:2; 61:5; Jeremiah 5:19; 30:8; 51:51; Ezekiel 3:6; 10:10; 30:12; 44:7–9; 1 Corinthians 14:10–12; Ephesians 2:19);
something foreign or unknown to you (char);
people looking for a country of their own; longing for a better country (see Hebrews 11:14–15);
enemy (see Ezekiel 28:7).

Friend:

if an unknown "friend," then possibly
indicates the Holy Spirit (see John
14:16–17, 26);

angel (see Psalm 91:11–12; Daniel
3:24–28);

if the friend is a Christian, possibly the
Holy Spirit or Jesus (see Matthew
26:50; John 14:16, 26; 15:15);

representing another who is like your
friend (rel);

the friend him/herself (rel);

look at the name—what does it mean?

Friends from the past:

represent themselves or other old
friends (rel);

look at where you were spiritually/
emotionally when you were with
these friends (func);

an old way that once made you happy
(func);

look at the name—what does it mean?

G

Gardener: see Themes/People and
Beings/Farmer.

General: Christ (Josh 5:4).

Generations, previous: something passed
down to a newer generation from an
older (see Genesis 9:12; 15:16; 17:7–9;
Exodus 3:15; Psalm 78:4; 145:4; Luke
1:50; Ephesians 3:5).

Genie: Satan (from Islamic faith—Satan
was a *jinn*/a genie).

Gentiles:

fellow partakers of the promise of
Christ Jesus (see Ephesians 3:6);

those whose hope is in Jesus (see
Matthew 12:21);

those who are "grafted" into Christ
(see Ephesians 2:11–13);

those outside the Word of Jesus (see
Matthew 10:5).

Ghost, bad: bad spirit/evil force (see Galatians 1:8).

Ghost, good: spirit/angel from God (see
Daniel 4:13; Mark 8:38; 12:25; Hebrews 1:14).

Gingerbread man: be careful what you
are hearing or "feeding on" (char).

Girl, if seductive:

Jezebel spirit; spirit of control and manipulation (see 2 Kings 9:22);

corrupts others (see 1 Corinthians
15:33);

demonic spirit (see Galatians 1:8).

Girl, young: spiritually immature person
(see Ephesians 4:13–15).

Girl, young, good, often with short hair:
angel (see Psalm 91:11–12).

God:

God (see Deuteronomy 32:39; Isaiah
45:5; Ephesians 4:4–6);

Trinity (see Titus 2:13);

only one true God (see 1 Timothy 1:17;
2:5);

Creator of everyone, but only a few
call Him Father (see Psalm 68:5; Jeremiah 3:19; Matthew 10:33; 11:25–27;
23:9; 28:19; Luke 2:49; 10:22; 11:13;
John 8:42; 10:14–38; 14:6–9, 23;
16:33; Romans 4:16);

idolizing our own job or works/putting
our jobs ahead of God (see Hosea
14:3);

idol (see Genesis 31:19; Leviticus 19:4;
26:1; Deuteronomy 29:17; 32:21);

enemy/demons (see Deuteronomy
32:17).

Governor:

Jesus (see Matthew 2:6);

one in authority over you (see Genesis
42:6; 1 Kings 4:7; Matthew 10:18);

sent to punish evil (see Zechariah 12:6;
1 Peter 2:14);

lays burdens on people (see Nehemiah
5:15–18).

Grandfather/grandmother/grandparents:

spiritual inheritance (see Psalm 145:4);

inheritance (see Deuteronomy
6:23–25);

passed down from a previous generation (see 1 Kings 15:3, 12; Psalm
145:4).

Groomsmen:

Lord (see 1 Samuel 2:9; Psalm 127:1;
141:3; Proverbs 2:8; 2 Thessalonians
3:3);

angels (see Genesis 3:24; Isaiah 52:12);
see Themes/People and Beings/Attendants of the Bridegroom [Jesus];

to actively protect work that has been done; do not sit on past laurels (see Ezekiel 38:7; Nehemiah 7:1–3);

a protector and nurturer (see Numbers 11:12; Matthew 27:54).

Guide:

God (see Psalm 73:24);

Holy Spirit (see John 16:13; Romans 8:14);

bad spirit (see Ephesians 6:12);

to speak on one's own initiative (see John 16:13).

H

Harlot: see Themes/People and Beings/ Prostitute.

Harvest workers: those evangelizing [harvesting others] (see Matthew 9:37–38; 13:30; Luke 10:2); angels (see Matthew 13:39).

Healer: see Themes/People and Beings/ Doctor.

Heir: shares in blessings and promises (see Isaiah 65:9; Ephesians 3:6).

Helper:

God/Jesus (see Deuteronomy 33:29; Psalm 118:7; 145:14);

Holy Spirit (see Luke 12:12; John 14:26; 16:13; Acts 9:31; Romans 8:26; 1 Corinthians 2:13);

angels (see Psalm 91:11–12; Daniel 3:24–28; Matthew 4:6; Hebrews 1:14).

Hired:

labors for hours and years (see Leviticus 25:53; Job 14:6);

hard work (see Job 7:1);

is due wages and should not be oppressed (see Leviticus 19:13; Deuteronomy 24:14; Job 7:2).

Holy Spirit:

spirit of wisdom (see Ephesians 1:17);

spirit of revelation (see Ephesians 1:17);

Helper given as a promise from God (see John 14:16–20; 20:22);

Comforter (see John 14:18; Acts 9:31);

leads you into truth and is a pledge of inheritance in God's kingdom (see John 16:13; 1 Corinthians 2:13);

will teach you (see Luke 12:12; John 14:26);

spirit of sonship with the Lord (see Romans 8:15);

given to praise God's glory (see Ephesians 1:13–14).

Homeless man: without a home there (char; note location/setting).

Household members: see Themes/People and Beings/Family.

Hunter: searches out those where they live (see Proverbs 6:5; Jeremiah 16:16).

Husband:

Jesus [as the Bridegroom] (see Jeremiah 3:14–20; 31:32; 54:5; Hosea 2:14–20 [*ishi*: husband]; Ephesians 5:22–32; Revelation 19:7);

God (see Isaiah 54:5);

actual husband (see Matthew 1:16; Colossians 3:18–19).

I

Idolater: those who value other things as more important than God (see 2 Kings 17:15; Jeremiah 2:5; Revelation 21:8).

Infant: see Themes/People and Beings/ Baby.

Intercessor:

Jesus (see Job 16:20–21; Matthew 11:27; Hebrews 7:25; 8:6; 9:15; 12:24);

one who stands in the gap (see Job 16:20 NIV);

one who tries to block access to God (see Hebrews 4:14–16).

J

Jesus:

Lord/God (see Isaiah 40:10; Matthew 9:14–15; 16:13–17, 20; 26:63–64; Mark

1:24; 5:7; John 4:20–26; 10:30; Titus 2:13; Hebrews 1:8);

Son of God (see Matthew 16:16; 17:5; 22:42–45; Galatians 1:16; Philippians 2:5–9; Hebrews 1:8; Revelation 5);

the Word (see John 1:1);

Creator (see Colossians 1:16);

the Rock (see Psalm 62:6);

Lamb (see Revelation 7:17);

Savior (see John 3:16; Acts 4:12);

the fullness of deity in bodily form (see Colossians 2:9);

the shepherd (see Psalm 23:1–4).

Jesus, a false one: will mislead many (see Matthew 24:4–5, 24).

Judge:

Jesus (see John 5:27–30; Acts 10:42; 2 Timothy 4:1, 8; James 5:9; 1 Peter 1:17; Revelation 19:11);

God (see Genesis 15:14; 16:5; Judges 11:27; 1 Samuel 2:3; 24:12; Job 9:15; Psalm 94:2; 98:9; Hebrews 12:23);

Holy Spirit (see Judges 3:10; Romans 8:20);

to discern/test against Word of God (see Genesis 42:16; 1 Kings 10:1; 2 Chronicles 9:1; Job 12:11; 34:3; 2 Corinthians 13:5–6; 1 Thessalonians 5:21; 1 Timothy 3:10);

resolves disputes (see Genesis 31:37; Deuteronomy 25:1; Matthew 27:19);

protector of those needing protection (see Psalm 50:4; 68:5);

opinionated/complaining (see Isaiah 53:12; 59:16; Matthew 7:1–5; Romans 8:34; James 4:12; 5:9);

casting condemnation on others (see Matthew 27:3; Romans 2:1).

K

King:

Jesus Christ (see Psalm 45:11; Isaiah 28:5; Matthew 2:2; 21: 5; 22:11; 27:11, 37; Luke 23:36–38; John 18:36–37; Ephesians 1:21–22; 1 Timothy 1:17; 6:15–16; Hebrews 2:9; Revelation 5);

God (see 1 Timothy 1:17);

strong, high authority (see 1 Samuel 2:10; Isaiah 52:15; Matthew 10:18; 1 Peter 2:13).

King of the North: Syria (rel).

King of the South: Egypt (rel).

L

Lahmi: brother of giant; to be closely related to strong person (see 1 Chronicles 20:5).

Lawyers: see Themes/People and Beings/Attorney.

Leader:

Holy Spirit (see Romans 8:14);

Jesus (see Matthew 2:6);

pastor/authority (see Numbers 1:16; Deuteronomy 1:15; 2 Chronicles 18:16; Mark 10:42);

one who keeps watch over and is accountable (see Numbers 25:4; Colossians 4:1, Titus 2:9; Hebrews 13:17);

authority of a nation/area (see Matthew 22:17–21);

will be held to higher accountability (see Deuteronomy 32:48–52; Matthew 23:14; Colossians 4:1);

note: what is controlling you? (see Matthew 27:1; 1 Corinthians 6:12);

see Themes/People and Beings/Elder.

Leper: one who is unclean (see Leviticus 13:45; Matthew 8:2–3; 10:8; Luke 5:12; 7:22).

Liar:

those who deny the truth of God's words (see Isaiah 57:4; 1 John 2:22; Revelation 21:8);

those who listen to malicious talk (see Proverbs 17:4);

devil (see John 8:44).

Long-haired man: strength (see Judges 16:17–19); vow (see Judges 13:4–5); defiance/dishonor (see Ezekiel 44:20; 1 Corinthians 11:14).

Lots of relatives:

bloodline blessings (rel);

family issues (rel);

harassment (see Genesis 37:1–36); bloodline curses (rel).

M

Magi: wise men (see Matthew 2:2, 7–12); see Themes/People and Beings/Wise man.

Magician:

doing things behind the scenes/hidden (char);

tapping into second heaven [demonic spirit] for miracles and information (see Deuteronomy 18:10–12);

see Themes/People and Beings/Medium.

Man:

other people (rel);

for a while a little lower than angels (see Hebrews 2:7);

angel/spirit (see Genesis 32:24–26; Daniel 3:24–28; Zechariah 5:9; Hebrews 13:2);

self [if dreamer is a man];

see Themes/People and Beings/Person.

Man, hired: see Themes/People and Beings/Hired.

Man, in linen: angel (see Ezekiel 9:2–3, 11; 10:2–7; Daniel 10:5; 12:6–7).

Man, in woman's clothes: not being true to self (see Deuteronomy 22:5).

Man, mature: see Themes/People and Beings/Mature.

Man, new: your new self, transformed by Christ (see Ephesians 4:22–24).

Man, nice looking, good:

represents a friend (rel);

angel helper (see Daniel 3:24–28; Hebrews 13:2);

someone who will be helping (char).

Man, old:

wisdom (see Job 12:12; Titus 2:2);

maturity (see Titus 2:2);

willing to go where you do not want to go for God's glory; putting self second (see John 21:17–18);

old self; before Christ's transformation (see Ephesians 4:22–24).

Man, seducing, attractive:

wooing/romantic (char);

controlling, manipulative spirit (see 2 Kings 9:22; Hebrews 13:2);

temptation (see 2 Kings 9:22; Hebrews 13:2);

deception (see 2 Kings 9:22; Hebrews 13:2);

witchcraft (see 2 Kings 9:22; Hebrews 13:2);

Jezebel spirit/demonic spirit (see 2 Kings 9:22; Hebrews 13:2).

Man, sleeping:

Jesus appearing not to be doing anything (see Matthew 6:24–25);

rest (see Psalm 127:2; 132:4);

not paying attention (see Psalm 121:3–4; Isaiah 5:27; Matthew 13:25; Ephesians 5:14; 1 Thessalonians 5:6);

physical death on earth but not spiritual death (see John 11:11; 1 Thessalonians 4:15–16; 5:10; 2 Peter 3:4);

see Themes/Actions/Asleep.

Man, strong and evil: Satan (see Matthew 12:25–29; Mark 3:27).

Man, strong and good: wise (see Proverbs 24:5); angel (see Joshua 5:13–15; Daniel 3:24–28).

Man, you dislike or feel uneasy around:

people not acting of God (see Matthew 27:1);

soul conflict (see Galatians 1:10);

demonic activity (see Matthew 27:3–5; Hebrews 13:2);

corrupts others (see 1 Corinthians 15:33).

Man, warm, friendly, helpful: angel (see Daniel 3:24–28; Hebrews 13:2); human friend (rel).

Man, wonderful, and possibly romantic: Jesus (see Matthew 9:15, John 3:25–31); Holy Spirit [if you do not see His face] (see John 14:16–20).

Man, young: knows the Lord and is strong, but still growing (see Exodus 33:11; Proverbs 1:4; 1 John 2:14); still following one's own desires (see John 21:17–18).

People and Beings

Master: employer (see 1 Timothy 6:1); see Themes/People and Beings/Leader.

Mediator: see Themes/People and Beings/Intercessor.

Mediums: not of God (see Leviticus 19:31; Deuteronomy 18:10–12; 2 Chronicles 33:6; Revelation 21:8); witch (see 1 Samuel 28:3, 7, 9).

Mentor: provides direction and correction.

Midget: small (char); humble (char).

Military:

God's angels and people (see Psalm 24:8; Hebrews 13:2; Revelation 19:14);

enemy's angels and people (see Hebrews 13:2; Revelation 19:19);

see Themes/People and Beings/Army.

Military leader: Jesus (see Joshua 5:14; Psalm 24:8; Matthew 8:8–13; Revelation 19:11); Satan and his representatives (see Daniel 10:13, 20; Revelation 19:19).

Military people: angels [good angels or bad angels] (see Joshua 5:13–15; 1 Chronicles 12:22; Hebrews 13:2; Revelation 19:14).

Mocker:

seeks wisdom but does not find it (see Proverbs 14:6);

creates a heavy chain (see Isaiah 28:22);

proud and arrogant (see Proverbs 21:24);

follows their own lusts (see 2 Peter 3:3; Jude 18);

abuse/disrespect (see Matthew 27:31–44; Luke 22:63);

ridicule (see Psalm 69:11–12; Matthew 27:31–44).

Mom: see Themes/People and Beings/Mother.

Mother:

your source/foundation (see Genesis 3:20; 17:16; 24:60; Proverbs 1:8; Ezekiel 19:2, 10; Galatians 4:26–27; Revelation 17:5);

mother in Christ (see Matthew 12:46–50; Mark 3:33–35; 10:29–30; Luke 8:21);

church (see Proverbs 1:8; Hosea 2:2–5; Matthew 12:48–50; Mark 3:33–35; 10:29–30; Luke 8:21);

caretaker of children (see Matthew 20:20–21; 1 Thessalonians 2:7);

mother-image (see John 19:27);

family (see Ruth 1:14; 2:11; Matthew 10:35; Luke 12:53);

older woman (see 1 Timothy 5:2);

old church family (see Proverbs 1:8; Hosea 2:2–5; Matthew 12:48–50; Mark 3:33–35; 10:29–30; Luke 8:21);

actual mother/biological mother (see Genesis 20:12; Exodus 20:12; Matthew 12:46–47);

parent (see Genesis 20:12; Exodus 20:12; Matthew 12:46–47);

mother-in-law (rel);

ambitious for children (see Matthew 20:20–21).

Mother, "like mother, like daughter": source (see Ezekiel 16:44–45).

Mother-in-law:

legalistic church (play on words);

mother image controlled by legalism (play on words);

our family (rel);

our loving church family (rel);

source by covenant (char);

meddler; trouble (char);

mother-in-law herself;

represents real mother (rel);

a mother-image (rel).

Murderer: one who destroys and kills (see Genesis 4:8; Numbers 35:16); kills God's will for others; inflicts hurt on others (see Job 24:14; Psalm 10:8; James 5:6; Revelation 21:8).

N

Nazi: demon/bad angel (char: army of the evil one; see Revelation 19:19).

Nazirite: set apart to serve God from birth (see Numbers 6:2; Judges 13:5).

Neighbor: someone nearby (see Galatians 5:14; Luke 10:28–30); one with mercy (see Luke 10:29–37).

Nomad:

finds nourishment [lives life] in a place
of little sustenance [desert] (char);

without a permanent home (char);

waiting to plunder (see Jeremiah 3:2).

Nurse: healer (see Isaiah 61:1; Jeremiah
8:22); angel [assistant to the Great
Physician] (see Psalm 91:11–12; Matthew 4:11; Luke 22:43).

O

Old love:

going back to an old way of doing
things (see Psalm 89:49; Revelation
2:4);

soul tie (char);

old issues (rel);

warning dream (rel);

Look at who the old love is. Was it a
good person in your life or someone
who was bad for you?

If the old love was good for you, then
it might be speaking of going back
to a good thing/a love you used to
have, etc. Probably not a romantic
love, as this is a symbol—not actual—but it could be a hobby you
loved, an estranged family member,
a relationship with God, or a friend
who used to mean a lot to you.

If the old love was bad for you, then it
is speaking of you going back into
a "bad-for-you" love. This could be
a bad habit. Are you smoking again,
etc.? Or are you involved in a bad
situation or with a previously toxic
person?

Old person:

mature (see 1 Corinthians 14:20; Ephesians 4:14; Titus 2:2–3);

wise; able to discern falseness and
hidden evil in others (see 1 Kings
12:6–15; Job 12:2; 2 Timothy 4:14;
Titus 2:2);

tests to discern truth (see Job 12:11–12,
34:1–3, 1 Timothy 3:10).

Orphan: without support (see Lamentations 5:3; John 14:18); without God/
without Jesus (see John 14:18).

Outsiders: those who are not of Christ
(see Exodus 29:33; Leviticus 22:10;
Colossians 4:5).

Overcomer:

Jesus (see John 16:33);

one who conquers (char);

whosoever is born of God and believes
Jesus is the Son of God (see 1 John
5:4–5; Revelation 2:7).

Overseer:

Jesus (see 1 Peter 2:25);

watches over (see Acts 20:28; Philippians 1:1; 1 Timothy 3:1);

see Themes/People and Beings/Leader;

see Themes/People and Beings/Elders.

Owner: one in power over you (see Nehemiah 5:5; Isaiah 1:3; Zechariah 11:5;
Matthew 21:40); responsible person
(see Exodus 21:28–29, 34).

P

Partner: fellow worker and equal (see
Proverbs 29:24; Luke 5:7; 2 Corinthians 8:23; Philemon 17).

Pastor:

pastoral message (see Jeremiah 3:15);

Holy Spirit (func);

not everyone who professes and calls
on the name of the Lord really
knows Him (see Matthew 7:21–23);

see Themes/People and Beings/Priest.

People, in the basement: someone doing
something "below the surface" (play
on words).

**People, where one person in the dream
is acting out parts as two different people:** doing something
self-destructive.

People, out of sight: angels (see Hebrews
13:2); Holy Spirit (see Exodus 33:23).

**People, a stranger who makes you feel
uneasy:**

not from the Lord (see Hebrews 13:2;
How does the person make you
feel?);

demonic presence (see Hebrews 13:2;
How does the person make you
feel?);

People and Beings

corrupts others (see 1 Corinthians 15:33).

Person:

a spiritual being—good or bad (see Hebrews 13:2);

what do you feel about them? Good or bad? This tells you who they are representing (see Revelation 4:2);

could represent others in a similar situation (see 2 Samuel 22:26–27);

look at who the person is, i.e., their name, their position, their relationship to you (see Matthew 16:13; 17:10–13; 25:31–45);

self (rel).

Person, fat [and not normally overweight]: satisfied/plenty (see Psalm 63:5; 65:11; 73:4); caught up in the flesh; someone who is acting out of the flesh or not following God (see Leviticus 8:16; Judges 3:17; 1 Samuel 2:5; Job 15:22–27; Psalm 73:3–7; Isaiah 10:27).

Person, without a face: Holy Spirit (see John 14:16–20).

Person, you can see them, but you do not know who they are:

angel [good/neutral feeling] or demon [bad/uneasy feeling] (see Hebrews 13:2; Revelation 4:2);

actual person dreamer might meet in the future;

representative of "others" (see 2 Samuel 22:26–27).

Pharisee:

legalistic advocate (see Matthew 23:23–25);

unproductive; a destroyer of God's church (see Matthew 21:33–46; 23:13);

will be held to higher accountability (see Matthew 23:14);

corrupts others (see Matthew 23:15).

Pharmacist, druggist:

if good, he/she might represent someone who is trying to control others for good reasons (func);

one who helps others get the medicine they need to get well (func);

if the person is unknown to you and not good, he/she might represent a witch or someone evil (a person who uses potions to control and manipulate others);

Do you know the pharmacist? Look at the name, relationship, etc. (rel);

control (char);

witch (see Themes/People and Beings/Witch).

Physician: see Themes/People and Beings/Doctor.

Pioneer: breaks through rough terrain so that others may follow (func); does not receive a welcoming committee (char).

Planter: one who plants God's seeds (see 1 Corinthians 3:6–8).

Plowmen: those who cause furrows [deep wounds] (see Psalm 129:3).

Police:

one who is in authority (char);

authoritative help (char);

angels (see 1 Chronicles 12:22; Hebrews 13:2).

Positional people: look at what they represent (rel); look at your *relationship* to these people or their positions (rel).

Potter: God (see Isaiah 64:8; Jeremiah 18:1–10; Romans 9:21).

Powers: those having high authority (see Ephesians 6:12); high spiritual authority with evil intent (see Ephesians 6:12).

Preacher: see Themes/People and Beings/Priest; see Themes/People and Beings/Pastor.

President:

Lord of hosts/God (func);

ultimate authority (func);

authority of the nation (see Matthew 22:17–21).

Priest/Preacher:

messenger of the Lord (see Malachi 2:7);

heads of families (see 1 Chronicles 9:13);

ministers in God's church/authority (see 1 Chronicles 9:13; Matthew 21:15–27);

Jesus (see Isaiah 11:1; Ephesians 1:21–22; Hebrews 2:17; 3:1; 4:14–15; 5:6; 7:24–28);

Christians or followers of Christ Jesus (see Exodus 19:5–6; Zechariah 3:7–10; 2 Timothy 4:1; 1 Peter 2:9; Revelation 1:6; 5:10);

should not go near a dead person (see Ezekiel 44:25);

self appointed authority (see Matthew 21:23–27);

not everyone who professes and calls on the name of the Lord really knows Him (see Matthew 7:21–23);

unproductive; a destroyer of God's church (see Matthew 21:33–46; 26:3–4, 14–15).

Prince:

Jesus (see Isaiah 9:6; Matthew 22:2);

high authority (see Genesis 12:15; 1 Samuel 2:8);

mortal ruler (see Genesis 12:15; Psalm 146:3).

Prince, of the air: Satan (see Ephesians 2:2).

Princess: the Church/Bride of Christ (see Psalm 45:13–15).

Principal:

authority (char);

starting point (see Proverbs 1:7);

choice part of knowledge (see Proverbs 1:7).

Prisoner:

look at who you are serving (see Ephesians 3:1; 4:1, 8; Colossians 2:8; 2 Timothy 1:8; Philemon 1);

imprisoned by debt (see Psalm 68:6);

in bondage/not free/in darkness (see Genesis 39:20; Job 3:18; Isaiah 61:1; 2 Timothy 2:26).

Prophet:

prophetic word (see Deuteronomy 18:18; Matthew 11:9–10);

one who speaks out what the Lord/Holy Spirit is saying (see Numbers 12:6; Deuteronomy 18:15, 18; Judges 6:8; Matthew 7:15; 11:9–10; 21:46; 1 Timothy 4:1);

without honor in his hometown and among his own family (see Matthew 13:57; Mark 6:4; John 4:44);

Jesus (see Matthew 21:11);

from Abel to Zechariah (see Luke 11:51).

Prophet, false: wrongful words attributed to God (see Jeremiah 5:31; 14:14; Ezekiel 22:28; Matthew 7:15; 24:11, 24; Mark 13:22; Acts 13:6; 2 Peter 2:1; 1 John 4:1; Revelation 16:13; 19:20).

Prosecutor: see Themes/People and Beings/Accuser.

Prostitute:

not faithful (see Judges 8:33; Psalm 73:27; Isaiah 1:21);

degrades self (see Ezekiel 16:25–26);

caught up in a sin of giving yourself for the wrong reason (see Joshua 2:1; Isaiah 57:3);

sells self for worldly things (see Deuteronomy 31:16; Judges 2:17);

replaces good for willful pleasure (see Judges 8:27, 33);

people who lust after other gods (see Revelation 17:1);

the worldly church gone astray and rebellious (see Revelation 17:1–6);

a great city with power (see Revelation 17:18);

a pit that seduces others (see Proverbs 23:27; Jeremiah 3:2; Nahum 3:4);

enslaves others/uses witchcraft (see Nahum 3:4);

perverse/rebellious; does evil/disgraceful things (see Leviticus 20:5; Deuteronomy 22:21; Judges 2:17; 1 Samuel 20:30).

Prostitute, scorns payment: adulterous wife (see Ezekiel 16:31–34); lower than a prostitute (see Ezekiel 16:34).

Purifier: God (see Malachi 3:3).

Q

Queen: held in esteem (see 1 Kings 15:13; Esther 1:11); in control (1 Kings 10:1–4; Revelation 18:7).

Queen of the South: those actively seeking the truth [Queen of Sheba who traveled to King Solomon to seek the truth] (see Matthew 12:42).

R

Rancher: one who watches out for others (see Zechariah 13:5; 2 Timothy 2:6); see Themes/People and Beings/Farmer.

Reaper: angels of the Lord (see Matthew 13:30, 39–42).

Rear guard: Holy Spirit (see Isaiah 52:12).

Rearview mirror: hindsight (func).

Rebel: against the Lord (see Numbers 14:9; 16:1–3; Deuteronomy 1:26; Joshua 22:16; 1 Samuel 15:23; Isaiah 57:4; Hebrews 3:15).

Refiner: God (see Psalm 66:10; Isaiah 48:10; Daniel 12:10; Zechariah 13:9; Malachi 3:2–3).

Reporter: may take it public (func).

Reporters, cameras flashing: something gone public (func).

Rescuer: God (see Exodus 6:6; Psalm 18:2, 19; 22:8; 35:17; 136:24; 144:7; Daniel 6:27; 2 Timothy 4:18); Jesus (see Colossians 1:13–14).

Revealer: Holy Spirit (see Ephesians 3:5).

Robber: waits to pounce on the unsuspecting with evil intent (see Judges 9:25; Hosea 6:9; Obadiah 1:5).

Ruler:
Christ (see Exodus 15:18; Isaiah 28:17; Matthew 2:6; Ephesians 1:21–22; Revelation 3:14);
leader/in authority (see 1 Chronicles 11:2; Proverbs 28:2; Jeremiah 51:46; Matthew 2:6; 9:34);
those having care and control over others (see 2 Samuel 5:2; Proverbs 28:2; Ephesians 6:12, Titus 3:1);
take measure of/analyze (see Ezekiel 40:3);
see General/Ruler;
see Themes/People and Beings/Leader.

Runner: swift (see Job 9:25); striving in life (see Psalm 18:29; Proverbs 1:16; 4:12; Daniel 12:4; Joel 2:7; 1 Corinthians 9:24).

Runner, in front: Jesus (see Hebrews 6:20).

S

Saint: follower of the Lord (see Daniel 7:27; Ephesians 1:15; 3:8; Philippians 1:1).

Samaritan: one who helps unexpectedly (see Luke 10:33); people of the world (see Matthew 10:5; Acts 8:25).

Satan:
a defeated foe who will still try to make trouble until he has to report to Jesus and be chained for all eternity;
tries to deflect and cause us not to receive what God wants to give us;
a representative of Satan, e.g., a dark angel, demon or human who is acting on satanic direction, etc.

Savior:
Lord (see 2 Samuel 22:3, 47);
Jesus (see Titus 1:4; Hebrews 7:25).

Scribe: one without authority who records (see Matthew 7:29).

Searcher: Holy Spirit (see 1 Corinthians 2:10–11).

Secretary: see Themes/People and Beings/Scribe.

Secular person, especially one hostile to God: the secular world.

Seer: one who has the ability to understand; one who can "see" into things spiritually (see 1 Samuel 9:9–19; 2 Samuel 15:27; 24:11; 2 Kings 17:13; 1 Chronicles 9:22; 21:9; Isaiah 29:10; 30:10; 2 Timothy 2:7); see Themes/People and Beings/Prophet.

Sensual people: those who are sensitive to others (char); those who seek their own ungodly lusts (see Jude 19).

Servant:
Christ (see Isaiah 53:11);
nature of Jesus (see Luke 22:27; Philippians 2:5–9);
see Themes/People and Beings/Slave.

Short-haired woman, good: messenger or helper from God; angel (see Daniel 4:13; Mark 8:38; Revelation 1:1).

Shearer: one who removes a bad covering (func); one who removes the covering from those who have no defense (func; see Isaiah 53:7).

Shepherd:

protector (see 2 Samuel 5:2; Isaiah 40:11; Ezekiel 34: 1–10; Zechariah 10:2–3; John 10:12);

leader (see 2 Samuel 5:2; 1 Kings 22:17; 1 Chronicles 11:2; Jeremiah 3:14; 6:3; 50:6);

elder (see 2 Chronicles 18:16; 1 Peter 5:2);

Lord/Jesus (see Psalm 23:1; Isaiah 40:11; Matthew 2:6; 26:31; John 10:11–14; Hebrews 13:20; 1 Peter 5:4; Revelation 7:17);

God (see Jeremiah 31:10; Ezekiel 34);

priest (see Jeremiah 3:15; 23:1–4; Ezekiel 34:1–10);

one who takes care of the flock (see Ezekiel 34:1–10; John 10:12).

Shepherd, chief: Jesus (see 1 Peter 5:4).

Sister:

young woman (see 1 Timothy 5:2);

sister in Christ (see Matthew 12:46–50; Mark 3:35; 10:30; 1 Timothy 5:2; Philemon 2);

biological sister (see Genesis 34:27; Matthew 10:21);

sister-in-law (rel);

a friend who is close to you (see Ezekiel 16:50–52; Mark 10:30);

others in the same position or on the same "path" as you (rel; see Ezekiel 23:31–33);

town/country (see Ezekiel 16:44–63);

see Themes/People and Beings/ Brother.

Sister (or brother) and you: generational bloodline (rel); sisters or brothers in Christ.

Sister-in-law: a fellow Christian who is legalistic (play on words—law, legal).

Slave:

prophet (see Jeremiah 7:25; Colossians 1:25–26; Hebrews 3:5);

look at who you are serving (see Philippians 1:1; Colossians 1:23; 1 Timothy 4:6; James 1:1; 1 Peter 2:16–18; 2 Peter 1:1);

follower of Christ (see Matthew 25:21);

look at what overcomes you (see 2 Peter 2:19);

in bondage (see Ezra 9:9; Galatians 4:7–9; 5:1; Philemon 16);

child (see Galatians 4:1–2);

ruled by others (see Lamentations 1:1; Galatians 5:1; 1 Timothy 6:1).

Sniper: one who deceives others and says, "I was only joking" (see Proverbs 26:18); one who "shoots" his power unexpectedly from afar (func).

Soldier:

army of God (see Philippians 2:25; 2 Timothy 2:3–4; Philemon 2);

one who serves with strength (see Philippians 2:25; Philemon 2);

people under authority (see Matthew 8:9);

God's people (see Joel 2:25);

angels;

Holy Spirit (see Isaiah 52:12);

see Themes/People and Beings/Army;

see Themes/People and Beings/Military People.

Son:

Jesus (see Psalm 2:7; Isaiah 42:1; Matthew 2:15; 3:17; 11:27; 28:19; Galatians 4:4; Ephesians 1:3; Colossians 1:13; Hebrews 1:1; 3:6; Revelation 12:4–5);

Son of Man (see Matthew 12:8; Revelation 1:12–20);

child of God (see Deuteronomy 32:19; Jeremiah 3:19; Matthew 2:15; 11:27; Galatians 3:26; Hebrews 1:8; Revelation 21:7);

Israel (see Exodus 4:22);

father's strength (see Deuteronomy 21:17);

descendants (see Exodus 1:1–5, 9; Matthew 1:1; 9:27; 12:23; 15:22; 21:9);

one who follows you (see 1 Samuel 24:16; Jeremiah 49:1; Matthew 5:9; 11:27; 1 Timothy 1:18; 2 Timothy 1:2; Hebrews 12:5);

has access to the father (see Matthew 10:32–33);

father's strength (see Deuteronomy 21:17);

People and Beings

one who is exempt (see Matthew 17:25–26);

heir (see Matthew 21:38; Galatians 4:1–9);

one who listens to you (see Proverbs 1:8);

biological child (see Matthew 1:21–25);

following in same footsteps (see Leviticus 21:1; Numbers 10:8; 2 Kings 8:9; Colossians 3:6).

Sorceress: evil/evil spirit (see Exodus 7:11; 22:18; Leviticus 19:26; Numbers 23:23; Deuteronomy 18:10–14; 2 Kings 17:17; 21:6; 2 Chronicles 33:6; Isaiah 47:9–12; 57:3; Acts 8:9; 13:6).

Sower:

one who throws out bits [money, love, nurturing, information, advice, etc.] so it has a chance to take root and grow (see Exodus 23:10; Leviticus 25:3–4; Deuteronomy 28:38; Job 4:8; Psalm 126:5–6; Proverbs 11:18; 22:8; Matthew 13:3; Luke 8:5–8);

doing actions that have repercussions—good or bad (see Job 4:8; Psalm 126:5; Proverbs 11:18; 22:8; Galatians 6:7–8; James 3:18);

Jesus (see Matthew 13:37);

see Themes/People and Beings/ Farmer;

devil (see Matthew 13:39).

Spirit, bad: demonic (see Matthew 12:43–45; Ephesians 2:2; 1 John 4:3–6); leads you astray (see 1 John 4:1, 3, 6).

Spirit, good:

Holy Spirit/access to God (see Matthew 1:20; 10:20; 12:32; John 14:18; Ephesians 2:18; 4:4; 1 John 3:24; 4:2);

Comforter (see John 14:18; Acts 9:31);

spirit of wisdom (see Ephesians 1:17);

spirit of revelation (see Ephesians 1:17);

not to be blasphemed (see Matthew 12:31–32);

leads you into truth (see John 16:13; 1 Corinthians 2:13; 1 John 4:6);

will teach you (see Luke 12:12; John 14:26);

will speak through you (see Matthew 10:20).

Spirit, unclean: see Themes/People and Beings/Spirit bad.

Spiritist: people who contact the dead are not representing God (see Leviticus 19:31; 20:6, 27; Deuteronomy 18:10–12; 2 Kings 21:6; 23:24; 2 Chronicles 33:6).

Stranger:

angel (see Hebrews 13:2);

not of God (see 1 Chronicles 29:15; Zechariah 7:14; Ephesians 2:12, 19; Hebrews 11:14–16);

not of Jesus (see John 10:5);

not of the status quo (see Hebrews 11:13);

others amongst you (see 1 Peter 2:11);

among other nations (see Psalm 69:8; 3 John 1:5);

see Themes/People and Beings/ Person.

Strongman: Jesus Christ (see Psalm 19:4–6); Satan (see Matthew 12:25–29).

Superman: appears to be great/intimidating (see 2 Corinthians 12:11).

Survivor:

came out of a bad situation (char);

remnant (see Isaiah 4:2; 10:20; Revelation 11:13).

T

Taskmaster: oppressing and abusing others through work (see Exodus 1:11–14; 3:7–9; 5:9–14); see Themes/People and Beings/Leader.

Teacher:

Christ (see Isaiah 28:29; 54:13; Matthew 11:1; 23:10; 26:49; Mark 9:5, 38; 10:17; Luke 18:18; John 1:38; 11:28);

Holy Spirit (see Matthew 23:10; John 14:26);

of authority (see Matthew 7:29);

helps others to learn (see Matthew 10:24; John 3:10; Hebrews 5:12);

first do no harm (see Luke 17:1–3);

should not lead others astray (see Luke 17:1–3);

receives stricter judgment (see Deuteronomy 32:48–52; James 3:1); instructs others (see Matthew 10:24–25; Galatians 3:24).

Tempter: enemy (see Genesis 3:1; Matthew 4:3); Satan (see Genesis 3:1; Matthew 4:3; 1 Thessalonians 3:5).

Terrorist: destructive person (char).

Thief: does things unexpectedly; without prior public knowledge (see 1 Thessalonians 5:2; 2 Peter 3:10; Revelation 3:3; 16:15); Satan's forces/enemy (see John 10:10).

Thief, caught: disgraced (see Jeremiah 2:26; 1 Thessalonians 5:4).

Tribe: types of people (see Hebrews 7:13–14; Revelation 5:9).

Twin: not alone (see Song of Solomon 4:2; 6:6); multiplied (Song Solomon 4:2; 6:6).

U

Unruly person: needs admonishing (see Jeremiah 31:18; Ezekiel 5:7; Hosea 11:12; 1 Thessalonians 5:14).

V

Vestry: leaders of the Church (func).

Virgin: twelve tribes of Israel/God's people (see 2 Kings 19:21; Isaiah 23:12; 37:22; Jeremiah 18:13; Amos 5:2); one unaffected by false doctrine (see 2 Corinthians 11:2).

W

Warriors:
angels (see 1 Chronicles 12:22; Psalm 120:4);
Lord (see Exodus 15:3);
those who fight for the Lord (see Judges 5:11; 1 Samuel 16:18; Psalm 24:8);

mighty fighter (see 1 Kings 12:21);
uses strong words to fight (see Psalm 120:4; 127:4);
ready to do battle (see Proverbs 16:32);
impatient (see Proverbs 16:32).

Watcher: angelic-like holy one from heaven who decrees heavenly decisions (see Daniel 4:12–17, 22–24).

Watchmen:
those with power over you (see Isaiah 56:10);
those of spiritual authority (see Psalm 127; Song of Solomon 3:3; Isaiah 52:8; 56:10; Jeremiah 6:17; Ezekiel 3:17);
prophetic (see Jeremiah 6:17);
one who must warn others (see Isaiah 56:10; 62:6; Jeremiah 6:17; 31:6; 51:12; Ezekiel 33:2–7);
those who are supposed to protect you (see Song of Solomon 3:3; Jeremiah 4:17);
those who hurt the ones they are supposed to protect (see Song of Solomon 5:7).

Whore: see Themes/People and Beings/Prostitute.

Wife:
covenantal relationship (see Genesis 2:24; 2 Samuel 3:14; Galatians 4:24);
pure Church (see Isaiah 54:6; Ephesians 5:25, 31–32; Revelation 21:9);
actual wife (see Genesis 2:25; Colossians 3:18–19).

Wise man:
one who journeys to seek the Lord (see Matthew 2:1–2; John 1:1–18);
one who builds on good foundations (see Matthew 7:24–25);
one who studies higher-level things (see Matthew 2:7).

Witch: one exerting control over (see Galatians 3:1); demon/not representing God/demonic spirit (see Deuteronomy 18:10–11; 1 Samuel 15:23; 2 Kings 21:6; 2 Chronicles 33:6; Micah 5:12; Nahum 3:4; Galatians 5:20).

Witness:
Christ (see 1 Samuel 20:23, 42; Revelation 3:14);

People and Beings

Holy Spirit (see John 15:26);

bond/tie (see Genesis 21:30; 31:44; 1 Samuel 20:23);

testimony (see Exodus 20:16);

see Themes/People and Beings/ Witness.

Woman:

angel (see Zechariah 5:9; Hebrews 13:2);

church (see Revelation 12:1–17; 17:18);

God's people waiting for Messiah or God's church/twelve tribes of Israel/ God's people (see Jeremiah 14:17; 18:13; Amos 5:2; Revelation 12:1–17; 17:18);

wickedness/sin (see Zechariah 5:7–8);

see Themes/People and Beings/ Person.

Woman, in childbirth: preparing to birth something or do something new (see Isaiah 42:14); in pain (see Jeremiah 50:43; Isaiah 13:8).

Woman, in a man's clothes: not being true to self (see Deuteronomy 22:5).

Woman, mature: see General/Mature.

Woman, nice looking: the Church/daughter of God (see Jeremiah 6:2; Revelation 17:6).

Woman, old:

old Church/Israel (see Revelation 12:4, 6; 17:4, 9);

reverent and mature (see Titus 2:3);

wise (see Job 12:2);

old self [before transformation by Christ] (see Ephesians 4:22).

Woman, pregnant, attractive and offering something: attractive new offer (char); seductive offer (char).

Woman, seductive, attractive, young:

temptation (see Ephesians 2:2; 1 John 4:1–6);

deception (see Ephesians 2:2; 1 John 4:1–6);

controlling (see Ephesians 2:2; 1 John 4:1–6);

manipulative spirit (see Ephesians 2:2; 1 John 4:1–6);

Jezebel spirit (see Ephesians 2:2; 1 John 4:1–6);

witchcraft (see Ephesians 2:2; 1 John 4:1–6).

Woman, warm and helpful: angel (see Hebrews 13:2); human friend (rel).

Woman, you dislike her initially, but then like: something God is walking you through (char).

Woman, you dislike or feel uneasy around:

demonic activity (see Ephesians 2:2; 1 John 4:1–6);

not of God (see Daniel 10:13; Matthew 25:41; Galatians 1:8; 1 John 4:1–6);

soulish conflict (rel).

Woodsman: people who do hard work on earth (see 2 Chronicles 2:10); people who are prepared to cut down God's people [trees may represent God's people, see General/Tree(s)] (see Isaiah 14:18).

Workers:

people (see Exodus 12:45; Ruth 2:21; 2 Kings 12:15; Matthew 9:37–38, 10:10; Luke 10:7; 1 Corinthians 3:9; 2 Timothy 2:15);

people who are assigned a task (see Ruth 2:21; 2 Kings 12:15; John 2:5; Romans 14:11–12; 1 Corinthians 3:9);

people who spread God's Word (see Matthew 9:37–38).

Y

You, as a child: old issues God wants to release you from (char); soul stunted in an area (char).

You, as someone else that you do not know:

not being true to yourself (rel);

changing in some way (char);

someone has placed a curse on you (func).

Youth: see Themes/People and Beings/ Children.

Numbers

- If you are given a number in a dream, use it to look up the Bible chapter and verses. For example, if *223* comes up in a dream, look at chapter 2 verse 23, or chapter 22 verse 3 of the relevant book, etc.
- A clock time such as 1:11 a.m. may be referring to Ephesians 1:11; similarly, 3:33 a.m. may be pointing to Jeremiah 3:33 or Jeremiah 33:3.
- Beware of non-Bible-based numerology teachings, which may introduce you to wrong symbols.

1:
God (see Deuteronomy 6:4; Matthew 10:37; Ephesians 4:4–6; James 2:19);
Jesus (see John 14:6);
first (see Ephesians 1:12; Revelation 6:1–2);
unity (see John 17:20–24; 1 Corinthians 12:12; Ephesians 4:4, 13).

2:
discernment (see Exodus 2:12–14; Matthew 18:19);
witness for confirmation (see Genesis 41:32; Matthew 18:16, 20; 2 Corinthians 13:1; 1 Timothy 5:19; Hebrews 10:28; Revelation 11:3);
double [blessing or trouble] (see Genesis 19:1; 2 Kings 2:9; Job 42:10; Proverbs 28:6; Isaiah 51:19; 61:7; Matthew 6:24; 10:10; Revelation 18:6);

division/multiplication (see Genesis 1:6–8; 15:10; 32:7; 1 Kings 12; 16:21; 18:21; Ezekiel 37:22; Matthew 6:24; 12:25; Hebrews 11:37; Revelation 6:4);
union (see Matthew 19:5; Mark 10:8; 1 Corinthians 6:16);
a helper (see Ecclesiastes 4:9–12);
it is established; it is going to happen (see Genesis 41:32);
double payback for trouble (see Exodus 22:9; Revelation 18:6);
to receive double for sins (see Isaiah 40:2).

3:
Godhead (Father, Son, Holy Spirit); Trinity (see Revelation 1:4–6);
a number signifying that something may be divinely established/a clue that this may be from God (see Deuteronomy 19:15; 2 Samuel 24:13;

Matthew 18:16, 20; Acts 11:10; 1 Corinthians 14:29);

Resurrection (see Matthew 12:40; 27:63; 28:6; Mark 8:31; 1 Corinthians 15:4);

produce/fruit/vegetation (see Genesis 1:11–12; 6:10);

perfect witness (see Deuteronomy 19:15; Matthew 18:16; 2 Corinthians 13:1; Hebrews 10:28; 1 John 5:7–8);

provides strength (see Ecclesiastes 4:12);

first geometric shape, therefore, the first completion (func);

to imitate (see Matthew 12:40);

a number of chances (see Titus 3:10; as in "three strikes and you're out");

time of famine (see 1 Chronicles 21:12; Matthew 16:21; Luke 4:25; Revelation 6:5–6);

time of oppression (see 2 Kings 17:5; 1 Chronicles 21:12; Matthew 16:21; Revelation 13:5).

3 1/2: time of famine (see Luke 4:25); time of oppression (see Revelation 13:5).

4:

God's creative works and redemption; earth (see Genesis 1:14–19; Zechariah 6:1–5; Revelation 4:6; 20:8);

reign/rule (see Genesis 2:10; Revelation 7:1);

to be reimbursed for sinful action done against you (see 2 Samuel 12:6);

all directions [all four directions] (see Daniel 7:6);

worldly things (see Exodus 25:34; Revelation 19:4);

nature and earthly things (see Genesis 2:10; Exodus 25:34; Leviticus 11:20–27; Isaiah 11:12; Ezekiel 37:9; Matthew 24:31);

plagues (see Revelation 6:7–8).

5:

grace (see Romans 5:2);

to serve (see Romans 5:2);

persecution (see Revelation 6:9–11).

6:

man; man was made on the sixth day (see Genesis 1:26–31; 2:7; Revelation 13:18);

humanity/weakness of man (see Leviticus 25:3);

time of man (see Matthew 27:45; Luke 23:44);

cataclysmic events and/or fear (see Revelation 6:12–17);

evil (see Revelation 13:18).

7:

perfection and completion; divine fullness (see Genesis 2:2–3; 4:15; Leviticus 8:33; 23:6–8; Numbers 12:14–15; 1 Samuel 6:1; 10:8; 2 Samuel 12:18; 1 Kings 6:38; 2 Kings 8:1; Nehemiah 8:1, 18; Ezekiel 45:21; Zechariah 4:2; Revelation 1:4; 4:5; 11:15–19; 15:1);

of God (see Revelation 4:2–6);

good; victory (see Joshua 6:4; Proverbs 24:16; Jeremiah 34:14; Hebrews 11:30);

covenantal sign [Sabbath day] (see Exodus 31:13, 17);

rest (see Exodus 20:11; Leviticus 23:3; Hebrews 4:4);

week (see Daniel 9:24–26);

a week of years, e.g., seven years (see Daniel 9:24–27);

cancellation of debts (see Deuteronomy 31:10);

to receive payback sevenfold for injury/theft you have endured (see Proverbs 6:30–31).

8:

new beginnings (see Genesis 17:12; 1 Peter 3:20);

manifest (see Philippians 3:5);

saved (see 1 Peter 3:20);

teacher (see John 20:26).

9:

harvest/fruition (see Luke 23:44);

divine justice/judgment/salvation (see Matthew 27:45–46; Acts 23:22–24);

evangelist (see Luke 15:4);

manifestation of spiritual activity (see Matthew 27:45–46).

10:

political completion; perfection of divine order (see Genesis 15:19–21 [God's covenant with Abram was to bestow upon him the complete ten segments of land—a new political empire for the descendants of Abram/Abraham]; Daniel 7:7, 20–24; Revelation 2:10; 12:3; 13:1);

political earthly power (see Revelation 17:4, 12–17);

pastoral (see Numbers 5:15; Nehemiah 10:38);

wilderness/trial/test (see Numbers 14:22, 34; Job 19:3; Daniel 1:13–15; Zechariah 8:23; Revelation 2:10);

tithe (see Genesis 14:18–20; Matthew 23:23; Hebrews 7:1–10);

law [Ten Commandments; the Lord's prayer in ten clauses] (see Exodus 20:1–17; 34:28; Matthew 6:9–13];

testimony [Daniel's ten-day test diet; see Daniel 1:12–16] (see Leviticus 25:9; Numbers 18:26).

11:

revelation/prophetic/transition (see Ezekiel 26:1; 30:20; 31:1; Zechariah 1:7);

ending (see Jeremiah 52:5; Matthew 20:6–12);

last (in the eleventh hour); transition time (see Jeremiah 52:5; Matthew 20:6–12).

12:

final completion (see Luke 22:30; Acts 19:7; Revelation 7:5–7; 12:1; 21:12–14, 21; 22:2);

apostle (see Matthew 10:1–2; Luke 18:31; 22:14; Acts 19:7);

united (see Exodus 39:14);

govern/leadership (see Genesis 17:20; 42:3; Exodus 39:14; Numbers 1:44; Joshua 3:12; 4:2; Matthew 19:28);

tribes of Israel (see Matthew 19:28; James 1:1);

represents all of God's people (see Numbers 17:2, 6);

healing (see Matthew 10:1).

13:

baker's dozen; an extra blessing (rel);

rebellion/revolution (see Genesis 14:4; Esther 9:1);

curse (see Esther 3:12–13).

14:

double anointing (see Esther 9:18–19);

disciple (see Acts 27:33);

deliverance/salvation (see Leviticus 23:5; Matthew 1:17);

a shift in course that brings a major change in life (see Matthew 1:17);

Passover (see Exodus 12:18; Leviticus 23:5; Numbers 9:3–5; 28:16).

15:

extra grace/reprieve/mercy ("I will add fifteen years to your life," see 2 Kings 20:6; Isaiah 38:5);

sin covered (see Hosea 3:2);

rest (see Esther 9:18);

liberty (see Ezekiel 32:17).

16:

ready to go forward [16 years old] (see 2 Kings 14:21);

ready for love (as in "sweet sixteen").

17:

elect of God (see Genesis 37:2);

beginning of a major work of God (see Genesis 7:11);

success/victory (see Genesis 8:4);

to buy land (see Jeremiah 32:8–9).

18:

bondage (see Judges 3:14; 10:8; Luke 13:11, 16);

judgment (see Luke 13:4).

19: loss/lack of (see 2 Samuel 2:30).

20:

redemption (see Judges 15:20; 16:31);

acceptance by the Lord (see Genesis 6:3; 31:38);

unable to meet the standards (see Genesis 6:3; 31:41).

21: sin/strong spiritual attack (see Daniel 10:13).

22: lack of discernment; fearful (see Judges 7:3; 1 Kings 16:29; 1 Chronicles 18:5); unsuccessful (see Judges 20:21; 2 Samuel 8:5).

23: death (see Numbers 26:62–65; 33:39; 1 Corinthians 10:8); not listening to the Word of the Lord (see Jeremiah 25:3).

24:

works accepted by the Lord (see Revelation 4:4; 5:8);

before the throne of God; priestly (see Revelation 4:4, 10);

elders (see Revelation 4:4; 5:8; 11:16; 19:4);

government (see 1 Chronicles 23:4; Revelation 4:4; 11:16);

military division (see 1 Chronicles 27:1–15).

25: to begin training for ministry (see Numbers 8:24).

26: fit for battle; valor (see 1 Chronicles 7:40).

27: kindness; mercy (in Hebrew).

30:

to begin ministry (see Genesis 41:46; Numbers 4:3; Luke 3:23);

return on an investment; harvest (see Matthew 13:8–23);

price paid for a slave gored by an ox (see Exodus 21:32);

time of mourning (see Numbers 20:29; Deuteronomy 34:8);

the mighty ones (see 1 Chronicles 11:15);

release; captive (see Jeremiah 38:10);

betrayal (see Matthew 26:15; 27:3–9).

40:

generational issues and completed rule (see Ezekiel 4);

temptation (see 2 Kings 8:9; Luke 4:2);

time of testing (see Genesis 7:12; 1 Samuel 17:16; Nehemiah 9:21; Matthew 4:1–11);

time of purification and teaching (see Genesis 7:4; Exodus 16:35; 24:18; 34:28; Deuteronomy 29:5; Matthew 4:2; Acts 1:3; Hebrews 3:17);

punishment (see Deuteronomy 25:3; Ezekiel 29:11–12; Psalm 95:10);

burden (see Nehemiah 5:15).

42: time period in which evil will exercise authority (see Revelation 13:5).

50: liberty (see Numbers 8:25); jubilee (see Leviticus 25:10–12).

52: completion of rehab; setting something right whether it is a structure or a behavior addiction, etc. (see Nehemiah 6:15—rehab of the wall completed after 52 days).

60:

noble (see Song of Solomon 3:7; 6:8);

good return on an investment; good harvest (see Matthew 13:8–23);

guardian (see Song of Solomon 3:7–8).

66: waiting for cleansing (see Leviticus 12:5).

70:

multiple forgiveness (see Matthew 18:21–22);

elders;

length of life (see Psalm 90:10; Isaiah 23:15);

time of captivity (see Isaiah 23:15–17; Jeremiah 25:12; 29:10);

to bring righteousness, seal up prophecy, anoint holiness, finish transgression, end sin, atone for evil (see Daniel 9:24);

desolation completed (see Daniel 9:2).

70 x 7: forgive as much as needed (see Matthew 18:21–22).

72: disciples to go out and teach with power (see Luke 10:1, 17).

77: multiple forgiveness (see Matthew 18:21–22).

80: length of life with strength (see Psalm 90:10); offering to the Lord (see Jeremiah 41:5).

100:

large count (see Proverbs 17:10; Ecclesiastes 6:3; 8:12; Matthew 18:12; 19:29; Mark 10:30; Luke 8:8);

large return on an investment; large harvest (see Matthew 13:8–23);

the power of synergy:

God: 1, man: 0;

alone, man is nothing;

beside God, man becomes large: (10: God [1] and one man [0]); or (100: God [1] and two men [00]); or (1000: God [1] and three men [000]);

synergy: God and one man puts 1000 demons to flight (see Deuteronomy 32:30);

synergy: God and 2 men puts 10,000 demons to flight (see Deuteronomy 32:30).

144: 12 x 12; perfection (see Revelation 7:4).

150: time of duration from an act of God (see Genesis 7:24).

153: different species of fish, which represents all nations (see John 21:11); fulfillment and advancement of the Church (see John 21:11).

200: large count of (see Themes/Numbers/2 characteristics—division, blessing, trouble, discernment); 2 x 100.

300: large count of (famine, oppression, etc.; see Themes/Numbers/3 characteristics); 3 x 100.

390: time to bear the results of sin (see Ezekiel 4:5, 9).

400: large count of (God's creative works, worldly things, etc.; see Themes/Numbers/4 characteristics); 4 x 100.

430: legalism/law/length of time under others' control (see Exodus 12:40–41; Galatians 3:17).

500: large count of (grace, persecution, etc.; see Themes/Numbers/5 characteristics); 5 x 100.

600: large count of (humanity, weakness, etc.; see Themes/Numbers/6 characteristics); 6 x 100.

666:
enemy or his work (see Revelation 13:18; 15:2);
Satan (encouraging man to fill Trinity roles (see Revelation 13:18; 15:2);
setting "self" as God; full lawlessness (see Revelation 13:18; 15:2);
number representing tripartite man: body, soul and spirit (see Revelation 13:18; 15:2);
beast's number (see Revelation 13:18).

700:
large count of (perfection, completion, rest, victory, etc.;
see Themes/Numbers/7 characteristics);
7 x 100.

777: Jesus (perfection: body is 7, soul is 7 and spirit is 7).

800: large count of (new beginnings, manifestation, etc.; see Themes/Numbers/8 characteristics); 8 x 100.

900: large count of (harvest, justice, etc.; see Themes/Numbers/9 characteristics); 9 x 100.

911:
help (func);
God's salvation (char); prayer/asking God's help (char);
destruction (see Revelation 9:11).

1,000:
sacrifices (see 1 Chronicles 29:21; 2 Chronicles 1:6);
reign (see Revelation 20:4, 6);
day (see 2 Peter 3:8);
large count of (pastoral, wilderness, trials, etc.);
completion (see Revelation 7:4);
see Themes/Numbers/10 characteristics.

1260: 3½ years—time that the dragon has authority (see Revelation 12:6; 13:5).

3,600: foreman/supervisor (see 2 Chronicles 2:2, 18).

7,000: those who have not bowed to Baal (see Romans 11:4).

10,000: large amount owed to others (see Matthew 18:24).

14,700: people dying from sin (see Numbers 16:49).

20,000: gifts to servants (see 2 Chronicles 2:10).

70,000: carriers (see 2 Chronicles 2:2, 18).

80,000: stonecutters (see 2 Chronicles 2:2, 18).

144,000: picture of the perfect church of God (perfection and completion of God's kingdom); 12^2 (see Revelation 7:4, 14:1).

153,600: aliens (see 2 Chronicles 2:17).

200,000,000: destroying troops sent out (see Revelation 9:16).

1/3: partial destruction due to sin (see Revelation 8:7–12); followers of evil (see Revelation 12:4).

1/10: God's portion (see Luke 11:42; Hebrews 7:6–9); portion of pastors/priests (see Hebrews 7:4–5).

Numbers

Actions

A

Accusations: enemy trying to create pain or dissension to thwart progress (see Nehemiah 6:1–9).

Adoption: become as a son/daughter (see Ephesians 1:5).

Adultery:

coming into agreement with (see Revelation 18:3, 9);

unfaithfulness (see Hosea 2:2);

unclean acts (see Deuteronomy 5:18);

betrayal (see Leviticus 20:10).

Affair:

in an intimate agreement with (see Genesis 4:1; Ezekiel 16:8);

breaking of intimate trust (see Exodus 2:21; Joshua 23:12; Malachi 2:11);

break in relationship (see Daniel 11:17; Matthew 19:12);

see General/Sex;

see General/Marriage.

Age-progression: symbol for "over a long period of time" (func).

Ambushed: to wait and pounce on the unsuspecting with evil intent (see Judges 9:25).

Angry: anger is not to be used as a fuel for revenge (see Ephesians 4:26); do not stay angry (see Ephesians 4:26).

Anxiety: in need of consolation (see Psalm 94:19).

Ask: actively seeking an answer (see Matthew 7:7–11).

Asleep:

not taking action (see Matthew 8:24);

died earthly death (see John 11:11; Acts 7:60; 2 Peter 3:4);

being unaware (see Psalm 121:3–4; Isaiah 5:27; Matthew 13:25; Ephesians 5:14; 1 Thessalonians 5:6);

has died on earth, but is alive in the spirit (see 1 Thessalonians 4:15–16; 5:10).

Awaken:

change direction/mindset (see Zechariah 4:1–2 NIV);

come out of a time of sleeping or inactivity; to resurrect (see Jeremiah 31:26; Daniel 12:2);

make aware/alert (see Psalm 108:2; Revelation 16:15).

B

Backslide: fall away from God (see Jeremiah 3:22; Matthew 7:24–27).

Bath: cleansing/repentance (see Psalm 51:2–3).

Bathroom, feeling the need to go: under pressure (see 1 Samuel 24:3).

Bathroom, using toilet:

getting rid of toxins or unclean things in your life (see Leviticus 8:16);

to relieve yourself (see 1 Samuel 24:3).

Battle:

life's struggles (see Ecclesiastes 9:11; 1 Timothy 6:11–12);

fight against sinfulness (see Revelation 3:5);

spiritual warfare (see Ecclesiastes 9:11; 1 Timothy 6:12).

Beat:

going through rough times (see Proverbs 17:26);

persecution (see Proverbs 17:26);

losing/not winning(see Proverbs 17:26).

Beat, breasts: feeling powerful; ashamed and humiliated (see Jeremiah 31:19).

Beat someone to get them to listen: force something on someone (func).

Belch: speak out offensively (see Psalm 59:7).

Believe: accept as truth and receive Christ Jesus as Savior by His grace (see John 3:16; Ephesians 1:19; 2:1–5); to have faith and take action (see Mark 1:14–15).

Belongings being slung about: things you are doing have caused your life or situation to need order (char).

Bend over: slaughter (see Isaiah 65:12).

Bent over: to humble oneself (char).

Bind: heal (see Isaiah 61:1).

Birthing: time of pain before joy (see John 16:22).

Biting: individuals who think they are right but use hurtful words (see Galatians 5:15).

Blame: not of the Lord (see Psalm 101:1–2).

Bleeding: defiled/hurt (see Genesis 4:10–11); covenant (see Matthew 26:28; 1 Corinthians 11:25; Revelation 7:14; 12:11).

Blind: unable to see the things of the Lord (see Matthew 12:22); unwilling to see the truth (see Exodus 23:8).

Bottle rocket, chasing you: being harassed by something larger than you know how to handle (char).

Bow:

honor (see 2 Samuel 1:2; Philippians 2:10);

humble (see Psalm 72:9; 1 Chronicles 29:20);

submit (see Numbers 22:31; Psalm 38:6; Ephesians 3:14; Philippians 2:10);

make request (see Matthew 18:26, 29; 20:20).

Bowed down: in distress (see Psalm 57:6).

Buying: believing (as in "buying into something"); accepting something that you will have to pay for (char).

Buying, not: not believing (char).

C

Call: what you are intended to do (see Ephesians 1:18).

Calling for help: praying to God (see Jeremiah 33:3).

Came out of cover: coming out from under God's covering (char).

Carrying a burden: weighed down by the Word (see Matthew 11:28).

Carrying water to others: being a servant to others (see Joshua 9:21).

Cast down: depressed (char); to be on your back, unable to get up [like a sheep]; needing help (char).

Celebration outside: church reaching out to the community (rel).

Change mind: not of God (see Numbers 23:19).

Changing into a psycho: to become self-destructive mentally (char).

Changing into someone else: in agreement with them (see 2 Chronicles 18:3).

Chasing:

will not let you alone (char);

oppressing the one who is being chased (char);

harassing (see 2 Samuel 2:21–23, 26–28).

Chasing a rabbit: going miscellaneous directions (char); not staying on task (play on words).

Circling: going around and around (char); dealing with something over and over (char).

Clap hands: joy (see Psalm 47:1); express praise for (see Psalm 98:8); signifying the end (see Ezekiel 6:11).

Clap hands over mouth: to stop exalting self and planning evil (see Proverbs 30:32).

Climbing to reach a rock: seeking refuge (see Psalm 61:2).

Clothing someone: to take care of (see Matthew 6:30).

Confess: how you plea [as in a courtroom—guilty or not guilty] (see 1 John 1:8–10).

Conscience:

good conscience toward God (see 1 Peter 3:21);

listening to God (see John 8:9; Acts 24:16);

see General/Conscience.

Cook: to prepare spiritual food (see Nehemiah 9:15; Proverbs 18:20).

Count: to take inventory of/care for (see Jeremiah 33:22; Philippians 3:8; Revelations 7:9).

Cowardly: to fearfully succumb to things that are not of God (see Revelation 21:8).

Crawling: under submission (see Numbers 22:31; Psalm 38:6; Ephesians 3:14; Philippians 2:10); submitting to (see Numbers 22:31; Psalm 38:6; Ephesians 3:14; Philippians 2:10).

Create: something that comes from no earthly thing and without human works, but rather comes from God (see Psalm 51:10).

Cringe: fear (see Psalm 66:3).

Crying:

repentance/sorrow (see 1 Samuel 30:4; 2 Samuel 1:12);

regret for the way life is going (see Genesis 27:33–35);

to regret you got caught, but not to regret the action (see Jeremiah 5; 11:9–14).

Curses: Lord will change it to a blessing for those who obey (see Nehemiah 13:1–2).

Cutting off: remove (func); kill (see Deuteronomy 25:18; 1 Kings 9:7).

Cutting self: see Themes/Actions/Self-abasement.

Cutting wood: servant to others (see Joshua 9:21).

D

Dance: taking the same view (rel); moving together (see Matthew 11:17).

Deaths, early, run in the family line: cursed by inheritance (see 1 Samuel 2:32–34).

Deploy: sent out against (see 1 Chronicles 19:11).

Devouring each other: hurting each other (see Isaiah 56:9; Galatians 5:15).

Die:

pertaining to the end of an era in your life (see Mark 9:21; Luke 15:4–32; Ephesians 2:1; Colossians 3:3);

life-altering (see Matthew 14:2; Mark 9:21; Luke 15:24–32);

salvation; individual has died on earth but is alive in heaven (see Matthew 22:32; Luke 20:27–40; Ephesians 2:1; Colossians 3:3; 2 Timothy 2:11).

Die, killed: a life-changing encounter [could be good or bad] (see Matthew 14:2; Mark 9:21; Romans 6:2–11).

Die, suddenly: sudden life-changing encounter (see Matthew 14:2; Mark 9:21; Romans 6:2–11).

Disciplining: helping others endure (see Hebrews 12:7); giving life and hope (see Proverbs 19:18).

Discretion: choices that guard you (see Proverbs 2:11).

Dishes, wipe: to wipe out, turning things upside down (see 2 Kings 21:13).

Disorder: not of God (see Matthew 9:23).

Divination: rebellion (see 1 Samuel 15:23).

Do not like, then like: something God is walking you through (func).

Dress you and lead you where you do not want to go: future experience of something being forced upon you (see John 21:18–19).

Actions

Drink: receive/share in (see Revelation 16:6); experience (see Matthew 11:19; Revelation 21:6).

Drink, alcohol:

becoming filled with the Spirit (see Acts 2:15–17; Ephesians 5:18);

filled with spirits (play on words);

receiving things that cause a distorted reaction (see Proverbs 20:1; 23:29–35; Isaiah 28:7; Hosea 4:11).

Drink, blood of men: conquer (see Ezekiel 39:18–19).

Drink, from a cup: following the path (see Matthew 20:22–23; Revelation 16:19; 18:6).

Drink, not joining in: not going along with worldly ways (see Matthew 11:18).

Drink, sweet: celebration (see Nehemiah 8:10).

Drink, wine: communion with God (see Isaiah 25:6; 55:1).

Drip, constant: quarrelsome (see Proverbs 19:13).

Driving: in charge of; in control (see Judges 2:23).

Driving a car full of water: the person in control is overwhelmed (func).

Driving, no one is driving the vehicle, but it is moving under its own power: the person sitting in the driver's seat may think he is in control, but he is not (char); something else is controlling things; possibly God is in control (char).

Driving, someone else driving car: someone else is controlling the work, ministry or family [or whatever the car represents] (char).

Drowning, saved from: baptism (char).

Drunk:

full of the Holy Spirit (see 1 Samuel 25:36; Ephesians 5:18; Jeremiah 23:9);

caught up in one's feelings (see Revelation 17:2, 6);

overwhelmed by (see Deuteronomy 32:42; Psalm 107:27);

unable to fight or think (see 2 Samuel 11:13; Isaiah 63:6; Jeremiah 51:39, 57);

drunkenness (see Proverbs 23:20–21; Isaiah 5:11).

E

Eat:

to learn; knowledge/understanding (see Jeremiah 3:15);

communion/relationship (see 2 Samuel 9:11; Matthew 9:10–11; 11:19);

partake in/experience/fellowship (see Matthew 9:10–11; 11:19; Revelation 3:20);

partake in the Word/presence of God (see 1 Samuel 21:4–6; Proverbs 13:25; Ezekiel 2:8; 3);

blessed (see Jeremiah 5:7–8);

overcome/conquer (see 2 Samuel 2:26–29; Isaiah 5:14; Jeremiah 2:30; Ezekiel 39:18).

Eat, children: abortion (see Deuteronomy 28:53–57).

Eat, not joining in: not going along with what is being done/spoken (see Matthew 11:18).

Endure: get through trials (see Hebrews 10:36).

Erase, name: death (see 1 Samuel 24:21).

Escape:

get free (see Genesis 14:13; 19:17; 2 Kings 10:24);

let loose (see Genesis 19:20; 2 Kings 10:24);

unable to control (see Deuteronomy 23:15; 2 Chronicles 16:7);

to miss out on (see 1 Kings 19:17; Job 11:20).

Examination, taking: being tested by Lord (see Psalm 26:2).

F

Face: look upon (see Deuteronomy 31:17).

Facedown, to be:

humbled (see Numbers 20:6);

in reverence to (see 1 Samuel 5:4);

mourn/grieve; to be vexed (see 1 Kings 21:4);

fear (see Numbers 16:4; Matthew 17:6).

Faint: in the Spirit of God (see Revelation 1:17); weakly fearful (see Hebrews 12:5).

Faith: grafts branches onto main tree; becoming part of God's family.

Fall down:

worship (see Revelation 5:14);

to humble oneself before another (see Revelation 5:8);

heading in the wrong direction (see Jeremiah 8:4; Matthew 7:24–27; Revelation 2:5);

succumb to (see Joshua 1:5; Lamentations 1:7–9);

unable to move forward smoothly (see Psalm 27:2; Jeremiah 13:16);

pride (see 2 Chronicles 26:16);

die (see Ezekiel 11:10).

Falling:

fearful and major change of life direction without control (char);

taking the "plunge"/stepping out into a new scary direction (char);

overwhelmed (char);

loss of support [financial, moral, public] (see Proverbs 11:28);

trial (see Matthew 7:24–27; James 1:2);

succumb/fail (see Proverbs 16:18);

backsliding (see Proverbs 22:14; Matthew 7:24–27).

Falling, forward: an issue caused by the fall will be perpetuated/will affect future generations (char).

Falling onto someone: coming down upon someone (see Matthew 21:44).

Fasting: reaching out to the Lord for answers or results; motivation for fasting (see Zechariah 7:5).

Fear:

respectful obedience (see Job 6:14; Psalm 112:1–10; 147:11; Proverbs 1:7; 10:27; Jude 12);

accountable to (see 2 Corinthians 5:11);

individual is afraid of what God is doing and tries to stop it; fear causes individual to back away from

what the Lord is doing (see Matthew 8:34);

afraid of not pleasing man (see Proverbs 29:25; Luke 21:25–26);

afraid of the unknown and unexplained (see Matthew 14:26; 28:4);

afraid of what the enemy will do (see Proverbs 3:25–26; John 7:13);

afraid God is angry; a crippling anticipation of punishment/retribution (see 1 John 4:18);

afraid of past mistakes (see Matthew 27:3–5);

afraid that you do not deserve success (see Matthew 25:14–27);

afraid of loneliness (see Psalm 25:16–17).

Fear the Lord: to be accountable to Him (see 2 Corinthians 5:11).

Feed: see Themes/Actions/Eat.

Feigned: your heart is not in it (see Psalm 66:3).

Fight: see General/Battle.

Finger in the dirt:

doing works that are unclean (char; see Isaiah 2:8);

unclean discernment (char; see John 8:7);

without conviction (see Proverbs 6:13; Isaiah 58:9).

Fishing: trying to help others (func; see Matthew 7:10; 13:48); trying to obtain information (play on words).

Fist, shake: anger toward another/situation (see Isaiah 10:32).

Flatter: compliment for sake of gain or advantage (see Jude 16).

Flirt: manipulation of people (see Ephesians 6:6).

Flogged: bad results of actions (see Deuteronomy 25:1–3; Psalm 89:32).

Flying:

high spiritual activity God is taking you to (see Isaiah 60:8);

call of God on your life (see Isaiah 40:31);

destiny to a higher spirituality (see Isaiah 40:31; 60:8; Zechariah 5:1–2).

Follow: to stay with (see Psalm 23:6).

Foot, slipped: in need of support (see Psalm 94:18).

Forgive: Lord will make you prosperous and give you double for your trouble (see Job 42:10).

Forgiven, not: blasphemy against the Holy Spirit (see Luke 12:10).

Full of food: embracing greatly the things of the world [as opposed to spiritual things] (see 1 Samuel 2:5).

G

Gathered to his people: to die (see Numbers 20:24–26).

Glutton: will come to poverty (see Proverbs 23:20–21).

Gnashing of teeth: torment (see Matthew 8:12; 13:50).

Gobbled up: devoured (func); birds devoured seeds; the evil one stealing (see Matthew 13:4).

Going up a hill: getting closer to God (see Psalm 24:3); going through a difficulty (as in "it's an uphill battle"; see Galatians 5:7).

Gore: displaying power (see Deuteronomy 33:17).

Graduation present, document received: you just passed a test (char).

Gravel, in mouth: to feed on things obtained by falsehood (see Proverbs 20:17).

Grieve: distress including sadness, wounding, heartbreak (see Ephesians 4:30; Acts 20:38); to mourn; a process of coming to terms with sadness, fear and pain from a loss (see Deuteronomy 34:8; James 4:9).

Grinding: working (see Matthew 24:41).

Groan:
longing for (see 2 Corinthians 5:2); wounded/hurt (see Jeremiah 51:52); in distress and need (see Psalm 77:3); broken heart; bitter grief (see Ezekiel 21:6–7).

Growl: not satisfied (see Psalm 59:15).

Guilt: a burden too heavy to bear (see Psalm 38:4).

H

Hand, raised threateningly: to come against (see 2 Samuel 18:27–29; 20:21; Zechariah 2:9).

Hang, person: in despair (see Matthew 27:5); under God's curse (see Deuteronomy 21:23; Galatians 3:13).

Hard to find: narrow is the way (char).

Head, toss: to mock (see 2 Kings 19:21).

Hide: in fear (see Genesis 3:10); not coming out or exposing self (char).

Hiking: being led by (char); living in (char); going through (char).

Honor: see Themes/Actions/Respect.

Hostile: against God's Church (see 1 Thessalonians 2:15).

Hug: embrace (char); agree with (rel).

Humble: God's grace (see 1 Peter 5:5); willing to let God be everything (see John 5:9, 30; 6:38; 7:16; 8:28, 42; Philippians 2:8–9; Revelation 4:10–11).

Hungry:
seeking righteousness and good teachings (see Psalm 107:9; Matthew 5:6);
able to receive (see 1 Samuel 2:5);
without sustenance (see Revelation 7:16);
no strength (see Isaiah 44:12).

Hurled to the ground: overcome (see Revelation 12:9; 13).

Hurry: haste causes you to miss the way (see Proverbs 19:2).

Hyperventilating: affects your ability to breathe in the Holy Spirit (see Isaiah 40:7; Ezekiel 37:9–10).

I

Intoxicated: full of the Spirit; caught up in one's feelings (see Revelation 6; 17:2); overwhelmed by (see Deuteronomy 32:42).

In bed: at rest (see 2 Samuel 4:5–7; Psalm 63:6; 132:3); see General/Bed.

In bed, with someone:
at rest together (see Job 7:13; Isaiah 57:7);

Actions

in close exchange with;
in cahoots with; in agreement with
(see Job 17:13; Isaiah 57:7; Revelation 2:22);
in unwise situation with (char);
see General/Bed.

In chains: those who rebel against God's Word (see Psalm 107:10).

J

Jealous: unyielding as the grave (see Song of Solomon 8:6).

Jobs, doing old jobs: look for parallels with the issues of the old job (rel); dealing with issues that were prevalent at that time (rel).

Joy: strength (see Nehemiah 8:10).

K

Kiss: in agreement with; to come together (see 1 Samuel 10:1; Psalm 85:10); honest answer (see Proverbs 24:26).

Kneel: submit to (see Numbers 22:31; Matthew 17:14; Ephesians 3:14; Philippians 2:10); humbleness (see 1 Kings 8:54; Matthew 17:14).

Knees, knocking together: frightened (see Daniel 5:6).

Knit: put together (see Psalm 139:13).

L

Labor:
preparing to bring forth; create (see Isaiah 66:7);
will not be in vain (see Isaiah 65:23);
pain (see Psalm 48:6).

Lay something in front of: submit to (see Revelation 4:10).

Learning: understanding right from wrong (see Isaiah 1:17); comes from the Lord (see 2 Timothy 2:7).

Leave the path/road:
going your own way (char);
stray from doing the right thing (see Proverbs 15:10);
off course (see 2 Samuel 2:19).

Lie down/lying back: resting (see Psalm 23:2).

Life, long: human satisfaction (see Psalm 91:16).

Life seasons, former places lived, tests taken, etc.: you find yourself back in old "seasons," dealing with the same issues you had at that time (char); look at the name of the town, the street you lived on, the color of the house; what did you feel then? (rel).

Lifted up: Spirit of God (see Ezekiel 43:5).

Lights go off: not being revealed/hidden (see Deuteronomy 5:23; Job 3:6; Psalm 97:2).

Listen:
brings wisdom (see Proverbs 19:20);
brings knowledge (see Proverbs 19:27);
to pay attention and try to understand (see Matthew 13:9–19);
to believe what you hear and act out of that belief (see Proverbs 29:12).

Listen, not: to ignore what is out there (see Matthew 13:9–19).

Looking at clouds: you are not going to reap (see Ecclesiastes 11:4).

Looking back: yearning for old ways (see Luke 9:62).

Looking for something: reviewing/analyzing (see Matthew 27:55).

Love: act of putting others first in action and in heart (see Ephesians 5:32–33).

Love, love those who hate you and hate those who love you: contrary (see 2 Samuel 19:6).

Lying/telling lies: the one who is lying is displaying hatred for those the lies wound (see Proverbs 26:28); will receive punishment (see Proverbs 19:5).

M

Man in woman's clothes [not a usual act]: not true to self (see Deuteronomy 22:5).

Measuring: comparing (see Deuteronomy 25:13–15).

Men coming against you: punishment for wrongdoing (see 2 Samuel 7:14).

Mercy: grace of God (see Nehemiah 9:28; Ephesians 2:4); given to those who are ignorant or disbelieving (see 1 Timothy 1:13–16).

Move, unable to: something hindering you from advancing (func).

Murder:

ending someone's old way of life (see Mark 9:21; Luke 15:4–32; Ephesians 2:1);

to kill the body, but not the soul (see Matthew 10:28; 2 Timothy 2:11);

killing God's will for others; separating others from God (see Luke 15:24; Ephesians 2:5; Colossians 2:13; Revelation 21:8).

Mute: cannot open mouth or speak out (see Psalm 38:13; 135:16); unable to pray (see Matthew 22:12).

N

Naked, in public: to have vulnerability; to be open and honest (see Genesis 3:7; Isaiah 57:8; Matthew 27:28).

Naked, start putting your clothes on in the dream under pressure: you are conforming to your environment (see Genesis 3:7).

Nagging: like a constant dripping (see Proverbs 19:13).

Neck, hurting: not listening; being stubborn (see Exodus 32:9; 33:3–5; Deuteronomy 9:6; Proverbs 29:1).

Network: interaction (see 1 Kings 7:17).

O

Obey instructions: guards your life (see Proverbs 19:16).

Obstinate: rebellion against God (see Isaiah 30:1).

Offended: stumbling block (see Proverbs 18:19; 1 Peter 2:8); negative thinking (see Matthew 13:57; Mark 6:3).

Overcome: conquering sin (see 1 John 5:1–6; Revelation 3:21); victory over worldly things (see 1 John 5:1–6; Revelation 3:21), endures without succumbing to things not of God [sin] (see Revelation 3:21), see General/Battle.

Overflowing: pouring out to others or elsewhere (see Colossians 2:7).

P

Pants: to thirst for (see Psalm 42:1).

Patience: has wisdom (see Proverbs 19:11).

People flying around from bombs: people being strongly affected spiritually by a powerful action [good or bad] (func).

People working: [if this appears to be good] people doing good works (func); [if this does not appear to be good] people in the church working, but not for God—or people accomplishing nothing for their works.

Playing: life (see 2 Timothy 2:5).

Playing instrument:

prophesying (see 1 Samuel 10:5);

ministering in the gifts of the Spirit (see 1 Corinthians 12:4–13);

worshipping (see 2 Chronicles 29:25–28);

manipulation (play on words, as in "playing someone like a fine violin").

Playing a sports game: going through life's struggles and competitions (see 2 Timothy 2:5).

Plea: how you confess (see 1 John 1:8–10).

Plow:

work to be done (see Luke 9:62);

to uncover things (see Judges 14:18);

preparing for harvest (see Psalm 141:7);

work that results in the upheaval or exposure of bad/soiled acts [dirt]/or people acting badly.

Poured: brought forth (see 2 Chronicles 34:25).

Actions

327

Poured out on: will happen to (see Daniel 9:27).

Power: walking with God/living with God (see 2 Chronicles 27:6); authority, guidance and might from God (see Matthew 28:18; Luke 24:49).

Prostituting: to come into an intimate relationship for gain (see Judges 2:17); to replace good with willful pleasure (see Judges 8:27, 33).

Provoke lion to anger: doing something that will cause a life-change; strong repercussions (see Proverbs 20:2).

Punch holes into: to see or create defects in something (char).

Push back: to win against (see Psalm 44:5).

Q

Quaking: fear (see 1 Samuel 13:7).
Quiet: inactive (see Psalm 83:1).

R

Race: competition (see 2 Timothy 2:5); life (see Hebrews 12:1).

Raise from the dead: taken to heaven (see Ephesians 2:5–6).

Ransacked: brought down (see Obadiah 6).

Raped: without power (see 2 Samuel 13:14); someone exerting power over another through force (see 2 Samuel 13:14).

Ready: what you have is enough (see 2 Corinthians 8:12).

Realize you are dreaming and change course: Lord telling you to change something so it does not happen (func).

Reap: to receive results from things you or others have done in past (see Deuteronomy 19:18–21; 1 Kings 21:19; Zechariah 1:6; Matthew 6:14–15; Galatians 6:7–9; 2 Thessalonians 1:6;

2 Timothy 4:14; 2 Peter 2:13; Revelation 18:6–7).

Rebellion:
stand against (char);
sin (see Exodus 34:6–9);
divination (see 1 Samuel 15:23);
witchcraft (see 1 Samuel 15:22–23).

Reclining: on a low level (char); rest (see Isaiah 14:30).

Remember: to grant favor toward (see 1 Samuel 1:19).

Repeated activities:
established by the Lord and will happen quickly (see Genesis 41:32);
trying to get you to know or understand (see 1 Samuel 11:5; Habakkuk 3:2);
to not leave your own follies (see Proverbs 26:11).

Repent: making tender (see 1 Kings 8:47; 2 Chronicles 6:37); to voluntarily turn away from (see 1 Kings 8:47; Jeremiah 31:19; Mark 1:14–15; Acts 8:22).

Rescue: God's help (see Nehemiah 9:28; Psalm 96:6); an escape from (see 2 Thessalonians 3:2).

Resist: to withstand the effect/oppose (see Galatians 5:1; James 4:7; 1 Peter 5:8–9).

Respect: honor and speak highly of (see Ephesians 5:33).

Rest: to receive the promise that God did everything and nothing more is needed (see Hebrews 4:1–5).

Rest, not: trusting in our own works; to try to fix things (see Hebrews 4:1–5).

Rested: died (see 1 Kings 2:10); with the Lord (see Isaiah 57:2).

Riding: writing (play on words); ministry (see Themes/Animals and Creatures/ Horse).

Rise up:
change direction and leave the old ways behind (see Exodus 12:13; Isaiah 60:1–2; Matthew 27:52);
to move higher toward God (see Matthew 27:52;
become active (see Deuteronomy 32:38; 1 Samuel 25:29);

Actions

come against (see Exodus 15:17; Deuteronomy 19:15–16; 2 Samuel 22:49).

Risk: faith (see Acts 15:26).

Roam: to forget your resting place (see Jeremiah 50:6).

Rob: to steal from the unsuspecting (see Judges 9:25).

Rockets shooting off: warfare (rel).

Ruffled: frustration/irritation (char).

Rule: to have dominion over (see Psalm 49:14).

Run: striving (see Isaiah 40:31; Galatians 5:7; Philippians 2:14–16; Hebrews 12:1).

Run, away from:
intimidated/afraid of something or someone (see Genesis 16:8; Joshua 8:6; Nehemiah 6:11; John 10:12);
escape (see Joshua 8:6; Jonah 1:10);
hiding a wrongdoing (see Genesis 31:19–21).

Run, slow motion [see limping]:
something that is not working completely (see Proverbs 26:7; Hebrews 12:13);
foundational issues are slowing you down (see Proverbs 26:7; Hebrew 12:13);
something is hindering you from advancing (see Proverbs 26:7; Hebrews 12:13).

Run, with: who is the dreamer running with? (ask this question); those you contend with (see Jeremiah 12:5).

Running race: following God (see Galatians 5:7).

S

Satisfied, not: not of the Lord (see Isaiah 55:2).

Scatter:
to fall away from Christ (see Matthew 26:31);
to harass (see Matthew 9:36);
to cause separation (see Matthew 12:30).

Scourged: to receive injury due to another's sin (see Matthew 27:26).

Scream, but nothing comes out:
circumstances choking off your passion for prayer (see Matthew 22:12);
feeling like prayer is not getting through (rel);
unable to ask for help (func).

Search: seek to know or understand (see Psalm 139:1).

See: understand (see Isaiah 6:10; 44:18; 52:15; Daniel 5:23; Matthew 13:13–15; Mark 8:17; Luke 8:10; Acts 28:26).

Self-abasement: to trap self in the "basement" by saying, "I'm evil" (see Colossians 2:16–23).

Sex with husband in church: intimacy with Holy Spirit (husband: Jesus/ Holy Spirit (see Jeremiah 3:14–20; 31:32; Hosea 2:14–20).

Shake: a shake-up from God (see Hebrews 12:26–29); afraid (see Psalm 62:2, 6).

Shake, clothes: a curse upon others to lose all (see Nehemiah 5:13).

Shaken: to remove things that can be removed (see Hebrews 12:26–29).

Shaving, beard: humiliation (see 2 Samuel 10:4–5; Isaiah 7:20).

Shaving, head: cleansed of past life (see Deuteronomy 21:12; Numbers 6:9); to humiliate (Numbers 6:9; Isaiah 7:20).

Shaving, legs: exposure (see Isaiah 7:20); conforming to society (char).

Shoes taken off: without peace (see Deuteronomy 25:9–10).

Shout: bring charges against (see Jeremiah 25:30–31).

Shrink back: falter in fear/without faith (see Hebrews 10:38–39).

Sick: in need of healing (char); the result of bad choices (see Psalm 38:3; 107:17).

Sigh: in need (see Psalm 5:1).

Signed certificate: just passed a test (char).

Silence:
calm (see Psalm 94:13);
patience (see Psalm 62:1);
inactive (see Psalm 83:1);
unwilling to defend (see Matthew 27:12–14);

Actions

death (see Psalm 94:17).

Singing:

praise [to God or idols] (see Judges 5:3; 2 Chronicles 5:13; Nehemiah 12:28; Revelation 5:9);

worship (see Psalm 98:4–5; 108:3); see General/Song.

Sit, alongside: stay and rest in the presence of (see Revelation 3:21).

Sleep:

resting (see Psalm 127:2; 132:4);

unaware (see Matthew 8:24);

without understanding (see Isaiah 56:10);

inactive (see Psalm 44:23; 121:3–4; Proverbs 20:13; Isaiah 5:27; Matthew 13:25; Ephesians 5:14; 1 Thessalonians 5:6);

not paying attention (see Psalm 121:3–4; Isaiah 5:27; Matthew 13:25; Ephesians 5:14; 1 Thessalonians 5:6);

not praying (see Luke 22:46);

unaware/inactive/not taking action (see Psalm 44:23; 121:3–4; Proverbs 20:13; Isaiah 5:27; Matthew 13:25; Ephesians 5:14; 1 Thessalonians 5:6);

dead/died and in the Spirit (see 2 Kings 4:31–32; 13:9; Jeremiah 51:39; Matthew 27:52; John 11:11; Acts 7:60; 1 Thessalonians 4:15–16; 5:10; 2 Peter 3:4).

Slept: had sex (see 1 Samuel 2:22).

Slide, backward: fall away from the Lord (see Jeremiah 3:22).

Slipping: in need of support (see Psalm 94:18); to lose your foothold; to lose the right of way (see Psalm 38:16; 73:2).

Smoking cigarette: pride/arrogance; saying, "Do not come near me, for I am too sacred for you" (see Isaiah 65:5).

Sniff: contempt (see Malachi 1:13).

Soaring: high spiritual activity that God is taking you to (see Isaiah 40:31; 60:8; Zechariah 5:1–2).

Sow: things done that will bring about results (see Genesis 26:12; Exodus 23:16; Psalm 126:5–6; Matthew 13:3–5, 37–39; Galatians 6:7–8).

Speak, unable to: unable to pray (see Matthew 12:22); unable to communicate well (see Matthew 12:22).

Speaking curses and bad words: speaking evil; "out of the abundance of the heart man speaks" (func; see Luke 6:45); an evil heart (char).

Spit: reject and disrespect (see Matthew 27:30).

Spit, in face: disrespect (see Deuteronomy 25:9).

Stab: pierce with grief (see 1 Timothy 6:10).

Stalk: lie in wait in order to come against (see Psalm 59:3).

Stamp feet: signifying the end (see Ezekiel 6:11).

Stand up: stand against (see Joshua 1:5).

Stone, turns into: suffering a stroke (see 1 Samuel 25:37).

Straightens out: to be made right (see Psalm 5:8; Ecclesiastes 1:15); to be put back on track (see Psalm 27:11; Proverbs 15:21).

Stray: not to be ignored or neglected (see Deuteronomy 22:1–3).

Stray person: not to be ignored or neglected (see Deuteronomy 22:1–3).

Striking out at an object: spiritual discernment and reaction to it (char).

Struggle: see Themes/Actions Battle.

Stubborn: rebellion against God (see Isaiah 30:1).

Stumble:

being refined and purged (see Daniel 11:35);

unable to go forward smoothly (see Psalm 27:2; Isaiah 5:27; 28:7; 59:14; Jeremiah 13:16; Matthew 26:31);

to fall into sin (see Psalm 73:2–3; 91:12; Proverbs 4:19; Isaiah 8:14–15; 31:3; Jeremiah 6:21; 31:9; Matthew 5:29; 18:6, 8–9; 1 Peter 2:8);

in a place of struggle/ to be down [as in "he is down and out"] (see Psalm 35:15);

weak (see 1 Samuel 2:4);

error (see Jeremiah 18:15; Daniel 11:35; Matthew 26:31; James 3:2).

Actions

Submitting to authority: receive power to resist the enemy (see James 4:7).

Suffer: problems/areas of oppression (see Revelation 2:9–10); our duty; the duty of soldier (see 2 Timothy 2:3–4; Romans 12).

Surround: go about seeking (char); protect (see Jeremiah 31:22).

Swallow: overcome (see Revelation 12:16).

Sweating: affecting yourself (see Genesis 3:19; Luke 22:44).

Sweet turning sour: sour side of the Gospel [condemnation to those who do not receive it] (see Revelation 10:9–10).

T

Talking, everyone talking at once: confusion (see Genesis 11:9; Acts 19:32).

Talking, in a seat behind someone: someone talking behind another's back (char).

Taste: experience (see Luke 9:27).

Teeth, lose: something one needs to understand (see Themes/Body Parts/Teeth).

Temper: anger that causes a penalty (see Proverb 19:19).

Tempted sexually: a Jezebel spirit [spirit of control] tempting you (see 1 Kings 19:2; 2 Kings 9:30).

Tests: [are there parallels with the issue?]

test, going to take it, but stop to help someone and miss the test: helping people to avoid what God has for you is no excuse (char); humanism or situational ethics (char);

test, but could not find the room: you are looking in the wrong place (char);

tests, missed: you are missing what God is telling you (see 2 Chronicles 32:31; Proverbs 17:3; 2 Corinthians 13:5);

tests, taking: you have recently gone through a test (func);

being tested by God (see Judges 2:22; 3:4; Psalm 26:2).

Thirsty:

seeking righteousness/seeking spiritual righteousness (see Isaiah 55:1; Matthew 5:6; Revelation 21:6; 22:17);

unsatisfied (see Isaiah 44:3–4; Psalm 107:9);

to become faint (see Isaiah 44:12).

Throw away: disregard (see Hebrews 10:35); remove (see Matthew 18:8–9).

Throw down: overcome (see Revelation 12:10; 18:21).

Throw self down upon: done by free will (see Matthew 21:44).

Tips over: goes over (char); falls (char).

Torment: evil spirit from the enemy or from God (see 1 Samuel 16:14–16, 23; 18:10; 19:9; 1 Kings 22:19–23).

Totter: ready to fall (see Psalm 60:2).

Transfigured: to become holy: face shines like the sun, clothes white as light (see Matthew 17:2); man turning into a woman/woman turning into a man: changing in a self-destructive direction, turning into deception (char).

Trip: unable to go forward smoothly (see Jeremiah 13:16).

Trodden on: beat down (see Psalm 44:5); destroyed (see Jeremiah 12:10).

Turn: going toward a new way of living or a different direction (see 1 Kings 9:6).

Turn left or right: to stray off of the path (see 1 Samuel 6:12); to turn away from (see Deuteronomy 28:14).

Turning back and forth into different people or different things: what appears to be one thing is really something else (char).

Two people having same dream: two or three witnesses are established from God (see Matthew 18:16).

U

Unable to move: firmly established (see Psalm 93:1).

Unbelief: not believing the promises/words of God (see Revelation 21:8).

Unconscious: not listening to God (see 1 Peter 2:19); denial of memories and attitudes that are affecting you (func).

Understand:

to know Christ (see Psalm 49:20; 2 Timothy 2:7);

brings compassion and favor (see Isaiah 27:11);

comes from God (see 2 Timothy 2:7).

Unfaithful: one who does not stay true (see 2 Chronicles 30:7).

Untie: to set the oppressed free (see Isaiah 58:6).

Unveil: reveal/cause to appear (see 1 Peter 1:7; Revelation 1:1–7); to cause to understand (see Matthew 11:25; 16:17; 1 Peter 1:12).

Urinate: cleansing toxins from your life (see Leviticus 8:16).

V

Vile: choosing ungodly ways (see Revelation 21:8).

Violence: an unwanted outcome (see Proverbs 16:29); an outcome reached by tremendous upheaval (see Genesis 6:11–13; Judges 9:24; Job 5:21).

Visiting: not where you "live" or emotionally stay, but where you are right now (char).

Vomit: getting rid of bad things (see Job 20:15); unclean words (see Isaiah 28:8); expunging sin (see Leviticus 18:28; 20:22; Isaiah 28:8; 2 Peter 2:20–22).

W

Wait: patience in the Lord (see Psalm 27:14).

Walk:

the way one is living/life/live (see Judges 2:22; 2 Chronicles 27:6; Psalm 101:2; Zechariah 3: 6–10; Galatians 5:16, 25; Ephesians 2:2; 4:1; 1 John 2:6);

the direction you are going—should be done in Jesus' name (see Zechariah 10:12);

journey (see Psalm 23:4).

Walk in muddy or rocky areas: living in ways that are not good (see 1 Kings 9:4; Isaiah 65:2).

Walk to a building: what you are involved in [look at the type of building] (func).

Walk, together: in agreement with each other (see Amos 3:3).

Walk, unable to: a method [that you are living in/working in] is not for you (see 1 Samuel 17:39).

Walk, upright: following the Lord (see Isaiah 57:2).

Wash: spiritual cleansing; to get rid of evil (see Exodus 30:17–21; Deuteronomy 21:6; Psalm 51:2, 7; Isaiah 1:16; Ephesians 5:26; Revelation 22:14).

Wash clothes: cleansing of things you are involved in (see Revelation 22:14).

Wash dishes: to clean out vessels of God (see 2 Kings 21:13).

Wash hair: cleansing of your covering; see Themes/Body Parts/Hair.

Wash hands: cleansing your work (see Themes/Body Parts/Hand); old traditions (see Mark 7:1–9).

Water, pouring down stairs: God's Word [judgment]; cleansing that starts at the top and goes down (see 1 Peter 4:17).

Weapons, not working: lost power (func).

Weary: discouraged (see Jeremiah 4:31; Matthew 11:28; Hebrews 12:3); in need of the Lord (see Psalm 63:1).

Weave:

to put together (see Psalm 139:15);

network (see 1 Kings 7:17);

to interact with others (see 1 Kings 7:17).

Weeping: distress/hurt (see Matthew 8:12; 13:50).

Weight lifting: lifting of weight or burdens (func).

Whipped: see Themes/Actions/
Scourged.

Wink:

expressing an interest in (see Proverbs
16:30);

plotting (see Proverbs 16:30);

plotting perversity (see Proverbs 6:13;
16:30);

causes grief (see Proverbs 10:10).

Withdraw: fleeing from evil (see Matthew 12:15).

Woman in man's clothes [not usual]: not
being true to self (see Deuteronomy
22:5).

**Words that come out of your (or anoth-
er's) mouth:** what you (or another) are
currently saying (see Matthew 4:4).

Work: acts of living (see Ephesians
2:12).

Wounded: healed (see 1 Peter 2:24;
through Jesus' wounds, we are
healed).

Wrestle: striving/fighting (see Colossians 4:12); spiritual warfare (see
Ephesians 6:12; Colossians 4:12).

NOTES

Foreword by Mike Bickle

1. Andrew Murray, *Abide in Christ: The Joy of Being in God's Presence* (Springdale, Pa.: Whitaker, 1979), 23–24.

Chapter 1: Where We Begin

1. I took *The Art of Hearing God* and *Understanding Dreams and Visions.* Learn more at https://www.streams ministries.com/home.

Chapter 2: Common Dream Questions

1. *Merriam-Webster,* s.v. "kook," accessed November 27, 2017, https://www .merriam-webster.com/dictionary/kook.

2. To learn more about Freud's theories, see J. Strachey, ed., *The Interpretation of Dreams (First Part),* vol. 4 of *The Standard Edition of the Complete Psychological Works of Sigmund Freud* (London: Hogarth Press, 1953); and J. Strachey, ed., *The Interpretation of Dreams (Second Part)* and *On Dreams,* vol. 5 of *The Standard Edition of the Complete Psychological Works of Sigmund Freud* (London: Hogarth Press, 1953).

3. To learn more about Jung's theories, see C. G. Jung, *Dreams,* trans. R. F. C. Hull (Princeton, N.J.: Princeton University Press, 2010).

4. *Merriam-Webster,* s.v. "scientific method," accessed November 27, 2017, https://www.merriam-webster.com/dict ionary/scientific%20method.

Chapter 3: The Steps of Dream Interpretation

1. John Paul Jackson, *Understanding Dreams and Visions* online teaching series, https://www.streamsministries .com/home.

2. John Paul Jackson, *The Art of Hearing God* online teaching series, https:// www.streamsministries.com/home; also Jackson, *Understanding Dreams and Visions.*

3. Jackson, *Understanding Dreams and Visions.*

4. Dorothy Astoria, *The Name Book* (Minneapolis: Bethany, 1997), 209.

Chapter 4: Types of Dreams

1. Maynard Solomon, "The Dreams of Beethoven," *Beethoven Essays* (Cambridge, Mass.: Harvard University Press, 1990), 59.

2. See https://en.wikipedia.org/wiki /Yesterday_(Beatles_song).

After amazing dream experiences, **Marsha Trimble Dunstan** began helping others understand their own dreams. With the Holy Spirit's leading, she uses biblical principles and symbols to explore what the dream world is speaking to the dreamer. Coming from a left-brain world (Marsha worked for years as an electrical control systems engineer and, prior to that, as an insurance underwriter and adjuster), her blend of left-brain approach to the right-brain world of dream interpretation creates a fun mesh of practical application and thought-provoking anecdotes.

Follow her ongoing postings and teachings of dream interpretation at www.mtdunstan.com.